T0301283

JEANNETTE GRAULAU

The Underground Wealth of Nations

ON THE CAPITALIST ORIGINS

OF SILVER MINING,

A.D. 1150–1450

Yale

UNIVERSITY PRESS

NEW HAVEN & LONDON

Published with assistance from the Louis Stern Memorial Fund.

Yale University Press books may be purchased in quantity for
educational, business, or promotional use. For information, please e-mail
sales.press@yale.edu (U.S. office) or sales@yaleup.co.uk (U.K. office).

Set in Times Roman type by Integrated Publishing Solutions,
Grand Rapids, Michigan.
Printed in the United States of America.

Library of Congress Control Number: 2019937183
ISBN 978-0-300-21822-0 (hardcover : alk. paper)

A catalogue record for this book is available from the British Library.

This paper meets the requirements of ANSI/NISO Z39.48-1992
(Permanence of Paper).

10 9 8 7 6 5 4 3 2 1

To Arístides Rodríguez Rivera
and José Pepe González Díaz, with admiration,
and Luis Vázquez González, *in memoriam*

CONTENTS

ILLUSTRATIONS

TABLES

PREFACE

'MEN OBTAIN WEALTH FROM THE bowels of the earth, and not from the sur-face-soil,' stated an English professor two centuries ago, a wrathful pedagogue contending with the weighty matter of capitalist improvements of lands. He had many reasons for agitation. How capital digged, usurped, and claimed the bowels of the earth in search of metallic wealth is an inquiry ignored by the political economy canon. This inquiry is the subject matter of this book.

The key to understanding capitalist mining comes from a view toward the 'complex totality' of mining history. Once mining promontories were drawn, with their varied geography, a pattern became discernible: empty feudal coffers in the long thirteenth century were to the mines what the Black Death was in the fourteenth century. They were obstacles to mining. This did not come as a sur-prise to feudal lords, who were aware of their incapacity to make the mines pro-ductive. Capital came to the rescue and 'ploughed back its gains' into the subsoil in unrepentant ways. The outcome was unequivocal: Europe's mining *feodum* dispensed with feudal lords from the thirteenth century onward, but never with capital. That this took place before the sixteenth century means that the ashes into which the mining question was burnt by Smith and Marx hide a fire beneath!

A few intuitions guided the inquiry of this book. First, that capitalist silver min-ing did not originate in the sixteenth century, with the beginnings of an ill and de-ficient nation-state. This, despite the indefatigable efforts by world system scholars to show otherwise. The capitalist heart of the mining business was born centuries earlier, from distinctive 'capitalist structures.' Second, that the 'toil and trouble' that mining requires, today as in the past, admits of no reductionist explanation. 'Perfect freedom,' of the type guiding the individual man portrayed in *The Wealth of Nations*, chose not to roam in the mines of the world. Liberty belonged instead to the medieval mining corporation, enjoying favorable conditions for taking over the mines from feudal lords. Third, that Emir Sader was right when he wrote 'that history moves swiftly from one mode of production to the next is no longer appealing' nor sufficient for studying the evolution of land, labor, and capital on a global scale.

The book is motivated by the conviction that capitalism took diverse *routes de terre* while in the making. That which took place in the mining lands of Western Europe eight hundred years ago will not happen again and could not be replicated anywhere else. There, mining societies and cultures seemed destined for the natural progress of wealth, but one that required turbulence and contradictions as well as social order.

The time is ripe for a dispassionate look at how capitalism transformed these mining lands, but only if one is willing to leave the weighty burden of 'the agrarian question' behind. This is as much a generational quest as it is a theoretical paradigm. Leaving the agrarian question behind means opening the door to new questions in the spheres of economic theory and history. The burden of patiently digging for a vein and following its course to the end means penetrating the underground world armed to the teeth, but vigilant and aware of the unexpected. Why did mining corporations succeed in the Latin West? Was Islam too rigid and inflexible toward the economic life of mining? How did the European medieval mining corporation lose its battle against the nascent state from the late fifteenth century onward? These are unexpected questions that occur over and over again in the book, and ones that admit of no easy answer.

This book is also guided by the belief that it is imperative to build an economic theory of mining, adhering to the procedure that many decades ago Sombart described as 'that of the mathematician, who takes out the letter recurring in all values and places it before a bracket, so that he says $a(b+c+d\ldots)$ instead of $ab+ac+ad$.' An economic theory of mining must start with general postulates and must explain the present state of affairs in connection to the past.

Lastly, there is a temperamental bias of mine that vindicates my asking the question of capitalist mining. I believe there is only one question that matters in political economy theory and history, at the expense of many other interesting but distracting affairs. It is a question that Marx borrowed from Thünen, and one that still lingers in the air: 'How has the labourer been able to pass from being master of capital—as its creator—to being its slave?'

ACKNOWLEDGMENTS

MANY PEOPLE HAVE CONTRIBUTED in one way or another to this book. My political science colleagues have supported my research and teaching interests in ways that make me feel very fortunate. My gratitude also goes to Dennis O. Flynn, for supporting unconditionally my quest. Many thanks to them for the times we have spent together arguing about how best to elucidate an economic theory of mining.

Research leading to this book was completed with generous support from the Research Foundation of The City University of New York. My thanks go to all grant officers who assisted my navigating through institutional procedures. My thanks to Dean Edward Jarroll, who was always supportive, as were my colleagues in the Political Science Department, especially Ira Bloom and Donna Kirchheimer. The generous support by the Lehman College Foundation allowed me to obtain image-licensing rights for many of the illustrations contained in the book. In the Office of the Dean, many thanks to Shawn Plant for his readiness in assisting me with grant matters.

A book of this sort is never the building of one individual. The disinterested assistance of scientists whom I have met along the way brought wise advice and much joy to my research endeavors. Petrologist Gabriele Cruciani, from Università degli Studi di Cagliari, allowed me to have firsthand unpublished pictorial material about geoheritage sites of Iglesias, Sardinia. The Associazione Amici della Miniera courteously responded to my information requests. The long hours of dialogue with economist Dennis O. Flynn were instrumental in my grasping of the significance of 'the silver question' in global and monetary

history. I am indebted to Dennis for the sagacity and candor with which he em-
braced my questions. The challenging and stimulating e-mail exchanges with
Peter Claughton, archeologist and mining historian at the University of Exeter,
allowed me to understand technical aspects of mining that were absent from my
training as a political economist. His keen eye for details proved that a single
fact was worth a shipload of arguments. These colleagues' support, kindness,
and rigor made them invaluable contributors to this book. The shortcomings
that this book may contain are only an expression of my faults, and they are in
no way the result of lack of my intellectual guidance.

I want to acknowledge the invaluable assistance of Eugene Laper, from the
Interlibrary Loan Department, Leonard Lief Library, Lehman College. The
thrill with which he accepted the challenges of assisting me with my requests
for obscure sources was encouraging and delightful. Gene proved that nothing
is difficult to the brave. Many thanks also to librarians of the New York Public
Library and Biblioteca dell'identità Toscana in Florence as well as personnel
from different institutions who contributed one way or another to my having
access to the sources and images included in this book.

My brother Jaime proved to be more than a map advisor. He patiently took
my cartographic data and 'massaged it' so that it would yield what I wanted
to portray. Jaime prepared the maps accompanying this book. The intellectual
debt I have with him for the many lessons on GIS and map-making software
is colossal. He was the Quixote of the map-making aspect of this book; I was,
simply, his Sancho. Also, I want to thank my parents, Irma and Jaime, and
Mayda and Orlando, my other siblings, for filling my life with love and excitement. To Peter N., my gratitude for helping me understand that one has to
endure what cannot be cured.

My sincere gratitude goes to all.

THE UNDERGROUND WEALTH OF NATIONS

Mining the Underground Wealth of Nations:
A Word on Theory and History

WHEN DID MINING BECOME A CAPITALIST business? This question poses a problem about the place of mining in the history and theory of capitalism. The problem seems quite obvious: as every student of political economy knows, the founding fathers of classical political economy had no intellectual grasp of the subject. Adam Smith dispensed with the inquiry at once: 'Of all those expensive and uncertain projects which bring bankruptcy upon the greater part of the people who engage in them, there is none perhaps more perfectly ruinous than the search after new silver and gold mines.'[1] Adam Smith could not anticipate the innovative industrial force that mining would have in nineteenth-century Britain. Nor did Smith see the force of mining in the movement toward land improvements in northern Europe. Other than reflecting negatively upon the coal mines of England, Smith said very little about the relationship between mining and wealth. Mining 'is perhaps the most disadvantageous lottery in the world, or the one in which the gain of those who draw the prizes bears the least proportion to the loss of those who draw the blanks: for though the prizes are few and the blanks many, the common price of a ticket is the whole fortune of a very rich man.'[2] 'A prudent lawgiver,' said Smith, 'who desired to increase the capital of his nation, would least choose to give any extraordinary encouragement' to silver and gold mining.[3] The 'strange delusions' of Walter Raleigh concerning 'the golden city of Eldorado' and those of Columbus and the many 'adventurers' who 'flattered themselves that veins of [gold and silver] might in many places be found as large and as abundant as those which are commonly found of lead, or copper, or tin, or iron' were to Smith proof that mining was bad for the wealth of nations.[4] 'The same passion which has suggested to so many people the absurd idea of the philosopher's stone, has suggested to others the equally absurd one of immense rich mines of gold and silver.'[5] Many of today's neo-classical economists reiterate that mining indeed traps countries into development dilemmas, such as 'Dutch disease' and 'resource course,' that leave no easy way out.[6]

Karl Marx, eager to challenge the tenets of bourgeois political economy, saw mining as a pre-capitalist economy that engendered exploitation and violence, trapped in the logic of 'primitive accumulation.' Like Adam Smith, Marx saw very little industry in mining: 'With the exception of the extractive industries, in which the material for labour is provided immediately by nature, such as mining, hunting, fishing, and agriculture (so far as the latter is confined to breaking up virgin soil), all branches of industry manipulate raw material, objects already filtered through labour, already products of labour.'[7] He reiterated in the first volume of *Capital* the following idea:

> All those things which labour merely separates from immediate connection with their environment, are subjects of labour spontaneously provided by Nature. Such are fish which we catch and take from their element, water, timber which we fell in the virgin forest, and ores which we extract from their veins. If, on the other hand, the subject of labour has, so to say, been filtered through previous labour, we call it raw material; such is ore already extracted and ready for washing. All raw material is the subject of labour, but not every subject of labour is raw material; it can only become so, after it has undergone some alteration by means of labour.[8]

Feudal surplus extraction, 'like other pre-capitalist economic arrangements,' made consumers and producers, 'lords and peasants,' independent 'from the imperative to respond to market opportunities by maximizing returns from exchange.'[9]

Political economists agreeing or disapproving of the ideas of these giants have since then been at ease with excluding mining from the history and theory of capitalism.[10] Marxists, however, carry this anti-mining bias even further. They are convinced that mining in medieval Europe was as Marx described it in the first volume of *Capital*, as an activity that relied upon exploitation of the 'free gifts of Nature.' The latter referred to the natural resources which created no value or surpluses when exploited in 'small-scale commodity production.'[11] In coercive feudal relations, peasant families exploited the 'free gifts of Nature,' allowing for the sustenance of lords, peasants, and serfs. To this day, and despite all we know about mining, Marxist scholars firmly cling to these ideas, turning them into classifying categories for studying the 'laws of motion' of capital. Robert Brenner's thesis on the 'agrarian roots' of capitalism concludes that mining was one of those pre-capitalist economies which had an inherent inability for innovation.[12] Feudal lords took advantage of 'extra-economic' conditions to coercively extract the surplus of their mines. It was easy to put miners under the 'lordship of untitled masters, many of whom treated them as virtually slaves, while for many more thousands of other peasants on the older domains of elite lords of the old aristocracy and the church, the proximity to penurious knights in threatening castles proved to be a harsh liability.'[13] Such was also the argument of Peter Kriedte, a critical Marxist who in his day launched the *Alltagsgeschichte* critique to orthodox Marxism.[14] John Cole and Eric Wolf saw in medieval Alpine mining communities the 'hidden frontier' or 'peasant sideline' that created the value needed to the rise of modern industry.[15] The 'technical barrier' of this 'pre-capitalist' economy, 'at which exploitation became unviable or deleterious,' pushed mining further into the feudal world, according to Perry Anderson.[16] He stated, with much conviction: 'The extraction of silver, to which the whole urban and monetary sector of the feudal economy was organically connected, ceased to be practicable or profitable in the main mining zones of Central Europe, because there was no way of sinking deeper shafts or refining impurer ores.'[17]

Yet, something about mining between the twelfth and fifteenth centuries announced a change with feudal mining. The word *argentifodina*, or silver mine, appeared in the text of a grant by Emperor Frederick I in A.D. 1189: *cum omnis argentifodina ad jura pertinent imperii et inter regalia nostra sit computata.*[18] Decades earlier, in A.D. 1158, the word *argentifodina* appeared in a decree pertaining to imperial rights to mines, *cum omnis argentifodina ad iura pertineat imperii et inter regalia nostra.*[19] The word was included in a statement by Frederick II in A.D. 1193: *argenti fodinae et omnes venae metallorum.*[20] Similar evidence is available today describing transactions related to *argentifodina* in medieval Tuscany, Bohemia, and Sardinia. A bishop in Volterra claimed jurisdiction over *argentifodinis latentibus & apertis* in A.D. 1217, as will be described later. The words *argentifodina, argentifodinae, argentifodinis, argentifodio*, and *argentifodii* were written in a mining law enacted by Přemysl Ottokar I King of Bohemia in A.D. 1227. Thereafter, the word appeared in the

Chart of Jihlava or Iglau in A.D. 1247 and 1249 and Bohemia's mining law of
A.D. 1300.[21]

In Siena, a private business contract of the year A.D. 1462 included the word
argentifodinas.[22] A will under the name of Baron Betto di Samminiato included
furnaces for *venam argenti et plumbi* in A.D. 1324.[23] In A.D. 1321, a receipt
was presented to the same man by a private corporation for expenses related to
colando venas argenti et plumbi.[24] A century earlier, in A.D. 1225, the phrase
venam argenti aut ramis was included in the text of a mining law in Massa
Marittima, Tuscany.[25] A private mining contract in Trento dated A.D. 1208 contained a similar phrase, *vena auferatur*.[26] In A.D. 1317, a document mentioned
the *venam argenti* in reference to a specific mine in Iglesias, Sardinia, mortgaged by a master of the *Ospedalle Novo Misericordia* to two private citizens
of Pisa.[27] The word also appeared in Sardinia in A.D. 1333, when the governor
of Cagliari imposed taxes to those *in exercicio argenterie predicte et colacionis
venarum argenti et plumbi*.[28] Later, a *mineriis auri et argenti* was included in
a notarized letter on behalf of a woman by the name of Doña Isabella de San-
remon in Iglesias in A.D. 1495.[29]

That the word *argentifodina* appears in legal documents of the twelfth to fifteenth centuries matters greatly. These centuries saw the ascent of global business houses from Italian and German origins, the development of accounting
techniques, the spread of written business records, the rise of guild and munic-
ipal statutes, and the expansion of trade circuits connecting the Latin West to
the East. Changes in property and contractual institutions were in the making,
including the disappearance of military service from contractual obligations
between lords and vassals in prosperous jurisdictions. These are the times of the
rise of autonomous city-states, large bureaucracies, urbanization, and demographic explosion at least until the fourteenth century.[30] Moreover, silver-based
monies were used in international trade transactions, indicating that a rising
speed of silver demand was central to the medieval economy. The simultane-
ity of these phenomena demands that political economists study the place of
mining in this world. Was mining a matter of exploiting 'free gifts of Nature'?
Did mining under feudalism contain a capitalist embryo? Did the times offer
favorable conditions for mining to become a capitalist industry allowing lords
to benefit from the underground wealth of their lands? These questions are the
theme of this book. Finding answers to these questions requires making sense
of the unit of study and identifying general principles about medieval mining.

Fig. 1.1. Man mining for alum (A.D. 1161), by Matthaeus Platearius. A miner employs a slightly curved swing-pick resembling a hoe to break alum-bearing rocks. A miner using this type of tool would not have been able to fully swing it over his shoulder, as he would have done with a short, straight-bladed pickaxe. Using this curved tool as leverage would have also been difficult. It is possible that the artist had in mind a typical tool used in agriculture. Wellcome Collection, CC BY.

The 'Great Tongues of Land' Encircling the Mediterranean: A Good Starting Place

We are confronted with the challenge of defining the 'smallest physical entity'[31] possible that allows for describing the state of mining in the medieval world. Drawing upon lessons from mining history, a mountain chain is the space and place that created the conditions determining the success or failure of capitalist mining. From the twelfth to the fifteenth centuries, the Alps, Carpathians, Apennines, and Sardinian and Balkan mountain ranges formed the worlds of mining. Mountains were the warehouses *par excellence* of metals, minerals, and raw materials. The *Alpes*, *montes*, and *valles* were the territories dotted by *argentifodina*, as stated in a grant by German Emperor Frederick I in

Fig. 1.2. Man mining for gold (A.D. 1161), by Matthaeus Platearius. A miner is shown digging for gold in an open field. A shovel, a lantern, and a sack for carrying ores are some of the tools of the miner, besides a curved pickaxe. The denuded hills in the background of the picture suggest that the site is a typical mining space, but iconography can be deceiving. Red-dyed woolen cloth was not within the reach of the ordinary miner, nor was fur headwear. It is possible that the illustrator was depicting an expert craftsman rather than an ordinary miner. Wellcome Collection, CC BY.

A.D. 1164.[32] Miners were mentioned in mining laws in relation to no meadow, pasture, marsh, or woodland, but to *mons*, as those working in *mons vaccae* in Monte Calisio, Trento, in A.D. 1206 or *mons argentarius* of Goslar in the Middle Ages.[33] Miners lived in Mons in Chutna or the mountain of Kutná Hora, stated the Bohemian king in A.D. 1300. *Montem drictum* was the term employed by politicians of Massa, Tuscany.[34] The Montagna di Chiesa—such was the place for German immigrant miners in fourteenth-century Sardinia.[35] Mining laws describe many *filone* and *fossa* in mountains perforated by *fondoratum* or digging.

The social and economic life that flourished in these 'great tongues of land'[36] and the ranges skirting them was a heat engine that provided the necessary energy to mining. The heat was non-uniform, producing great differences in the speed at which mining progressed, but everywhere it meant that *montes*[37] and *eminentes*[38] formed the space of mining, mines, and miners. It was a space of challenges posed by geography and geology to the feudal world. Transformation of nature through labor had many spillover effects affecting the legal, political, and social life of lords. Feudal ruling classes of the twelfth and thirteenth

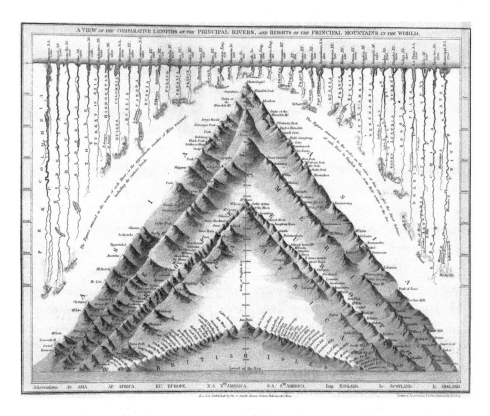

Fig. 1.3. Heights of the principal mountains of the world (A.D. 1846), by engraver Augustus Mitchell. The engraver took great care in identifying the highest habitable mining towns known at the time. The *Ciudad imperial* of Potosí, number 65 on the map, lies in an Andean valley situated at 4,300 meters above mean sea level. Real del Monte, a silver-mining town in colonial Mexico, occupies one of the highest habitable places of the Sierra Madre range but is still below the highest peaks of the world. The mining colonization of high-altitude valleys inspired men of science to develop theories to explain the geographic roots of 'American clinical entities' or 'maladaptation of mountain [American] people to normal life,' as Carlos Monge and E. S. Guzmán did not so long ago. David Rumsey Map Collection, www.davidrumsey.com.

centuries suffered a certain incoherence when governing and managing natural resource economies which were changing at accelerating speed, as this book will discuss.

Mountains gave birth to mining towns. Indeed, the symbol of the action of incessant labor upon ore-yielding mountains was the mining town and settlement. The *communis, commune, castri, ville, villa,* and *intervilla* represented the space of land and mine improvements, colonization, and long-term habitation.

Starting in the tenth century but gaining momentum in the twelfth century, a wave of urbanization swept across the best mountain lands of Europe.[39] Mountain towns were mosaics of different settlements that exploited resources needed for sustaining life at a time of rapid economic changes. Mountain soils, pastures, woodlands, and forests of higher altitudes than those exploited in the ninth and tenth centuries were the sites of new towns specializing in mining and extractive production.[40] In the central Alps, rural towns sprang up in the high mountain valleys bathed by rivers, such as the valleys around Trentino. A patchwork of *castelli* or *castri* dotted the Apennines of Tuscany by the twelfth century, dominated by a *signori di castelli*, which were lords who built fortresses at altitudes of 600 to 1,000 meters above sea level, one of which was the castle in Benabbio.[41] On the Czech side of the Carpathians, towns proliferated in altitudes of 400 meters above sea level or more, as waves of migrants colonized the best agrarian lands.[42] The mountains of Sardinia experienced demographic growth in the twelfth century, when two superpowers of the Mediterranean fought for control of the island and pushed the natives inland. Population had nowhere else to go; plains constitute only one fifth of the island's territory.[43] The mountains of the Balkan Peninsula experienced rapid urbanization in the thirteenth century, when village population 'ran into mountains,' escaping Mongol invasions and colonizing valleys at altitudes exceeding the 900 meters elevation above sea level, as in the case of Trepčain Kosovo.[44]

Mining towns had economic and political functions different from those of port and coastal cities and medieval capital cities.[45] Extraction and processing of ores took place in mining towns. It was there that continuous improvement and drainage of mines took place. Today, we are still far from fully evaluating the real footprint left in mining landscapes by peoples of different ethnic stock cultures, after many centuries of toil and trouble in exploiting mines. One thing is certain: that mining created a dense and complex economic and social life that could not be contained within the walls of medieval towns. Parishes, market places, communal castles—as well as the *placita*, the place where lords concentrated tax collection and administrative functions—were everywhere linked to the mining industry.

New contractual and legal arrangements setting the laws of motion of a new way of doing mining were born in rural mining towns, where societies felt the real pressure of exploiting nature to their advantage. Even when good geology trapped some rural towns in the neo-classical dilemma of precious metal-driven growth, it still endowed such towns with a powerful economic base for challenging the politics of their times. It was in montane towns and settlements endowed with geological and geographic bounties where old feudal mining laws endured their most significant change. From a monopoly right of feudal lords, mining became the right of private citizens. A new onomastic system emerged from the local experience of land and mine improvement in rural communes: the mining *societates* and *communitas foveae* and *consilium Wercorum*. This transition as it took place in montane mining towns and jurisdictions is the theme of this book.

Mountains encircling the Mediterranean became the world mining regions of the medieval period. Dotted by *argentifodina* exploited by *societates foveae*, these world mining regions yielded everything that lords wanted: the best resources, the easiest resources to discover and exploit, with prospects for good rent of mines. Enjoyment of mining rent, however, was no free gift of Nature.

First Principle: Mining Required Capital

A lord's sovereign rights over mines made no mine, in the same way that discovering 'a mere bunch of ore' today makes no mine.[46] Something else was needed for transforming geological bounties of a *feodum* into the underground wealth of the land. The missing element was money. Ore geology accounts for part of the problem. Silver is rarely found in its native state. Evidence of metallurgical activities indicates that miners extracted silver from various silver-bearing minerals associated with lead ores, usually in the form of galena. Galena is a lead sulfide found in 'nearly every country of the globe and in nearly all the geological formations.'[47] Galena was only one of the many silver-bearing ores that miners exploited, some were high-quality when compared to galena.

Diverse silver-bearing ores meant different exploration and processing costs, a theme that need not concern us here except to point out that ore diversity meant that mining costs, processes, and techniques varied across mountain regions. The exploration methods used by miners in this period left very little historic record behind. 'We have no clear record of the guiding principle of [early] prospectors,' stated Forbes.[48] One can confidently assume that exploration required sinking shafts and extracting and testing ore samples. If today's exploration-cost principles are of any help, especially the idea that 'only an

Fig. 1.4. Galena crystals with chalcopyrite, siderite, and ankerite-dolomite (Erzgebirge specimen). The variety and amount of associated minerals entangled with galena ore veins depend upon the mining location. Miners dig shafts for mining the most abundant mineral associated with galena, in this case chalcopyrite, a major copper ore. The amount and diversity of associated minerals and unwanted substances determine the process of silver recuperation. Courtesy of Thomas Witzke, X-Ray Application Laboratory, Malvern Panalytical, The Netherlands.

exceedingly small proportion of the locations made ever develop into mines, probably not more than one in a hundred,' then it is safe to assume that exploration costs were not insignificant.[49] A method described by Agricola, the 'forked twig,' which afforded 'the greatest use in discovering veins,' was possibly used only by miners with no access to professional land-surveying techniques. Ac-

Fig. 1.5. Galena crystals (Halsbrücke specimen). Miners and mineral collectors agree that galena is easy for even the untrained to identify. Galena's lead-grey color, cubic shape, relatively high density, and heavy weight when compared to samples of other minerals of similar size make it a sought-after silver-bearing ore. Courtesy of Thomas Witzke, X-Ray Application Laboratory, Malvern Panalytical, The Netherlands.

Fig. 1.6. Examples of shaft-lining (Fig. 1, top) and mine galleries (Fig. 2, bottom), as depicted in *L'Encyclopédie* of Diderot and D'Alembert. Most of the illustrations of mines included in *L'Encyclopédie* were copies of the beautiful drawings done by German mine surveyor Balthasar Rößler (Rössler) in *Speculum Metallurgiae Politissimum* (A.D. 1700). The figure shows advanced mine-engineering works in underground shafts. Courtesy of ARTFL Encyclopédie Project, University of Chicago.

Fig. 1.7. God the Father Measuring the Universe, Bible Moralisée, mid-thirteenth century. The medieval evolution of mathematics worked to the advantage of early capitalist mining businesses. These relied upon expert land-surveyors, a technical class with a professional ethics heavily regulated in medieval mining laws. 'God himself was a master mathematician,' as historian William McNeill noted. His design of the world was ordered by reason and mathematical principles. One succeeded in finding hidden ore veins if one applied the same principles. Österreichische Nationalbibliothek. Erich Lessing / Art Resource, NY.

cording to Agricola, miners 'grab the forks of twig with their hand, clenching their fists'; 'clenched fingers should be held toward the sky in order that twig should be raised at that end where the two branches meet.' Then, miners wander 'hither and thither at random through mountainous regions.' 'When they put their feet on a vein the twig immediately turns and twists.'[50]

Traces of old mining works possibly lowered exploration costs. Chronicles of the period praised old Roman mining ruins of the central Alps as late as A.D. 1230, suggesting that prospectors followed surviving Roman relics.[51] Silver rushes also guided prospectors and most certainly lowered prospection costs, but only in the short run. Everywhere, the principle that governed exploration costs was that without pains, there could be no gains. Economic returns were possible, but only after considerable 'toil and trouble' was expended in the mine. Expenditures included the initial cost of partitioning or dividing a mining claim as well as the costs of replacing diminished capital, such as replacing old tools, and re-timbering shaft walls in the case of old mines to be reclaimed.

Timbering shafts and tunnels for the transport of miners, rocks, tools, and beasts of burden required money. The high price of timber in regions like the Alps and Lombardy was the net result of scarcity, as will be described later. Surveying land was a necessity, so that 'workmen may not encroach on other people's possessions,' as Agricola stated.[52] Mine-surveying depended upon money besides legs and triangles, since surveyors were men physically able to walk the fields. These experts were knowledgeable of mathematical principles in vogue including Euclidian geometry, a corpus available in Europe after 'translations of the entire text of the *Elements* from Arabic appeared in the twelfth century.'[53] The surveyor's role was to walk the mining field with instruments in hand, and measuring distances and depths connecting shafts and tunnels by applying the following method:

> The surveyor either measures the interval not yet wholly dug through, which lies between the mouth of a tunnel and a shaft to be sunk to that depth, or between the mouth of a shaft and the tunnel to be driven to that spot which lies under the shaft, or between both, if the tunnel is neither so long as to reach to the shaft, nor the shaft so deep as to reach to the tunnel, and thus on both sides work is still to be done.[54]

Afterwards, a surveyor's role in mining sites was not cost-effective.[55] The law determined when a surveyor was required *in situ*. A sixteenth-century description of surveyors by German mathematician Erasmus Reinhold (A.D. 1511–1553), author of *Gründlicher und warer Bericht vom Feldmessen*, offers a glance at the lucrative business of land surveying: 'Nearly all underground surveyors are so guarded and distrustful, that they let no one examine their methods, even though their actions affect them less than the mining enterprises; their mistakes reach directly into the pockets of [their employers].'[56]

Lords needed more money for 'extirpating them [metals] from the foreign bodies with which they are entangled,' as a French naturalist stated. 'The ore must not only be pounded and washed, but it must also be mixed with certain earths, and certain salts, and in a certain proportion.'[57] Long before Alonso Barba discovered the metallurgical process of amalgamation in sixteenth-century Potosí,[58] processing silver-bearing ores required two essential stages: smelting of silver-bearing lead ores, and 'de-silverization' of lead bullion and recuperation of silver. Smelting was possibly 'cheap and versatile' but had a high environmental cost.[59] It required a process of 'dressing' the lead sulfide before the mined ore could be separated from the vein minerals and unwanted rock.[60] Generally, there were two options for the process of smelting. The first option required heating the dressed ore at approximately 600 and 800 degrees Celsius, which 'recovered from 40 to 75% of the metal and left a lead-rich "grey" slag.'[61] Boles were employed in this first step, which created an oxidizing atmosphere. A bole was a 'windblown hearth fueled by wood and built on a prominence to catch the wind.'[62] Bole hearths varied. Rippon, Claughton, and Smart observe that the bole hearths employed at Devon 'appear to have been of substantial construction using masonry and brocks or tiles (*tegula*), although some were described as being earth structures (*bolas terreas*).'[63] There, adaptations were made to allow boles to be turned for facing prevailing winds, but this remarkable innovation seems to be unique to Devon.[64] Also at Devon, 'a bole structure had been mounted on a moveable platform capable of being rotated about a vertical central axle to face the wind.'[65] Excess of oxygen was essential for chemical reactions to occur between liquids or gases and solids.

Evidence of boles at English mining sites indicates that their use was limited to the smelting of large pieces of ore. Since the slag carried amounts of silver-rich lead, a re-smelting of the slag was needed for recovering all the silver from the ore as mined. Bellows-blown furnaces were the second smelting option, and they were also used for the re-smelting of the slag. According to Peter Claughton, 'these were developed extensively in Central Europe where they became the primary smelting process for the rich silver-bearing minerals found in association with galena.'[66] The bellows-blown furnaces required crushing and washing the slag for separating the lead-rich material from the waste. At Calstock, England, horse-powered millstones were used for the crushing, and a water-wheel was used for driving the bellows. Since bellows-blown furnaces were used for re-smelting small pieces of ore but 'consumed large amounts of charcoal,' those in charge of operations had to decide between the expenses of transporting charcoal to smelting sites or the expenses of carrying ores to woodlands. The decision was by no means a random choice, but a matter that depended upon rights to woodlands.

The final process was cupellation, which required 'converting lead to litharge or lead oxide before it could be separated from silver.'[67] It was a 'high-temperature metallurgical operation aimed at refining the noble metals.'[68] The process of creating litharge worked in two ways: 'it oxidized other base metals present, and reacted with metal oxides to form fusible compounds.' 'As a result, the noble metals, which do not react with oxygen or lead oxide, separate from the melt as a discrete button.' The smelter employed a cupel for this metallurgical operation, which was a small thick vessel frequently made of ashes from calcined bone, a material that allowed for a 'neat separation' of silver since 'the mineral bone apatite does not react with the oxidized metals but mechanically absorbs them by capillary action.' Silver was then separated from the metal melt and was left relatively 'free' from impurities.[69] Much remains to be fully understood about the design and efficiency of cupellation hearths employed in large-scale refining of silver since few have survived.[70] However, the tools and process used to recuperate silver from mined ores show that an advanced industry with capital requirements was in the making.

Inputs were expensive, since the amount and composition of unwanted materials determined the amount of fuel required for smelting.[71] Access to high-quality charcoal at favorable prices, which depended upon networks of montane producers and suppliers known as *carbonari, colliers, colemen,* or charcoal-burners, was a plus.[72] Because not all types of charcoal yielded high amounts of carbon, the poorer the carbon yield, the higher the amount of charcoal required. Experiments by an English engineer by the name of Mushet showed that 'the woods before being charred were thoroughly dried, and pieces of each kind were selected as nearly alike in every respect as possible.'[73] Appendix B summarizes Mushet's findings about diverse types of charcoal available in Europe and their carbon yields. Only in Westphalia were ten loads of wood required, according to Blanchard, indicating high demand for wood.[74] But this number was by no means a general rule. Certainly, charcoal-making industries reduced much of the ancient coniferous forest-covered area of central Europe—a point that no doubt further increased expenses and living costs in a mining town.[75]

Labor was not a free gift of Nature either, even if nominally, lords provided labor as they did for improving agrarian lands.[76] The cost of mining labor was real, as it was the net result of specialization. Laborers hammered crude ores;

they separated the larger stones or 'bing' from the smaller stones.[77] This group of laborers moved the remaining 'bouse' to a 'knocker stone.' This was a large, flat, round stone on which a laborer crushed the rock using a 'bucker,' a heavy piece of iron with 'a curved under-surface and a handle.' Another group of laborers specialized in treating this ore in a large water trough. Using a long-handled 'scrubber,' laborers scrubbed the 'bouse' until the heavier element, lead, was deposited at the head of the trough and limestone was deposited at the base. The lead deposit was graded by another group of laborers. This step required dividing the ore for smelting with a sieve. Another group of skilled laborers were in charge of book accounting.

While miners extracted ore-bearing rocks from the mines, other laborers transported ore-bearing rocks to smelting factories. Other laborers specialized in charcoal-making; others were responsible for transporting processed ore to the mint and other designated places. Another specialized group of manual laborers was in charge of controlling for 'the vagaries of the wind' in cupellation factories.[78] The more specialized a mining task was, the higher the possibility that those engaged in it were free miners remunerated with fees or salaries in metallic currency, as will be described later. Laborers that made up the bulk of the medieval mining economy did not belong to the category of serfs but came from diverse groups of free and 'semi-free' labor. The most advanced forms of labor were the skilled and semi-skilled tradesmen, technical experts, and business auxiliaries or fee-takers with public duties in the towns. In general, good prices for labor, opportunities to migrate, and the possibility of living in a mining town without formal citizenship status were conditions that could increase the expenses of opening and exploiting mines.

If one adds to the picture the fact that the silver content of the galena commonly exploited in many regions is, as a general rule, astonishingly low, one must concede that mining required a great deal of money. Galena is generally 80 percent lead, with silver, sulfur, and other metals forming the rest. The average amount of silver in galena ores varies from 20 to 200 ounces of silver per ton of lead.[79] When expressed in percentage per ton of lead, galena ores contain less than 0.5 percent of silver.[80] The table below summarizes some occasional silver yields of galena ores. The classical works on lead metallurgy by Forbes and Lamborn agree that the average ratio of lead to silver in galena deposits of the ancient world was approximately 400 to 1. In the nineteenth century, the ratio was approximately 550 to 1.[81] Today, the majority of galena ores contain fifty

Table 1.1. Occasional maximum silver yield of
selected galena ores, in percentage per ton of ore

Ore sample location	Ag yield
Bulgar Ma'den, Turkey	1.84
Ala Dagh, Turkey	1.00
Val di Castello, Italy	0.72
Ikuno, Japan	0.60
Montefondoli, Trentino, Italy	0.60
Bottino, Lucca, Italy	0.56
Przíbram, Czech Republic	0.50
Ciudad Real, Spain	0.40
Campiglia Marittima, Italy	0.30
Clausthal, Germany	0.30
Fojnica, Bosnia-Herzegovina	0.20
Montevecchio, Chiesa, Sardinia	0.17
Graz, Styria, Austria	0.06
Tarnowiskie Góry, Poland	0.03
Derbyshire, England	0.004
Argentiera, Montieri, Italy	0.002
Cava del Piombo, Italy	0.0015
Cornwall, England	0.001

Sources: D'Achiardi, 'La miniera del Bottino nelle Alpi Apuane';
Hall, *Lead ores*; Lamborn, *The metallurgy of silver and lead.*

ounces of silver per ton of lead (0.15 percent silver) with the most improved techniques for metal recuperation, although an ore containing eight ounces of silver per ton of lead (0.02 percent silver) can be considered profitable.[82] The numbers suggest that for centuries miners have removed incalculable amounts of rock to furnish relatively modest quantities of silver.

The costs of mining leave us with one certain conclusion: that turning ores into the underground wealth of lands required capital. Fixed money was the missing factor in a lord's goal of enjoying the rent of mines.

Second Principle: Lords Had No Capital for Mine Improvement

Neither large numbers of serfs and free laborers nor the size of fiefs endowed a lord with all of the conditions needed for keeping mines in continuous operation. As lords discovered, shaft flooding was a serious problem.[83] Mines flooded when extraction works reached the water table of a mine, the fate of mining almost everywhere deep shafts anticipated an abundant ore yield. When it happened, lords faced the problem of how to turn 'wet ores' into 'dry ores' and prevent destruction of mining works by flooding. It was not easy for lords to simply reallocate their inputs and resources once specialization took off; mountain geography afforded no easy way out.

The pressure of gaining rents from mines was real. Thus, lords everywhere adapted old Roman hydraulic techniques and machines to drain mines. The Romans, many centuries earlier, employed the Archimedean screw when haunted by a similar problem.[84] Diodorus of Sicily (90–30 B.C.) described the improvement that the Archimedean screw brought to mining works in Spain in the following words:

> Sometimes at a great depth they meet with rivers underground, but by art give a check to the violence of their current; for by cutting of trenches underground, they divert the stream; and being sure to gain what they aim at, when they have begun, they never leave off till they have finished it; and to admiration they pump out those floods of water with those instruments called Egyptian pumps, invented by Archimedes the Syracusan, when he was in Egypt. By these, with constant pumping by turns, they throw off the water to the mouth of the pit, and by this means drain the mine dry, and make the place fit for their work.[85]

After spreading through European lands, the Archimedean screw underwent several adaptations during the Middle Ages. At the mine of Santa Bárbara, in Cordova, Spain, the Archimedean screw was used in a gallery measuring 300 meters in length, 2.7 meters in width, at an angle of thirty degrees.[86] The invention of the Egyptian pump was by no means the only hydraulic technique used for draining lands and mines. There was also the *noria,* a wheel that raised water from the bottom of a shaft to its surface entrance. Archeologists have discovered many examples in Rio Tinto, Tharsis, Lagunazo, and Murcia, in southern Spain, as well as Romania and Dolaucothi in Wales. Only in Rio Tinto, thirteen water wheels were discovered some time ago, measuring 4.5 meters in diameter 'with all their parts carefully stamped with numbers for facilitating assemblage.'[87] The Rio Tinto *noria* elevated water to approximately thirty meters. The Roman *noria* varied in diameter, but none were moved by animal power.[88] Bellow-pumps and the Heron fountain continued to be adapted and used in mining regions of Europe.[89] Similar hydraulic techniques were employed outside Europe. In the Middle East and Central Asia, miners used the swape or Egyptian *shaduf* for removing water from shafts.[90] Possibly invented in Alexandria between the third and first centuries before the Common Era, this pumping machine facilitated bailing out water by using vertical wheels that contained buckets, driven by a horizontal wheel.[91] Ismāʿīl Ibn al-Razzāz Jazarī (d. A.H. 602 / A.D. 1206) illustrated fifty complicated hydraulic machines in use in northern Iraq, in *The Book of Knowledge of Ingenious Mechanical Devices* or *Kitāb al-Ḥiyal* (A.D. 1206). Most were moved by animal power.[92]

The Archimedean screw became inefficient for solving the problem of underground water in silver mines from the twelfth century onward.[93] Miners responded to hydraulic challenges by innovating with mine geometry in the hope of solving the problem of flooded shafts. Miners built cross-cuts and cuniculus or drainage tunnels at deep levels in the mines.[94] Sloping tunnels in areas of steep topography, incessantly cutting through mountains, were also built in mines. A sloping tunnel lowered the local water table, reducing the potential of flooding; however, it was efficient only if firmly built. A slightly inclined tunnel driven from the base of a cliff or a deep valley facilitated drainage.[95] But the design and construction of tunnels required adaptions 'to deal with the strata pressure.'[96] Inclined tunnels and gravity did most of the work in young mines, but the danger of poor infrastructure increased the expenses of mine drainage. This was especially the case in mountain chains that had multiple streams or large lakes or were highly vulnerable to climate change, such as the Alps.[97] There, ore extraction became 'governed by the presence of an aquifer and its depth.'[98]

While many techniques for draining agrarian lands were 'simple and could be organized locally by peasants,'[99] cheap and effective drainage of shafts depended upon the thickness of the roof built inside mine shafts, the types of rock and materials forming the roof, and the condition of the mine roof and walls at the time the mine was flooded and abandoned. The freezing of flooded shafts in winter could make matters worse. No one needed or wanted the work of digging out ice, a task that had to be done during the 'unwatering period' of a mine when the weather was favorable to men and beasts alike. Mine drainage works required incessant labor. It required supervision of works by mine foremen with experience and knowledge about mine geometry. While miners excavated a mine rockwall searching for the orebody, other miners removed rubble and

Fig. 1.8. Miners at work, in *De proprietatibus rerum* (A.D. 1482). An ecclesiastical lord or possibly his *gastaldionibus* (tax collector) observes a miner at work. The scene is too feudal to explain the spectacular development of silver mines in world mining regions where capital plowed its gains back into the subsoil. At the close of the fifteenth century, remnants of feudal mining grants remained in England, France, and parts of Spain, lagging behind the rise of capitalist mining elsewhere. British Library. Granger.

rocks from drainage tunnels. Others were charged with the toil of keeping the oil lamps well fed, since proper and sufficient lighting was needed for work to continue. Lords expected that the work of draining a shaft created no interruption in the work of exploration and extraction taking place in neighboring shafts.

Water, however, proved to be a formidable opponent. *Fodinae aquaticae, argentifodium submergentem, argentifodium cum aqua submergente*: such were the terms that miners employed to refer to shaft flooding.[100] The terms indicate a fearsome situation: *argentifodium desolatum,* the shutdown of mining works.[101] The solution required fixed money and much 'toil and trouble.'

The problem of shaft-flooding presented lords with one urgent question: was it possible to benefit from the underground wealth of their lands while firmly clinging to feudal mining rights and privileges? The answer to the question took different paths; yet, it firmly announced a radical change in the organization and system of production of mining. Lords desperately called for private money for solving the problem of shaft-flooding. The feudal mining grant, based upon a prince's need of money,[102] soon reached a point of diminishing returns.

Getting Rid of Inadequate Explanations about Mining

Economists studying medieval silver prices have looked at mining in a very narrow sense. They study mining as if mining were an extension of minting, responding to the same business cycle as minting. The problems with this approach are fairly visible. Minting and mining were different industries. They required different inputs, and owners of mints and mines responded to different stimuli to enrichment, despite the general capitalist feeling that bonded them together. The cost of money and the ascent of a single coinage greatly determined the rise and fall of mints in particular regions, as the work of monetary historian Peter Spufford shows. But these factors alone never determined the opening or closing of mines. Even if one assumes that the owners of mines were fully aware of the purchasing power of money, this knowledge was not enough for achieving success with mining. Accessible mineralized deposits and availability of water and timbered lands in regions with affinity to transport and road networks were key factors that determined opening or closing of medieval mines. Besides, experienced prospectors were interested in finding high-grade ores rather than the cost of money.

Lifespans of minting and mining industries were different, too, with mining generally enjoying a longer lifespan.[103] High demand for coined money in a particular region usually led to the proliferation of small competing mints which turned foreign or old coins into new coins. The same factor was of no important consequence to the mining industry. Detailed research on medieval mints shows that organization and production varied, depending upon the character of mints—communal, royal, imperial, feudal, and episcopal mints were not all the same.[104] A mint was not always located close to a mine, and when it was, 'there was no compulsion to use it.'[105] Yet, some economists insist that it is correct to estimate growth and decline of mining production by drawing upon the price of money in a particular place.[106]

The economists' narrow view of mining owes much to their obsession with identifying tradable surpluses as evidence of a capitalist industry. According to this view, mining became a capitalist enterprise around the eighteenth century, when it produced metal surpluses traded in 'integrated' global markets. The argument is based upon the idea that mining centuries earlier relied upon 'free gifts of Nature' and thus created no wages, no profit, no rent. But tradable surplus is a difficult category when used for studying mining because mining was never predicated upon the principle of self-sufficiency. Mining was an export-oriented economy. Ores were rarely mined for exclusive domestic consumption from the eleventh century onward, when ecclesiastic orders ceased to be the dominant metal producers of feudal Europe.

Archeologists oftentimes offer an explanation of mining that emphasizes discoveries of technical innovations and inventions. Although it sheds much light on the history of medieval mining and smelting techniques in specific localities, their work is based upon the general proposition that techniques say it all. Slags are the evidence *par excellence* of medieval mining in archeological studies.[107] A slag is the waste product of smelting, 'primarily the non-metallic content of the ore which is separated as waste.' Through the application of scientific techniques including carbon dating, archeologists elucidate questions concerning rates of metal recovery and outputs, fuel consumption, and surpluses of certain mining sites.[108] Albeit rich in technical knowledge and empirical possibilities, scientific scrutiny of slags contains its own dangers.[109] Slags studied in the last decades, according to archeologist Claude Domergue, allow for a miscellany of conclusions lacking a coherent research question: 'the lack of a field of mining archeology'; 'the need to find continuity of mining between the Bronze Age and the Islamic period'; and the 'lack of archeo-metallurgical analysis of slag samples collected in different sites.'[110]

There are other problems with the hypotheses and explanations based upon 'technical evidence' that discard 'non-technical' evidence. Slag discoveries can lead to contradictory conclusions about mining, raising questions about the use of 'smelter sites as archives of history,' in the words of German archeologist Lothar Klappauf.[111] A more urgent problem is the gap that separates First World universities, with world-class archeological facilities and training, from Third World research institutions with interests in developing an agenda for mining research. The very limited archeological data available today for certain mining regions, such as Western Arabia, is perplexing and disappointing, and the same can be said about many regions in Africa and the Asian world. The luxury of studying and preserving slags belongs to a small group of European universities, and there, national authorities, laboratory facilities, easiness of funding, among others, can play a role in setting research agendas.[112] Besides, some slag discoveries have been purely accidental. Among the most spectacular of such accidents was the collection of slags found in Populonia and Piombino on the island of Elba. The slags were discovered while Italian engineers worked on underground excavations.[113] Thus, the problem of 'asymmetrical evidence' sets in explanations about mining.[114]

Historians studying medieval economic development continue to add new evidence for making generalizations about mining. The medieval traveler diary, in absence of or as supplement to archeological evidence, is a case in point. The use of Arab and Islamic medieval diaries seems to be the norm for discussing the big East-West question. The virtues of this evidence have been sufficiently praised elsewhere.[115] But traveler narratives need to be handled with caution when used for studying mining. The 'patronization of history-writing' by eleventh-century dynasties meant that 'the likes and dislikes of the ruling class' guided chroniclers' presentation of past events.[116] Islam's tradition of peregrination to holy sites, which required a vast network of well-maintained roads, also determined certain views by Arab chroniclers about distant lands and kingdoms. Most travelers visited only principal commercial cities, especially in the case of the Maghreb: Al-Qayrawan and Tunis in Tunisia, Annaba or Bona and Béjaïa in Algeria, and Fez and Marrakesh in Morocco. Very little they knew about Africa beyond the Sahara or west of Saudi Arabia into the al-Hijaz Mountains.[117] The large output of work from the third to the sixth centuries of the Islamic era is 'genuine as well as unreliable,' states historian Siddiqi.

After studying fourteenth-century travel diaries, Del Mar emphatically concluded: 'geography runs mad.'[118] Medieval Arab accounts about the Ma'din 'Awwām silver mine display genuine confidence when locating the mine in Morocco. In the same place, Leo Africanus (A.D. 1494–1554), the great traveler from Andalusia, 'who passed that way,' saw an iron mine.[119] The point, coming from this accomplished writer, was no *lapsus calami*. With the exception of Ibn Ḥawqal, author of *Book on the Routes and Kingdoms*, none of the Arab writers ever visited Morocco.[120] And not even Ḥawqal could dispense of using other authors' accounts in his own written work on Morocco.[121] Accounts by a chronicler from Cordova, Aḥmad al-Rāzī (d. A.H. 344 / A.D. 955), 'the authentic prince of all the Andalusian historians,' followed the *jabar* genre. It consisted of compiling different testimonies of the same event and at different times, without describing sources or chronology.[122]

With respect to the historical geography of the Atlas Mountains, 'Arab geographers lack precision and, like Strabo, often apply the name to the mountain chains otherwise called Adrār n-Deren, a term in fact reserved for the High Moroccan Atlas and the Saharan Atlas of Algeria [. . .] some authors erroneously extend it as far as the Nefūsa, to Egypt and even beyond.'[123] They located the eastern boundaries of the Maghreb in different places. Some included Egypt and the Red Sea, while others excluded Egypt. Other writers included Sicily and Spain as part of the Maghreb. 'All descriptions of Al-Andalus' from the time of the Caliphate were indebted to al-Rāzī. His work, used extensively by Arab and Persian writers, 'usually without acknowledgement,' is 'only known to us in a Castilian version,' published by the famous Spanish Arabist and historian De Gayangos in the nineteenth century. Even the work by De Gayangos originated in a fourteenth-century copy of the writings of al-Rāzī commissioned by King Denis (A.D. 1261–1325) of Portugal.[124]

Bryer recently challenged the 'alleged literary evidence for medieval Gümüşhane (Argyropolis) and its silver mines.'[125] Arguments about the existence of the mine come from four medieval diaries or accounts, as follows:

> In 1293 Edward I of England's envoy, Nicholas of Chartres, visited 'Dymesho' (which has been taken to be Gümüşhane). In 1294 Marco Polo noted a silver mine on the Trebizond-Tabriz route in, or near, Paperth (Bayburt), and in at least one version, an abundant silver mine at 'Argiron' (which has been taken to be Argyropolis). In 1332 come two references. On his way from Amasya to Erzincan, Ibn Battutah visited the then-Turkish silver mining town of 'Kumish' which was in the hands of Eretna, while the Moroccan geographer, al Umari, reported mines near Badhert (Bayburt) and at 'Gumush Saray' (which has been taken to be Gümüşhane).[126]

Bryer's conviction is encouraging: Gümüşhane never existed, despite the medieval literary accounts that insist upon it. Moroccan traveler Ibn Baṭṭūṭa (A.H. 703–770/A.D. 1304–1368), hailed as *el Marco Polo de los árabes*, was wrong.[127] There could have only been two mining centers in medieval Turkey: Tzanicha and Torul, northwest of Kovans.[128] Many historians, however, still insist that the original four literary accounts are more or less accurate, as the

British Orientalist Gibb did, when he insisted that the name of the town said it all—Gümüşhane literally means 'house of silver.'[129]

The Safest Road Ahead: Studying Mining Laws

One must choose the safest road ahead: the study of contractual and legal arrangements governing medieval silver-mining works. Mining statutes and contracts show how medieval societies addressed problems of productivity, economic efficiency, and even the profits of mining. They show that exploitation of mines did not follow a plunder mode of production, but a highly advanced set of rules and institutions without which lords could not enjoy the rents of mines. This is evidence ignored so far by Marxist and liberal political economists alike. One mining statute available today is the *Codex Wangianus* (A.D. 1185/1207), a compilation of grants and contracts for mines located in the central Alps and Lombardy. Nineteenth-century historian Rudolf Kink, from the University of Vienna, transcribed and translated the *Codex*. His voluminous study included in its first edition all legal documents recording the history of the Principality of Trento from A.D. 1082 to 1281. For this reason, Kink's edition is pertinent and continues to be used today by historians.[130] Recently, a new Italian edition of the *Codex* appeared, expanding greatly the study of the history of Trento and based upon new archival and archeological evidence. This edition was prepared by medievalists Emanuele Curzel, from the Università degli Studi di Trento, and Gian Maria Varanini, from the Università degli Studi di Verona.[131]

A second mining statute that offers invaluable information about medieval *argentifodinam* is *Constitutiones juris metallica* (A.D. 1300). This was enacted by Vaclav II (d. A.D. 1305), king of Bohemia and Poland, for the city of Kutná Hora or Kuttenberg, today in Czech Republic. A small number of works have appeared by Czech, Slovak, and Hungarian historians commenting on aspects of this mining statute.[132] The edition of *Constitutiones* prepared by nineteenth-century legal historian Hermenegild Jireček is the one used in this book. Recently, a small number of Czech archeologists and historians have dug into the pages of the statute, looking for answers to pressing questions on the medieval history of Bohemia. Their work will be cited in the next chapters.

A third mining statute, entitled *Ordinamenta super arte fossarum* (A.D. 1225), appeared in the city of Massa Marittima. For almost thirty years, the statute underwent revisions starting in A.D. 1294. It became a lengthy and comprehensive

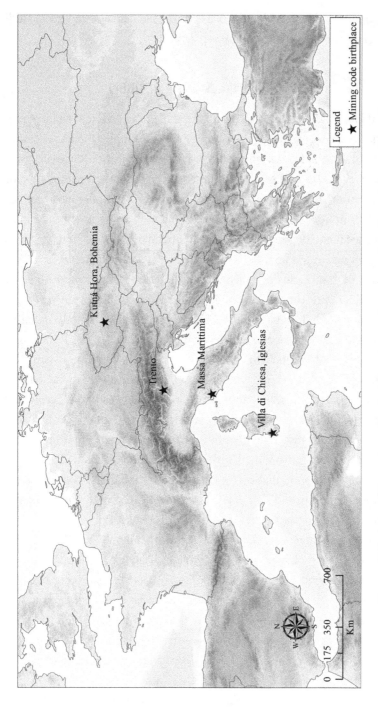

Fig. 1.9. Birthplaces of Europe's medieval mining statutes. Laws governing silver-mining works are the offspring of mountainous landscapes. Coastal lands, ports, and commercial cities, all privileged spaces by world-system analysis, had a role to play, but all were subordinated to montane life.

legal code containing a total of eighty-six articles. Several editions of the statute appeared in the nineteenth and early twentieth centuries, the most widely
used being the one including commentary by Niccolò Rodolico, historian from
University of Messina, and published by the Regia Deputazione di Storia Patria
per la Toscana in the nineteenth century. In the last four decades, European historians have added much information to Rodolico's edition, in works that will
be mentioned in the following chapters.

A fourth statute is the famous mining law of Iglesias, Sardinia. Entitled *Breve
di Villa di Chiesa e Sigerro* (A.D. 1327), the statute is a hybrid legal document.
It contains juridical principles that originated in the medieval city-state of Pisa,
as well as laws coming from the medieval kingdom of Aragon, for reasons
that will be described later. The edition of *Breve* most widely used is the one
authored by nineteenth-century Italian scholar Carlo Baudi Di Vesme.[133] The
work by the late Marco Tangheroni and his students shed light upon aspects of
the statute and brought to the attention of European historians unsolved questions on the medieval history of Sardinia.[134]

Relying upon the study of mining laws and legal institutions can present
some real dangers. Medieval mining contracts and grants are the ideal piece
of evidence. A fire that destroyed Iglesias, Sardinia, in A.D. 1355 consumed
valuable documents about the silver mines of the island.[135] Historian Peter King
states that most records stored at the Cistercian monastery of Cîteaux in Dijon,
France, were destroyed by soldiers of the French Revolution: 'what happened
to records of endowments is a mystery.'[136] Much was possibly lost about their
feudal mining grants. The Cistercians 'carried the Empire financially, admin-
istratively and politically'; yet, time has been implacable with their early medieval
footprint.[137] No written record exists of the Novelese Abbey's estates situated in
Piedmontese mining lands, which Muslims conquered after crossing Mount Cenis
Pass in the early tenth century. The only things we know for certain are that 'the
monks had barely time to escape' when the Muslims conquered their monastery
and that 'the two monks in charge of the Abbey were given a sound beating.'[138]

Neither mining laws nor mining contracts of medieval Central Asia have survived. The Ikh Zasag, or the Great Yasa, the 'unbreakable code of the steppe'
and first written Mongol code of law, disappeared centuries ago. It was, according to Hodgson, 'more than the decrees of a given ruler, it was the sum of such
decrees and was to stay in force as long as the family bore rule.'[139] Mongolian
tribes kept this system alive by war, custom, and tradition. Laws concerning

metal trade and craft industries enacted by Chinghiz Khân have long since dis-appeared.[140] Virtually nothing survived on the early Seljuḳ Turk or early Otto-man mining laws for the districts of Pandjhīr, Ghorband, and Khorāsān in north Afghanistan.[141] Lindner, in a recent historical account of the early Ottoman state, entertains no vain hope: 'to seek the origins of Ottoman history is a bit like eating cotton candy, with a fuzzy, tantalizing exterior and, perhaps, the taste of cardboard at the end.' No secure dates exist in Ottoman history before A.D. 1302. 'Given this difficulty,' he continues, 'how far back can we go? The Ottoman sources redacted after 1420 give a very confident response: back to Noah.'[142] All, however, is not lost.

Fortunately, Ottoman mining laws for the Balkans have survived. These laws derived from regulations enacted by the Kovačević Voivodes and the Serbian despot Stefan Lazarević (A.D. 1377–1427), available today in legal compila-tions commissioned by Sultan Bâyezîd II (r. A.D. 1481–1512). The compila-tions include administrative acts enacted by Bosnian and Serbian rulers and are confirmed by the Thunderbolt, Sultan Bâyezîd I (r. A.D. 1389–1402), and Sul-tan Mehmed II (r. A.D. 1444–46, 1451–81). Working with Paris manuscripts,[143] Nicoară Beldiceanu, expert in Turkish language and literature, translated the documents into French. A facsimile German edition of the same Paris doc-uments by the late Franz Babinger and a Turkish annotated transcription by historians Robert Anhegger and Halil İnalcik are also available.[144] Beldiceanu's work is an invaluable tool to the student of mining history for its comprehensive and copious explanations on historical aspects of Ottoman mining based upon an extensive bibliography, and it is the one used in this book.

The mining statutes mentioned above contained regulations about all aspects of mining production. From mining geometry specifying dimensions of private claims to methods for timbering adits and galleries, salaries and payments to land surveyors, and ore testing and smelting, everything was contemplated by the law. Mining bureaucracies emerged, sometimes in public-private forms of governance, other times as private citizens' initiative, but always overseeing mining operations. No aspect of mining was left unattended: banning Jews from 'wandering' in certain mining fiefs, prohibiting mine judges from relying upon witness accounts by women, enforcing the use of land surveyors for solving disputes over stake boundaries, fixing the number of times that a man on trial for ore theft has his name proclaimed in the court and general assembly, dictating the size of candle offerings that miners prepared for religious holidays. Nothing was viewed as 'extra-economic casualty,' in the words of Pierre Vilar.[145] Every-thing was considered relevant for making the mines productive at a time when silver was the 'oil that moved the wheels of the global economy.'[146]

How to avoid answering the question about the social origins of the under-ground wealth with a legalistic argument? To avoid this tension, one must recog-nize that statutes are not enough for studying the 'complex totality'[147] of capitalist mining, à la Braudel. Collating additional sources from the fields of geography, environmental and economic history, and archeology is in order for identifying the state of mining in Islamic Andalusia, Liao China, medieval France and Japan, and the rest of the known world. The work by Spanish Arabists on medieval Is-lamic *fatwā*, old and new generations of Sinologists, and medievalists will come in handy. A lengthy digression is unavoidable, if one wants to return back to Europe's mining *feodum* with a bird's-eye view of the world of medieval mining. Unexpected discoveries await the patient reader. Why most mountains of Europe were ruled by advanced laws while feudal maladies suffocated other ranges of the world is a question that can only be addressed after a long voyage through the world's mining regions. The end of the voyage will possibly not surprise many readers: mining was advanced in the Latin West and more feudal in the rest of the world. The *why, how,* and *when* we reserve for the next chapters.

The comprehensiveness of mining laws reveals that something was taking place in the mines of the *feodum* located at the heart of the mountains that en-circle the Mediterranean. *Consilium* or *societas* appeared as a legal category, referring to a corporate body formed by private citizens with money for in-vesting in mines. The mining statutes allow us to identify how corporations were organized as well as their rights and duties vis-à-vis the rights and duties of sovereign lords and princes. A general pattern is discernible: that miners, organized in associations of producers or corporations, yielded not to God, not to emperors, nor to feudal lords, but to a law that recognized the role of private money in the silver-mining industry. Patriarchal lines, blood ties, feudal alli-ances, military ties, and old feudal relations allowing for coercive extraction of surplus came under attack. These antagonized the capital needs of mining. The 'feudal utility' of mining was undermined, even when some remnants of the old feudal order remained, as will be described later.[148] The story of the medieval *argentifodinam* started when miners pierced the mountains of the world. Many questions of the uneven development between Europe's *argentifodinam* and mines elsewhere remain deep and complex for my understanding of this matter.

2

World Mining Regions before the Rise of Modern Capitalism

WHILE GEOLOGY SET IN MOTION THE primary 'law of attraction'[1] that pulled miners into the wombs of mountains, geography cultivated and turned this excitement into an economic force. Geography, thus, set in motion the conditions for turning ore deposits into the underground wealth of Europe. The results were astonishing: the low elevations of Europe's mountains were transformed into world mining regions.[2]

The Central Alps and Lombardy: A Region of 'Copious Silver Veins'

The central Alps and Lombardy constituted a world mining region from the twelfth to the fourteenth century. Mining fields extended into the Austrian Alps and the *territori montuosi* that encircle Lake Lugano, between Lake Maggiore and Lake Como.[3] Later in the fifteenth century, mining fields shifted slightly to the east, in Padova, Vicenza, Verona, Treviso, Feltre, and Belluno, north of Venice, controlled by diverse *società tedesca*.[4] Miners were immigrants who found themselves in the midst of feudal battles among German emperors, local aristocracies, petty lords, and factions prone to alliance with Byzantium.[5] It was a *grandi invasioni alemanne*, as Italian historian Agostino Perini described the eleventh-century German immigration to the central Alps and Lombardy.[6] Immigration by *Welsches* continued until the fifteenth century, when the newly opened mines of Venice became the center of mining activity.[7] Their continuous migration added unity to their ideas about mining businesses. There were Italian immigrants, too, who came from Padua, Milan, Bologna, Verona, Cremona, and Florence. Their settlements transformed Lombardian valleys into *un paese italianizzato* in which rich Florentine immigrants exerted 'moral and financial authority' at the dawn of the fourteenth century.[8]

The impetus with which immigrants excavated Mons Argentarie or Monte Calisio suggests that feudalism was no deterrence. Situated between Fersina and Avisio, Argentarie ran between Orzano and Bosco, north of Civezzano and overlooking Trento.[9] 'Here were situated,' stated an Austrian geographer, 'the richest silver mines of the time [A.D. 1400] in all Europe' where 'dug and delved at one time thirty thousand miners.'[10] The mining laws of Trento, written by Bishop Frederick Wanga (c. A.D. 1194–1250), unleashed the rapid development of capitalist mining works. Argentarie was 'entirely perforated by subterranean adits.'[11] Evidence that miners found much silver here is the fact that the north side of the mountain facing Trento was a *monte calvo,* or 'bald hill,' entirely denuded of vegetation by the thirteenth century.[12] Today, experts estimate that Argentarie contains more than two thousand kilometers of underground galleries and more than twenty thousand mining shaft relics.[13] Certainly, this is an archeological feast waiting to be dissected by mining historians.

'Copious silver veins' were found hidden in a black carboniferous limestone that 'climbs up' into the Alpine foothills.[14] Veins were pregnant with lead and zinc ores. Further to the east, miners exploited silver ores up to the first decades of the fifteenth century, and if it were not for this event, stated Baillie-Grohman, 'we of the twentieth century would have never heard' of the Fuggers from Augsburg.[15] The Alps of Carinthia contain the largest lead deposits of the entire Alpine range, with deposits extending 'over an area nearly 100 miles long and several miles wide.'[16] 'In the course of time huge masses of this waste accumulated on dumps, and when the rich pockets became exhausted, and smelting processes improved, the waste was worked over and over again, so that for some three hundred years men made a living out of what previous generations had thrown aside as worthless, as happened in our own days before the invention of the cyanide process.'[17] Then, 'only the richest stuff was treated, the poorer ore being thrown aside as waste,' as in the Falkenstein mine in Schwaz.[18] The mine's ores reached English markets in the form of ingots known as "Suasburgh logs"; they were bought for minting purposes.[19]

Miners exploited other ores in Tyrol, a region 'famous for [its] former wealth of precious metals.'[20] Aussee and Sandling and Hallstatt were profitable salt

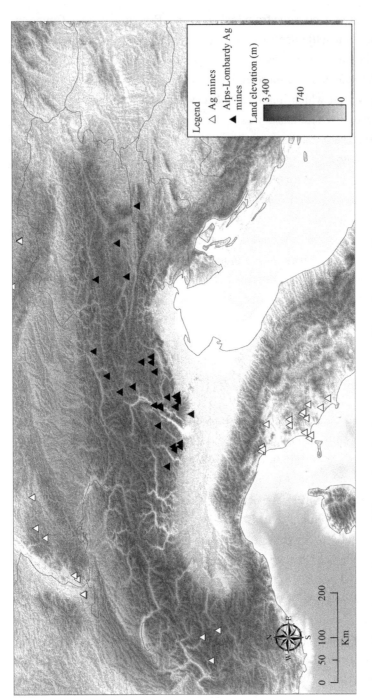

Fig. 2.1. Silver mines in the central Alps and Lombardy, A.D. 1150–1350. 'Come here man, if you dare, scale our summits and sow your corn in the furrows of our brows,' exclaimed Engels, describing the spirit of Alpine nature against the domination of man. Unfortunately, he was ignorant of topography and latitude. The Alps are the 'classic *hochgebirge*' that Germans speak of, in contrast to the medium mountain chains or *mittelgebirge*. The fact that timberlands 'tend to increase from coastal areas to continental interiors,' in the words of Price, turned the Alps into habitable mountains and one of the most enduring mining regions of Europe.

deposits.[21] The fame of the salt mining business of the Austrian towns made the
Salzkammergut a widely known market in A.D. 1379. Ischl, Hallein, Berchtes-
gaden, and Hall were prominent salt-producing towns located in the vicinity of
silver-mining towns.[22] Sandstone and brown coal deposits, running in the direction of the Ager and Traun rivers, were also exploited. Iron mining flourished
north of this area, in the famous town of Vordernberger in Leoben. Adjacent
to the town is the Styrian iron mountain, the Erzberg, reaching an elevation of
approximately 1,533 meters.

Having copious silver veins and other valuable ores was not enough for developing a capitalist mining business. Geography had to play its part.

Water, Timber, and the Green Costs of Mining

Improvements to the land à la Adam Smith were present everywhere. Alpine valleys were not the *secano* valleys of Islamic Andalusia, nor the sali-
nized lands of Sâsânid Iraq. The north and south borders of the central Alps
furnished 'wide valleys suitable for cultivation.'[23] The valley of the Estch River
in Tyrol, enclosed by medieval walls, developed extensive gardens. 'Mulberry-
trees, garlanded with the wild wine, alternate with peach and almond-trees,
among the foliage of which may be seen churches, villas, and castles, the whole
being overshadowed by towering walls of grey limestone.'[24] Quite picturesque,
in the eyes of an Austrian geographer. Fresh green meadows in the valleys of Upper
Rhine, Ursern, Formazza (Toce), and Vedretta (Tessin) made the region suitable
for agriculture and pastoralism. In Torino, farmers cultivated almonds and grapes,
and in other communes, farmers planted the *grano turco* or maize introduced to the
region later through the Columbian Exchange.[25] The legacy of German immigrants
was palpable in lands planted with hops, spinach, and artichokes.[26]

Oxen or castrated bulls were preferred in the Alps. These were cheaper to
feed than horses, which required oats.[27] The first medieval Italian treatise on
agriculture, written by the Bolognese Pietro Crescenzio (d. A.D. 1320), describes
how the use of a 'plough drawn by only one ox' and other 'different kinds drawn
by two and four oxen' led to improvement of agrarian lands of Lombardy.[28] Farmers employed drives or wagons with 'a wooden axle and low wooden wheels;
each wheel formed either of one piece or four pieces joined together.'[29]

The high Alpine valleys, situated at two thousand meters elevation, offered
abundant grazing pasture for the propagation of herding activities. The word
alps means, 'in the language of those who live amongst them, the grassy slopes

above the tree line, the grassy areas in hanging valleys, the pastures on the mountain spurs.'[30] These alps were consumed by levels: first, cows were driven to lower pastures in April, moved to middle pastures in early summer and higher pastures by July, before returning to lower pastures in early fall. Everywhere, Alpine pasture made possible 'cattle breeding, milk and cheese production.'[31] It made human habitation possible. Between A.D. 1140 and 1160, people's livelihoods in the Ardesio and Brenta valleys depended upon pastoralism, charcoal-making, mining, and timber cutting.[32] Pastoralists provided beasts of burden for transporting ores under various contractual relations. They probably played a pioneering role in discoveries of ore veins, as an Italian historian suggested a century ago.[33]

An additional geographic advantage of this mining region is that gorges and low elevation corridors opened the Alps in every direction. The Alpine range is 'a more or less solid mass,' a 'girdle' with valleys and passes, uniting continental Europe, Lombardy, and the Mediterranean.[34] Labor mobility was the norm, a point that Marxists missed. 'Despite the depth of snow and the frequency of avalanches,' Pounds states, 'the Alps were crossed at all seasons of the year,'[35] even when 'complaints of the dangers and difficulties of Alpine travel were frequent.'[36] True, north-to-south travel 'from the basins of the Rhône, the Rhine, the Danube' was 'relatively easier' than south-to-north, in the words of Földváry.[37] The Great St. Bernard Pass, the oldest pass of the western Alps, connected Lombardy's Aosta Valley, 'the pearl of the Alps,' to the Swiss valleys surrounding Lake Geneva. From Aosta heading southwards, the famous Roman road Via Francigena connected the communes of Lombardy and Tuscany to Rome.[38] 'Until the sixteenth century, the remains of a temple to Jupiter Poeninus were still visible beyond the highest point of the pass.'[39] The Great St. Bernard Pass was best known for the famous hospice built in the ninth century, which made it one of the most elevated inhabited buildings in Europe. The hospice belonged to the Augustine Order, with monks who did 'noble service in sheltering travelers, and in rescuing those in danger from the snow, with the help of the splendid St. Bernard dogs.'[40] Symbol of a time gone by!

The low-altitude Simplon Pass, at 701 meters, connected Germany's Rhine district with Italy.[41] According to legend, the Pass was used under Roman Emperor Septimius Severus (c. A.D. 145–211) and contained numerous stations, called *mansions,* for the imperial postal service.[42] Further to the east, the Brenner Pass offered 'an infinitely more direct passage from Italy to central Europe.'[43]

The Brenner Pass connects two of the largest valleys standing on opposite sides of the Alps: the Inn Valley in the heartlands of Tyrol with the eastern valley of the Po River. This mountain pass, barely reaching approximately 792 meters elevation,[44] was built to the taste of the capitalists of the times. German merchants preferred this pass when they brought spices to Nuremberg from Venice. Bypassing competitors headquartered at Bruges was possible when traveling through the Brenner Pass.[45]

A unique hydrological feature is noteworthy: none of the four largest Alpine rivers flow into the Atlantic Ocean or the Baltic Sea. The Rhône River rises in the Swiss Alps and discharges into Lake Geneva before running through valleys of the western Alps and then to the Mediterranean Sea. The Rhine rises in the Swiss Alps, enters Lake Constance, and moves northwards, bordering the western side of the Black Forest until it reaches the North Sea through the Netherlands. The Po River crosses Lombardy, runs along the southwest fringe of the Alps, and discharges near Venice into the Adriatic Sea.[46] The Estch or Adige River as Italians call it, rises in southern Tyrol and crosses Trento and Verona, before reaching the Adriatic Sea.

Besides the numerous small streams and tributaries of the largest rivers, the Alps contain a high number of lakes.[47] There are twenty-seven lakes in the high plateau of St. Gotthard; thirteen in the fringes of the mountains surrounding St. Gotthard; forty in 'the little Swiss canton of Uri'; twenty-eight in the Val Piora; twenty-two in the Tessiner mountain area; eight in the Adula mountain range.[48] No other mountain range of the world has this geographic asset, pivotal for human habitation and land colonization. One is led to believe that this abundant water supply aided the internal diffusion of smelting and cupellation factories; the evidence, however, is inconclusive.[49]

In addition, it is probable that the lakes were never frozen, until the worst years of the 'Little Ice Age' that descended upon Europe later in the sixteenth century.[50] Moreover, the largest Alpine lakes are found only in the central Alps. These are Geneva, Constance, and the *lagos* Maggiore, Como, and Garda in Lombardy. Maggiore, the Romans' Lacus Verbanus, reaches 197 meters elevation and is 'the deepest of all European inland lakes' at 853 meters deep.[51] Lake Como, to the east, was the Romans' Lacus Larius. 'The beauty of its color and the luxuriance of its shores have caused its praises to be sung by the poets in all ages, from Virgil to Manzoni.'[52] Lake Garda is situated in the chain that reaches down to Verona. It was known as Iacus Benacus to the Romans and Gartensee to the German merchants, who navigated the lake more than seven centuries ago to reach their warehouses at Venice's Fondaco dei Tedeschi. This, before German capitalists vanished from global trade, was replaced by the 'vast warehouses of the Dutch East India Company' in the seventeenth century.[53]

Abundance of water, however, was not always an absolute advantage. Over the long run, it is possible that water challenges increased the green costs of mining. The 'deranged regimen' of Lombardy's rivers is responsible for much landscape change and the high costs of land improvement. Lombard valleys are irregular valleys, subject to erosion and continuous change.[54] Here, 'ancient grape-vines have been found, buried in sand and clinging to elm-trees, many feet beneath the surface soil.'[55] Settlers of the Po Plain cleared and drained the lands east of the central Alps for centuries, in order to make them useful for pastoralism and agriculture; however, expansion of pastoralism depended upon destruction of forest woods by burning. The lands surrounding Lake Garda required 'much tillage and fire,' in the words of Niccolò Machiavelli (A.D. 1469–1527). The Florentine writer added:

> Unhealthy countries soon become salubrious, by being rapidly settled; the earth is purified by tillage, and the air by their fires, which nature alone never could have effected. . . . Venice . . . was built on marshy and unhealthy ground, but its rapid settlement soon remedied this defect.[56]

Deforestation made the area more vulnerable to extreme climatic events and intense flooding. 'Rain did not help either,' states environmental historian Guidoboni. Heavy rain in spring and autumn was the prelude to what Italians call *siccitosi*, or intense dry periods in the Po Plain.[57] Miners and farmers grappled for centuries with the difficulties created by torrential waters. The lower Po Basin suffered a series of floods throughout the sixteenth century, forcing towns situated in the Plain to devote 'much care to the problem of waters and their control.'[58] The Paulini family, landowners from Veneto, sent in A.D. 1601 'a project to the Republic of Venice' that explained the 'plain's water disorder and the consequent hydrological problems.'[59] It suggested intensive reforestation of the affected areas, a technique destined to become integral to economic life in the valleys of the Po River.

Settlers were forced to pay the costs of flooding and deforestation: wood became, from the eleventh century onward, a 'precious commodity.'[60] Lombard masons and builders had relied upon cheap construction materials—brick, wood, and stone—obtained from the mountains centuries earlier at favorable prices. Even 'the most modest house,' says architectural historian Porter, was 'built of bricks and buildings' vaults were built with wood.' The situation changed after the eleventh century, when wood prices became 'prohibitive.' High prices became a sign of resource scarcity. The latter exacerbated the region's environmental vulnerability: 'it is probable that the trees were seldom allowed to grow large enough to supply timbers for a church roof.'

The relation between prices and people's behavior fell here under one of Rostow's astute insights: that irrationality fits well into short-term economic history. Contrary to the wishful thinking much in vogue today that pricing nature minimizes its degradation, high wood prices led to a rapid spread of the timber industry and increased the pace of deforestation. The situation favored capitalists from abroad: Venetian merchants bought timber in the Adriatic and sold wood to ore-processing factories located in Lombardy.[61] Local mining and smelting factories also imported charcoal from as far as Crete, a move that increased the running costs of production of a diverse group of industries, including metal-armor makers from Milan and Brescia.[62] By the fifteenth century, wood demand had reached unprecedented levels, to the point that in A.D. 1557, King Ferdinand (A.D. 1503–1564), soon to become emperor, reserved the woodlands of Primiero or Primör in Trento for exclusive consumption by the mining industry.[63] High wood prices and discoveries of silver mines in Mexico and Peru played decisive roles in the decline of the mining industry of Lombardy.

Medieval mining corporations built an industry which lasted in the region for centuries. The mines of Bovegno, Collio, and Preseglie, in the province of Brescia, and those located in the Selva di Cadore and Rivamonte in Veneto were large-scale operations that depended upon Venetian monetary interests by the fourteenth and early fifteenth centuries. It was the mines of Trento, Bergamo, and Sabbia Valley, nonetheless, where the capitalist corporation based upon mining shares emerged for the first time in the twelfth century, as will be described in the next chapter.

The Carpathians: Lodes and More Lodes

The Carpathian Mountains formed a second world mining region. The range forms a great mass that stretches for roughly 209,250 square kilometers, from

Bratislava in Hungary to the Iron Gates of the Danube River on the Serbian-Wallachian border.[64] It has 'the form of a bow, of which the Danube is the string.'[65] The range surrounds the Hungarian Basin and Transylvania's Bihar mountains, in a northwest to southeast direction. The western Carpathians formed the core of this world mining region. It was a melting pot, where different cultures and peoples came into contact with one another, in 'hierarchical webs of social and economic life.' German migrants, the *colonii principalii* or peasant tenants of the region, played protagonist roles.

German peasants migrated into the western Carpathians in the twelfth and thirteenth centuries. Historian Walter Kuhn estimates that between 2,000 and 2,500 Germans and 'other crowds' made an annual migration to the East in this period, colonizing land on behalf of Hungarian rulers.[66] German miners were their 'own geologists.'[67] They sank shafts everywhere in layers of granite, metamorphic rocks known as the Flysch Belt, limestone and karst, searching for ore veins while prospecting the Carpathians' 'champion lodes.'[68] They surely found an unparalleled ore bonanza, with lodes as wide as twenty-seven meters—good cause for more migration.[69] The lodes were a source of a commercially and financially valuable ore, silver, enjoying high demand from craftsmen and silversmiths manufacturing ceremonial swords, jewelry, fine artistic and decorative pieces for domestic and export markets, and tithe payments.[70] On the Czech side, the most famous lodes were those of Mons in Chutna or Kutná Hora. They contained veins of feldspar and quartz, calcium spar with iron pyrites, copper pyrites, argentiferous galena, blende, and silver ores.[71] A mining rush to Kutná Hora in the last decades of the thirteenth century began with 'a small group of miners in the Abbey of Sedlitz' or Staré Sedliště; 'at the end of the fourteenth century it was reported in Styria that some 10,000 miners had been attracted to the Kutná workings from Poland, Pomerania, Meissen and Upper Hungary,' according to Ian Blanchard.[72] The town grew to 18,000 inhabitants after the *sbeh ke Kutne* or the rush to Kutná.[73] Today, a visitor to the town can stand at the starting point of the medieval rush in the Church of the Virgin Mary.[74] From here, the silver rush spread, determining the layout of the medieval city.

On the Slovak side of the Carpathians, German miners exploited the Spitaler lode in Banská Štiavnica and Kremnica, yielding gold and silver, 'its gold quantity decreasing while that of galena increasing the deeper the lode became.'[75] They also reached Kremnica's champion lode, twenty-seven meters wide, and

Fig. 2.2. Medieval miners of Kutná Hora, as depicted by nineteenth-century painter Karl Ritter von Siegl. It is believed that the mines located at Kutná Hora supplied approximately a third of the silver that reached European continental markets. The Osel mine was a honeycomb, which by the last years of the fourteenth century reached a depth of approximately five hundred meters. The garb of miners here appears clean and free of stains, a sign of the painter's romantic ideal of miners and mining labor. Österreichische Nationalbibliothek, PK1131, 2017, Vienna, Austria.

found native gold, silver, iron pyrites, stibnite ores, and brown and heavy spar. The Theresia lode in Banská Štiavnica, with the oldest silver ore veins, was worked by Carpathian miners. Immigrant miners worked the Hodstrich champion lode, with veins of silver glance, galena, and pyrites that reached a width of thirty-seven meters in some areas. Working wide and deep lodes meant that miners' self-preservation was guaranteed if they continuously went 'up and down' the mines, *ilyen a bányász Elete*—'that is the life of a miner.'[76]

The Carpathians yielded salt deposits in generous amounts, an invaluable commodity of the medieval world. Transylvania's salt mines 'were exploited at least since the Roman times,' states Romanian historian Alexandru Madgearu.[77] Miners exploited iron, copper, clay, and other minerals in the Slovakian side of the western Carpathians. Iron ore was extracted in the famous mine of Koterbachy in Rudňany in central Slovakia. Copper was mined at Banská Bystrica or Neusohl, Špania Dolina or the old German mining settlements of Herrungrund, Rožňava or Rosenau, and Košice. In Štiavnica, 'kaolinite clays were locally extracted at several spots, in the area of the so-called "Beluj" pottery'; this was an area of gold-porphyry mineralization.[78] Miners took advantage of red cinnabar and antimony deposits found in Košice. 'Hardened clay,' a rock formation found in the western extremity of the Carpathians, was used as building stone in Hungarian towns. It was known among geologists as *argilla indurata Germanorum* well into the nineteenth century.[79]

Miners laboriously pierced the Transylvania Mountains located in the center of the Carpathian arc. They worked gold mines at Roşia Montană, or the German Goldbach, and Fazebay, in the Apuseni Mountains of western Transylvania. Here was a real medieval Eldorado. 'The gold of Botza in the country of Liptov is found in a gray schistus, mixed with silver; it is considered the finest of any in Hungary or even in Europe'; 'the same metal is carried down all the rivers in Transylvania, and the largest pieces are found in the Aranyos.'[80]

Miners prospected the Munţii Metallifere, formed by the Mureş, Drocea, and Trascău mountains, mining for gold.[81] Relics of medieval mine portals still lie on some hills.[82] In Csétatye Mountain, an irregular and columnar network of gold veins or Katranza can still be seen. The veins have been excavated for centuries.[83] Abandoned workings remain today, and by their dimensions—128 meters in length and approximately thirty-six meters in width—the visitor feels perplexed and insecure, thinking about the depth of mining works. 'An ordinary

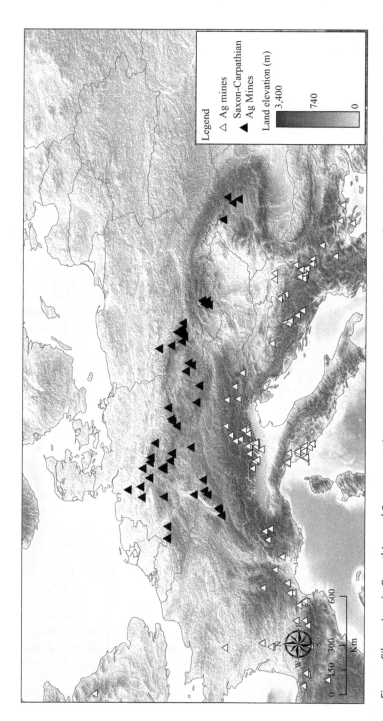

Fig. 2.3. Silver mines in Carpathian and Saxon mountain ranges, A.D. 1150–1400. Most mines were located in the small mountain ranges that extend from the north of the Danube to the northern plains of Europe. Miners took advantage of mountains with relatively low elevation and multiple trans-montane corridors connecting commercial centers to mining sites.

mining-lamp does not reveal the extent [of the caves], and reaching to so great a depth, that a stone thrown in, takes several seconds to reach the bottom.'[84]

A Mining-Induced Urban Boom

Medieval mining in the Carpathians laid the foundation for the development of cities with their own legal charters, an urban phenomenon unrivaled by any other mining region.[85] German colonists played a pivotal role in the foundation of mining towns; however, theirs was by no means an exclusive role. Hungarian kings put in place laws that treated German colonists as guests or *hospites* who enjoyed land rights denied to Slavonic, Magyar, Vlach, or Romanian peoples, among others.[86] Host peoples were displaced from mining regions, even when mixing of genetic pools took place.[87] Newly founded towns in the northern slopes included Banská Štiavnica and Banská Belá, the latter known to the Germans as Dilln, in Slovakia, and Baia Sprie or Felsöbanya, founded in A.D. 1376. These were followed by Baia Mare or Nagybánya and Cavnic.[88] 'A union of 25 Zips [that is, German] towns was formed, and constituted German settlements,' noted Schröcke. King Stephen V (r. A.D. 1270–72) of Hungary gave this union its freedom in A.D. 1271. One hundred years later, the Hungarian king confirmed the privileges granted to 'the Zips country' in a medieval town-chart known as *Zipser Willkür*.[89]

Another chart appeared in Uničov, a town founded 'by word of mouth,' according to Czech archeologists Martin Moník and Pavel Šlézar.[90] The original town district ranged from 'the Czech-Moravian border to the middle course of the Moravice River and from there to the middle course of the Byst ice River.'[91] Slags discovered recently in Rudabanya, Hungary, confirm that the town was a large mining settlement from the late twelfth century onwards.

The Mongol raids of A.D. 1241 contributed to the urban boom. Coming from the eastern steppes, the Mongols pushed miners to the west, deeper into Carpathian and Transylvanian mining towns.[92] In Romania, immigrants escaping Mongol invasions settled under the protection of King Bela IV (A.D. 1235–1270) of Hungary.[93] Baia de Arieş, known as Offenbánya or Offenburg, was founded in A.D. 1325, followed by Zlatna or Schlatten in A.D. 1357, in central Transylvania. Germans arrived at the region 'via the Moravian Gate'; Germans in route to Spiš in northeast Slovakia came from the north via the Popper gorge in the Carpathians.[94]

The urban core of the western Carpathians was the Siebenbürgen, or seven

German burghs located west of the Transylvania Basin: Hermannstadt, today's Sibiu; Klausenburg or today's Cluj-Napoca; Kronstadt or Braşov; Bistritz or Bistriţa; Mediasch or Mediaş; Mühlenbach or Sebeş; and Sighişoara or Schässburg.[95] The Siebenbürgen originated in legal privileges granted to German immigrants; only Germans enjoyed the status of burghers.[96] On all sides of the Carpathians, German towns were free towns nominally ruled by the Saxon count of Hermannstadt and had enjoyed political autonomy since the twelfth century. This exclusive migration added unity to their mining practices. It is, hence, no surprise that mining laws grew in tandem with the laws and customs brought by German immigrants. Germanic cultural influence was palpable in the mining lexicon that Bohemian kings added to the kingdom's mining statute (see Appendix A: German loanwords).

The Siebenbürgen attracted foreign merchants, who crossed Bohemia and Poland on their way to Kiev from Mainz. Jews from Central Europe, Walloons from today's Belgium, Dutch, Flemish, Italians including Florentine experts in minting, Poles, Armenians, Tartars, and even Muslims in the case of eastern Poland found their way into the towns.[97] In the words of Piskorski, towns became 'melting pots . . . where production increased most swiftly and from where new organizational, technical and technological advancements spread.'[98] 'Prague is the richest city by reason of its trade,' stated Ibrahim Ibn Yaqub, the renowned Jewish traveler from Catalonia in the late tenth century. He added: 'Russians and Slavs come to it from Cracow with their wares, and Moslems, Jews and Turks come from Turkey with goods and money, and they take away slaves, lead and various furs.'[99]

Geography added singular advantages to this world mining region. Waterways in all directions afforded communication to the Siebenbürgen with one of the following markets: northern Europe and the Hanseatic League, Venice and the Adriatic, the eastern Mediterranean and Anatolia, and the Black Sea. The Vistula or Wisla River is the largest river of the western Carpathians.[100] It rises in the Baranai Góra Mountain in Poland and runs northwards for more than a thousand kilometers—until it reaches the Baltic Sea through Danzig, after passing by diverse cities of the Silesia region, including Cracow and Warsaw in Poland. In the fourteenth century, copper from the western Carpathians traveled through the Vistula to Flanders via the Baltic Sea. The Dniester River rises in the Ukrainian side of the Carpathians and runs south and eastwards into the Black Sea. The Barzava River in the Banat of Transylvania empties into the

Serbian province of Vojvodina. The Timiş River, navigable for small crafts, rises in the western extremity of the southern Carpathians and runs northwest and then south until it reaches the Danube River east of Belgrade. The abundance of river waterways, starting with the Danube, which generously adds a great volume of water to the region, possibly facilitated diffusion and adaptation of lead smelting and cupellation factories in some regions.[101]

How many travelers crossing these routes visited the mines of the region is difficult to say. With certainty, their businesses in the region added direct and indirect stimuli to Carpathian mining industries, with the inevitable high costs to the mining industry that followed.

Immigrants, Emigrants, and Unequal Access to Resources

German immigrants were happy to leave behind the 'notoriously ferocious' climate of Saxon forests.[102] The Carpathians are a mountain chain with no glaciers, nowhere covered by perpetual snow, and much lower than the Alps.[103] These features made habitation possible at elevations ranging from 183 to 1,000 meters. The climate is continental, especially in the southern side of the range, bringing severe winters and warm summers. The Jablunkov Pass is the principal corridor connecting Czech Republic, Poland, and Slovakia, situated in a chain of primitive limestone. On the eastern side, there are the Dukla, Lupkov, and Uzsok passes, connecting Poland and Slovakia. Elevations of these passes never exceed 843 meters.

In the southern Carpathians, higher corridors connected towns to trade routes leading to Byzantium and the Central Asian steppes. The Vulcan Pass in Romania was 'one of the *plaiuri* [flat ridges] frequented by shepherds.'[104] The pass connected the mines of Petroseny to a market town situated on the banks of the Jiu River.[105] An internal road network connected Transylvanian mining settlements with Danube settlements in the west. The Mureş Valley road, on the western fringe of the Apuseni Mountains, included river tracts over the Tisza and Danube. Small boats and rafts made possible the transport of ores, salt, and other commodities. Salt traffic from the eleventh to fourteenth century relied on this road.[106] A second road crossed the Portile Meseşului Pass to the Someş Valley, connecting Hungary to Romania.[107]

Nonetheless, the urban boom exacerbated the unequal access to forest resources. German immigrants settled in the farming lands of the highest basins, where they built 'a dense network of agricultural villages' north and south of the Tatras range, between Poland and Slovakia, and the Liptov basin.[108] Their towns enjoyed the advantage of proximity to one another. Other farmers lived 'in individual holdings, hamlets or small villages, scattered through the utilized landscape, and owing an allegiance to an elite who variously displayed their power through rich burials, or by building hillforts, castles, or grand country houses.'[109] Slavs occupied the lowest parts of the Carpathian basin, where they bitterly encountered the Mongols.[110] The Vlachs, forebears of the Romanians, had limited opportunities: they migrated with their herds deep into the Carpathians, escaping Slavic and Mongol raids, until the year A.D. 1241, when the Mongols forced 'the ruling [Romanian] monarch to cross the Danube on the ice'—on Christmas day.[111]

Magyars or Hungarians, a Finno-Ugric tribe from southern Russia, migrated into the Carpathians in the late ninth century and 'settled somewhere between the Pruth and Dniester rivers.'[112] Northeast of the Hungarian Plain became 'the home of the Magyars,' where cultivated wheat in the black soils only found in the 'gentle slopes of the mountains,' with loess that extends up to a height of 396 meters. They 'occupied the grassy plains and left the oak and beech forests of the Carpathian basin to the Slavs.'[113] Their economies, based on 'wheat, cattle, and large herds of swine,' afforded Magyar settlements the advantage of diversification of production—an asset not to be underestimated in the competition against German merchants.[114]

Vlachs bore the heaviest weight. Forced to emigrate many times over the centuries, Vlach shepherd culture flourished only in the mountains. Initially, the *plaiuri* of the southern Carpathians offered extensive grazing grounds.[115] Later, the Vlachs moved as far as the Dinaric Alps, where they 'managed to exist through the centuries almost exclusively by the herding of livestock on mountain pastures; agriculture played little or no part in their lives.'[116] Still in the nineteenth century, 'the sheep that are taken to the Baragan Steppe and even to the Dobrudja are often owned by peasants from Transylvania, and many of the shepherds are Transylvanians.'[117] A Vlach shepherd from the mountains of Montenegro put it in the following words:

> Life on the mountains is not easier or more comfortable, but it is loftier in everything. There are no barriers between man and the sky. Only the birds and the clouds soar by. . . . On the mountain there is something for everyone—for the young, brightness and play, for their elders, sternness and constraint. Sorrows are more sorrowful there, and joys more joyous, thoughts are deeper, and follies are more innocent.[118]

Land colonization based upon mining, agrarian, and pastoralist economies intensified demand for natural resources.[119] Intensive grazing, charcoal-making, and mining created 'rapid deforestation not only from the mountain foot upward but also downward from the Alpine meadows,' in the words of Slovak geographer Pavol Plesník.[120] The beech tree yielded charcoal of average quality, as compared to charcoal of the Laburnum tree of the Pennines, or the chestnut tree of Tuscany, or even the oak tree of the Jehol of China and the Dinaric Alps. Yet it afforded 'good food for goats' and 'a very fit timber for machinery, for the stocks and handles of tools, and for many other purposes.'[121] Beyond the northern slopes of the western Carpathians, poor settlers extracted the oil of the beech tree and used it as a substitute for butter. 'The nut is sometimes burnt, for the purpose of making an infusion, which somewhat resembles coffee'—a traditional practice observed by an eighteenth-century traveler.[122] The fact that beech trees have a short life when compared to other trees added speed to the rate of deforestation.[123] 'The shepherds attacked the timberline in the West Carpathians most intensively during the Vlach colonization, but especially in the fifteenth and sixteenth centuries.'[124] In the words of Martonne, 'woods were cleared, small villages established, and little houses built here and there along the rivers or on the edges of the shoulders representing the floors of the sides of the old Miocene valleys.'[125] The result of wood scarcity was high wood prices.[126]

Intense pressure on water resources created other challenges. Water marks on the medieval walls of Toruń, in southern Poland, bear testimony to floods of the lower Vistula River since at least A.D. 1570.[127] According to Baron Ignaz Edler von Born, the notorious eighteenth-century Austrian mineralogist, 'the chief town [of the Banat region] and the center of the country is Temeswar, a regular, fine, and strong place, but unwholesome on account of its swampy situation.' He continued: 'Agues and inflammatory fevers of all kinds rage here every season, and procure to the physicians uninterrupted business.'[128] The seven hundred Danube lakes, covering an area of 920 square kilometers, made flood control possible by functioning as a natural channel system.[129] Water was, nonetheless, a force to be reckoned with. Geology afforded protection against floods to some Czech towns. Litovel, a town founded in A.D. 1213, on the River Morava route from Olomouc to Bohemia, was strategically positioned to take advantage of the transit that crossed to the neighboring large city of Uničov; however, much drainage work was required. Inside the urban center, continuous changes in the geological makeup of the terrain, what Klápště called a 'stratigraphic accruement,' elevated the terrain by two to three meters throughout the fourteenth century.[130] 'It certainly did not improve everyday life, but in times of floods it provided the only effective protection.'[131]

Underground water problems affected Carpathian mining works. In Upper Silesia, miners frequently talked about 'ores running to water,' or flooded shafts.[132] In the silver mines of Olkusz, miners built large networks of long galleries that included drainage infrastructure.[133] Agricola, who spent six years serving as doctor in Joachimsthal or Jáchymov, a Czech mining town, observed that pumps 'turned by ninety-six horses; these horses go down to the machines by an inclined shaft, which slopes and twists like a screw and gradually descends' in mines of the region.[134]

Still, miners and settlers of the western Carpathians made of this vast landscape a world mining region. The amount of silver mined by generations of immigrants from the Carpathians' champion lodes is astonishing. The mines of the Czech side of the Carpathians yielded 1.5 tons of gold and 22.2 tons of silver in the High Middle Ages.[135] It is possible that mines located in Slovak, Hungarian, Polish, and Romanian sides yielded comparable quantities. As late as the sixteenth century, Banská Bystrica yielded 'red silver,' or pyrargyrite, a silver antimony sulfide, possibly processed in a smelting factory annexed to the mine during A.D. 1395–1415.[136] The most significant mining works were those of Kutná Hora, running with brief interruptions from A.D. 1300 to 1560. Kutná Hora's late German Gothic architecture and medieval urban plan, which differs from that of Prague and Jihlava, indicate that the city adjusted its tempo 'to accommodate the mining complex and its relics.'[137] Miners made fortunes exploiting Kutná Hora's lodes, at a time when the economy of continental Europe was entering a recession.[138] 'Dumps of mining waste and slags several meters high' still lie in Kutná Hora's soil.[139] This was where the medieval mining corporation emerged, an unequivocal sign of the early capitalist beginnings of the business.

The Ore-Rich Veins of Tuscany's Colline Metallifere

Giovanni di Zaccharia (A.D. 1474–1544) once 'observed a large quantity of slag which, on being pounded and put into a crucible, yielded silver.'[140] This Volterra sculptor possibly found the slag while scrutinizing for the best porphyries and rocks of the Apennine valleys. Giovanni's slag discovery was proof of

Fig. 2.4. Silver mines in Tuscany and Sardinia, A.D. 1200–1400. Medieval silver-mining works were in a privileged location. The most extensive flat alluvial valleys are found west of the Apennines. The only large islands in the vicinity are located west of the Italian coast, a feature that aided in the technological transfer and diffusion from the peninsula to the islands and vice versa. On both sides of the Tyrrhenian Sea, mining mountains do not exceed 1,524 meters above the mean sea level. In Sardinia, elevation is lower—914 meters above mean sea level. The small, rounded Apennines leave behind the high peaks of the Alps as the chain moves southwards, a feature that facilitated the formation of population nuclei in the region.

Legend

△ Ag mines

Tuscany-Sardinia

▲ Ag mines

Land elevation (m)

3,400

740

0

N
W E
S

0 50 100   200
Km

the prosperous medieval mining industry that proliferated in the Ore Hills or Colline Metallifere of Tuscany.

The Ore Hills belong to the Apennines, the mountain range that traverses the Italian peninsula in a north-south direction.[141] The range starts as a branch of the Maritime Alps in the north of Genoa and moves eastwards and southwards, forming an arc within a short distance of the Adriatic before descending in a southeast direction through the center of the peninsula. The Apennine hills form calcareous eminences that branch off from the Ligurian Alps in Savona and continue south. Water springs and torrents continuously carry matter from the oldest part of the Apennines to the lower-elevation hills to the west. 'The quantity of matter brought into the valleys had been so great,' remarked a nineteenth-century observer, 'as not only to have raised the beds of the rivers, and choked the port of Pisa, but also to have considerably elevated the valleys.'[142] It is this matter, *sasso morto* as an Italian geologist called it, that becomes over time the dry lands of Tuscany, forming the geological makeup of the Ore Hills.[143]

When this waste descends from the Apennines, it brings beds of various natures.[144] Sediments containing metalliferous ores begin in the eastern hills of the Bay of Spezia or the Carrara Mountains, extending into Pisa, Siena, Grosseto, and Massa Marittima.[145] Ore lodes occur in streaks of four and a half meters to nine meters broad and up to twenty-seven meters long, with veins of argentiferous galena in hornblende formations. Decomposed matter also forms iron pyrites, as in Rocca San Silvestro, and copper pyrites, as in Temperino. In Cava del Piombo, it forms mostly blende and galena.[146] 'The mass of the lodes is often firmly joined to the wall-rock, and so intimately combined, that it is difficult to state where the limits are: they appear to have melted together.'[147] And almost everywhere, this waste contains veins of argentiferous galena.

Generations of immigrants and native miners pierced the hills of the Apennines in search of metals. The Gran Cava mine located in the Temperino Valley still shows impressive galleries and narrow and almost vertically inclined tunnels. The following description, written by a nineteenth-century traveler, gives an idea of the scale of mining works:

> The descent of the mine of Temperino is by short and nearly perpendicular ladders, not more than 30 feet in length, a great mistake to my mind, being so very fatiguing to the men; and after proceeding a few hundred feet in depth we arrive at the workings; we then enter the Galleria Fortunata, a large chamber, 44 yards high,

communicating with ancient Etruscan excavations, which are, however, chiefly
situated at a higher level, having been commenced from the surface at a distance
of 220 yards from the present shaft. Farther on is an excavation called the Grande
Cava. These are no longer accessible from above by the original openings, without
risking oneself by descending with ropes and other appliances. . . .[148]

Veramente grandiose, praised Italian geologists Carobbi and Rodolicco.[149]

Galena was found almost everywhere, from the Livorno coast to Pisa and Grosseto. A 'fine lead-lode' containing argentiferous galena was found in Campanella
di Garfagnana in the north Apennines.[150] Argentiferous galena was mined at Ruosina south of the marble district of Carrara. In Val di Castello, limestone rocks
contain bedded veins of argentiferous galena. The Versilia coast in Pietrasanta,
facing the Ligurian Sea, yielded a *complesso sistema filoniano*, extending from
Canale dell'Angina to Galena sulla Vezza, with veins of galena, blende, chalcopyrite, and pyrite.[151] Masses of galena were in Canalle dell'Angina. Further south, in
Campiglia in the Cornia Valley, the amphibole rock of the Cava del Piombo quarry
'appears almost black,' a sign of blende and galena formations.[152]

Tuscany's feudal lords hardly remained idle in the face of the plentiful geological endowments of the Ore Hills. When in A.D. 896, Margrave Adalberto of
Tuscany donated to a bishop of Volterra jurisdiction over Montero, Berignone,
Casole, Sasso, and Marciano, he was motivated by the ready cash that he would
receive from the mines. The date is by no means irrelevant: in the same year,
miners discovered galena veins at Mons Aeris or Montieri.[153] Montieri's location near Massetano and Boccheggiano promised much underground wealth
to Volterra's bishopric. Massetano and Boccheggiano contain massive homoge-
neous deposits 'made up entirely of sulphides' mined at Capanne Vecchie and
Fenice Massetana.[154] Ores found at Gerfalco knew no political boundary: they
continued into Spannochia and Chiusdino, in Massetano, and broke into the subsoil of Siena—a feature that fueled a centuries-long battle for the mines of the
region.[155]

Miners exploited other ores in a smaller mountain chain encircling the Arno
River. The chain yielded alum, coal, antimony, sulfur, and cinnabar, mined at
Pereta, Santa Fiora, and Rocca Albegna. For centuries, miners exploited a yel-
low marble 'streaked and spotted with black' in the Montariente quarries near
Siena. Miners have exploited amethysts of 'small value' in Potestaria di Massa,
too. Wolfram was mined in Gherardesca and saltpeter at Sorano.[156] Everywhere in

Tuscany the landscape was dotted by mining works. This vibrant mining activity confronted, notwithstanding, geographic challenges intrinsic to the region.

Good Food and High Living Cost

Twelfth-century Tuscany became a region of a rare duality: cheap food and high living costs. Expansion of commercial farming reduced over the century absolute prices of food, improving peasants' living standards.[157] Farmers planted olive trees in the western slopes of Monte Albano, facing Lucca, and the communes of Larciano and Lamporecchio. They cultivated the *oliva d'ogni mese*, the olive tree that furnishes olives several times a year—an uncommon feature in Mediterranean agrarian regions.[158] In time, Tuscany's olive oil was superior to that of Lombardy, 'amid the pestiferous marshes of Maremma.' A nineteenth-century English traveler noted that Tuscany's olive trees are 'of astonishing age, and immense size, conjectured [. . .] to have been planted by the ancient Etruscans.'[159]

Numerous irrigation projects contributed to the expansion of commercial agriculture.[160] Such was the case of thirteenth-century Pistoia, where crops achieved an average return of six to one on the seed, and 'returns of ten to one were not impossible.'[161] Wine was produced in Pistoia's middle hills, Montecatini, Arezzo, Montepulciano, and throughout the Arno Valley.[162] Not always, of course, was wine sold at favorable prices.[163]

In Garfagnana, at the basin of the Serchio River in north Tuscany, a different climatic zone furnished ideal conditions for cultivation of *castagno,* or chestnut.[164] 'Up to the middle of the present century, the valley was the *civiltà del castagno.*'[165] While in most parts of Tuscany 'wheat was the standard,' 'chestnut flour was a basic staple here, often more important than grain.'[166] An Italian encyclopedist put the importance of Apennine chestnut culture in global perspective: *le palme dell' Affrica, le agave dell' America, i fichi dell' India, castagno e leccio appenninico.*[167] A sixteenth-century estimate of the harvest of 'white, dried chestnuts gives an astonishingly high number 100,000 staia'; 'a century later, another estimate set the volume of chestnuts gathered and ground into flour at 300,000 staia per year, not including those eaten fresh.' The *starium* or *sextarium* was a unit of measurement of solids and liquids and varied from region to region, approximately equal to twenty-one liters.[168] Harvests were consumed by the domestic market, 'as chestnuts did not acquire much commercial importance and were not exported in substantial quantities.'[169] Harvest failures were the natural Malthusian check on population. In the fourteenth century, failures 'brought black hunger to the mountain communes.'[170]

But before the fourteenth century, expansion of agriculture aided other extractive economies. Settlers found abundant timber resources in Mount Cornate in Gerfalco, with an elevation of 1,058 meters, and Poggio di Montieri, situated at an elevation of 1,051 meters. The abundant *selva di castagne* in the high hills became the stock from which peasants made charcoal for local consumption and the export market. Metallurgical factories located in Follonica and Valpiana in Massa relied upon charcoal coming from bordering forests.[171] By the eighteenth century, Marradi and Montajone were still exporting charcoal made from the chestnut tree to the rest of the Italian peninsula.[172] The high-carbon yield of the chestnut tree justified the charcoal-making business, as long as the *selva di castagne* was sustainably managed. Only the laburnum trees found in the Pennines and central Europe surpassed the carbon yield of the chestnut tree, as summarized in Appendix B.

Land clearances after the eleventh century aided the expansion of silvo-pastoralist activities.[173] Tuscan meadows fed large flocks of animals and furnished lumber. Annual transhumance of sheep was observed in 'every part of the seacoast from La Spezia to Grosseto.'[174] Animal herding was controlled in cultivated valleys, aimed at sustaining the growing demand for food.[175] A Tuscan prelude to Malthusian thinking? The *turmas pecorum de Carfagnana* or sheep flocks of Garfagnana 'fed in the San Rossore forest near Pisa in A.D. 1156'; 'on the pastures of the Bishop of Luni near Brugnato in A.D. 1197'; and 'on pastures in the Maremma Massetana in the late twelfth and thirteenth centuries.'[176] This was truly a feudal lord's enterprise—'no peasant initiative,' according to Herlihy. In time, the peasantry recognized that 'economic development of any use to them would come with the exploitation of the silvo-pastoral economy, not with vineyards on north-facing mountain sides.'[177] By the fifteenth century, mules, pigs, sheep, chickens, and oxen were found almost everywhere in the region.[178]

Floods and malaria, however, were constant reminders that life was a costly strife against nature. Almost all coastal lands are swampy, as historian Wickham observes.[179] With frequent flooding, malaria became a permanent feature of this landscape. *Di Maremma e di Sardegna i mali*—such was Dante's description of malaria.[180] Malaria was the perennial enemy of the inhabitants of the Chiana Valley in central Tuscany.[181] The first mention of malaria came from a letter by Sidoine Apollinaire, who traveled from Lyon to Rome, around 4 B.C. He wrote about 'fevers' that affected Etruscan lands.[182] Peasants sought 'refuge in the Tuscan hills against "the bad air" or the *mala aria* of the poorly drained lowlands.'[183]

Landlords did the best they could, transforming malaria-infested marshes into real estate. Such was the case of the Chiana Valley, leased to Cósimo I de Medici for an annual sum of fifty *scudi* starting in A.D. 1573.[184] Two centuries earlier, Giovanni Boccaccio had declared the region as *infame palude*.[185] Machiavelli had said something similar: 'The malaria of Pisa kept it thinly populated, till the Ligurians, driven out of their territories by the Saracens, flocked thither in such numbers, it soon became populous and powerful.'[186]

The problem of malaria was exacerbated by the 'hydrological chaos' endemic to the peninsula. 'The very existence of a great part of Tuscany depends on the power the people may yet have to keep the waters under control.'[187] These were the words of a nineteenth-century Italian historian. A reliable statement, considering the fair number of pages the Romans devoted to commenting upon Tuscany's water problems.[188] The Arno River rises in the Apennines, at Mount Falterona east of Florence, bisects the city, and flows westwards to Pisa, before merging into the Tyrrhenian Sea. The river is fed by torrents from both sides of the Apennines. Most of its 240-kilometer course was navigable in the fourteenth century, which is why rich merchants settled their business headquarters close to the Arno Valley.

Yet, the 'convenience' of settling in the Arno Valley, as Machiavelli once put it, required much toil and trouble.[189] The Arno River has 'sinuous' channels that migrate laterally and constantly, generating networks of abandoned channels that are 'typical of low-gradient slopes.'[190] Roman waterworks controlled much of this phenomenon, and canals, ditches, and levies were built centuries later. However, with heavy rains in spring and fall, the Arno Valley from Florence to Pisa and Leghorn can completely flood. It was in the waters of the Arno River where military commander Hannibal of Carthage (247–183 B.C.) lost all his elephants, commented fourteenth-century Florentine Giovanni Villani in witty fashion.[191] Periods of high flood frequency resulted in 'persistence of wetlands and much more difficult management of waterlogged soils.'[192]

Swollen rivers running through the Ore Hills respected no feudal boundary and unleashed their fury equally against all towns. Lorenzo de Medici noticed the '"poor wealth" of highland families,' affected by the flooding of the Ombronne River.[193] Copious rains transformed the Cornia River into a destructive force, affecting everything in its northwest course from the Sasso Pisano hills to the northern side of the Ore Hills. Inhabitants of Monterotondo Marittimo and Massa Marittima are too familiar with landslides that cover the city streets in mud when the Turbone, Milla, and Risecco effluents swell. The Bruna River, rising south of Massa Marittima and running southwest into the Tyrrhenian Sea, was kept under control only after the Republic of Siena built a dam in A.D. 1468.[194]

Despite these geographic challenges, miners probably achieved a higher standard of living than the rest of the rural population. Today, the Parco tecnologico ed archeologico delle Colline Metallifere is a government initiative for promoting and protecting the region's geological heritage.[195] The five main communes of the park—Montieri, Monterotondo Marittimo, Massa Marittima, Roccastrada, and Sassetta—still display mining ruins that leave the student of mining history in awe. Massa Marittima was the most famous medieval mining commune. In A.D. 1200, Massa registered a population that reached ten thousand inhabitants. After more than a century of industrial growth, a war between Massa and Siena broke out in A.D. 1326. Not only did the war efforts against its enemies empty Massa's coffers, much in vain, but a wave of plague starting in A.D. 1328 greatly diminished the city's population. In A.D. 1396, silver-mining operations completely ceased.[196] In the first years of the fifteenth century, after a series of wars against Siena, only four hundred inhabitants made up the city's population.[197]

Massa's economy for most of the fifteenth century depended upon raw materials and short-lived positive spillovers from investments by Tuscan capitalists. The Medici had rebuilt mining and smelting works in Argentiera, an abandoned mine in Ruosina, Lucca, near Massa. The Florentine bankers did everything they could to revive the glory of the mining industry, even bringing ores from adjacent mines in Bottino and Val di Castello for refining in Massa.[198] The experience of the family with a profitable alum cartel possibly inspired Cósimo in his dealings with Massa's silver mines.[199] However, Cósimo was about to learn a bitter lesson: that alum and silver mines were totally different industries. In the last decades of the fifteenth century, Cósimo reopened the old mine of Pietrasanta in Lucca. He hired German miners. Cósimo's sons, Francesco and Ferdinando, were the sole owners of the mine. They also held mining claims in Val di Castello.[200] Fortune denied her hand to Medici's new enterprise. In the early decades of the sixteenth century, the enterprise ran at a loss. The mines yielded in their best year 208 silver pounds and 13,263 lead pounds at a cost of 32,690 *lire* in A.D. 1565.[201]

Silver mining became by then a bad business. Costs of production were too high, even for one of the greatest banking families of the medieval world.[202] Prohibitions on the use of wood throughout the second half of the sixteenth century did not alleviate the problem of high production costs. A new mining bonanza appeared only after the nineteenth century, when a modern mining company worked the Capanne Vecchie and Fenice Massetana deposits with much success.[203] The most glorious moment was the thirteenth century, when private mining *societas* exploited the underground wealth of rich Italian city-states.

Sardinia: An Island of Irregular Silver Veins

The islands of the Tyrrhenian Sea, Sardinia, comprising only twenty-four thousand square kilometers, formed a world mining region by itself.[204] An 'offspring of Hercules' named Sardus was the founder of the island, according to Isidore of Seville. 'Sardus . . . having set off from Libya with a great multitude, occupied Sardinia, giving his name to the island.'[205] The island offered a unique geological bonanza, observed Isidore of Seville, who wrote that its 'hot springs heal the eyes, and make thieves known; for their crime is revealed by blindness.'[206]

Sardinia lies on a meridian line from the Gulf of Genoa to Africa and, along with Corsica, is 'a remnant of an ancient submerged land mass.'[207] An island of mountains, its *graniaco promontorio* stands on the east side—a massive granite formation that runs 'in the form of amphitheaters [in Barbagia] from the seashore to the summit of Corruboi.'[208] This mountain forms a 'brusque escarpment' that limits access to the eastern coast, giving one the impression that the island 'turns its back upon Italy.'[209] The mountain becomes gentler when running westwards toward the mainland. The island's northeastern and southeastern mountain ranges are short, when compared to the great masses of the Alps and the Carpathians. They meet at Gennargentu, the Gate of Silver massif, the island's highest summit at 1,290 meters and located southeast of Sardinia. Separated by a flat plain, there are the mountains and hills of Sulcis-Iglesiente in the southwest, the center of the medieval mining district.

'The great number of metallic veins seen everywhere in great profusion' were exploited in an area roughly covering 2,500 square kilometers.[210] This quadrant included today's Montevecchio, Fluminimaggiore, Iglesias, Carbonia, San Giovanni, and Nuxis.[211] Sulcis was the origin of the medieval mining district of Iglesias. Miners found here innumerable topographic fixes bearing evidence of ancient mining works. A nineteenth-century Italian mining engineer put it

Fig. 2.5. Fine nineteenth-century masonry building complex, Piccalinna mine, Guspini-Montevecchio, Sardinia. In the mid-nineteenth century, mule-drawn carts were employed in transporting Montevecchio ores to the port of Cagliari. The journey lasted three days, according to Cruciani. Courtesy of Professor Gabriele Cruciani, Università degli Studi di Cagliari.

succinctly: *il travaglio delle miniere nella Sardegna è d'una data anteriore alla memoria d'uomini.*[212] Archeological evidence confirms that Roman mining works spread throughout southwest Sardinia, in Guspini, Fluminimaggiore, San Nicolao, Antas, Grugua, Malacalzetta, Iglesias, Monteponi, Gonnesa, and Arenas. Slaves, convicts, and forced laborers including condemned Christians worked the island's mines; 'the harsh condition of their internment would have allowed little or no opportunity for proselytizing except among their fellow convicts,' states Hirt.[213] Many found 'their route to martyrdom' serving sentences of forced labor in Sardinia's mines, as the life of Roman presbyter Hippolytus in the third century A.D. illustrates. Indeed, the Romans coined different names for the island, all evoking images of mines and metals—*Plumbea, Metalla, Argentiera, Argentaria, Montiferru,* and *Calapiombo.* It is possible that mining continued into the Vandal and Islamic periods up to the tenth century, although evidence of intensive mining works is still missing. Archeologist Rowland suspects that the evidence might lie in 'a late tenth century legal compilation preserved in a twelfth-century copy from Greek Southern Italy.' The compilation contains a document that mentions 'that lower class purveyors of love potions or abortifacents were to be sent to the mines, upper class ones to the island, while those of the former status who gave love potions to a woman were to be sent to the mines, to Sardinia or Corsica.'

The most spectacular medieval mining works took place in Montevecchio. Today one of the eight mining districts of Sardinia's Parco Geominerario, Montevecchio was 'the richest province of Italy.'[214] The district's ore deposits consist of irregular veins traversing clay slates and overlaying granitic rocks. Veins vary from stringers to lodes and can reach thirty and a half meters in width. The veins that run north of Arbus's granite mass are among the most remarkable of any Mediterranean region. They can reach a thickness of fifty meters and contain galena mixed with blende, iron pyrites, heavy spar, siderite, and copper pyrites.[215] Their argentiferous galena contains no modest amounts of silver— between 0.08 and 0.17 percent. The primary ores of Monteponi and Malfatano consisted of galena and blende with calamine.

Miners also discovered profitable silver veins in the district of Tulana, yielding 'seventy percent of pure silver.' Nurra and Sarrabus formed two additional mining districts, which generally yielded silver and antimony with galena.[216] Orlando Paglia, a Genoese merchant, with a 'Luccese financier in Genoa, and three partners,' invited two German capitalists to work the Nurra mine in the early years of the fourteenth century. This was no business for idle feudal lords: the starting capital was 200 Genoese pounds.[217] The 'hundreds of veins' of Sarrabus in southeast Sardinia yielded galena, native silver, and *argento rosso* or pyrargyrite.[218] In A.D. 1622, miners were still exploiting ore veins at Monte Narda in Sarrabus, where they found *galena ricchissima in argento*.[219]

Mountains furnished other valuable raw materials. The *mares* or *massacà*, a sedimentary rock prevalent in Majorca and the Baleares Islands, was used by Catalan masons in the construction of the Gothic-Catalan buildings that adorn some of the island's historic settlements.[220] Limestone was used in Cagliari's public works, while recently earth was used in buildings standing along the Campidano plain. Campidano yielded a clay 'adequate to the specific purpose of adobe production,' making it 'possible for the private builder to use the materials excavated *in loco*.'[221] Mediterranean limestone yielded beautiful marbles exported to Italy.[222] There, masons used it for building 'the columns adorning the Baptistery of the cathedral of Pisa.'[223]

Peattie's idea that 'mountains have an essential suggestion of republican-ism'[224] fits neatly to Sardinia's mining mountains. The latter, occupying three fourths of the island's surface, refused to subjugate easily to foreign invaders. The island's underground wealth, ideal harbors (especially at Cagliari), and strategic location made it a natural target of Mediterranean powers. Pope Bon-iface VIII (c. A.D. 1235–1303), allied with Aragon, granted jurisdiction of the island to King Jaime II. Boniface granted Sardinia and Corsica 'in perpetual fief' to the Aragonese king 'after two years of secret negotiations.'[225] His was no trivial political achievement: a mortal blow to foreign policy interests of other Mediterranean powers, in exchange for 'an annual payment of 2,000 marks of silver' in A.D. 1297.[226] Five Aragonese kings would rule the island between A.D. 1327 and 1410.[227]

The Aragon Crown conceived of Sardinia and Corsica as rightfully belong-ing to a Catalan-Mediterranean area of influence ruled by Aragon.[228] Aragon's expansionist policy clashed with the commercial interests of Pisa and Genoa, two genuine Mediterranean superpowers. Through alliances with the island's native ruling families, the city-states had gained power through four judicates: Cagliari in the northeast, Gallura in the south, Arborea in the west, and Torres and Logurodo in the center-north. These were nominally Sardinian kingdoms but had loose territorial borders. As Sardinian ruling families 'intermarried with Pisa and Genoese noble families,' the influence of the city-states in the eco-nomic affairs of the island grew.[229]

Legally, the Papal donation officially sealed the fate of Genoa and Pisa in the island—'the triumph of neither,' stated geographer Greville.[230] Genoa obtained some lands outside the southern mining districts, while Pisa's navy was forbid-den for a period of fifteen years.[231] *Piaccia al diavolo, che vengano questi Cat-alani!* ran the bitter cry by a Pisa citizen after listening to the news in Cagliari. Agrarian lands situated in the center of the island, necessary for sustaining min-ing settlements, were left outside the direct control of the king of Aragon.

The king of Aragon was busy with succession problems at home. However, his son, the future King Alfonso IV (r. A.D. 1327–1336), did pay attention in time to Sardinia's situation, pressured by continuous threats of external attacks by Pisa and Genoa. Alfonso IV invaded the island in A.D. 1323, with an army consisting of 1,500 soldiers, *e gente a piè grandissima.* Giovanni Villani, wit-nessing the events, calculated that more than 12,000 men died in the battles that ensued.[232] The island surrendered, with the exception of Iglesias and Castello di Castro, and became part of the Aragonese kingdom.[233] Notwithstanding, the king was forced to tolerate Pisa's presence in Trexenta and Ghippi.[234]

Yet no feudal institution was strong enough to suffocate the rising capitalist mining industry. Sardinia's mining flourished in the fourteenth century. Miners were immigrants from the Italian city-state of Pisa, long before the king of Aragon imposed restrictions to migration after he took possession of the island in A.D. 1323. They gained undisputed fame. *Ducere de Germania operarios practicos et expertos ad loca mineraria laborandum*, proclaimed Pope Sixtus IV (A.D. 1414–1484).[235] Many mining experts or *sardis Magistris* traveled to Catalonia in the mid-fourteenth century, hired by the king for prospecting the *crosos* or silver mines of Catalonia.[236] By then, their mining laws and techniques had gained undisputed fame in the medieval world.

Water and Malaria

Geography added distinctive challenges to Sardinia's mining settlements. The principal malaria vector of the island is the *Anopheles labranchiae,* one of the three vectors that affect Mediterranean European populations. It 'made every ecological zone vulnerable to its presence.'[237] An American geographer who visited the island a century ago stated, 'all regions have more or less malaria, an evil which has hardly abated since ancient times, in spite of the advance of science and distributions of quinine by the Italian Government.'[238] The island's population endured a centuries-long adaptation to endemic malaria, a factor that explains the high rates of Cooley's anemia and favism among Sardinians.[239] Found in other Mediterranean coastal lands, Africa, and Southeast Asia, Cooley's anemia causes 'severe anemia, facial deformities, and usually death at an early age.'[240]

Diverse hydrological features exacerbated the environmental vulnerability of mining settlements. Rivers 'are short and rapid, in the plains swelling so quickly in rainy weather as to become entirely impassable.'[241] Remains of Roman hydraulic machinery discovered at Rio Canonica, S'acqua Arrulla, Flumini, and Riu E'leni bear evidence that the Romans expended much toil and trouble domesticating the island's rivers.[242] Before the dams built in the first decades of the twentieth century, rivers tended to become torrential in the rainy season and overflow the plains.[243] The Tirso River rises in Buddoso in the north, and runs southwest into the Gulf of Oristano, near the ancient city of Tharros. The Flumendosa River rises in 'the mountains of Barbagia' and is approximately

113 kilometers long. It flows into the sea in southeast Sardinia. This river 'often causes disastrous floods, but leaves in its track a rich alluvial soil.'[244]

When swollen, rivers transformed valleys into marshes and lagoons that benefited the spread of the *Anopheles* mosquito.[245] The fight against malaria in the lowlands near the sea took people up into the dry plateaus. In a sense, malaria drew the mountain habitation line. No doubt, this was malaria's significant contribution to the island, many centuries before the disease vector was eradicated in the mid-twentieth century.[246] People settled in the island's hills and crests and 'looked down upon the watercourses below, dry or nearly dry in the Summer, wild and roaring during the brief rainy season.'[247] Swamps that were seen everywhere, including high elevations, 'frequently dry up in summer, remaining covered with shining salt crystals or decaying weed, and they are often shrouded in dense fogs.'[248]

Malaria-infested coastal swamps contrasted with the scarcity of water streams in the hinterlands. An Italian geologist lamented that the 'geographical environment has been hostile to Sardinian prosperity'; 'position, climate, relief, hydrography, and geology have all combined to retard the island's progress.'[249] This was a scornful lament from a peninsular man. He continued: 'The engineer Omodeo, therefore, does not exaggerate when he asserts that from the point of view of agricultural meteorology, the region of Campidano in Sardinia is the least favoured of the entire kingdom.' According to this expert, 'even Foggia itself in "dry Apulia"' received much more precipitation and hence, more water than Sardinia.'[250]

The island's rainfall patterns are 'more characteristic of truly desertic regions' and fail to compare to other Mediterranean locations.[251] The feature was aggravated by the low elevation of mountains, which made them inadequate for water storage. Frequent winds increase the rate of water evaporation. This wind pattern makes the island 'a garden with water, without water, a desert.'[252] 'Herbaceous plants tend to die in the hot summer, and the life of the trees themselves becomes dormant.'[253] One can speculate that ore-washing and smelting were, thus, expensive operations. Miners transported silver ores to places with fluvial networks, but only rich argentiferous veins justified the high transport costs. The cut-off grade, a point 'below which ore samples are not included in reserve estimations,' was certainly high.[254] However, ore-washing was much more extensive and important in medieval Sardinia than in any other previous period. The high diversity of specialized tasks related to ore-washing and cleaning further confirms this point, as will be described later.

Agriculture flourished, despite the fact that, unlike the Alps, Carpathians, or Apennines, Sardinian mountains are cut everywhere by ravines impeding the formation of long valleys. The Campidano plain southwest of the Gennargentu Massif and the Logudoro region in the northern foothills were agrarian lands. Campidano, extending for over ninety kilometers and reaching a breadth of sixteen kilometers, was the most important agrarian plain. It was here that the Roman *latifundia* took off.[255] The northern agrarian landscapes resembled those of 'Provence and Central Italy, well adapted for olives.'[256] Grains flourished in the south. Forests yielded timber resources. Proof comes from the mining statute, which details tax exemptions to miners for *legname dei boschi e salti di Kallari*, salt and timber from Cagliari.[257]

Coastal plains provided necessary salt impregnation for the growth of saltwort, sea-lavender, glasswort, and orach. The flora of Sardinia ranges from 'the products of Central Europe to those of North Africa.'[258] Willow, poplar, ash, oak, cork-tree, and ilex are common. Each tree species yielded other comparative advantages to Sardinian industries. A parasite affecting the ilex tree allowed Italians to produce a red dye, which was exported to Italian markets. The dye was inferior to the *coccus* of Spain but good for business.[259]

Shepherds made of the Barbagia Mountains the place of inverse transhumance pastoralism.[260] Here, 'permanent settlements are located in the mountains and flocks travel down to the lowlands for Winter'; shepherds spent most of the year, from November to June, in winter pastures.[261] Herding of sheep, goats, and small cattle became prevalent. The *musmo, musimo,* or mouflon, the island's sheep, has 'long, shaggy hair like a goat' and 'horns which curled round the ears instead of projecting outwards.'[262] Donkeys and mules also populated the island and were used by miners as beasts of burden. The Corsican red deer, wild swine, fox, hare, and rabbits were abundant in the mountains and provided miners with a source of protein and fat up to the early twentieth century, when Sardinia became 'a hunters' Eldorado' to rich Europeans.[263]

The strategic location of the island, coupled with its good harbors, offered several trade advantages. 'Its southern shore forms, together with the western tip of Sicily and the promontories of Tunisia, the triangular straits barring the passage from the western to the eastern Mediterranean.'[264] The southern port of Cagliari afforded direct communication with Tunisia and North Africa.[265] Silver from Sulcis found an ideal outlet in Cagliari, controlled by the Aragon Crown.[266] The flourishing trade of Cagliari was but one side of the relations

of unequal exchange that kept Sardinia in poverty, according to Marco Tangheroni.[267] The Aragon Crown built a port in Alghero, 'in the northwestern
corner of the island,' populated by Catalans; 'an attempt was made to exclude
Sardinians from holding land or even lodging there: when a trumpet sounded in
the evening at sundown, every non-Catalan was required to leave the city.'[268]

A typical mining field possibly resembled a busy booming town, in which
a diverse population of immigrants met. Indeed, the island became a frontier
land for displaced populations of continental Europe. Jewish communities attempted to move to Mediterranean islands, after French King Philip IV (A.D.
1268–1314) expelled them from France and confiscated their property.[269] Many
presumably found their way to Sardinia. The policy prohibiting Jewish men
from acquiring mining shares or settling in Iglesias suggests that Jewish men
were already in Sardinia's mining towns.[270] The rationale of the law, originating
in the *Breve anteriori,* the statute enacted by Pisa, was to 'solve the problem of
thefts of silver ores that the said Jewish do in the said silver mines.'[271]

Details about how the native Sardinians mixed and coped with immigrants
cannot be easily found in available sources. It is possible that native Sardinians
still occupied a role in the Iglesias mining economy. The fact that *sardo*, the
tongue of the native Sardinian, was maintained as written language for administrative and ecclesiastical purposes until the eighteenth century suggests that the social
fabric favored some melting of the pot. A cohesive culture ensued, if one considers
that the islanders spoke a tongue that outside Sardinia *niuno lo intendeva!*[272]

Changes in Mediterranean economic circumstances by the beginning of
the fifteenth century affected the fabric of mining towns. The period of the
infamous autos-da-fé in the Iberian Peninsula probably created momentum for
Aragon rulers to extend their crusading mission into Sardinia.[273] The mining
business by then had started to experience declining returns, after their early
capitalist start a century earlier.

Balkan Mountains: 'Silver Even Better than the Indies'

According to a Slavic legend, 'the Almighty, when shaping the Earth, carried
a great bag filled with mountains, which he has sown as a farmer sows grain.'[274]
The bag broke east of the Adriatic, and mountains fell out; the Dinaric Alps
were thus born. This is how the mountains south of the Alps running into the
Balkan Peninsula were formed. Known in antiquity as *Dalmatian* or *Darda-*

nian, the Dinaric mountains contained 'large deposits of the precious metals in great quantities and even better than those in the Indies,' in the eyes of court historian Kritovolous of Imbros writing to Sultan Mehmed II.[275] The historian's patron was not to miss this bounty.[276] The rugged terrain of the peninsula promised much reward to those who could conquer it.

Geology set the primary law of attraction that pulled miners to the Balkans, but in capricious fashion. Not everywhere was galena the main source of silver. The famous Fojnica deposits in Bosnia contain veins of quartz, pyrite, siderite with galena, and native gold.[277] Vrtlasce, situated in Bosnia's 'schist mountains,' contains pyrite and galena.[278] Čemernica deposit, consisting of quartz veins with galena and cinnabar, belongs to the mountains that lie in central Bosnia. The main minerals of the Srebrenića deposit in east Bosnia-Herzegovina are lead, zinc, silver, and sphalerite and galena ores, and the Čumavići deposit in the same region contains many sulfides including galena, sphalerite, pyrite, and chalcopyrite as well as sulfosalts and native gold and silver, among others.[279] Barite, hematite, and cinnabar are found in Bosnia's Dusin area.[280] Ore deposits in Kopaonic Mountains in Serbia include lead-zinc, antimony, copper, molybdenum, iron, and gold, among other formations.[281] Bordering Srebrenića, the Cer and Boranja sulfide deposits yielded, besides zinc and antimony, many sulfides including sphalerite and galena, pyrite, and chalcopyrite, various oxides, and gangue minerals, among others.[282] Further south, deposits in Kavala, Livadia, Chalkidikí, and Eleftheroúpolis in the Greek peninsula yielded silver, lead, and gold.[283]

Ottoman expansion was the second force that gave impetus to mining. While Turkic principalities rose and fell in Anatolia between the fourteenth and fifteenth centuries, the Ottomans continued their expansionist campaigns toward southeast Europe. Sultan Mehmed II put his eyes first upon the mine of Novo Brdo before conquering Prizren in A.D. 1455.[284] In Bosnia-Herzegovina, the mines of Fojnica opened after A.D. 1349, sometime after the early Ottoman expansion into the peninsula. Srebrenića and Olovo mines also in Bosnia were exploited around this time.[285] Serbian mines were mentioned in A.D. 1339, in a document granting foreign merchants the right to export metals.[286] Brskovo or Brescoa, today's Mojkovac in Montenegro, appeared in a document in A.D. 1254 in relation to immigrant miners, even though it was after the mid-fourteenth century when the mine became an important source of silver ores. A medieval chronicler wrote about mines located in Rascia, Serbia: 'there are indeed five

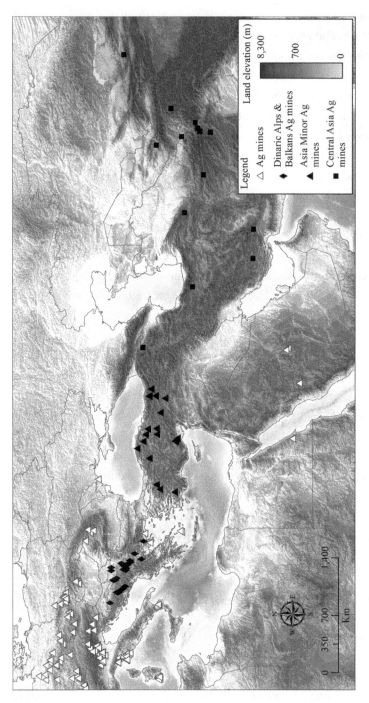

Fig. 2.6. Silver mines under Seljuk Turk and Ottoman jurisdictions, A.D. 1150–1500. No long river connected the western and eastern portions of the vast Ottoman lands. The Tigris and Euphrates run southwards, east of the Taurus chain. The route followed by the Araxes River lies northeast of the Pontic chain, between the Black and Caspian seas. No vast or extensive plain forced aggregation of mining sites into one single spot. The mountains were unprotected, opened on too many fronts to forces that hindered the early capitalist growth of mining.

gold mines and an equal number of silver mines in which expert miners toil without interruption'; 'there are also mixed deposits of silver and gold, which have recently been discovered at various and soundry sites, and huge dense forests.' He concluded with no hesitation: 'whoever owns this kingdom will have a veritable jewel in his possession, select and precious for all times.'[287]

Large-scale mining operations flourished in Kopaonik, Zeleznik, and Os-truvznica.[288] Along with Rudnik in Serbia, Srebrenića was under continuous operation until A.D. 1454.[289] Under Sultan Mehmed II, the mines Srebrenića, Kratovo, Prichtina, Serres, Selanik or Thessaloniki, Sofia, and Novo Brdo were leased for 120,000 *pièces d'or* every year, possibly as part of a grant of land usufruct rights known as *timar*.[290] Mines in Madenkhorio, Macedonia, were worked in the late sixteenth century. Small furnaces were built 'of solid masonry behind and fragile in front, and reconstructed once a week.' They were spread over a vast mining field in the Kholomonda Mountains, 'from Erissos to Makhala north of Lake Vilvi.'[291]

Mining was not to be limited to silver or gold. Bosnia became the 'land of salt'; Herzegovina, the 'land of stones.'[292] Salt mined at Kotor was an important commodity in the incomes of the Ottoman military class known as *'askerî*.[293] It had been a profitable commodity also for pre-Ottoman ruling classes. A treaty between Bulgarian tsar Michael II Asen (r. A.D. 1246–1256) and the city of Dubrovnik signed in A.D. 1253 stated that 'half of the profits from the sale of all the salt sold to the people of Rashka' went to the former.[294] Tar, a soft stone, was produced in Albania, in 'the mountains of Dukagjin in great quantities,' according to a sixteenth-century source. The anonymous author observed how tars 'are often transported down to the wharves at Lezha on the Drin.' He continued:

> I have seen them being sold at three or four big pounds for a *soldo*. The region of Vlora produces hard tars from the earth, which nature offers much as it does minerals. There is an infinite amount. I remember that in Vlora, tar was being sold at forty-five aspers for a *miaro*, and in recent times, it has become quite expensive because of certain individuals who have taken over all the tar trade.[295]

Antimony and arsenic were mined at Alšar and Rožden; iron at Rudino and Slatino, where a castle was built 'to protect the mines.'[296]

The third force was the waves of migrants who sought their destinies in Bal-

kan mountains and valleys. Venetians and Lombardians made the Balkans a
geographic catchment area.[297] Bulgarian tsars extended tax privileges to 'Venetian Franks.' Tsar Ioan Alexander (r. A.D. 1331–1371) made an 'oath and
treaty' in A.D. 1347 guaranteeing 'safe conduct to my friends and brothers, the
Venetian Franks, and my Tsardom swears in God the Father [. . .] that all the
Venetian merchants might come and go on their ships throughout my entire
Tsardom and be safe and sound.'[298] Merchants from Genoa enjoyed 'extensive immunities and extraterritorial privileges' granted by Bulgarian tsars; their
businesses flourished in the Black Sea and allowed Bulgaria to profit from 'the
affairs of the lands of the East.'[299] The Sasi or Teotonici, names by which the
Saxons were known, brought 'technical expertise,' according to historian John
Fine.[300] King Stephen Uroš I of Serbia (A.D. 1223–1277) welcomed the first
Sasi colony from Transylvania in A.D. 1243–1276.[301] Saxon immigrants gained
prominent position in the administration of the silver mines of the region.[302]
The Court of Serbian King Dušan reflected this hierarchical melting pot, 'with
Serbs, Bulgarians, Greeks, Albanians, Saxons from the mining towns, German
knights, revenue officers from among the patricians of Kotor (Cattaro) and Du-
brovnik, as well as merchants of Venice and Florence.'[303]

Migrants made of the peninsular mountains part of their lives and patrimony.
When the Ottomans reached these lands, they found mining associations that
possibly resembled those found in Latin Europe. The thirteenth-century association nested in the hinterlands of the Balkans was organized in a general assembly of miners, the *rudarski sabor*, which 'presided over causes related to mining: boundary, property and mining issues, arguments between associates.'[304] A
council or *curia Teutonicorum* composed of twelve members was the supreme
civil authority of the mining settlement. The miners' assembly was headed by
the *comes*, which possibly referred to a technical expert with experience in
mining. 'He was not based in any town hall and worked in his own home,'
states Rădvan. The king possibly participated in trials of the assembly through
a *vojvode*; 'he had the right to acquire products from townspeople at half the
price.' Custom officers or *carinci* 'acted as middlemen between the central authority and the local ones.' This officer had the right to 'one part of the mined
ore, one part of the refined metal, the right to mint currency, and to tax the mar-
ketplace.' The *curia Teutonicorum* and the officers linked to it disappeared after
Ottoman expansion into the Balkans. The geography of the Balkans pulled in
the opposite direction of a capitalist mining industry.

Geography Mixes All Extremes

The capricious features of the region placed unlike entities cheek by jowl, with vassal kingdoms neighboring autonomous lands ruled by chieftains and Christian villages bordering Muslim settlements. The triumphant progress of Bâyezîd I in the peninsula owed a great deal to this situation and the internal strife it triggered. Serbia and Bulgaria rejected Byzantine sovereignty very early, in A.D. 1167 and A.D. 1187, respectively, only to be at war with each other.[305] Bosnia, a cultural and political nest surrounded by different Slavonic peoples, became their 'coveted object.'[306] Bulgaria was an 'exhausted petty Tsardom,' with close diplomatic relations with Venice and the Papacy.[307] The old Vlachia was a fragile vassal state surrounded by independent principalities of less importance.[308]

By the last decade of the fourteenth century, most territories became vassal states of the Ottomans. Bulgaria as well as the Macedonian highlands fell under Bâyezîd. The warlike prince of Serbia, Stefen Lazarević, 'kept his throne by unswerving loyalty'—'his 'sister became Bâyezîd's wife.'[309] Greek territories, left defenseless by a weakened Byzantine empire, fell to the Ottomans before the mid-fourteenth century. In A.D. 1326, Ottoman armies took 'Adrianople (Edirne), and two years later they had advanced up the Maritza Valley as far as Plovdiv (Philippopolis).'[310] The *pomaks*, Bulgarians who escaped the Turks by hiding in the Rhodope, had little chance of surviving; they converted to Islam while preserving their language. Locals considered them to be 'collaborators.'[311] As for Albania and Montenegro, after battles that left the lands in devastation, the Ottomans learned a bitter lesson: better to recognize autonomy than to increase the war bill. These mountainous territories proved too difficult to conquer and remained ruled by 'independent minded chieftains' that 'proved difficult to control.'[312]

Christianity coexisted with Islam in uneven ways. Conversion to Islam took place in most lands, although its pace was slow. Noble families were assimilated into the Ottoman society in a process in which Islamization was 'a psychosocial phenomenon,' in the words of İnalcik.[313] Conversion was by no means a prerequisite to belonging to the privileged Ottoman *'askerî* or military class. The only prerequisite was loyalty to the Sultan, an extraordinary development that the early Ottoman state forged in Anatolia for religious but also geopolitical reasons. The state developed the practice of recruiting soldiers from conquered

Christian lands. Thousands of children were put under the direct tutelage of the Sultan, received the best education at the time, and became the Ottoman elite infantry soldiers known as janissaries and paid regular salaries by the Sultan. The janissaries had no alliance to land, caste, places, or Muslim families rivaling the Sultan in the rest of the Turkic world; their loyalty was to their patron, the Sultan. In time, they weakened the Ottoman state with 'insubordination and mutinies,' but this need not concern us here.[314] At its time of splendor, the class of janissaries ascended to the *'askerî* class, providing candidates to high political and administrative posts anywhere in the empire.

Payments to the military class came from taxes and land usufruct rights known as *timar*. Only special decrees by the Sultan could make members of the *'askerî* class become *timar*-holders. A *timar* had no territorial integrity; it was a fiscal unit for purposes of the Ottoman state, one that gave birth to the extraordinary Ottoman bureaucracy. This system made the Balkan noble families powerless in front of the Ottoman ruler. Nominally, loyalty to the Sultan in the form of military service generated income rewards in the form of *timar* grants. Leaving aside any treacherous host, *timar* rewards extended to everybody, and not only noble families. The lowest-paid soldiers were still rewarded: 'Those who have distinguished themselves, and carried off tongues and heads got a one-per-ten-akçe increase of their incomes,'[315] stated a sixteenth-century decree. 'Ten to fifteen tongues or heads' awarded a larger increase.[316]

Ottoman land laws were based upon one fundamental principle: that conquered lands belonged to the Sultan. The Balkans were conquered lands or *miri* land, which meant that revenues from land economies belonged to the state, and thus, the state or the Sultan rightfully used them for sustaining the *'askerî* class. Because the *'askerî* had no aristocratic origin and thus no historic claim to land, the Ottoman state, personified in the Sultan, owned and distributed resources that allowed this class to organically renew itself while fulfilling the military demands of the state. Naturally, *miri* lands were also instrumental in feeding the Sultan's personal coffer.

A *timar* was not hereditary and could be revoked at the discretion of the Sultan. Christian *timariots* or *timar*-holders were numerous in Albania, according to a *defter* of A.D. 1431 scrutinized by many historians.[317] The largest number of Christian *timar*-holders were found in border or strategic regions at the time of Ottoman expansion, 'while their number was considerably lesser in the regions situated deeper inside the Ottoman state territory.'[318] By the sixteenth century, Christian *timariots* were rarely found; 'in fact, the Christian origin of some of the *timariots* is only revealed by their rarely used family names such as Kurtik Mustafa in Albania, who was undoubtedly a descendant of the famous Slavo-Albanian lord, Pavlo Kurtic.'[319] Bishops became owners of *timars* in Albania 'with no liability for military service.'[320] While the latter were found in small numbers, this development shows that the rapid expansion of the Ottomans in the Balkans required these extremes.

The state retained pre-Ottoman territorial borders, but these would acquire different meaning with colonization of land based upon the *timar* system. Distant villages could form one *timar*, and villages belonging to one *timar* could be spatially separated by settlements belonging to a different *timar*.[321] Nominally, the view of land was that of a pool of taxable incomes to be surveyed and administered by appointed officers.[322] But this view was more of an ideal; one must assume that the reality was more complex. Certainly, 'by the first half of the fifteenth century, the timar-system had taken shape by and large.'[323] Mine revenues formed no category of their own but were added to other land revenues and taxes and measured according to imperial instructions and accounting methods—which varied with time. An Ottoman *sancakbeği* administering the conquered province of Bosnia reported in A.D. 1516:

Near Sokol [central Bosnia] are mines, like those of Srebrenica, they could quickly be put into production, and would supply the wages for all the fortresses of Bosnia. To travel to the Imperial Fortresses would become easy, so that one could go from the Well-Protected Territories to Sokol with just one or two men, and then on to Ključ and Kamengrad. Thus the troops and all the *re'āyā* in that region would live in tranquility, praying for the welfare of the Pādishāh.[324]

Thus, economic significance of ores varied depending upon how the land was surveyed for taxation. If the Serbian case is a general tendency, one can conclude that a *timar* represented the smallest census unit, representing an annual revenue of 19,999 akçe; *zeaments* yielded revenues equivalent to 20,000 to 99,999 akçe; and *hasses* yielded the highest incomes, starting at 100,000 akçe.[325] It is expected that the Sultan possessed *hass* land, as he did in Smederevo, which included incomes from the mine of Novo Brdo, various taxes, and customs by A.D. 1476–1477.[326]

To some extent, geography facilitated mixing extremes. The Balkan Peninsula lacks what the Iberian Peninsula has, waterways for accessing the world beyond. There is only one great internal highway, the Danube River.[327] The Danube flows in a west-east direction toward the Black Sea, a region that was to be dominated by the Ottomans. South of the Danube the Ottomans established border provinces, which acquired military relevance at different times during Ottoman expansion campaigns. The earliest Anatolia migrants deported to the Balkans became *sipâhîs* or cavalrymen, 'the main force of the Ottoman army,'[328] occupying garrisons in this region. They 'formed a solid belt extending from the Straits northward to beyond the Danube.'[329]

In the rest of the peninsula, the Ottomans found only short rivers, flowing either northwards or southwards. The Iskar River goes straight into the Balkan hinterlands and flows to the north instead of to the east. The Maritza, Mesta, Struma, and Vardar rivers flow southwards from the south side of the Rhodope, bringing water from many streams into the Aegean Sea; only the Maritsa 'was largely navigable prior to the 19th century.'[330] The Struma River, 'which would appear destined to the Black Sea, bores through the Rilo range' and flows into the Aegean Sea.[331] A tributary of the Danube, the Morava River rises close to Belgrade and forms the main line of communication between the Serbian highlands and the Danube. The Drin, Boyana, and Narenta rivers run toward the Adriatic Sea through limestone hills and caverns. Only the lower Drin in Albania was navigable for small boats. The river 'flows southwards through a very beautiful plain called the Sadrina (Zadrima) and continues on to the ancient town of Lezha which now has a fortress at the top of the mountain.'[332]

Ottomans found no great transport infrastructure in the hinterlands of the peninsula but trans-montane trade routes in 'miserable condition.'[333] The Roman road Via Egnatia had survived the Middle Ages; after 'a tenuous connection' between the Dinaric and the Pindus, the road 'serpentined its way up ridge after ridge of difficult mountain ranges' along the Adriatic coast.[334] The mountain pass connecting Konjic in Bosnia-Herzegovina to Sarajevo was the only main avenue of communication between inland Dinaric settlements and the Adriatic coastland. The Kačanik Pass connecting the Kosovo Plain to Macedonia was one of the many 'vertiginous mountain paths' that the Sultan's army crossed in its march toward Bosnia.[335] Bandits awaited merchant convoys in mountain passes. The Pljevlja plain in northern Montenegro, also known as Breznik or Tashlidja by its Turkish name, is the largest plain found between the Adriatic coastland and the Moesian and Dardanian staples. Ragusan and Venetian caravans passed through Pljevlja before reaching Niš and Constantinople. Venetian

traveler Ramberti, writing in A.D. 1541, described Pljevlja as 'large and well-fa-
voured, according to the country'; with the problem that 'robbers a few years
earlier, had plundered a Venetian caravan of about a hundred horses, and slain
two nobles of the Serene Republic, a Nani and a Capello.'[336]

Forces behind landscape formation conspired in the making of *chaos inex-
tricable*, in the words of a military geographer.[337] No long valleys in the Dinaric range; here, the great plains occupy the heights of mountains—unlike the
Apennines, where plains occupy the foot of mountains. Mountain peoples did
the best they could; 'inverse' transhumance became the norm. Animal herding
took place in the high mountains in the summer and the lowlands in the winter. The summer-burnt brown pastures were 'irresistibly tempting.'[338] Transhumance was practiced by Vlach families after their successful acculturation
to the mountains surrounding the Rhodope.[339] By the end of the fourteenth
century, the wandering life of the Vlachs of Bosnia and Herzegovina started
to disappear, as herders increasingly established permanent settlements on the
lower slopes of the mountains.[340] Vlachs of Bosnia-Herzegovina followed the
traditional routes from the lowland in the Adriatic coast in the summer season
to the mountains cut by the Neretva River to the south of Sarajevo.[341] Here, no
Mesta was possible, that medieval Castilian guild with muscle power against
kings and princes alike. No Arte della Lana emerged either, the wool guild
that became the symbol of the rising economic and political power of the city-
state of Florence. Balkan herders, the most vulnerable of the mountain peoples,
eventually succumbed to the fiscal intervention of the Ottoman State.

If herding communities retained their customary laws over the use of *bjeshkë*
or 'mountain pasture,' they did so because animal husbandry was inseparable
from farming.[342] One subsidized the other. Pig transhumance developed in Bosnia, a form of pastoralism that found no analogue in Europe.[343] Dense oak forests in the eastern fringe of the Dinarides afforded thick foliage and shrubs. The
hinterland vegetation includes oaks, beech, pine, and hemlock, making the land
suitable for pig transhumance. Dairy cattle were infrequent.[344] Olives supplied
the fats 'elsewhere derived from milk and butter.'[345] Sedentary village herding
and seasonal long-distance transhumance developed in the southern Dinaric.[346]

The erosional coast was one extreme, compared to fertility of inland valleys,
where cultivation of wheat, rye, oats, flax, and orchard fruits took place. According to historian Kaser, *timar*-holders enjoyed revenues coming from rice
plantations, which flourished in the Maritza Valley and the Sofia Basin.[347] In

Serbia, the most important grains cultivated were 'winter and spring wheat, oats, barley, and millet,'[348] species that tolerated calcareous soil and warm conditions. 'Cereals were grown together,' states Borojević. The term used by locals for indicating 'growing an intentional mixture of cereals' was *sumješica*; another word, *suražica*, denoted 'rye-wheat maslin.'[349] Rye and wheat were cultivated at Starigrad, Oldenburg, and Groß Lübbenau, all medieval Slavonic places. The local saying *nema žita bez kukolja*, 'there is no wheat without cockle,' suggests that corn cockle or *agrostemma githago*, the weed that contains toxic glycosides, was present in small quantities in wheat; its handpicking and elimination before consumption was not always possible.[350]

The silver-mining businesses that flourished in the fourteenth and early fifteenth centuries benefited from all extremes, if judged by the impressive record of silver production in the Ottoman Balkans. In Sidrekapsi, there were by the sixteenth century six thousand miners and 'numerous processing installations' including '500–600 furnaces.' The city was 'the largest Macedonian industrial complex and most productive of the Balkan centers.'[351] Its annual output of 347 kilograms of silver went to Constantinople. Military corps located in the region of Skopje, close to the Kratovo mines, 'received each year their wages from the *maden emîn* (mine director) of Kratovo who commanded silver and iron mines in other regions as well.'[352] Earlier in A.D. 1417, despot Stevan Lazarević leased the incomes of the mines of Srebrenića, with an estimated profit of thirty thousand ducats starting the same year.[353] Silver mined in Bosnia and Serbia found its way into Florence, Pesaro, Sicily, and Alexandria, according to Kovačević-Kojić.

There was, however, the Ottoman bureaucratic administration of the mining business. Mines belonged to *timar* grants, thus, *timariots* administered mines as they did other sources of revenues from the timar. This by no means suggests that there was no mining regulation but rather that mining was to be deprived of the legal autonomy that it enjoyed elsewhere, as will be discussed later.

3

Digging the Underground Wealth of Europe

In Defense of Private Monopolies: The Case of Trento

The mining business in Trento shared one essential condition of capitalist businesses: it was a monopoly of production. Some feudal maladies stood in the way, but private producers firmly took hold of the mines of the region. Everything started when Bishop Wanga was appointed to the bishopric by German Emperor Frederick II (A.D. 1194–1250) in A.D. 1206.[1] Wanga belonged to an aristocratic family from Bolzano and was a distant relative of the Emperor. For his loyalty to the Germanic Emperor during the campaigns into Italy, Friedrich Wanga, or Federico Vanga by the Latinized form of the name, obtained monopoly rights over Trento's forests and fishing and coinage rights along with the bishopric seat and its assets.[2] Emperor Frederick II also granted Wanga *in perpetuum* the title of Prince Bishop of Trento. This was a 'disinterested' gift, which made Wanga the city's supreme political authority.

Grants obtained by Wanga's predecessors starting with Bishop Udalrich in A.D. 1027 firmly gave bishops sovereign power over Trento.[3] It was sovereign power granted by imperial law and aimed at containing communal liberties and territorial ambitions of the secular lords of Tyrol, Brescia, and Bolzano.[4] By the time Wanga came to power, Trento was 'an island of ecclesiastical immunity,' where the Bishop Prince enjoyed 'uniform and compact jurisdiction' over the city's affairs.[5] Bishops were by then outside the traditional feudal chain of command; they responded to no secular lord, no Count or Duke, but were accountable only to the emperor if and when needed. Legally, bishops were vassals of

Table 3.1. Mining grants and acts of the Bishopric of Trento, A.D. 1181–1214

Bishop	Year	Content
Solomon	1181	Gold mines of Tassullo donated by the Count of Eppan.
Adalbert	1185	Silver mines of Tione donated by the Count of Eppan.
		Mining rights granted to *silbrarii*.
		Mining rights conditioned to payment of *fictum* and other taxes.
		Citizenship as requirement for holding mining claims.
		Bishop's right to claim subsidy from *silbrarii* under 'imminent necessity.'
		Bishop's obligation to defend and protect *silbrarii* and their businesses.
Conrad	1189	Donation of silver, copper, iron mines by Emperor Frederick I.
Conrad	1206	Donation of mines by Philip of Swabia.[a]
Wanga	1208	Confirmation of previous act.
		Recognition of mining corporation called *consilium wercorum*.
		Bishop's *gastaldia* to settle mining disputes and oversee mining works.
		Rules and fines on mine geometry, labor, ore sales, and mining shares.
		Rules and fines on taxes, fraud in mining sites, and abandoned shafts.
Wanga	1213	Fines against encroaching upon a corporation's property.
		Rules and fines on drainage adit at *mons Vaccae*.
Wanga	1214	Rules and fines on smelting furnaces.
		Mortgage of mining *gastaldia* by Bishop.
		Silver mine enfeoffed to *Wisca da Casalino*.
		All abandoned mines belong to the Bishopric of Trento.

[a] Son of Emperor Frederick I and King of Germany in A.D. 1198–1208.

Sources: Curzel and Varanini, *La documentazione dei Vescovi di Trento*, pp. 172–174, 184–187, 326–327, 350–354, 480–482, 490–491, 498–499; Kink, *Fontes Rerum Austriacarum*, pp. 430–454.

the emperor and as such were subjected to the *ius feudalis*. Their rights were not hereditary rights; however, as sovereign rulers of Trento, they enjoyed absolute freedom for disposing of the city's assets and property, including minting, military fortifications, castles, taxes, *dogana* (customs), and mines.[6]

The novel element under Wanga was his compilation of documents about the mines of the bishopric, entitled *Carta laudamentorum et postarum epis-*

copi factorum in facto Arzentarie (A.D. 1185/1207), undertaken by the notaries working for the bishop.[7] It contained in chronological order all mining laws regulating the businesses of *silbrarii* in *Arzentarie*, *Mons Vaccae,* and other silver mines of Trento.[8] The *Carta* belongs to *Codex Wangianus*, a comprehensive compilation of notarized grants, feudal investitures, and donations dealing with real estate and assets of the bishopric. The compilation was Wanga's 'mechanism of defense' against Lombardy's city leagues and the Pope's claims on Trento lands.[9]

Silbrarii appeared for the first time in Trento in A.D. 1185, in a contract concerning the mines of Mons Arzentarie. Count Henry of Eppan donated to Bishop Adalbert or Adalberto da Campo (A.D. 1184–1188), Wanga's antecessor, rights over the silver mines and *vasalli* of Breguzzo, Bondone, and Tione. An exception was made for the lands under the jurisdiction of aristocrats by the names Galapino da Lodron, Gumpone da Madruzzo, and Bozone da Stenico and the city's *milites*. The donation required give-and-take on the part of Bishop Adalbert. He had to give up *in perpetuum* his right to a tenth of the agrarian produce in Latsch, located in Trentino Alto-Adige. He also had to make a one-time payment of 800 pounds in Veronese *denarii* to the Count.[10] The Veronese *denarius* or silver penny was one of the moneys widely used in Lombardy, Tyrol, and Friuli, along with the Venetian *denarii*.[11] The Veronese standard weight was a *marca* or mark, counted as ten *libra* or pounds. Each pound was equivalent to 240 *denarii* or eighteen *solidi* or shillings.[12] The payment transferred the curia of Duomo and San Paolo Appiano, today's Saint Paul Eppan in the Estch Valley, to the bishopric's jurisdiction.[13] The Count's motivations are not relevant here; what is significant is that engrossment of lands under Trento's bishopric had started. And the lands were pregnant with metallic ores. The move sent an unequivocal signal to neighboring *milites*: the Bishop and supreme authority of Trento held mining lands.

The Bishop had one problem: he lacked money, and the mines were affected by *fodinae aquaticae,* or shaft flooding.[14] Mines required drainage. Adalbert could not afford idleness; thus, he made a contract with *silbrarii* on March 24, 1185, for exploiting the silver mines granted to the bishopric by the Count of Eppan.[15] He knew that his serfs could not bring the mines back to work after the shutdown of mining works due to shaft flooding.[16] He was thus in a rush when he summoned private producers to the Court to make a deal for bringing the mines back in operation.

The *silbrarii* that came to meet with Adalbert were Henricus Erfingar, Rip-
randus de Telue, Trentinus Covalat, and other *Argentariis, qui solent appellari
Silbrarii.*[17] They belonged to the urban aristocracy of Trento, and agreed to
invest money in Arzentarie, solve the problem of shaft-flooding, and restore
mining operations. We know nothing further about relations among these early
pioneers; it is safe to suppose that for flesh of wolf, tooth of dog, as the old
saying goes. They shared the goal of plowing money into the mines of Trento
to generate profit, and this common objective in time empowered them against
the bishop.

It is in Wanga's mining act of June 19, 1208, a *Carta*[18] notarized by Ercetus, where one finds details about the conditions under which *silbrarii* enjoyed
mining rights. Entrepreneurs legally became *socii affidati* of a corporation after
they took an oath. The oath made them members of a *consilium suprascriptorum wercorum*. Membership was voluntary, an aspect that signals an essential
distinction between *consilium* and other feudal economic institutions. Obligations of *socii affidati* included paying for mining expenses on a weekly basis,
deciding over matters pertaining to mining works, and sharing costs of infrastructure improvements.[19] How exactly they decided these affairs is a question
with no easy answer. The law only states that citizenship was a requirement that
applied to *Werchi* or German mining specialists and defined a minimum penalty
of fifty pounds against any *silbrarii* violating the law.[20] Thus, only citizens of
Trento and members of a *consilium suprascriptorum Wercorum* enjoyed ownership of mining shares or *partem* in Mons Arzentarie.[21] They enjoyed freedom
for investing in mining works in all lands under the Bishop's jurisdiction.[22] The
mining act established a condition that became essential to private mining business: it was 'necessary to belong' to the *consilium* formed by *silbrarii* in order
to enjoy mining rights in Trento.[23]

Wanga's *Carta* also reveals that no absolute economic freedom was possible. First, Wanga conditioned mining rights to payment of the *fictum*. If *silbrarii*
were going to enjoy a monopoly in Trento, they had to accept some intervention in their mining affairs by the Prince of Trento. To start with, *silbrarii* paid
the *fictum*, a tax that originated in A.D. 1155, when the German Emperor ceded
income rights to the bishopric.[24] Wanga defined the *fictum* as a rent owed by
silbrarii, in exchange for their enjoying the right to work the mines of Arzentarie.[25] The *Carta* states that if anyone avoided or fraudulently denied the
Bishop's right to the *fictum*, that person was bound to pay a fine of twenty-five

pounds and was punished according to the rules of the city.[26] Under Wanga, the *fictum* changed from a one-tenth to a one-ninth share of the mines' incomes.[27]

The second restriction imposed upon *silbrarii* was oversight of mining works by *Gastaldionibus* or *gastaldione*. The latter was an institution which, because of its long history in Lombardy, admits of no easy generalization—a point that mining historians have missed.[28] By the tenth century A.D., *gastaldia* appeared almost everywhere, exercising administrative duties as well as certain economic functions.[29] From the eleventh century onwards, *gastaldia* was an institution for the exercise of jurisdictional rights.[30] Those belonging to the 'office' of *gastaldia* were *gastaldo*, administrative officers with specific judicial and economic duties over villages and lord's courts. The place of residence of a *gastaldo* was a castle, 'from where he exercised military (*Waita*) and judicial functions.'[31] The *canipa* was the place where diverse tithes or *fictum* owed to the Bishop were collected.[32] In Trento, a *gastaldo* was an officer with specific legal, administrative, and tax-collecting duties over a village or court. In many cases, a *gastaldo* exercised judicial power. The institution belonged to the feudal history of Lombardy, which developed some anomalous institutions with no comparison anywhere.[33] Not only the Bishop of Trento had a *gastaldo*, but powerful secular lords, such as the Castelbarco family, had their own *gastaldia*.[34] It is intriguing that *gastaldia* appeared in relation to mines only under Bishop Wanga. Did previous bishops see little need in stating the obvious, that *gastaldia* responsibilities included mine administration? We can offer no definite answer to this question. It is possible that because previous bishops came from the local aristocracy, only Wanga felt the need to write readily about his *gastaldia*, so as to avoid future conflicts with his neighbors.[35]

Bishop Wanga added a role to his *gastaldia*: general supervision of mining works and representation of the bishopric's interests in the mining industry. In Wanga's *Carta*, a man by the name *Ambrosio* was identified as the Bishop's *gastaldione*.[36] His duties included settling disputes arising among *silbrarii* and general oversight of mining works. The text adds no further commentary on how the *gastaldione* exercised his jurisdiction. Certainly, the *silbrarii* were in no position to object to the jurisdiction of the Bishop's *Gastaldione*. Based upon the text of the law, one can infer that the *gastaldia* were a powerful institution, a sort of police force with the power to punish transgressions to the law, and one which *silbrarii* feared only because of its jurisdiction over taxation affairs. Any *Werchi* who rejected the rule for which he was brought to the

Bishop's Court or a decision by *gastaldione* incurred a penalty of 100 *solidi*.[37]
Gastaldia was an office that came with a salary, drawn from taxes collected by
this officer. We shall come back to this point.

Settling mining disputes possibly became an institutional affair, centralized
in the Bishop's Court. No other city's court served as dispute-settlement court
for Trento's *Werchi*. One can speculate that the intent of this provision was to
prevent freedom from degenerating in excess, which in this case meant preventing the absolute alienation of the Bishop from sharing in mining profits.
The job by *gastaldione* probably entailed some difficult situations, given that
miners sometimes brought their weapons to mining sites. This we infer by the
fact that the *Carta* prohibited miners to carry weapons—*lanceam, cultellum
cum puncta, et omnia alia fraudulenta arma*—to underground works.[38]

A third restriction to absolute economic freedom was the prohibition of
selling silver ores outside the medieval city walls or at night. This, of course,
means that ore sales did take place outside the city, most certainly at high frequency, given Trento's strategic location at the center of Alpine international
trade routes. Economic revival of Lombardian cities after the eleventh century
attracted silver ore, cloth, and raw materials traders from the Alps and the rest
of Italy. An exception was made for cases where drainage works required the
constant presence of *Werchi* in the mines, which were located outside the city's
walls.[39] Certainly, the Bishop felt vulnerable when policing expanding ore-
trade relations. Sales done in the city facilitated surveillance against fraud and
brought mining affairs within the city's catchment area. Bishop Wanga was
in no mood for tolerating transgressions to the law, even when mines did not
belong to him personally.[40] The law punished violations by confiscating illicitly
traded ores. In addition, the buyer paid a fine of ten pounds to the bishopric, and
the seller 100 *solidi*.[41] Any citizen who could not pay or refused to pay faced
'extreme punishment.'[42] The text possibly implied physical punishment, not
uncommon to feudal laws. How or who delivered punishment is an intriguing
question.

The *Carta* makes no further mention of the subject; however, there is reason to
believe that the Bishop's rights to exercise criminal law were not absolute rights
either. The Lombardian institution of the *avvocatus* was in charge of the ordinary
administration of justice and criminal law, even dictating the sentence in death
penalty cases.[43] In Trento, the *avvocatus* had different roles due to its Germanic
and Italian legacies. It is possible that this officer became increasingly relevant

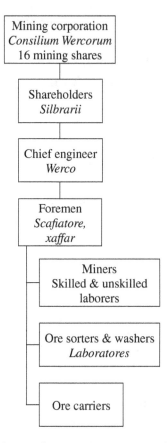

Fig. 3.1. Organization of mining corporations in the central
Alps and Lombardy, according to *Codex Wangianus*

before and during Wanga's tenure and exercised a wide array of district rights
that included criminal law.[44]

Previous mining acts give details of other conditions that at least nominally
Trento's *silbrarii* fulfilled. *Silbrarii* paid an additional tax based upon occasional gains of mining operations, determined in agreement with the Bishop.
One of the most peculiar obligations of *silbrarii* was a *subsidium* to be delivered at the request of the Bishop and 'under imminent necessity.' The *subsidium*
possibly referred to auxiliary forces, provisions, or assistance in case of war.
It first appeared under Bishop Adalbert in a document dated March 8, 1185.[45]
Was the *subsidium* a form of tallage such as that which flourished in many
parts of Europe? Not necessarily, since there was one distinction between the

subsidium defined in the *Codex Wangianus* and typical tallages elsewhere.[46] At first, the *subsidium* seemed an ideal lordly instrument of surplus extraction because of the impossibility of anticipating the amount and date of the charge; however, the same document stated that Bishop was forbidden from coercing *silbrarii* into the payment of the *subsidium*. The Bishop possibly thought that the *silbrarii* were too powerful as to be subjected to the arbitrary charge of the *subsidium*.

Additional taxes established under Bishop Adalbert ensured the bishopric's participation in mining revenues. Each association paid two talents for each Werhe or Werch employed in its mining business. Two talents were paid for each *Xaffar* employed in a corporation; two for each *Waffar*; one for the Master of *Waffar*; two for each *Smelzer*; and ten *solidi* for *in situ* mining operations, twice every year.[47] The latter were laborers of the mining corporation, below the *Werchi*. A *xaffar*, from the German noun *Schaffer*, was a mine foreman or administrator. He was hired by Werhe. *Waffar*, a word that comes from the German *waschen*, referred to ore-washing laborers. Below these occupations, there was a diverse group of skilled miners, hired by foremen for sinking shafts or *xafetus*, digging tunnels, and ore extraction. The work by Philippe Braunstein cited earlier clarified much of these labor categories for the case of Lombardy.[48] It is possible that some ore-washers worked independently, especially when located in proximity to large lakes. At the bottom of the hierarchy, there was a diverse group of miners whose tasks included ore crushing and hammering, transporting materials, and manual tasks in foundries. If, as Braunstein stated, a small number of the most experienced workers were owners of refining furnaces, these probably paid additional taxes to the Bishop.

In return, the Bishop's Court extended special protection to *silbrarii*, their property, and their businesses. There is no doubt that the old taxes still applied under Wanga's term. His lawyer, Ercetus, confirmed the act of A.D. 1185, where these taxes appeared for the first time, adding to his copy of the document the distinctive legal formula that indicated that the document was law: *breve recordationis pro futuris temporibus ad memoriam retinendum*.[49]

The *Carta* contained articles pertaining to mining works. It mandated that *silbrarii* divided each mine into sixteen parts. Each *partem* or share represented a fixed amount of money expended by each investor in a specific shaft or section of a mine and was calculated on a weekly basis by a technical expert. The weekly cost of all sixteen shares equaled the total expenditure in mining works undertaken in a mine.[50] *Silbrarii* could buy and sell their shares, which were nominally pieces of paper that could be seized by court action when share-owners defaulted on payments and contractual obligations.[51]

A shareholder had fifteen days to bring his shaft into work.[52] If anyone owning a claim in Mons Arzentarie neglected investing money into it, while the rest of the members of the corporation paid the total expenses of mining works, the shareholder was responsible for reimbursing expenses. This could end his participation in mining works. Possibly, the majority of the corporation had to agree for this decision to be enforced. 'The very real independence' of individual members of a medieval corporation was contained in the spirit of the statute.[53] If a shareholder was not able to pay off or reimburse the members of the *consilium* in a period of fifteen days, including payments owed to technical specialists and workers, his share 'in total' was transferred to other members of the same *consilium*. Nominally, gains were proportional to expenditures.

Silbrarii paid to the Bishop one tub of extracted ore every week, from each one of the sixteen parts that constituted a mine. A tub was an open flat-bottom container used for ore-packing and storage, with a volume capacity of almost one hundredweight.[54] If mines were productive and there was no easy way for *silbrarii* to cheat on tax accounts, one tub was no immodest amount of ore. New shafts had to keep a distance of at least ten *passus* or paces from existing shafts, equivalent to approximately fifteen and a half meters.[55] The penalty against this rule was fifty pounds reckoned in Verona *denarii*. In addition, the mining act established that mining rights granted for abandoned shafts were granted to anyone working at least one *passus* of the abandoned shaft, after such a shaft was abandoned for fifteen days.[56]

New requirements for keeping the mines under continuous operation were added.[57] In cases where miners encountered a hard-rock wall that could not be easily broken, miners had to identify softer limestone or *falumberg* and break and cut through it, until reaching the point where the hard-rock wall allowed them to dig no further.[58] Miners were required to open slits in shafts prone to be affected by shaft-flooding and poisonous vapors. In addition, in cases when conflict arose over a gallery connecting several shafts, identified as *dorslagum*, all parties involved in the dispute had to reach an agreement concerning the disputed gallery. Work in the shafts ceased, the text reads, 'until the lawsuit or quarrel is settled by our *Gastaldiones*, and if anyone contravenes this rule, incurs in a penalty of twenty-five pound.'[59]

The mining act of Wanga granted additional advantages to *silbrarii*. It prohibited any one man outside the *consilium* from hiring *manuales* for working either the mines or the *rotam* or water-wheel used for draining the mines of Arzentarie. The law granted one *manualem,* or salaried laborer, for working under a *Wercus*.[60] Wanga made sure to protect the mining sites owned by *consilium* by adding penalties against anyone destroying mining works or committing fraud by setting fire or creating a shaft flood in detriment to the work of *Werchi*.[61]

A new mining act dated May 26, 1213, established regulations concerning the drainage adit of Arzentarie.[62] It stated that efficient operation of drainage adits required incessant labor. The act created a mining tribunal composed of technical experts, whose duties included settling controversies among owners of mining claims in cases when a shaft was sunk in the direction of a drainage adit. The act originated when a *consilium* formed by 'Gandolfini et Odolrici Maji et suorum sociorum' brought to the Bishop's tribunal complaints concerning the drainage adit of Montis Vace.[63] Bishop Wanga possibly consulted with the most influential *silbrarii* who acted as a tribunal of technical experts and, as a result, enacted new rules concerning drainage adits.[64] According to Wanga's act, the Gandi and Odolrici *societas* was dissolved after *gastaldia* intervened in the dispute—*decidendas et terminandas predicti gastaldiones*—and a new *societas* took over the drainage adit.[65]

The new *Carta* prohibited miners from performing work that in any way obstructed a corporation's drainage adit. It made no reference to any drainage adit owned by the Bishop. Yet the tribunal of technical experts was to issue a warning against any attempt at monopolizing drainage adits. The text of the decision clarified that miners working drainage adits could sink no shaft close to drainage adits, irrespective of prospects or actual discoveries of ore veins. Miners were forbidden from abandoning their work in drainage adits for the sake of exploiting ore veins discovered (or to be discovered) near the adit. The astonishingly high fine that violators paid—300 pounds—shows the importance that the law gave to drainage works.[66]

The *Carta* established rules for ore sales. It stated that any shareholder accepting payment in exchange for his share of the ore vein was bound to give up and sell his share to the person who advanced the payment. Under no circumstance could the original shareholder rescind from the sale of his share once he collected payment. The act of receiving money for a share meant a contractual obligation. This regulation suggests that the Bishop had one unforeseen problem: a speculative market for buying and selling mining shares. Certainly, as mining profits grew, aristocrats and merchants from neighboring communes fixed their eyes on Trento's underground wealth.

A fixed amount of ore was to be paid to the Bishop, but only after technical experts designated by the *consilium Wercorum* evaluated the silver content of extracted ores. A fixed share of mine incomes was to be delivered to the Bishop. The subsidy owed to the Bishop 'under imminent necessity' mentioned earlier disappeared. The Bishop enjoyed the right to receive 10 percent of the final sale price of mining shares.[67] Mine management and administration were in the exclusive hands of foremen designated by *consilium Wercorum*, conditioned to the payment of a tax known as *jus custodiae*. The latter gave *Werchi* exclusive oversight of underground mining operations; the Bishop's *gastaldione* lost the right to enter or conduct on-site supervision of mining works. Mine and shaft portals were closed to them.

Also in A.D. 1213, Wanga established penalties against anyone invading *Werchi*'s property in *montis Arzentarie*.[68] The fine was not an immodest amount of money: fifty pounds to be paid to the Bishop and his *gastaldioni* and an additional amount of twenty-five pounds to be paid to *Werchi* to compensate for their loss. It is possible that by then the *Werchi* had expanded their smelting factories. The *Codex* makes no reference to smelting furnaces, other than a short but meaningful act written in A.D. 1214. Wanga declared that *Werchi* had the obligation of working the *rotam* or crushing mill with only one furnace, corresponding to taxes paid by them, and not with two furnaces. The text of the act allows one to feel the Bishop's anger: if *Werchi* wanted to work with two furnaces instead of one for smelting ores, those *Werchi* had to pay the *fictum* to the bishop for two furnaces. Any *Werco* violating the law was to taste the bishop's revenge: a fine of fifty pounds.[69]

A feudal monopoly was still possible. On July 20, 1214, Bishop Wanga declared that all abandoned mines in Trento belonged to the bishopric, possibly influenced by his urgent need for cash. He needed money for his crusading campaign in Africa, an important part of his missionary goals before he left the bishopric in A.D. 1218. The text of the grant reveals that the most important tax, the *fictum*, was in effect at one talent and three *edonodas*, justified as *iusta racione*.[70] Several years earlier, in A.D. 1214, Wanga mortgaged his rights to the mines of Trento to several *gastaldione* by the names Alberto of Seiano, Riprando of Ottone Ricco, and Ulrich of Rambaldo in exchange for a loan of two thousand Veronese pounds. These creditors enjoyed the right to collect two hundred pounds every year until the loan was canceled.[71]

Wanga left outside his compilation any note on small sharks; only big creditors attracted his attention. Alberto, Riprando, and Ulrich belonged to the high world of banking. Their names suggest that they belonged to a typical banking *societa*, composed of rich merchants from different territories. Most likely, small-scale creditors sprang up everywhere, taking advantage of money-lending opportunities of a smaller scale and benefiting from mining profits. *Prestatori,* or *prestatore* in singular form, were small-scale money lenders. They frequently interacted with foremen and well-to-do miners. Other mining statutes contain brief commentaries about *prestatori*; thus, there is no reason to believe that they never made it to Trento. Because total expenses of mining works were canceled on a weekly basis, a constant influx of money was needed, and *prestatori*, who could be anyone with liquid money, delivered cash where needed. Foremen and contractors presumably played the role of *prestatori* among miners and owners of furnaces.

The basic principle ruling credit relations was that a moneylender had the right to seize extracted ores when loans went unpaid.[72] Loans *ad usura* existed for a long time in Lombardy and Alpine cities, where they were known by different names—*premio, dono di tempo, merito, interesse, cambio, civanza, baroccolo,* and *ritrangolla*, among others.[73] The Church looked favorably on usury in cases of money exchange. This included money exchange *in situ*. Money-changers charged a fee for exchanging gold currency into silver currency and vice versa. The transaction was licit, 'as long as the fee was moderate.'[74] Those at the top of the mining business needed no law to specify interest rates. Bankers knew in advance 'the rate at which he was going to be able to make his "returns."' Was this the case of loans given by *prestatori*? Most likely, considering the interest rates that prevailed in Lombardy. In Trento interest rates varied between 12.5 and 20 percent, similar to other Lombardy cities in the thirteenth century. In the fourteenth century, interest rates in large Lombardy cities reached astonishingly high levels, 35 percent and up.[75] Legitimate *usura* also included situations where 'bankers sold letters of credit and undertook to pay the value thereof abroad,' as De Roover stated.[76] It is not totally clear how usury prohibitions increased the toil and trouble of *silbrarii*.[77] Without a doubt, *silbrarii* with experience in moneylending enjoyed the upper hand. And their legacy had an enduring impact not only in the mining industry of Lombardy but also in Trento's urban landscape. The inscription of the Vanga Tower, located at the center of the old medieval town is a testimony to the history of the silver mines of the bishopric: *Montes argentum mihi dant, nomenque Tridentum.*[78]

Trento was by no means an exceptional case. In Friesach, Carinthia, contracts between the Benedictine Abbey of Admont and silver producers started in A.D. 1185 and lasted until A.D. 1216.[79] The problem of *fodinae aquaticae* forced the shutdown of the mine located in *mons Zezzen*, until *socii* and *magistri fodinarum* came to the rescue.[80] Initially, the Abbot's *fictum* was a one-ninth, and an additional one-tenth of total mine revenues on behalf of the Archbishop of Salzburg. The *socii* of Friesach enjoyed the right to buy and sell mining shares. The Abbot collected 10 percent of the final sales price. A superintendent of mining works was in charge of the general management of the mines of Friesach and represented the Abbey's interests. After A.D. 1186, the one-tenth paid by *socii* to the Archbishopric of Salzburg was eliminated.

Contracts signed in A.D. 1202 and 1216 included the one-ninth owed to the Abbey but eliminated the Abbey's right to supervise mining operations.[81] Instead, oversight of mining works was delegated to elected officials, a governance structure peculiar to Lombardian cities. It was not uncommon for political bodies elected by citizens to take over functions related to infrastructure investments, such as building bridges.[82] The momentum had a price: *socii* of Friesach paid the *jus custodiae* and gained exclusive oversight rights of underground galleries. Neither the Abbot nor his superintendent of mines could descend into a mining gallery.[83]

What did a miner look like in Trento? It is possible that the ordinary miner included free serfs, although there is no mention in the *Codex* of serfs allocated to *silbrarii*. Ordinary miners included German and Italian immigrants and seasonal migrants, the *servi* and *manimorte* in the agrarian fields of each commune. Certainly, serfs who fulfilled mining obligations lived a harsh life. Did the tyranny of feudal agriculture make mining more attractive to the more well-to-do serfs? This is a weighty matter. Italian historian Luigi Cibrario stated more than a century ago: *Nondimeno nell'Italia alpina e subalpina, e negli stati d'oltremonte e d'oltremare, la condizione degli agricoltori liberi era in generale assai più dura, molto angariata e molto imbrattata di servitù.*[84] In the case of Sermide in Mantova, close to Trento, serfs had to till the lands of Sermide for three days every year. Each serf had to deliver to the lord the following: two large pigs and two large sturgeons from the Po River; one hundred *carra* of wood; one third of all other fish caught in the Po River; one tenth of the serf's agrarian produce and wine; half a bushel or *staio* of wine, for each wine jar; one bushel of each sowing; one bushel of slaughtered pigs and lambs; of each deer, the head until the middle of the neck, loins, the tallow, one-fourth of the right rear, and one-third of the sale of each deer; the head of each boar; of each hare, the head up to the middle of the neck; one-third of any other animal's body; and accommodation to the lord if and when needed.[85] The modern weight conversion for a bushel of wheat or sixty-three pounds might not apply here, considering that 'medieval grains were almost certainly less full in the ear than modern ones.'[86] The numbers indicate that lords squeezed their serfs but by no means prove that mining was a more convenient labor path.

Mines were located in the hills situated among pastures and meadowlands, in areas traveled by local armies. This was the case of the mine of Mount Giaú in San Vito di Cadore. Because of this geographic aspect, the mine yielded the utility of fixed capital, *à la* Adam Smith; the mine afforded some revenue or profit without changing masters.[87] Nominally, this notion of revenue also applied to Lombardy's farmland. The produce of agrarian lands, however, was more vulnerable to the old feudal problems of boundaries and jurisdictions. Secular and ecclesiastical lords continuously contested each other's titles of property, while in mining, ownership of shares allowed for private money to come into the mines.

Two additional conditions allow us to infer that life in mining villages took a different path than in agrarian fiefs. The fact that there is no mention in the *Codex* of leprosy or medieval diseases that took a high toll in the cities of Torino, Bologna, and Pepino suggests that a miner's livelihood in the mountains was a shelter from unwholesome urban environments.[88] In addition, the salary of a miner in the valley of Lazon was ten florins per month, or six *denarii* per day, by A.D. 1373.[89] A valid comparison is the salary of the archer of the army of Hungary, twelve florins per month, or seven *denarii* every day.[90] Mining was an attractive business.

Cartels and Government Regulation: The Case of Kutná Hora

Kutná Hora stands on the top of a hill, rivaling Prague with its magnificent German Gothic architecture. The fine structure of Saint Barbara Church, built by architect Peter Parler in A.D. 1358, is evidence of the fortunes made by

German miners in Kutná Hora's silver mining industry.[91] Its most distinctive urban feature is Palackého Náměstí Plaza. Nearby stands the building that once housed the royal mint established by King Vaclav II. Here, the first Bohemian silver *groschen* appeared in A.D. 1300.[92] Fortune smiled at miners in this world mining region, guided, however, by decisive government intervention.

The city belonged to the medieval kingdom of Bohemia, occupying a large territory which included modern-day Czech Republic, parts of Poland and Germany's Thuringia region, and northern Hungary. The earliest city statute was put in place by King Vaclav I (A.D. 1205–1253) in A.D. 1247. It granted to Jihlava the title *cives montani* or autonomous city, at a time when 'the Houses of Saint Maria, a church of the Teutonic Knight order, and Saint Joannis Baptist were located left of the Jihlava river.'[93] A decade earlier, Vaclav I legally recognized the authority of the city's judges, or *urborarius*, as Jihlava's chief mine officers—*judex, urborarius ceterique jurati montium in Igla*. By virtue of this law, Jihlava's citizens elected the city's chief mining officers: the *urburarii, magister montium*, and *jurati montanorum*.[94]

The preamble to *Constitutiones* did not stop there. Vaclav I expanded Jihlava's statute in A.D. 1249, and included regulations about mine geometry, as well as rights and responsibilities of *colonii* or miners.[95] Fifty years later, in A.D. 1300, the regulations appeared in a new and expanded mining law enacted by Vaclav II. Its full name was *Jus regale montanorum*; it is known today as *Constitutiones juris metallica*.[96] The law became the 'foundation stone of all legal relations in the Bohemian mining industry' until A.D. 1518, when the Mining Law of Jáchymov was enacted.[97]

Vaclav II's rule coincided with a silver rush to Kutná Hora that forced the royal court to address the problem of competing and overlapping jurisdictions. Kutná Hora's silver rush was just the tip of the iceberg: two royal towns, Čáslav and Kolín, separated from each other by twenty kilometers, heavily contested the mining lands under the jurisdiction of Cistercian Sedlec Abbey.[98] The monks were much concerned about maintaining order in their lands, and rightly so. Vaclav II had other concerns: to reorganize the urban fabric of silver-mining towns and to centralize mining operations in Kutná Hora.

Constitutiones recognized freedom to all subjects of the kingdom for exploring and mining Bohemia's *campo libero* or 'unclaimed' lands. 'Our silver mines, in the whole territory are to be worked freely, and be occupied peacefully and orderly by anyone'; 'a colonist that is obedient to natural law and

Fig. 3.2. Surveyors sitting in a circle. The fourteenth-century miniature depicts a meeting by agrarian experts possibly discussing technical matters about land boundaries, a theme of much concern in the period. Surveyors wrote treatises about land surveying techniques and paid special attention to defining common units of measurement, no doubt inspired by disputes about the boundaries of tribute-paying lands, private and Church estates, and commons. Album / Art Resource, NY.

works the mines enjoys our royal protection.'[99] The message was meant to appease those with enough money to plow back into the subsoil. The law recognized that mining rights belonged to the *colonii principalii*, a term that denotes possession or ownership of a spot of land.[100] This is not the *colonus* who tilled the land; the law was very clear on this point. This was the *colonus* of *argenti fodinam* or silver mines.

Immigrants made up the bulk of the mining workforce; however, *primi fossores Theutonici fuerint*. Germans were the earliest miners. They were the *colonii principalii* of the Carpathians who enjoyed some economic freedom, but no absolute freedom. They were organized as a society identified as *Gewerken*.

Fig. 3.3. A surveyor marks a boundary while another measures the field, from *Treatise of Land Surveying* (fifteenth century), by Villeneuve. One surveyor employs a medieval *decempeda*, a measuring pole approximately three meters long, while the other marks the land. Medieval surveying instruments and techniques relied upon the basic methods known in antiquity. These allowed the surveyor to divide an area after measuring and marking its boundaries. Instruments were simple and easy to build. By the fourteenth century, surveying was a professional field, and its practitioners wrote treatises that circulated throughout Western Europe. Bibliothèque Inguibertine. © DeA Picture Library / Art Resource, NY.

Gewerken were private citizens organized in a mining society. Membership in a *Gewerken* society was strictly voluntary and not determined by birth. Possession of a mining claim was valid as long as its owner kept the mine in operation. Incessant labor, day and night, was the sole standard.[101] Bohemia's mining statute defined a mining concession as a loan granted when a miner discovered ore veins. For claiming a stake, prospectors identified 'ores in sight' after following the outcrop and building a vertical shaft, as illustrated in the following illustration from Stretch's work.[102]

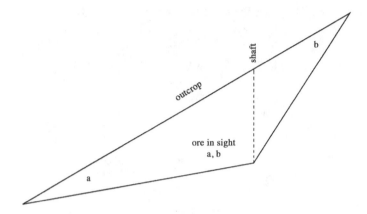

Fig. 3.4. Ore in sight: schematic representation by Stretch. Until recently,
geologists believed that identifying the ore in sight of a mine was an
indicator of the amount of exposed ore and profits. Today, geological modeling
of ore deposits is more complex. When Stretch wrote his 'practical treatise'
Prospecting, locating, and valuing mines, his aim was to show miners the importance
of sinking more than one shaft to estimate the length and breadth of valuable ore in
sight. Stretch, however, warned miners that profits from ore in sight of different metals
depended upon multiple factors; in the case of gold and 'to a lesser extent' silver, competition mattered little. Location, 'want of capital,' and 'business tact' mattered most.

The first task of a *colono* was to dig a shaft; however, a shaft only proved
that 'at that particular point and to a certain depth' some amount of ore could
be found.[103] More work was needed for making estimates of thickness of an ore
bed. This task presumably required sinking a second shaft traversing the vein
outcrop. When a second shaft was sunk, it was possible to determine which
shaft section yielded the best ore. Then, the *colono*, by now a prospector, sent
extracted ores from each shaft to smelting factories for testing. A chief mining
engineer or *magister montium* examined the ore samples. Afterwards, technical experts or *scansores*, officers appointed by the king, tested the samples by
cupellation. They made final decisions determining profitability of an ore vein.
If *scansores* decided that ores were profitable, a *colono* hired a surveyor for de-
marcating the area to be worked, in the presence of *urburarii*, the chief mining
officers of Bohemia. Thus, a mining claim was granted only after a *colono* expended much toil and trouble demonstrating the existence of a sufficient quantity of ore, enough to justify granting the stake.

A mining claim granted rights to extract ores in pre-defined areas of the vein's
hangingwall and footwall. The hangingwall, or *hangundez*, refers to the roof

or top surface of layer overlying an ore bed. It is also known as headwall. The footwall, or *liegundez*, is the foot or bottom surface of layer underlying the ore vein. Agricola defined it in the sixteenth century in simple terms: 'When we descend a shaft, the part to which we turn the face is the footwall and seat of the vein, that to which we turn the back is the hangingwall.'[104] A mining claim encompassed a total area of seven *lanei* along the strike of an ore vein. This area was the 'measured mine,' according to Jánošíková.[105] Royal surveyors added an additional *laneum* to be worked on behalf of the King. After all, the Crown held ownership of mines, and the King conceded mining rights only for private persons to work *nostrum argentifodium*, 'our mines.'[106] The *laneum* used in Jihlava was equivalent to approximately fourteen meters, a unit possibly used throughout Carpathian mining cities.[107] Once a concession was granted, the law mandated sinking a minimum of three shafts. The prospector who first discovered the ore bed was *colonii principalii* and enjoyed the right to work two *lanei* in the concession area. A second miner, leasing mining rights from *colonii principalii*, enjoyed the right to work one *laneum* out of the total seven *lanei* of the claim area. *Colonii tertiarii*, or third colonists, hired by *colonii secundarii*, enjoyed the right to sink a shaft in the remaining area, keeping at least one *Lachter* of distance from existing shafts.[108] The *Lachter* or German fathom was equivalent to approximately one and three-fourths meters.[109]

A good prospector could estimate the average width of an ore vein resting between the hangingwall and footwall. The assumption was that not all the area covered under the seven-*lanei* rule was to be worked, at a profit, by the first discoverer. Because outcrops in the Carpathians rarely show uniformity in thickness and length, it is possible that after costly exploration works, miners targeted only the sections in each shaft yielding the highest-grade ores. No work for amateurs, inept serfs, or idle feudal lords. After years of practical experience with Carpathian ores, miners learned to calculate the appropriate vertical and horizontal length of the ore lode—with some acceptable margin of error.

Once an extraction shaft or *stollo* was sunk in the claim area, the owner of the mining stake had a period of six days for starting ore extraction works.[110] Not the speed of a typical feudal grant! Otherwise, the city's *urburarii* transferred mining rights for that *stollo* to another miner. *Urburarii* required proof of an ore-digging agreement among miners, in cases when a miner, after enlarging his shaft, discovered an ore vein at the point of contact with a neighboring shaft. Right of transit in underground tunnels belonged to those who expended toil and trouble building the tunnel. This regulation applied even to discoveries of new ore veins. Flooded shafts had to be drained in three days. Drainage adits had to fulfill the following condition: that they effectively 'purged' shafts by removing water away—*et foveas suas debito modo purgaverit.*[111] Miners had only three days for starting drainage work once their shafts were affected by *fodinae aquaticae.*

Historian Jánošíková believes that, in general, a mining field owned by a *Gewerken* association was as extensive as ninety-eight meters by sixty-four meters and contained several shafts.[112] Extraction sites opened during the silver rush of A.D. 1296 measured three by nine kilometers, if the calculations of Czech archeologist Jan Klápště are correct.[113] The above numbers insinuate an incredible enlargement of the surface area of private mining claims. How these compared to the average size of a fenced agrarian plot owned by a small-scale farmer is difficult to determine. Kutná Hora was established in lands not suitable for agriculture, a fate it shared with other mining cities of the Carpathians. Here, 'we cannot manage with an emphasis on the agrarian and non-agrarian prerequisites,' as Klápště stated.[114] It is possible that because of the length and width of ore lodes, an average mining *feodum* was larger than an average agrarian field.

The typical mining corporation of the Carpathians was formed by *Gewerken*, or mine specialists, who were the German *hospites* described in the previous chapter. It is possible that Vlach men of property joined some mining corporations, given that it was only after the reigns of King Louis and King Sigismund when the Vlach were subjected to expropriation of lands and deprived of their noble status.[115] Only *Gewerken* or *colonii principalii* owned mining shares; thus, the tendency of the mining corporation born in the Carpathians was to assume functions of today's cartels: to restrict competition, promote mutual interests, and control ore prices. *Constitutiones* portrayed *Gewerken* associations as seeking to monopolize discoveries of ores and mine profits by any means possible.[116] These were agents who profited from 'secret agreements about ore prices with the purpose of eliminating competition' by their 'detestable conspiration against the common good.'[117] The mining statute denounced the *conspirationes illicitas* formed by *Gewerken* in smelting factories and granted a period of fourteen days for correcting 'fraudulent' practices concerning ore prices.[118]

Most certainly, *Gewerken* corporations were beyond the control of feudal lords; however, they were subjected to hidden antagonisms. Associations varied from eight to thirty-two *Gewerken* members. The total number of mining shares held by an association was thirty-two *pars* or *tál*, implying that a member could hold as low as one share or as high as four shares.[119] The value of a mining share was calculated upon the expense of work-shifts. The duration of the working day was divided into *schichten* or working-hour shifts, each consisting of four hours. The concept of *schichten* corresponded to a twenty-four-hour cycle, divided equally into two twelve-hour periods accounting for day and night. Each *schicht* contained a *prima hora*, *secunda hora*, *tertia hora*, and *quarta hora*, all of equal length; however, the real duration of each hour depended upon the season of the year, with winter and summer solstices affecting the length of the daylight hours. Miners were required not to exceed one shift, each day.[120] Origins of this work-shift concept are possibly found in the *kost* contract that German *hospites* and immigrants from Flanders, Luxembourg, 'and the valley of the Moselle' brought to the Carpathians centuries earlier.[121] This was an early process of Westernization aided by Germanic written law; it governed elements concerning urbanization, trades, craftsmanship, and mining.[122]

Two types of *kost* contract flourished in mining settlements in Saxon forests after the tenth century. In the first type, a technical specialist leased a shaft or section of a shaft to poor miners, who paid the lease with a share of extracted ores. Whether these poor miners were the serfs that Marxist historian Perry Anderson described as 'united to the soil' is not easy to decipher.[123] What is most probable is that the *Lehenschaft*, as this type of contractual relation was known, originated in cities with abundant labor supply, such as Goslar, Freiburg, Schneeberg, and Annaberg.[124] The second type of *kost* contract referred to a lease paid back in coined money. It is possible that this type flourished in mining fields that needed ready cash for investments, at times of abundant coined-money supply, and when landlords charged their rents in coined moneys.[125] In exchange for ready cash delivered to a landlord holding a mining grant, lease holders enjoyed the right to settle close to mining sites, hire workers, and retain whole or part of the extracted ores. None of these privileges appeared in contracts between *Gewerken* and poor miners in early fourteenth-century Carpathia. Mining towns were most likely saturated; by then, opportunities for moving up in mining towns by late immigrants were scarce. Later, amendments to *Constitutiones* recognized a six-hour work-shift, divided into a number of units equivalent to 128 *kuks* or shares.

The legal instrument of the share probably came earlier to Bohemia with Germanic migrants. In Saxon cities, the *Gewerkschaft* was a shareholder's association, formed by a minimum of eight *Gewerken*. The association owned 128 *kuxe* or mining shares. A mining share represented a unit of certain value corresponding to the value of one share of a mine's immovable assets. It could be divided, mortgaged, and sold by *Gewerken*. Each shareholder covered the expenses of mining works and made investments in infrastructure while mining works continued; 'the mine gave no returns' and 'shared in profits as soon as such were realized.'[126]

Almost all amounts of ores collected by the *urburarii* went to the Kutná Hora mint factories. Every association had to deliver a ninth of its total amount of extracted ores to the kingdom's smelting factories and mints. In addition, they paid an eighth of extracted ores; 5/32 of associations' gross returns; an amount of ore equivalent to the income generated by one of every four *schichta*; and 1/16 of what the *Gewerken* collected from *colonii secundarii*. All colonists working a mining claim had the responsibility of dividing equally among themselves the incomes collected from one *schichta*.

Constitutiones introduced a monetary law that reorganized the seventeen small mints formerly spread in Carpathian cities into one large mint factory at Kutná Hora, with the intention of establishing the *moneta grossorum Pragensium et parvorum*, the Kingdom's official currency.[127] The mint became 'a vast establishment' composed of workshops spread in the thirty square kilometers surface of Kutná Hora, under the direction of a Florentine mint master.[128] It minted between 6.4 and 6.7 tons of silver annually between A.D. 1300 and 1305.[129]

In addition, *Constitutiones* recognized the following rights: the right of the *popolus montanorum* to work; salary in currency *solos remunerari volumus cum metallo*;[130] a work week of four consecutive periods or *schichta* of six hours per day and five days a week; free legal assistance in case of conflicts about payment and salaries; and a prohibition on taking a pledge on anticipated incomes of mining works. Whether these rights were enforced is open to interpretation. In towns that suffered environmental calamities, seasonal mining laborers probably found themselves in limbo, unprotected by the law. The law, however, recognized the *Lehenschaft*, an institution that probably originated in Saxon mining towns.[131] It restricted to a period of six months the time that tenants could be assigned to specific extraction sites of the mine shafts. Hardly a typical lord-serf relation. A rotational work pattern allowed laborers to work in different sections of the mine. The goal was to prevent a situation where tenants were the victims of unpredictable geological variations that determined the silver content of ores or difficulties of unequal digging and extraction.[132]

Gewerken corporations were heavily regulated by the Bohemian government, as described below.

Mining Officers and Governance

The *urburarii* were appointed to *pauperes defensare* and to enforce the rights of mountain people. *Constitutiones* defined the *urborariorum* as the officer in charge of *urbura*, or 'faithful and loyal administration of the mining affairs of mountain cities.' His job was to 'protect mountain citizens' by 'saving them from danger of injustice.'[133] *Urburarii* were the highest mining judges, the super-czars of mining, and sat below the King.[134] The jurisdiction of the *urbura* office extended only to the affairs of the mining cities, while the courts of law of the kingdom intervened in all other affairs. It was in the power of *urburarii* to remove mining judges or *magistri montium* in cases of negligence and release any *colono* from a judge's wrongful sentence.[135] Along with mining judges, they were in charge of all matters concerning the mountain of Kutná, 'diligently correcting anything that puts obstacles to the development of the mountain.' No *urburarii* could examine a cause, dictate a sentence, or act as a judge unless he did so in the presence of at least two persons confirmed by oath. The statute added: 'safer to dictate sentence in the presence of many.'[136]

The responsibility of *urburarii* included granting mining concessions, executing the kingdom's mining law, and correcting any wrongdoing by corporations in pricing and valuing ores—*pretium et mensura*.[137] After a court ritual in which *urburarii* publicly swore to 'abide by and defend the kingdom's mining law,' these officers were ready to do their job.[138] The law reminded them that their decisions had to be the outcome of a 'composed mind,' unperturbed by 'fury,' 'dominated by reason,' and prone to 'deliberation.'[139]

The office of *urbura* was significant in many ways. The impression the text gives is that the King of Bohemia was highly suspicious of private mining corporations and their ways of siphoning ores outside the kingdom's mints. German migrants monopolized the underground wealth of the kingdom, after decades of urbanization of the Carpathian Mountains. Even if social classes admitted some mobility, there was a hierarchy in which apprentices, craftsmen, technical experts, and newly arrived migrants stood below a propertied German merchant class.

Urburarii reached decisions to the point of law, sometimes relying on wit-

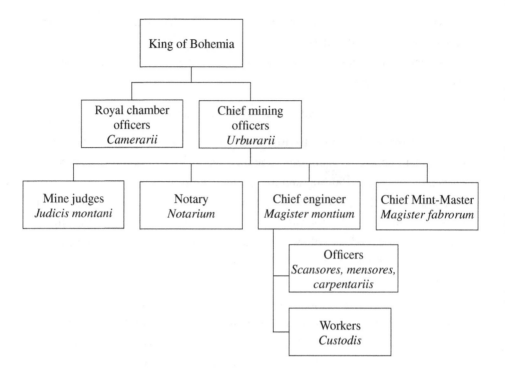

Fig. 3.5. Organization of Bohemia's mining governance, according to *Constitutiones*

ness accounts. The principle that 'all men are born free by natural law' justified the use of witnesses—*quia ab initio jure naturali omnes homines liberi nascenbatur.*[140] The article on witnesses states that because of the faculties that natural law imbues in all men, there cannot be any prohibition to the service to justice. There were, however, some exceptions. The law strictly prohibited judges to rely on testimonies and witness accounts by women, because 'a woman's mind is inconstant.'[141] Judges also could not rely upon witness accounts by *impuberes*, because they 'lack judgment.' *Impuberes* were defined as males below the age of fourteen and females below the age of twelve. A judge was expected to identify *impuberes* 'based upon the modesty of their bodies.'[142] *Furiosus* or madmen, 'incapable of discerning right from wrong,' served no purpose to judges seeking witness accounts. The law made a similar prohibition targeting 'men of bad reputation' or *infamis*, infidels, 'Jews, Sarracens, and heretics.'[143]

Below the *urburarii*, there was a chief mining judge or *magistri montium*. The *Magistri montium* was a royal officer with ample jurisdiction in mining

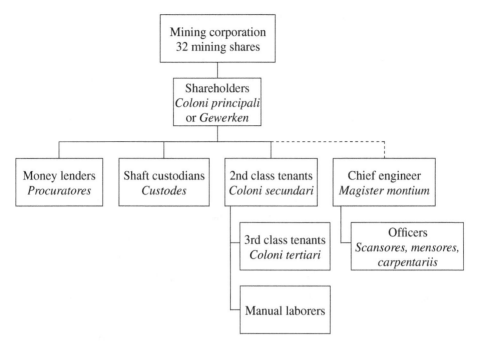

Fig. 3.6. Organization of mining corporations, according to *Constitutiones*

affairs. His salary was fixed by law at seven *groschen* or *denarii grosso* per week, funded with taxes and minted ores.[144] The responsibilities of *magistri montium* included inspecting mining works; overseeing works in underground shafts, tunnels, and galleries once a week; and 'correcting' any wrongdoing concerning mine geometry.[145] The *magistri montium* intervened in cases when hired miners and the *colonis multitudine* received no salary. In such situations, the *magistri* granted each miner the equivalent of two *schichta* in ores, and a 1/32 extraction area, *in monte vel laneo llo vel etiam concessione.*[146]

Magistri were guardians of the well-being of *carpentarii et custodes*, and all other workers of the mines. They fixed a subsidy for the welfare of the *pauperibus laboratoribus*, or impoverished workers. The mining statute explicitly stated that impoverished workers committed delinquent acts because of lack of food.[147] The money of the subsidy came from mine earnings. There were mining judges or *judicis montani*, and notaries or *scriptoribus urburae*, all below the *magistri montium*.[148] Judicial decisions by these officers had to demonstrate *moralis maturitas et constantia perfectorum* and that judges were 'obedient to reason' and 'prudent in action and word.'[149] It is possible that these judges came from the colonies of German merchants that dominated the mining cities of Bohemia, although the statute makes no reference on this point.

The statute forced the notion of the 'common good' not only upon mining corporations but also upon government officers, reminding them that the Prince stood on top of the feudal and seigniorial orbit of political power and that it was his role to bring the private and public sectors closer to a new political understanding of law, crime, and justice. Vicious and despotic feudal lords might have erratic wishes, but never the Prince. Thus, neither *urburarii* nor *magistri* were above the *lex humana*. They could not grant mining concessions at their own will.[150] The *magistri* could not dispose freely from mine incomes either. This was *unam odibilem consuetudinem* which corrupted the judicial institution of the kingdom. *Nostrae republicam laessionem*, stated the law.[151]

On the technical side of the mining bureaucracy, there was a diverse group of craftsmen, such as *scansores*, *mensores*, and *carpentariis*. The first two were land and mine surveyors, 'rigorous and assiduous' officers who were needed in disputes over boundaries of mining claims. They were paid by the litigant parts, although it is unclear if litigants hired them directly, or if they were appointed by the king or royal officers.[152] Three surveyors and a member of the *urbura* office, possibly an assistant of an *urburarii*, intervened in disputes over shaft depth. A mine supervisor inspected shafts and tunnels. Exercising *cautelam maxime*, he ensured that mine geometry requirements were fulfilled and that mines were kept under continuous operation.[153]

Carpenters were responsible for timbering shaft walls *pro utilitate colonorum* —to the colonist's utility. They were men of 'sagacity and ingenuity,' much 'useful for working old mines.'[154] Carpenters were ordered to provide robust timber pillars 'without which a mine could be ruined'—*providere robustis firmando sustentaculis, quidquid in argentifodinis ruinosum appareat et caducum.*[155] Theirs was a task that required experience, because miners preferred to use timbers in the 'state in which they left the forest,' excluding bark.[156] It is possible that some shafts and tunnels were in a state of decay, considering that wood was continuously exposed to water vapor in underground fields. *Procuratores*, representing absentee colonists, registered their transactions with the *magistri montis*.[157]

The relation between monopolies formed by *Gewerken* and ore prices as portrayed in *Constitutiones* makes this mining statute one of the most remarkable laws of any world mining region. The statute suggests that the times called for

Fig. 3.7. Miners digging shafts in a mountain, in *Splendor Solis* (A.D. 1532–1535), by Salomon Trismosin. The artist, Nikolaus Glockendon from Nuremberg, here depicts miners working with pickaxes as they search for the raw material for the Philosopher's Stone. The miners are dressed in the colors of gold and silver metals. A story from the Book of Esther sets the scene, showing perfect union between polarities, according to Völlnagel. bpk Berlin / Kupferstichkabinett, SMB / Jörg P. Anders / Art Resource, NY.

kings to be vigilant against rising capitalists. *Constitutiones* appeared at a time when the idea of the just price had reached its zenith in scholastic economics, long before David Ricardo hinted at the relation between 'value and the difficulty or facility of production.'[158] The just price referred to a price established between buyer and seller in the 'freedom of bargaining,' arguably determined by abundance or scarcity of commodities.[159] Thomas Aquinas (d. A.D. 1274) defined prices as 'a social phenomenon not arbitrarily determined by individuals, but by the community.' 'The price of the commodity can be fixed either by the public authorities for the common good, or by the estimation currently arrived at in the market.'[160] *Constitutiones* echoed some of these ideas: prices were the result of demand and supply, without 'any frauds, restraints, and conspiracies.'[161]

The text of the law, written by an Italian professor of civil Roman law by the name of Grozio of Urbino,[162] states that the King intervened in the silver mining industry because of *conspirationes contra nostram rempublicam* perpetrated by *Gewerken*.[163] Royal appointment of mining officers was the duty of the King. It was the intervention of the king in the mining affairs of feudal lords that represented the essence of the *publicae utilitatis* of the Crown.[164] Thus, appointing *urburarii* was the king's responsibility, given that they 'restore harmony' in the mining lands of the kingdom, 'in order that our public interest (*rei publica*) and gains of labor prevail.'[165] Grozio adorned the text of the law with references to Roman jurisprudents, philosophers, and emperors and explicit sentences about human dignity, reason, justice, and the common good. And all with refined scholastic taste. For introducing the duties of *urburarii*, Grozio wrote: 'Man is the worthiest of all creatures because reason is of his exclusive competence, so we wish all these things [articles] to be followed as reason mandates, because reason is the mother of all virtues.'[166] 'Violence is the enemy of law'—the admonition that Grozio added for justifying the jurisdiction of *urburarii*.[167] From Isidore of Seville, Grozio added the following sentence in an article concerning mining judges: *Non est judex, si non est in eo Justitia*.[168] One finds this language in no other medieval mining statute, something that suggests that Carpathian mining had a role in the making of a secular view of the state.[169]

Was the intention solely to establish reparation payments, medieval style, to minorities displaced by centuries of German migration? The text of the law is clear: *Constitutiones* was written for *montanis suis per regnum Bohemiae universis*.[170] All people living in the Kingdom of Bohemia were to abide by the law. In the centuries of Germanic migration to Carpathian mining cities, the native propertied class never relinquished its claims to the best lands of the kingdom, including mining lands. Privileges granted to German migrants and their towns created a center-periphery relation in the towns of the Carpathians, with ethnic and cultural overtones. Slovak mine workers were in a subordinate relation with respect to German laborers. Germans and their descendants, indeed, enjoyed the fame of being the most qualified miners. Slovaks were 'mountain workers,' or 'auxiliary workers'; Germans were *Hauer, Häuer, Flötzer,* or *Trentscher*.[171] Probably also from Slovak origins were the carpenters and craftsmen responsible for the safety of pits, or the *Zimmermanni*. For historian Peter Kalus, this ethnic division was reflected in a geographic hierarchy of mining towns in the region: rural settlements around the cities of Slovakia were of Slovak origins, while the urban centers were distinctively Germanic. These formed the 'under-privileged' settlements in the hierarchy of mining cities.

In Slovakia, *Lehenhäuers* hired by *Gewerken* belonged to a group of free entrepreneurs. They possibly functioned as contractors after the fourteenth century. Below them was a group of laborers whose craft was trade, but circumstances pushed them to sell their labor in the mines. This group performed different tasks and, unlike poor miners, enjoyed different rights. The highest occupation in a Slovakian mining site was that of shaft foreman, a worker who supervised all miners. This worker was known as *Steiger, Bergschaffer,* or *Schaffer*. There was the *Hutmann*, or guardian of tools and instruments, according to Kalus. It is most likely that if the *Hutmann* was 'a mountain worker in a leading position,' as Kalus concedes, he was much more than a guardian of tools.[172] The root *Hut* signifies enclosure or a spot of land, denoting 'appropriate spot, or Earth, guarded, fenced.'[173] The *Hammermeister* supervised workers cutting limestone and owned some mining tools. The *Gossenfüller* was in charge of filling ore-dredging crushers with water. The *Schlämmer* or *Schlemmer* was hired for washing refined ores and clearing away dust. The *Zuschütter* was in charge of different tasks related to ore crushing and mills. *Zuwarter*, or general workers, occupied the lowest stratum of the hierarchy.[174]

In the mining towns of Transylvania, the small fortunes that German miners made had an enduring presence, as Weber observed:

> Saxon representatives appeared in Royal Congregations in 1291, 1317, and 1357. In 1464, we find the Saxons of the town helping to elect a judge in Orâste. Saxons appear as parties in law cases and judicial documents dated 1383, 1385, 1413, and 1419. In almost every case, the local inhabitants who had lost pasture or other rights for the benefit of Saxon burghers or farmers tried to get their own back by raiding and spoiling the German lands. In almost every case the authorities are on the side of the Saxon settlers.[175]

Kutná Hora contained rich veins, with a silver concentration of 2.5 percent.[176] Between twenty to thirty smelters sprang in the city in A.D. 1300.[177] The old Marxist explanation on the 'crisis in the East' put forward by Perry Anderson seems incomplete, when one looks at the booming mining industry. 'The momentum of settlement now slackened and died out,' stated Anderson about feudal industries in eastern Europe.[178] The evidence presented here suggests that in the Carpathians, mining enterprises experienced a radical change earlier. By the fourteenth century, the mining business was a profitable capitalist affair.

A Government-Regulated 'Invisible Hand': The Case of Massa

The center of the mining industry in thirteenth-century Tuscany was the city of Massa Marittima. This was the second place in Italy dedicated to *coltivazione delle miniere*, after Lombardy, in the words of an Italian observer.[179] The city of *inestimable opulenza* was built on top of a hill for easy defense, at a time when the communes of Volterra, Siena, and Pisa had the habit of encroaching upon neighboring lands.[180] Here, miners built an industry that supported the commune's early growth and traveled as far as Calabria, when the Duke of Calabria asked for one hundred miners, *magistros centum sufficientes ad cavas facendum ante castra, et fortellicias destruendas* on August 15, 1326.[181] The Count of Savoy in A.D. 1300 made a similar request.[182]

Ordinamenta super arte fossarum was the mining statute of the commune of Massa. It was Massa's response and stance against territorial claims by Siena and the Bishop of Volterra to the mines of the region. Both Siena and the Bishop would face the fate that old feudal interests faced elsewhere: they were incapable of exercising claims over mines that demanded capital.

The statute established an environment favorable to the development of private mining businesses, while recognizing the role of the elected officials in mining governance. It established that private persons who enjoyed mining rights were subjected to two conditions. First, a claim holder was required to waste no time and keep the mines in operation—*fovea que erat viva et tempus non perdiderat.*[183] Second, ownership of a mining claim required proof of citizenship. From the moment of staking a claim, indicated by the planting of a cross in a prospection site, a miner had a period of three days for starting ore extraction. This time period could be extended, after a *magistri montis* or mine clerk declared the claim valid.[184] The cross could not be removed by anyone, not even the landowner,[185] suggesting that feudal landlords had a tough time keeping miners away from their agrarian lands. A stake was licit if, after one month and three days, the land showed signs of improvement, *hedificando et abbocando dictum signum*, and such improvement was new. The owner held mining rights as long as work at the site continued. This applied to *foveis et buctinis*—adits, shafts, and galleries. The condition of continuous operation was non-negotiable, and one must conclude that this condition originated in the practical experience of the mining corporation. A constant presence of miners was mandated by law, even when disputes over shaft boundaries arose. The rationale was that 'unexpected situations occur in the mines.'

Work-shifts started Monday morning and ended Saturday morning. The statute divided mining labor in work-shifts and recognized that a miner's labor *in situ* was divided into specific tasks that included digging, ore extraction, charcoal transport, and ore-washing. The time that each laborer spent in the mine was determined by the length of time of his work-shift. Laborers could not interrupt their work as long as their shift ran unless ordered to do so by a *magistri fovea* or master of the mine. Violators faced a penalty of ten *solidi* in addition to losing their salary.[186]

The law required that new shafts kept a distance of twelve to fifteen paces from neighboring shafts, ten to twelve paces for tunnels and galleries. Massa's *passum* was equivalent to three *brachia*, equivalent to approximately 5.7 'English feet' or less than two meters. The *brachium* or arm unit was equivalent to sixty centimeters. The arm unit used in Massa and other parts of Tuscany was equivalent to 0.6 meter. A pace was equal to 1.80 meters. This number approximates the *Lachter* unit used in the central Alps, Lombardy, and Carpathian mining regions.[187] This means a distance between twenty-one and seventy-four meters separated neighboring shafts. Mine geometry in Massa was slightly different than in Trento. The land surface of Massa, in the Tuscan coastland, with layers of unevenly spread *sasso morto*, prevented perfect symmetry in shaft and mine design. Archeological research confirms that shafts generally reached one hundred meters in depth and 1 to 1.2 meters in diameter, and that the minimum distance separating shafts was fifteen meters, the maximum twenty meters.[188] Enforcing mining geometry would have required constant presence of surveyors in exploration lands, something that was not feasible. Any *Communitas* owning shares worth at least sixty pounds per share was required to 'raise shafts' in a stone house.[189] This meant that *partiarii* paid the expenses of constructing the *capannas* sheltering workers and tools in shaft entrances.[190]

Massa's mining business was more advanced than that found in Lombardy or the Carpathians. Corporations, known as *communitas foveae* or *societas foveae*, were formed by *partiarii*. The latter were owners of mining shares. Their membership into a *communitas* was a voluntary affair, as in the case of Trento's

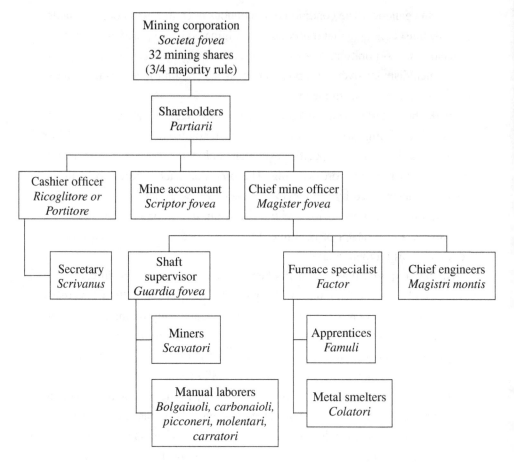

Fig. 3.8. Organization of mining corporations in Tuscany, according to *Ordinamenta*

consilium and Bohemia's *Gerwerken* corporations. Economic freedom enjoyed by an individual *partiarium* was limited by the prospective gains of the rest of the corporation. Aggressive individualism was still in the making. A mine was divided in thirty-two *trente* or shares,[191] the maximum number of shares owned by a corporation. A master of the mine or *magistri foveae* calculated production costs at the end of every day's work and registered the sum in an accounting book. Every three days, he aggregated expenses to be claimed and expenses 'lost to the mine.'[192]

A share was part of a mine's assets, as shafts, veins, and *coffari* or crude ores; however, unlike other assets, a share was not fixed to the mine. Shares were movable assets that could be sold and were ready to be delivered anywhere.[193]

Partiarii enjoyed the right of leasing or selling his mining shares, but such transactions could not obstruct or hamper mining works owned by all other corporation members. The statute strictly forbade shareholders to sell shares to persons not subject to city laws.[194] The fewer enemies with access to Massa's underground wealth, the better. There is one example of leasing of mining shares that gives us an idea about how the transaction worked. An investor owned shares for a shaft identified by the name *le Meloni*. He leased the shaft, with its tools, to a man named Ganterino da Cugnano, a member of another *Communitas*. Ganterino's *Communitas* assumed the responsibility of mining operations for *le Meloni*. The *partiarii* obtained three-fifths of the final product of *le Meloni*, and Ganterino and his society kept two-fifths.[195]

Partiarii followed certain rules for making decisions about mine investments. They required a vote representing three-fourths of the total number of mining shares for withdrawing investments. Only one vote was required for making the decision to continue mining works, irrespective of the total number of shares represented by such a vote.[196] This meant that the majority of shareholders were obliged to cover expenses of mining works, even if only one shareholder actually invested in the mine.[197] White beans were used for expressing affirmative votes, and black beans for negative votes, with a quorum of one third of the corporation's members.

Because ore refining took place *ex situ*, there were several penalties against 'untimely' ore deliveries. No ore buyer could receive a *molentaro* or *carratore*, laborers responsible for the transport of materials, if the ore delivery and transport to a previous client was not completed.[198] Ore transporting and delivering was prohibited unless permission was granted by two men elected for this job by the *Signori Nove Gobernatori del Popolo*. The latter were ten governors, selected by the nine *anziani* or council of nine men, who embodied the *laudable officio* or council that ruled over all affairs of Massa.

The law required that silver ores from mines located in a circumference of approximately nineteen kilometers be sold in the Massa. This means that *Ordinamenta* successfully combined under the same administrative regime all mines situated beyond the walls of the commune.[199] Merchants trading galena ores outside the city paid the *dogana* or customs tax. In practice, it was a ban on silver exports.[200] It is difficult to know the extent to which Massa's mining industries sold ores exclusively in Tuscany, or if their product traveled far. It is possible that high quantities of silver ores were sold to metallurgical and art workshops all over Tuscany. The magnificent medieval art objects made of silver today conserved in many cathedrals and palaces of the region indicate that this was the case. The beautiful *tabula argentea* or silver altarpiece in Pistoia's Cathedral of Saint Zeno, was made with native silver ores. The altarpiece was 'constructed to accommodate a piece of the apostle's head.' The Cathedral is dedicated to Saint Zeno, of whom it is said that he saved Pistoia from floods.[201] The altarpiece was commissioned by the special *magistri* of the Opera di San Jacopo in A.D. 1287. It is possible that what historian Stuard calls 'dotal strategies' also absorbed some quantities of Tuscan silver ore.[202] These are hypotheses that require further research.

There were other restrictions to absolute economic freedom. It was strictly forbidden to remove discarded ores or mine tailings from areas surrounding mine shafts. It is possible that some miners expended much toil and trouble sorting discarded rocks that piled up in mining sites, hoping to find unprocessed ores. The *Breve* stipulated that extraction of such material 'could cause harm and injury to mining operations.' It ordered miners to devote 'no time to this material.'[203] Punishments against violators of the law showed a draconian, feudal legacy difficult to be rid of: in cases of ore theft, a thief's hand could be chopped off if the culprit could not pay the penalty imposed by law against such crime—ten Volterra pounds for assayers, fifty pounds for miners taking property from inside and outside the pits, one hundred *solidi* for thefts in shaft houses.[204] Undercover agents or guards were in charge of monitoring mining sites for this purpose, and their word was taken without question.[205] They enjoyed no further power, nor the authority to punish violations to the mining statute. They were 'sent to each mine for spying' on workers and 'denouncing any violation' to *Ordinamenta* laws.[206] Their presence in mining sites, however, was a symbol of the robust bureaucracy governing mining affairs.

A Large Mining Bureaucracy

The majority of mining officers were elected, signaling the participation of the propertied class of the commune in mining affairs.[207] The Council of Nine Men or *anziani* was Massa's highest political body. It held the keys to the city's chest, where Massa's documents were kept. Ten citizens formed the *Gobernatori del Popolo* or 'People's Governors' noted earlier, which intervened in matters concerning military defense and citizens' rights. It is possible that this body intervened in certain mining affairs, although the text does not mention

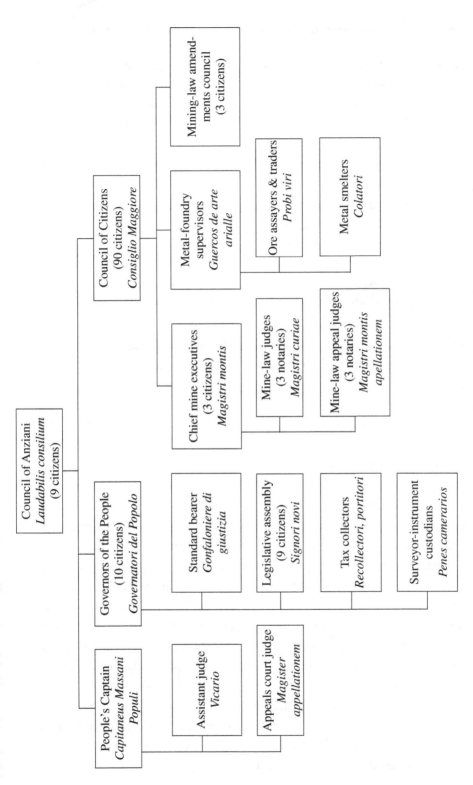

Fig. 3.9. Organization of Massa's mining governance, according to *Ordinamenta super arte fossarum*

anything further. A citizens' council, composed of ninety men and appointed for a one-year service starting every December, selected a five-member council which was very active in war. The *Gobernatori* and the citizens' council, along with the 'Captain of the People,' intervened in matters concerning abandoned mines.[208]

The Captain of the People was the highest-ranking civil servant. He could be reelected, but only after two years of his last day at the job. He authorized mining concessions, executed the mining law, and exercised jurisdiction over Massa's *societas foveae*. He attended the meetings held by the Consiglio Maggiore and was in charge of daily policing of the city. This was a very nice job for ambitious citizens, with a 1,000-florin annual salary.[209] No Captain could own shares in any mine or have any participation in mining works.

In front of this officer, all *magistri*, *partiarii*, and anybody with interests in the mines of Massa swore oaths. He declared final sentence with respect to shafts available for sale: 'shafts that reach the ore source, and show no sign of work, are open to partitioning'—*ad petitionem partis petentis*. It was the Captain's duty to sell shafts, observing the *primum fondoratum* or 'first discoverer' principle established by the law.[210] He met with *magistri* for gathering information on mining works, prepared official reports, and ordered changes to mining works if and when needed.

A Captain inspected shafts, tunnels, and underground works when disputes over claim boundaries occurred. His observations were cross-checked by *magistri* who joined him while conducting mine inspections. He made a decision that could include a new division of shares. This officer was expected not to remain lenient in cases when *partiarii* 'negligently' set fire in a mine or flooded a shaft. In such cases, a Captain imposed a fine of twenty-five pounds reckoned in Volterra *denarii* to the *Communitas* to which the *partiarii* belonged.[211] *Malleficium, fraude, iniuria, offensiones, frustra:*[212] these were the situations that provoked a Captain's fury and intervention in the affairs of mining corporations. A Captain punished *partiarii* who obstructed ventilation galleries, blocked access to another *partiarii*'s work in a *fovea stantiale* or a common shaft or hampered a mining shaft that followed an ore vein strike.

The Captain of the People, with nine *Gobernatori*, elected three men, *bonos, sapientes, discretos et legales viros*, to study the statute and recommend amendments. The election of these public servants took place every December. Their term started immediately after their appointment. By January, these men recommended, in writing, amendments to the mining statute and submitted them to the citizens' council.[213] Amendments to the statute in A.D. 1294, 1295, 1298, 1299, 1301, 1303, 1310, 1311, 1324, and 1328 suggest that the mechanism worked.[214]

The *magistri* belonged to a professional and technical class that enjoyed association rights.[215] This officer belonged to the judicial branch of the political system of Massa. A *magistri curiae* was responsible for ensuring that boundaries of mining claims were valid. Its members visited mines and ore-smelting factories and made recommendations on how to improve mining works.[216] *Magistri curiae* officers were judges who mediated among 'stakeholders' in conflicts over mining works. They were accountable to the Captain of the People.

Members of the *magistri primae et secundae apellationis* were chosen among 'practical men who were familiar with the art of mining.'[217] *Magistri appellationum* were experts responsible for hearing appeals by *partiarii* to *magistri curiae* decisions. Another body, the *magistri montis* or *magistri artis rameriae et argentariae*, was responsible for executing the decisions of the *magistri curiae*. It was formed by three officers who also inspected mining works and submitted their decisions to the city's governors. Most likely, the nomination of *magistri curiae* by the Captain meant appointment, given the importance of a Captain in mining governance. Simonin interpreted the role of the *magistri montis* as that of 'ordinary engineers,' while the *magistri curiae* was a chief engineer or project manager, and the *magistri primae et secundae appellationis* were mine inspectors. The former had jurisdiction over mining affairs—imposed fines for violations of shafts and ore stealing, punishable with a fine and hand removal, as in the *Codex Wangianus*.[218] Mine judges and administrators worked *in situ,* supervising bookkeeping tasks, inspecting mining infrastructure, and 'denouncing and punishing fraudulent works.'[219]

The *Gobernatori* appointed two mine accountants known as *guercos de arte arialle*.[220] These *guercos* were responsible for the *custodia arialle*. Entrance to metal foundries was forbidden to these supervisors during holidays and days of rest.[221] The noun *arialle* originated in the German word *Erzhalle* and designated the city's metallurgical office.[222] The office functioned as a warehouse, protected by city laws, where ores made a brief stop for accounting purposes while en route to smelting factories. Arialle officers registered in an accounting book all details about ore deliveries. We know nothing further on the exact method of accounting.[223] Today, the Porta all'Arialla identifies a site southwest of the city of Massa coming from Follonica, where the remains of the city's public metal foundries were visible up to the early nineteenth century.[224]

Book accounting was essential for 'avoiding litigations, quarrels and scandals,' in the words of a fifteenth-century merchant from Naples.[225] It allowed for easier monitoring of the quality of ores that arrived at metal factories, including copper ores.[226] The statute allowed Massa to buy copper ores, over a radius of approximately twenty kilometers. Copper from neighboring mines was assayed in Massa's furnaces. It could not contain more than 2.5 percent of impurities. This was known as *rame di fusione*. A second type of refined copper was sold, known as *rame di polzone*. The latter was reduced in the form of bars or grains, *panectolis* and *exgranatum*. The letter *M* was stamped on Massa's copper bars, which measured 10 by 2 inches.

Additional accounting officers were needed. Officers known as *recollectoribus* and *portitoribus* undersigned all pecuniary affairs concerning mining works and kept two different accounting books.[227] One book went to Massa's civil registry, and the other to the commune's chamberlain. Accounting officers kept a book recording date of ore extraction, name of *partiarii*, amounts of ores owed to each *Communitas* member based on number of shares, ore quantity delivered to factories for cupellation and assaying, and carriers' names.

These accounting officers had additional responsibilities. The *portitore* was the officer in charge of city customs. He brought tax debts of shareholders to *magistri*, which allowed him to seek *solutio* or cancel debts. Afterwards, the *magistri* seized the debtor's mining assets and canceled the tax debt. The city held the prerogative to confiscate a *partiarium*'s property in cases of tax evasion, and it was the role of the *portitore* to collect payments in coined money as well as refined silver ores from the confiscated property.[228]

Surveying instruments were under the custody of city officers known as *penes camerarios comunis*.[229] Surveyors belonged to a class of technical experts with offices located in the city quarters. They measured mines *ad planum* and *arhipendolum*, that is, using plumb lines, quadrants, and compasses.[230] Instruments included rods, squares, and levels, instruments employed by medieval 'army corps of engineers' throughout Europe.[231] Who paid surveyor salaries in Massa is not sufficiently clear in the text of *Ordinamenta*. Most likely, salaries came from incomes of mining corporations.

Partiarii sat at the top of the mining hierarchy. Its public counterpart was the *magistri foveae*. Below each, there were diverse groups of semi-technical

Fig. 3.10. Miner's surveying instrument, A.D. 1590. The side circle attached to the rotatable column contains an engraved semicircular arc divided into degrees. A surveyor mounts two of these devices on stands of equal height at two different points of a shaft. On the first device he attaches a cord to the circle's hook, walks with cord in hand to the point where the second device is mounted, and attaches the other end of the cord to the circle's hook. He reads the numbers on the side arc and the base of the instrument and determines the shaft's vertical inclination and horizontal orientation, according to Michael Korey. bpk Berlin / Staatliche Kunstsammlungen Dresden / Jürgen Karpinski / Art Resource, NY.

and manual workers or *laboratores*. The *bolgaiuolus* was a worker in charge of removing extracted ores from shafts; the *carbonaiolo,* responsible for working with charcoal, measured and recorded amounts of charcoal used in the commune's furnaces in every stage of the cupellation process.[232] The most unskilled laborers were the *picconerio* or ore digger, a worker with a pickaxe; the *molentaro* or *carratore*, in charge of transport of materials; *colatores,* or metal smelters; the *factor,* or general mine worker; the *famulus,* or apprentice; and the *guardia,* or shaft custodian.[233] The latter enjoyed no association or guild rights.

The enactment of *Ordinamenta* coincided with a period of intense mining activity. Costs of mining the underground wealth were high, in a region affected by river floods and malaria, as described earlier. The fact that commercial farming took off in the region meant that private capital was available and ready to plow back its profits into the subsoil. Also, an interventionist policy made

Fig. 3.11. German compass, A.D. 1591. The circular scale is divided into hours, rather than degrees, a feature common to mining instruments. A thin wax ring encircling the compass permits the surveyor to mark directions underground and read off angular positions above ground. The compass itself occupies one-sixth of the total diameter; the rest is fine artistic work representing the seven classical planets of antiquity. The instrument was possibly commissioned as a gift for a wealthy and princely mine owner. bpk Berlin / Staatliche Kunstsammlungen Dresden / Jürgen Karpinski / Art Resource, NY.

sense to a newly independent commune surrounded by a hostile enemy, Siena, eager to wage war and annex Massa's territory. The largest mining operations were the Poggio alla Cave, located in Pozzoia or Poczorio Valley, and Poggio di Serra ai Bottini, on a hill close to Pozzoia.[234]

Was the large mining bureaucracy the symbol of enduring feudal roots? In A.D. 1072–1118, the Sestina Abbey received a one-tenth of mines in the frontier of Massa.[235] Bishop Bernardo of Populonia obtained a papal donation of income rights from the mines located in Elba Island in A.D. 1066 from Pope Alexander II (d. A.D. 1073). The grant included the tenth owed to the church of the incomes of the iron and silver mines of Elba's *cava*. In A.D. 1134, the Bishop of Volterra received the Castle of Montieri and jurisdiction over its court, from the Pannocchieschi, a family with extensive landed property in Siena. Three years later, the Bishop gained a mining grant for the silver mines of the region. In A.D. 1194, Bishop Martino of Populonia, who also held the title of Prince of Massa, obtained in feudal grant the city of Massa by Emperor Henry VI (A.D. 1165–1197). By then, and because of an ecclesiastical decree, the Bishop of Populonia was also the Bishop of Massa—*Episcopus Populoniae & Massae.*

In A.D. 1151, the citizens of Montieri made an agreement with Siena merchants, against the Bishop of Volterra. They swore to guard and defend, on behalf of Siena, half of Montieri's castle and tower, the plaza or court, and silver mine. In the meantime, Siena merchants took over a silver mine in Montieri, claiming that they discovered it in A.D. 1180. In the same year, the Archbishop of Magonza, the Imperial Vicar representing the interests of Emperor Frederick Barbarossa, donated to Siena all his income rights over Siena's *contado* as well as half of the Montieri mine. The citizens of Massa opposed this grant, arguing that its commune had obtained in A.D. 1160 a grant by the same Emperor over half of the mine of Montieri. The Volterra Bishop also argued against this grant, based upon the A.D. 896 grant by Adalberto, Margrave of Tuscany. The year after, Ugone, Bishop of Volterra, 'donated,' under military pressure, a one-fourth share of the mine of Montieri to Siena, his powerful enemy. He received a feudal-style compensation package: 330 pounds. The Pannocchieschi family appeared on stage again, claiming rights over the silver mines.

In A.D. 1188, the family received from Emperor Frederick I a chart of privileges, which included jurisdiction and rights over the Diocese of Montieri, regalia rights, and the silver mine of Montieri. In A.D. 1214–1216, the Bishop of Volterra, already at war against Siena, had no other option but to buy from Siena the rights over the Montieri castle and the silver mine, under a penalty of 1,000 pounds. The Bishop obtained a donation grant of a one-tenth of the incomes of the silver mines located in the districts of Massa and Monte Valle-Buja in A.D. 1217. Still, in the year of independence of Massa, the Bishop claimed jurisdiction over the city's silver mines.

The Bishop and the Chapter of Canons of Massa sold to the commune rights over the court—*jus eligendi potestatem, sive consules, jurisdictionem.* The commune paid 100,000 pounds in Pisa money, the dominant money of Tuscany then. However, the Bishop excluded the silver mines from the agreement—*Item excipimus ac reservamus nobis, & successoribus nostris omnem iurisdicitonem & consuetudines, quam, & quas habemus in Argentifodinis latentibus & aper-*

tis. The Canon Chapter received from the citizens of Massa 600 pounds in the same year; it did not renounce jurisdiction over its silver mines of Massa. The phrase *argentifodinas nostras* leaves no doubt on this point. The Canon's jurisdiction over the silver mines was confirmed in a Papal Bull by Pope Alexander IV in A.D. 1254. The Bull announced the excommunication of Massa's captain of the people and council for 'occupying' the silver mines that belonged to the Church.[236]

Later, in A.D. 1253, and with the consent of Pope Innocent IV, Ranieri, the Bishop of Volterra, still held half of the Montieri mine and its court. The Castle of Montalcinello was included in the agreement. He had an agreement with Siena to pay 215 pounds in Siena *denarii*. The penalty for violating the agreement was 200 pounds. Later, before the end of the century, Siena took over Montieri as well as Montalcinello. By then, the Bishop of Volterra had gained two powerful enemies: the merchants and aristocrats of Siena and those of Massa. The subsequent war between Massa and Siena in A.D. 1326 was a period of decline for Massa; not only did the war efforts against its enemies empty its coffers but a wave of plague starting in A.D. 1328 greatly diminished the population of the region. Faced with increasing economic problems triggered by wars and the plague, the city's inhabitants abandoned mining.

The early capitalist mining industry that took off in Massa could not eradicate the deep-seated feudal roots of Massa. Roots of trees rarely feel the violence of storms, says an old Mediterranean proverb. Feudal lords held dominion over the mines surrounding Massa; investors seeking to exploit the mines had to yield to a lord's wishes. A Ragusan entrepreneur, with 'Maestro Allegro of Imola, Jew,' petitioned the Lord of Montieri 'to be allowed to mine in the territory of Montieri, that is, in the villages of Boccheggiano and Roccastrada.'[237] The letter was sent from Siena in A.D. 1455. The letter established the following 'pacts, conditions, and procedures':

> [T]hat where they begin to mine no other person be allowed to mine within a mile from them for a period of twenty-five years; and if it should happen that two years pass without their mining anything, then, this grace is to be understood to be null and void; and they offer forever to give your Commune out of anything they mine or find one part out of twelve. Also, in regard to everything they mine-that is, gold, silver, and any other metal-they promise your Commune that they will have it melted and refined by artisans living in your town, that is, by goldsmiths; and if [the goldsmiths] themselves wish to do this, they promise not to send [the

metal] to others, that is, outside your city. Also, [they promise] that they will have
it all struck in the mint of your Commune. Also, we wish to be allowed to use any
water in the said localities and to erect there any building [needed] to work the said
metal, and to be allowed to cut wood without detriment or damage to any of your
communities or to private persons, [since] this grace is not to be understood to be
detrimental in any part to them.[238]

The letter 'pacts' promise a capitalist beginning for Montieri's mining industry.
No fifteenth-century lord could have resisted the tempting offer, after the wars
that destroyed Tuscany's mining industries after the fourteenth century. The
glory of the early capitalist mining business was maintained in the memory of
merchants of Europe.

The Happy Marriage between Banking and Mining: The Case of Iglesias

The *Statuto di Villa di Chiesa e Sigerro*, also known as *Breve di Villa di
Chiesa*, appeared in Iglesias, Sardinia, in A.D. 1327. At the time, Iglesias belonged to the Arborea judicate, an old Pisa ally. The mines, however, were
located in the dominions of the Donoratico counts.[239] Between the most influential politicians of the region[240] on the one hand, and absentee landlords[241] on the
other, capitalists found the ideal crack for making their way to the city's mines.

Most of the statute's articles appeared in A.D. 1302–1304, in a *Breve anteriori* enacted under Pisa's rule and *redatto in volgare italiano*, in the words
of Mattone and Ferrante.[242] From this *Breve*, the Aragonese statute copied the
principle of freedom to all citizens for exploring and mining in Iglesias.[243] Staking a new claim required planting a cross in the prospect site and registering the
claim with a *camerlingo*, the officer who authorized mining claims. A mining
claim was granted if the shaft kept a distance of twenty-one *braccia* or arms
from existing claims.[244] If a prospector opened a new quarry, shaft, or water
channel in *montagna nuova* and discovered silver ores, which, after deduction
of expenses, were worth five pounds per *corbello*, he paid a tax of ten pounds
per una robba to the city's *camerlingo*.[245] He enjoyed a five-year period of tax
exemption.[246] Payment of the ore-discovery tax made the prospector a holder of
a private mining stake.[247]

Claiming an abandoned shaft required planting a cross in the site. The cross
indicated that a prospector had three days for what the *Breve* called *ripiglia-*

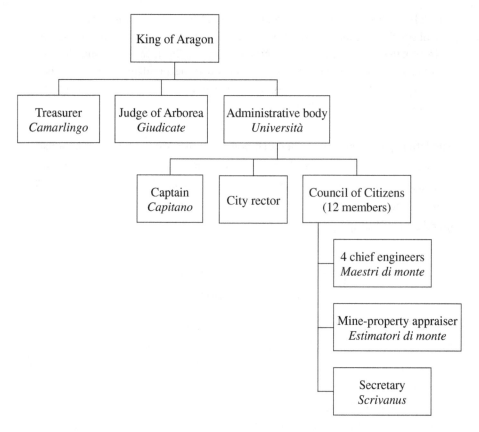

Fig. 3.12. Mining governance structure in Sardinia, according to *Breve di Villa di Chiesa*

tura, or the opening of an abandoned shaft.[248] The cross could be replanted or *rinfrescarsi*, which gave a prospector three additional days for starting ore extraction. Time was of the essence. A prospector could work during holidays and the days of rest observed in Iglesias, with the exception of the day when the *magister montis* declared a suspension of all works under extraordinary circumstances.[249] If the shaft showed no sign of improvement after six days, a *magister montis* or chief mining engineer allocated the shaft to the miner who offered the best bid for it. The magister collected one silver mark after re-leasing the shaft. The weight of the Sardinian silver mark or *marco sardesco* was approximately 238.022 grams.[250] Work on a reclaimed shaft was expected to run uninterruptedly for a minimum of three months.

There were other conditions under which a prospector could claim abandoned shafts. If a shaft was sunk at a depth of one pace, it was not considered

abandoned, unless fifteen days passed and the shaft showed no sign of improvement.[251] If the same shaft yielded two or more *corbelli* of silver per day, holders of the mining claim had the right to present cause for keeping their claim.
Shareholders in this case had one month and three days to present their legal
case in the court of Iglesias. For a prospector's claim over an abandoned shaft
to prevail or the cause of *ripigliatura* to succeed,[252] the prospector had to work
the shaft for seven days and register the claim with the Iglesias court. The court
granted eight days to previous investors for settling debts concerning the shaft
under question.[253] The goal was to allow new miners to acquire mining shares
free of debt while avoiding disruption in the prices of mining shares. Investors
were mandated to attend personally to the Court of Iglesias or courts in *Do-
musnovas, o Baratoli, o Bagniargia, o Conesa, o Bareca, o Sigulis, o Antasa, o
Ghiandili*,[254] villages that were absorbed into Iglesias's catchment area.

Investors still enjoyed the right to sell half of their shares to the new prospector claiming the abandoned shaft. Otherwise, the total number of shares
belonged to the new prospector. If a prospector failed to submit to the Court the
ripigliatura claim and worked an abandoned shaft for a period of two months,
for which no investor claimed shares, the prospector had no right to demand
from any investor the sale of mining shares. The *Breve* was firm on this point:
if a mining engineer, notary, or *parzonavile* or shareholder failed to prove that
ripigliatura conditions had been observed, the investor lost the claim to the
abandoned shaft. He could do so if a shaft showed no sign of improvement
in fifteen consecutive days. When there was no sign of improvement for four
consecutive months, the shaft belonged to the first prospector. He became the
parzonavilii or shareholder of a *segno morto* mine and was exempted from
ripigliatura conditions. There was only one condition a prospector had to fulfill: he had to register the claim for a *segno morto* mine in fifteen days.

Shafts belonged to a *societas* or *communita*s, the medieval mining corporation of Sardinia.[255] Mines were the *partitura communale*, the property to
be divided in thirty-two *trente* or shares among members of a corporation.[256]
These shares were further divided into quarters, for purposes of Court procedures and accounting. Shareholders were the *parzonavilii* mentioned earlier,
and their forming a corporation was a voluntary affair. They enjoyed the right
to claim their shares within a month after the division of *partitura communale*
took place. This period was valid in cases where a *societas* was formed for
working newly opened mining shafts. In cases where the division of shares was

completed, the one-month period took effect after the date of the promise of
the *trente*. In any case, an investor's duty included registering the claim in the
Iglesias court. Rights of ownership of *trente* were valid only after a claim was
registered in court. A shareholder could rescind from ownership of *trente* and
liberate himself from spending additional amounts of money into his part of the
mining works. This right, however, did not exempt him from canceling debts
incurred in mining works.

A *parzonavile* also enjoyed the right to donate or transfer his *trente* in inheritance to a family member. He could give shares in dowry, and women could
legally hold them.[257] A shareholder also enjoyed the right to lease his mining
shares while retaining his economic obligations to the mining corporation. A
lease was a contract that fixed the price of mining shares. It consisted of selling
anticipations of metal outputs, in amounts proportional to the number of shares
held by the seller. The buyer paid in advance for metal outputs that were going
to be produced in the future, as part of the weekly mining outputs of the mine.[258]
The advantages of the lease contract are evident: a *parzonavile* obtained ready
cash proportional to the value of his mining shares before silver ores material-
ized. This lease contract became prevalent later in the sixteenth century, as the
portfolio of the Augsburg family of the Fugger illustrates.[259]

It is likely, as it did in the sixteenth century, that leasing mining shares led
to speculative bubbles. In response to this problem, the *Breve* stipulated other
conditions applying to leaseholders. If a *condutore*, an investor outside a *communitas*, bought a lease at a fixed price and the number of shares equaled the
majority of *trente* held by the corporation, that investor could buy the remaining *trente* at the same price, if these were to be sold. This price privilege only
applied if *trente* were not to be returned within fifteen days after the lease was
done.

Information about relations between buyers and sellers of mining shares is
still scanty. Yet all we know is that they are totally ignored by Marxist historiography. The archetype of medieval land leases, those of manorial lands
in twelfth-century England studied by Postan, operated within the realm of
control of the landlord.[260] These were contracts between landlords and their
tenants. This archetype seems inadequate for the improvement of the medieval *argentifodina*. Forced by their lack of capital, feudal lords in Iglesias
became dependent upon revenues derived from leasing their mines. One example of share-leasing has survived. On March 9, 1317, the *Ospedale Nuovo*

della Misericordia di Pisa or Hospitaller Order of the Mercy of Pisa, today the Ospedale di S. Chiara, leased shares for the Giumentaria mine in Monte Barlao, today's Monteponi. Giacomo Puccio del Boninsegna, bought the lease at five florins per year, for two years. In exchange, Giacomo retained a third of the extracted silver ore. In less than a week, on March 15 of the same year, Giacomo advanced a payment of fifty florins to the Order.[261] We hear from the Order again in A.D. 1335, when it leased the same mine to 'Gaddo of the late Cerio Patroculo,' a relative of Bonifazio Donoratico. The lease was done 'at the fixed price' of twelve and a half florins per year. In exchange, Donoratico obtained two *trente* of the mine at half price.[262] The Hospitaller had to catch up with the times.

The mine located in Monte Barlao had a privileged location, which suggests that the Order was desperate to lease the shares. Only in Monte Barlao, with its continuation in San Giorgio and Is Fossas or *Seddas de Is Fossas*, and Monte Malva or *Narda*, ore-washing took place *in situ*.[263] In Narda, the *Breve* prohibited fabrication of *piazza da lavare* or ore-washing facility in an effort to prevent damages to mining works.[264] The Nasella and Galatta *fossas* in Monte Barlao already had ore-washing installations; however, the river in the vicinity was dry for most of the year and water ran short. Miners used an additional *piazza da lavare* in Monte Barlao. The mining law prohibited rechanneling the water stream that fed the Barlao *piazza* and defined water rights that prevented monopolizing this precious resource.

The right to sell and lease shares exempted no investor from paying off mining expenses. And these had a lot to do with an investor's credit relations and capital gains.

Did Mining Shares Yield High Capital Gains?

Mining the rich geological endowments of Iglesias required credit, given the changing costs of mining operations.[265] The apogee of moneylending of the twelfth-century Italian Renaissance infiltrated the mining business culture.[266] Mining expenses here had the flair of the high world of Renaissance banking. Total expenses of mining works were legally defined as debts of *parzonavilii*. A *francatura* or bill of payment, written by a master of the mine or *magister di monti*, was presented in the Iglesias court every week for debt cancellation. Information written in the bill note was also written in the mine's accounting book.

The *francatura* bill was calculated based upon the price of one *corbello* of ore. Expenses incurred in producing one *corbello* of metal output, measured in money, were multiplied by the total number of *corbelli* produced in the mine; the number was then divided among the number of mining shares.[267] The bill was presented by a notary at the Iglesias court every Saturday. A *francatura* represented a debt cancellation claim for the entire mine account, since valuing mine incomes required that expenses and earnings be calculated for the mine as a whole. The *Magister* of a corporation collected payments from *parzonavilii* every Saturday, based upon the number of *trente* each *parzonavilii* owned. Promise of payment was accepted if a shareholder could not pay his *francatura* but was committed to make whole the debt in the near future. The principle at work here was 'that a debtor can, will, and must pay.'[268] A shareholder lost his *trente* if he was unable to pay his debt. The law granted a period of fifteen days for *parzonavilii* who lived outside Iglesias to make payments. Otherwise, the *trente* was granted to any other *parzonavilii,* if requested.

Calculations of debts, however, required relying upon practical mathematical artifices and experience. To start with, a *corbello* was a unit of volume used for measuring ores, equivalent to approximately 370 pounds in Massa.[269] But it was not the only unit used in Sardinia, as will be described later. Second, the prices of ores varied, depending upon the number of *corbelli* obtained from each ore-extraction shaft. As described in the previous chapter, Sardinia's veins were irregular and carried unpredictable ore quantities. There were cases where one shaft yielded less than one *corbello*, while other shafts yielded sixty-three *corbelli* of silver ore on a weekly basis, for each *trente* of the *communitas*. Some estimates and averages had to be taken for granted by a master of the mine when calculating the bill of payment. The results of the *francatura* payments say something about the 'invisible hand' that guided the economy: *trente* prices varied significantly among *societas*, according to metal output, the amount of silver recuperated through cupellation, and the purity of the silver ores.[270] *Trente* values could vary within the same mining corporation, too, considering that investors nominally could hold claims over different sections of the same extraction shaft.

A *francatura* bill was by no means the only debt haunting investors. If an investor borrowed money for cancelling his *francatura* debt, his credit relations included a *bistantaria* contract. The latter was an agreement whereby a creditor or *bistante* advanced money to *parzonavile* only for paying mine expenses and collected payments *ad usura*.[271] Under Pisa's rule, interest rates reached four *denarii* per pound every month, a number equivalent to 20 percent every year. The value of the *denarius* was based upon the standard of Pisa. In the new *Breve, usura consueta* was equivalent to two *denarii* per pound every month.[272]

A *bistante* became a partner of the mining company, providing very specific financial services. Once a notarized letter appointing a *bistante* was issued, the name of the *bistante* was added to a mine's accounting book. Information contained in the letter could be changed, after a party's request, within two months after the notarized letter was issued. Once a *bistante* contract was registered in the Iglesias court, the letter could not be changed. A copy of the letter was held by *parzonavilii* and *bistante*, both copies stating the amount of loaned money. A *bistante* stayed with the society as long as the contract was active. The contract, naturally, came first, so that in the event of a mine shutdown, debts and payments could be settled. A *bistante* paid salaries of workers by the end of each week, charged debt payments to the mine's incomes, and seized a debtor's property if he could not meet his payment obligations.[273] He was not, however, part of the decision-making body of a *communitas*. Property that could be seized included a debtor's shoes, bed, guns, and horses. The most important responsibility of a *bistante*, after he became a partner of a mining society, was to deliver the promised money advance every Saturday. Violators paid a fine of one silver mark.

It was not easy for a *bistante* to confiscate a debtor's property. Seizing property required a public notice on Fridays and Saturdays, the Court's session days, for a period of one month and three days. A debtor enjoyed the right of appeal, but he had the responsibility of publicly promulgating a payment declaration three times, at the S. Chiara Church and the Court's assembly.[274] If the debtor could not fulfill his payment obligation, his property was confiscated and declared to be liquid capital belonging to *bistante*.[275] Four elected public servants, including two mining experts, estimated the value of the seized property using the following property-appraisal formula: three *denarii* for every five *denarii* of property value. Unlike *Ordinamenta*, where only money was accepted for debt cancellation, the Iglesias statute allowed a *bistante* to accept *trente* for payment cancellation—afterwards the *trente* acquired new value.

Creditors, however, enjoyed certain rights. A creditor was never to be forced to capriciously advance money for mining works. A *Magister* submitted a written request to the Court for additional amounts of money from a *bistante*, and the request remained open for three days. If in this period of time, the *bistante* refused to advance the money, the *Magister* and *parzonavilii* could agree to a new contract with another *bistante*. In such cases, the *Magister* cancelled the debt with the first *bistante* with silver ores processed while the contract with the first *bistante* was in place. He could add newly mined ores for payment purposes if necessary. According to the general formula, the last *bistante* paying for mining operations was paid before any shareholder. A continuous renewal of credit relations worked to the benefit of a corporation. Another financial partner, known as a *portitor*, was a 'service provider,' elected by shareholders. He performed minor roles, such as delivering cash advances.[276]

Certainly, investors recuperated extraction costs with minor problems. Most mining works took advantage only of the richest silver ores; thus, *parzonavilii* spent no money processing low-quality galena ores.[277] This made sense in Iglesias, where only in Fluminimaggiore and Sarrabus[278] producers recuperated amounts of silver that ranged between eight and nine ounces of silver per *cantaro* of ore. The *cantaro* was a medieval unit of volume used in Aragon equivalent to forty-six kilograms.[279] The lack of interest by Iglesias industrialists on lead ores is still intriguing, given Europe's high demand for lead.[280]

Credit relations also suggest that running costs tended to increase, not decrease, in the short run, because mines were located in highly uneven terrain. Miners built most shafts in inclined levels, which required costly construction of drainage infrastructure and experts for managing underground waters. Miners also equipped shafts with a wide range of tools and materials, from thick ropes used to connect each shaft's bottom with its portal, to other tools needed for easy transport of men and materials. Miners rented beasts of burden for transporting ores to washing facilities. The law allowed miners to change the course of a water stream as long as the digging did not hinder any wagon road or roads used by donkeys and mules, the preferred beasts of burden. The law required that any person hampering a path or road build another path for beasts of burden to come and go at ease.

A Mining Hierarchy

A *guelco* or *guelchi* was an expert in ore smelting and the *forni di colare vena*. Having an expert eye for weighing and measuring was a requirement for working in ore smelting. The smelter was most likely a literate man, as he played a pivotal role in debt accounting. He bought galena ores from either

Magistri or shareholders and denounced illicit ore sellers in the Iglesias court. The statute granted them a monopoly for buying ores produced in Iglesias: *et la vena di quelle montagne* [. . .] *vendere e dare alli guelchi di Villa di Chiesa, et non a 'ltri guelchi.*[281]

A *guelco* cancelled debts incurred by *parzonavilii* for cupellation expenses. The formula used on this side of the mining business was the standard price to be paid for the ore brought to the smelting factory. There was, nominally, not much room for cheating. A *Magistri di Monti* was responsible for registering the debt in the mine's accounting book before the ore reached the smelting factory, if a *parzonavile* wanted to cancel his debt with a *guelco.*[282] The accounting exercise was not done at random. The *guelco* cancelled a shareholder's debt before he calculated the amount of ore to be sent to smelting factories. This provision was put in place for avoiding any 'market disruption' in the price of ore veins, according to Baudi di Vesme.[283] We shall come back to the question of ore market and prices later.

No *guelco* could be harassed by shareholders, once ores were processed. In those cases, a *guelco* had eight days to present a case against a shareholder. The book account kept by the *guelco* was the legal document used in the Iglesias court. Temptations to fix the book account were probably too many; thus, the *Breve* imposed a fine against anyone removing mine accounting books outside Iglesias. It is possible that legal conflicts between shareholders and *guelco* were common and time-consuming, given that the statute specified that no shareholder could demand money from a *guelco* after a two-year period.[284] One need not have Ricardo's keen eye to notice that prices of unrefined ores owned by debtors were artificially lowered. What separated debt-plagued from debt-free shareholders was a sea of conflicts.

The tenure of a *guelco* lasted three months. This officer enjoyed the right to bear arms—*offendivile* and *deffendivile*—when working in smelting installations.[285] This privilege made the *guelchi* a very important officer in the public opinion of Iglesias, comparable to the *homini del Signore Re.*[286] Below the *guelchi*, there were the *mastri colatori* or *mastri smiratori* and the *fancelli*. The latter were followed by *smiratori, trattatori, lavoratori*, and their assistants. A *societas* hired these laborers for diverse ore-processing and smelting tasks. The law subjected them to fines in case of 'ore damage' or fraud, including punishment for violating work hours of factories, running from Monday morning to Saturday noon.[287]

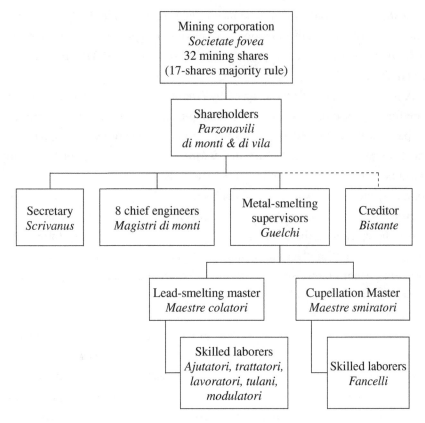

Fig. 3.13. Organization of mining corporations, according to *Breve di Villa di Chiesa*

Eight chief mining engineers, or *Magistri di Monte*, were elected by the city council, but only four were sworn in to carry out the job. The chief engineers adjudicated disputes concerning boundaries of underground works.[288] For this purpose, five out of the eight *Magistri* held a mining court for two days in a row every week, either Saturdays and Sundays or Sundays and Mondays. The job tenure lasted three months. *Magistri* enjoyed the right to bear arms and received payments from mines' earnings.[289] Their office was located in the city's *palazzo*. With a minimum of five years of experience in mining affairs and three years of legal residence in Iglesias, these engineers were experts in principles of mine accounting.[290] *Magistri* supervised mining works in Sulcis and Sigerro, both of which belonged to the judicate of Cagliari. They could own *trente* only after they ended their official term in the mines of their interest.

Shaft masters or *Maestri di fossa* supervised mining works in shifts that ran from Monday noon to Friday noon. They were different from *Magistri di Montis*. First, *Maestri di fossa* were hired by *parzonavilii* and not elected by the Iglesias city council. Second, their responsibilities included being physically present in mining sites. Shaft masters performed the role of expert miners with ample experience in ore geology. They supervised ore-extraction works in conformity with the interests of *parzonavilii*.[291] They had to demonstrate a minimum of five years of experience for hiring—a condition that probably was rarely fulfilled.[292] A *Camerlingo* licensed metal processing factories and authorized mining claims. He administered the *libri dell'argentiera*, the commune's treasury. The city's chief judicial officer was known as *Rettore*, and had general jurisdiction over the mining industry. The *Università* or commune, a *Camerlingo*, and the Donoratico counts were at the top of the governance structure in Iglesias.

At the bottom of the mining hierarchy, there were ordinary miners, including a mixed group of urban patriciates.[293] Miners and metallurgical laborers participated in the procession of the Church of *Sancta Maria di Mezo Gosto*, held (as the name indicates) every fifteenth of August. *Due operarii argentierii* built a processional candle or *candelo*, in representation of miners. The *candelo* weighed eighty pounds of 'new wax,' at the expense of the King, and was presented to the Church of St. Maria in festivities held every year.[294] Workers of metal smelters, known as *lavoratori di truogara, et tulani, et modulatori*, built a second *candelo*. This one was smaller—seventy pounds of *cera nuova*—also made at the expense of the King. Iglesias associations representing the most influential families headed the religious procession, according to Braunstein. Associations representing mountain towns, district representatives, and lastly, artisans and miners followed.[295]

It is possible that miners achieved mobility, albeit with limited possibilities. Iglesias 'witnessed a population explosion during the latter half of the century as immigrants, even delinquent debtors, were actively sought and granted asylum to cultivate communal lands and to prospect for mining sites.'[296] The price of labor was comparatively low, possibly because of abundant supply. 'A Sardinian laborer cost six to eight times less than a Florentine laborer before the plague, twelve times less afterwards, and a unit of grain in Sardinia was valued at about one-third of the same unit in Florence,' observed historian Rowland.[297] Modest amounts of money went to payments of labor. High amounts of silver went in the direction of banking. As late as A.D. 1553, taxes collected over silver and lead ores from the mines of Iglesias amounted to 2,400 tons per year, based on a letter from Iglesias' Rector to the Viceroy.[298] One thing was certain: mining dominated the economic landscape of Iglesias. Agrarian and land laws were subordinated to mining. The statute established freedom to individuals to *lavorare et beneficiari tucte et singule montagne, boschi, valle et acque,* in Iglesias and adjacent villages.[299] Ambassador Bacciameo Muglione da Putignano complained that the population of Iglesias did not take care of cultivated fields of cereals because *intendunt magis ad laboreriam argenterie.*[300] Mining absorbed all forms of labor. Fortune blessed the happy marriage between banking and silver mining in Sardinia.

A Fiscal View of Production: Ottoman Mining in the Balkans

Mines were no mere fruits of victory; they were to be a continual stream of revenues. The Ottomans found ideal conditions in the Balkans for taking advantage of mining revenues while firmly imposing their view of society and government. The state borrowed from the Saxon tradition the principle that prospectors enjoyed exploration rights.[301] Medieval Serbian laws granted privileges to Saxon miners, not only for mining enterprises but also settlement and metal-trade rights. The *Zakonik* or Law of Stefan Dušan, enacted in A.D. 1349, granted Saxons the following:

> Wheresoever Saxons have cleared forest up to the date of this Council, that land let them have. And if they have unlawfully taken any land from any lord, let the Lord use them according to the law of the Sainted King. But from henceforth a Saxony may not clear and that forest which he clears shall not belong to him, nor shall they settle people there, but it shall stand empty, so that the forest grow. Let no man forbid a Saxon so much timber as he needs for his business, so much let him fell.[302]

Charters granting privileges to German immigrants in the thirteenth century have not survived.[303]

Exactly how much freedom an Ottoman miner enjoyed for prospecting lands is a matter of controversy. Certainly, mineral exploration required sinking shafts, building underground tunnels, timbering and fortifying mine galleries, and ore-sampling and testing. The law mandated miners to sink shafts from the surface to the point of contact with an ore vein strike or *tchah.*[304] The quartz rocks of the Balkans, hosting galena ores, did not give up easily to miners' pickaxes.

**Table 3.2. Ottoman mining laws of Saxon-Balkan origins,
fourteenth and fifteenth centuries**

Mine	Law year	Origins
Kratovo	1390[a]	Bosnian and Serbian laws, 1300s[b]
Novo Brdo	1455[c]	Ancient Serbian custom[d]
Cetate-Albă	1484[e]	Ancient Moldovan tradition
Crnča	1488	1352 Bosnia law[f]
Sasse	1488	1352 Bosnia law[g]
Srebrenica	1488	1352 Bosnia law
Belasica	1488	1423 old 'model' law
Plana	1488	1346 old 'model' law
Zaplanina	1488	1390 old 'model' law
Trepča	1489	1303 Serbian law
Janjevo	1489	1303 Serbian law
Novo Brdo	1494	1391 Serbian law[h]

[a] Enacted by Sultan Bāyazīd I. [b] Acts originated in laws enacted under Bosnian *ban* or governors of the Kotromanić House before A.D. 1350. The latter ruled Bosnia from A.D. 1322 to 1376. Ottoman laws mention the Byzantine *perper* currency as well as the *asper*, a currency common in Black Sea cities. Spufford, *Money and its use in medieval Europe*, p. 147; see also Miller, 'Bosnia before the Turkish conquest,' pp. 651–660. [c] Enacted by Sultan Mehmed II. [d] The Serbian law enacted by Prince Stefan Lazarević in A.D. 1391 was drafted after a meeting of twenty-four men 'who knew the ancient law of Novo Brdo,' according to Beldiceanu. [e] Enacted by Sultan Bāyazīd II. [f] Enacted by King Stephen Tvrtko I of Bosnia (A.D. 1353–1391), nephew of King Stephen Kotromanić. [g] Enacted by the Kovačević voivodes who emerged by the end of the fourteenth century during the reign of King Tvrtko I. In the early fifteenth century, Kovač Dinjičić held the title of Voivode. His descendants held the title for a short period of time after the conquest of the region by Sultan Mehmed II. [h] Enacted by Prince Stefan Lazarević.

Source: Beldiceanu, *Les Actes des Premiers Sultans*, vol. 2, pp. 43–47, 53–58.

In Janjevo, today part of Kosovo, miners spent between three and six months sinking shafts and building underground galleries, a mining engineering feature that figured prominently in Ottoman mines.[305] At Trepča, miners spent between two and four years sinking different shafts before reaching the mine's *tchah*.[306] Miners in Novo Brdo dug through hard limestone: they spent between ten and fifteen years sinking and digging before reaching the mine's *tchah*, measuring fifty to sixty *ḳulaç*, or between 85.5 and 102.6 meters in length. Time meant money. Miners' experience digging through hard limestone could be useful for besieging enemy cities and was not to be missed by Ottoman Sultans prone to war. Miners of Novo Brdo were mobilized to the Golden Horn in the Muslim campaign against Constantinople.[307]

Considerable variations in shaft length could be found in Ottoman mines, from fifty to one hundred *kulaç*, or between 85.5 and 171 meters.[308] The Ottoman *kulaç* was equivalent to 1.7 meters, making it comparable to the German *Lachter*, or fathom.[309] Shaft and adit portals were fortified with timber, and a *qram* or warehouse was built close to a mine's portal for storage of materials and ores prior to sale or transport.[310]

A mine was divided in sixty-four, sixty-six, or sixty-eight *ḥiṣṣe* or shares. The reason for this unusually high number of shares is not easy to interpret, given that the history of extractive economies for the early Ottoman period is still controversial.[311] One sensible explanation is that costs were high in lands ravaged by military campaigns. It is also possible that the high number of shares was the outcome of a practice of mergers in earlier periods of Ottoman expansion. The scenario is plausible, especially given that Ottoman laws recognized rights over individual components of a mining complex, from surface land, to shafts, ore-washing machines, smelters, and refineries. Another possibility is that high production costs, in lieu of coin debasements and silver shortages, led to partnerships with a higher number of members.

A *varaq* provided investment capital covering exploration and ore-testing costs.[312] It is possible that neither ethnicity nor religious affiliation of a *varaq* mattered, at least nominally. As in all other mining regions, this entrepreneur enjoyed no absolute right of property.[313] The law required mines to be under continuous operation.[314] *Varaq* had six weeks for starting mining works.[315] Another partner, known as *varaq lenkhovar*, was responsible for leasing shafts or parts of a mine. The word came from the German noun *Lehenhäuer*, a linguistic borrowing that the Ottomans absorbed from Serbian laws (see Appendix A). After leases were sold, this *varaq* registered all *yoldaş* or partners of the association and their investments in the mine's account book.[316] *Yoldaş* were 'fellow travelers' who possibly came from the Turkish military elite, without excluding local powerful groups, as in Egypt, Rumelia, and Anatolia. The scanty evidence unfortunately allows for too many speculations.[317] A *timar ṣāhibi*, if and when included among shareholders, represented the Sublime Porte.[318] Nothing impeded a *mülk* or landowner from owning mining shares, as an account written in A.D. 1484 for the silver Kavala mines in Greece indicates.[319] And nothing impeded the Sultan from ordering certain investors to put their money into the mines. A law enacted for the mines of Kratovo ordered that the *sahib*, an owner of mining shares representing the Sublime Porte, paid for everything necessary for ore extraction. It also mentions a commitment by owners of forgery factories to fabricate iron tools needed for excavation works.

Nominally, a *varaq* could invest money in abandoned shafts, but only after a *qāḍī* and *emîn* certified the abandoned state of shafts. The process required interviewing *varaq* of neighboring shafts and completing a written report. The report's final destination: Constantinople. In lands of conquest, abandoned shafts were certainly not infrequent. The law could be understood as a license for entrepreneurs to act like predators and take over mines, as long as government bureaucrats were informed. The Ottoman army captured fortresses in strategic valleys and trade routes, bringing ambitious and entrepreneurial soldiers close to mining towns. Novo Brdo, the Novobërda, Nyeuberge, or Newburgh of Saxon colonists, was not distant from an old Dalmatian road probably crossed by the Ottomans, since the road was identified in the thirteenth-century map known as *Tabula Peutingeriana*.[320] On the right bank of the Markova Reka River, close to the Skopje plain and Mount Karšjak, there was an old mining town, located 'little below the village of Sušica,' that was 'still worked by the Turks' in the late seventeenth century.[321]

Rights of a *varaq* over his mining claim were protected against takeover or appropriation by the mining partnership, as well as other *varaq*. This protection extended also to the Sultan when he was a shareholder. Are we to conclude that the mining partnership entailed joint ownership of mines? Islamic contract law was not unfamiliar with the idea of joint ownership. This idea implied 'inheriting or purchasing anything together,' as treated by jurist Ahmad, also known as Muhammad al-Qudūrī (A.H. 362–428 / A.D. 972–1037).[322] The contradiction between the principle of Sultan's ownership of mines and al-Qudūrī's view of common ownership is evident to all. But in al-Qudūrī's interpretation, there is slight room for doubt. Al-Qudūrī stated that in a proprietary ownership contract between two people, 'neither of them is permitted to dispose of each other's portion, except with his permission.'[323] It is plausible that a similar idea of joint ownership of mines developed in practice among *varaq*, albeit vague and not always consistent with legal theory.

Shareholders could sell mining shares owned by the Sultan, but only if authorized by a *qāḍī* and an *emîn*.[324] The law stated that no *varaq* could be forced into an expense regarding infrastructure against his will. A *varaq* could offer his mining shares as securities, but only if the purpose of the loan was to invest in mine improvements. The latter included paying the costs of sinking and timbering shafts and setting up galleries, ventilation, and drainage works. It was not impossible for a *varaq* to own a 'perpetual lease' of shares, as in the Zirniče mines in the late fifteenth century. In a mid-sixteenth-century report about the Srebrenića and Sasse mines, a *mülk* was identified as owner of an underground gallery, after he invested money for improvements of such a gallery for a long period of time.[325]

Decision-making in a mining partnership probably followed majority rule, although the laws studied here establish two cases dispensing of majority rule. The first case stated that a shareholder who owned one share had the right to undertake mine improvements when necessary and to be compensated accordingly when total mine earnings were calculated.[326] The second case established that a shareholder could fire another shareholder from the partnership in case of debt default. If a member of a mining association refused to pay his share of expenses for improving a specific section of the mine, he was excluded from profits coming from the improved area. When a shareholder died, his shares were sold to members of the same partnership or were mortgaged to outside investors. Mortgages required payment of a yearly tax to the Sultan that varied in different times between a fifth and a tenth. In addition, a *varaq* paid the *'ōšr*, or the tenth that the state collected from silver refined through cupellation, lead ores, and mercury ores. The tax changed in different periods, to a sixth, a seventh, an eighth, and a fourth of extracted silver ores.[327]

As in other world mining regions, mine earnings were directly proportional to the number of shares that each partner owned, conditioned to shares being debt-free. In the mines of Srebrenića, Sasse, and Belasica in Macedonia; Zaplanina in Slovenia; Prizren in Kosovo; and other mining centers, a *varaq* could also own shares in metal foundries.[328] In these cases, a *varaq* could transfer the equivalent of two shares of mine earnings into his metal forgeries.

High costs of production meant that newcomers enjoyed but small chances of joining a mining association. A typical investment required between 120,000 and 250,000 akçe, for a period of ten to fifteen years.[329] The akçe was the basic monetary unit of the Ottoman Empire, equivalent to one Venetian ducat starting in A.D. 1326, although it was devalued frequently in the fifteenth and sixteenth centuries.[330] Mobility of technical experts was virtually impossible in Ottoman mines by the fifteenth century, unless there was a connection with the bureaucratic-military establishment.

The profitability of a mining partnership depended upon income. What remains difficult to ascertain with the available evidence is whether incomes were calculated on a weekly basis, as mining corporations did everywhere else. It is difficult to assert if accounting for 'running capital costs' entailed standard formulas or simply involved a distinction between 'cost' and 'asset.' These distinctions were relevant considering the time and expense that Ottoman mines entailed. It is impossible to know if accounting for costs of new shafts differed from old shafts, as was the practice in mine accounting until recently.[331] All we can infer is that without mine accounting, financial comparability of mining operations was not possible.

Unfortunately, not much is known about the map of a typical Ottoman mine. Drawing upon the work by Beldiceanu and others, one speculates that a typical Ottoman mine was a labyrinth of galleries with a central gallery or transport corridor, connected to prospection and extraction shafts.[332] A typical mine had a ventilation gallery connected to an adit leading to a surface entrance. Other galleries connected high- and low-elevation shafts. Beldiceanu observes that in most mining laws, the term *ichlagh* identified an exploitation gallery built in the area where ramifications of an ore vein met one another. 'The principal feature is that both end points of the gallery are underground.'[333] If a mine contained several levels of galleries and shafts, the work by *ḥutman* or foreman was among the most important works.

Shareholders hired a foreman or *ḥutman* or *ḥudman*, who was responsible for ensuring that miners' payments were duly delivered in specie for most laborers, salary to technical specialists, and shares under extraordinary circumstances, or an amount of extracted ores in some cases.[334] A foreman's salary was ten akçe per week in Belasica. In Novo Brdo, a foreman received forty akçe per week. Foremen of the Plana and Zaplanina mines received two out of sixty-eight shares into which the mine was divided. In Sidreqapsa, a foreman was paid one sack of unrefined ore per week, equivalent to the amount of ore that could be carried by one horse. It is safe to suppose that foremen and other laborers did their best to find complementary sources of income. The likelihood of them accumulating petty sums or small capital is, at best, questionable. Money was a source of great anxiety.

A *vodar* inspected drainage-adit works, and a *šafar* supervised ore extraction in shafts.[335] He only supervised ten shafts in each mining field, although it is possible that in some Ottoman lands a *šafar* supervised all shafts. This mining post survived into the eighteenth century, when the Ottoman *šafar* was appointed by the Treasury. In the fifteenth century, the šafar was appointed by a varaq. In A.D. 1488 mining acts, the salary of a šafar varied, depending upon locality. The same applied to the *urbarar*, a simple officer, says Beldiceanu, in charge of policing mining shafts and workers.[336] An *ismuičar* or *smiačar* was a technical cupellation expert. He was assisted by *otkapar* or junior experts.[337] A *vatroq* or metal factory specialist was responsible for buying ores from *varaq*. This worker appears in mining laws of Sidreqapsa, Kratovo, Trepča, Novo Brdo, Fojnica, and Janjevo.

It is impossible to say if a typical Ottoman mine was simply a 'confused labyrinth of galleries'[338] rendering drainage impossible, as the Heraclea mine was in Anatolia, where surface water constantly accumulated. Drainage was not the central concern of Ottoman mining laws. The most plausible explanation is that miners had ample time for adapting drainage machinery and techniques to their geological circumstances before the Ottoman conquest of the Balkans. The advanced development stage that mining reached in Serbia, Bosnia, and Kosovo exempted the Ottoman state from enacting a coherent mining industrial policy. The goal of the Ottoman state was, after all, to increase the flow of silver tax revenues. Thus, mines that produced gold and silver had different levels of fiscal importance to the Ottomans. In Trepča, starting in A.D. 1303, and Sre-brenića, late in A.D. 1352, producers shifted to extraction of silver ores, in response to the fiscal needs of the Ottoman state. In the rest of the Balkan mines, silver ores occupied a second and even third place, after gold and (sometimes) copper.[339] Venice's monetary and foreign policy in the Balkans probably had a lot to do with this situation.[340] In Bosnia, toll rights for the mines of Srebrenića and Ponor were sold by King Stefan Lazarević to Ragusan merchants in A.D. 1389, for 425 pounds of silver. In A.D. 1417, the toll rights of Srebrenića were sold for 3,100 pounds of silver; in A.D. 1458, these rights were leased for 30,000 ducats per year.[341]

A Burdensome Bureaucracy

Two imperial officers had plenary powers over all mining affairs: the *emîn* and the *qāḍī*. These were the central officers in charge of statistical surveys of lands and peoples, essential to the Ottoman system of government.[342] The *qāḍī* and *emîn* kept written records of all transactions pertaining to mining shares, an obligation that they exercised even in the case of shares owned by the Sultan. It is possible that they confirmed transactions with mining shares in official mine accounting books.[343] Drawing upon sixteenth-century evidence for the eastern provinces of Anatolia, one can see a neat division of labor between *qāḍī* and *emîn* to the advantage of the good Ottoman policy of fiscal centralization.[344]

A *qāḍī* represented 'a Law that came from God and was in essence not subject to the whims of mundane and transitory sultans,' in the words of historian Ergene.[345] He was a regional judicial chief with the right to select his own court and appoint local religious officers.[346] He 'adjudicated on the basis of his own reading of the law,' but his decisions created no precedent 'not even for later judgements of his own.'[347] One must conclude that judicial decisions concerning mining found a certain homogeneity and continuity needed for mining to flourish.

The *emîn* collected data for preparing the *defter* or survey and included information on all lands, peoples, transactions, and resources for taxation. The law authorized the *emîn* and his clerk to collect a modest sum of money in the surveyed districts for meeting their expenses. Thus, surveyed peoples subsidized the instrument of Ottoman survey. The first task of the *emîn* was to gather 'all timar-holders or their trustees and instructed them to hand in legal documents on their possession.' Then, the *emîn* accompanied by his clerk visited all villages of the surveyed district 'and began inspection on the spot.' The survey, then, became a *defter*, legitimate only after confirmation by the Sultan. It is possible that the *emîn* employed the same surveying technique he used when completing agrarian surveys, as follows:

> A special diploma which empowered him [a surveyor] with all necessary authority, and ordered the subjects and local officials including the *qāḍī* to obey and assist him in his task. In the diploma, the procedure to be followed is described in detail. The surveyor started his investigation on the spot, comparing the actual situation with what he had found in the previous survey book. In a village, for example, he invited into his presence the elderly, the *vakf* trustees and the military with all the documents in their hands.[348]

All mining officers were appointed directly by the Sultan or by designated bureaucrats. The Sultan appointed an *urubār*, an expert in mining geometry responsible for recording and supervising the calculations pertaining to opening and sinking of mine shafts. He intervened in conflicts regarding mine boundaries, demarcation, and exploitation rights.[349] The *urubār* was subordinated to a *yasaqdjı*, an overseer of mining works and metal factories, also appointed by

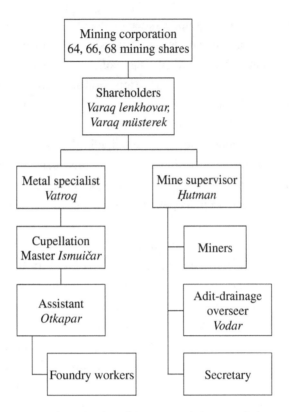

Fig. 3.14. Organization of Ottoman mining associations,
according to fifteenth-century laws

the Sultan. The roles of this officer varied from mine to mine, but in all places the main function of a *yasaqdjı* was to supervise mining and metal production and punish violators of mining laws.[350] Most likely, the men appointed to serve as *urubār* and *yasaqdjı* came from the ample group of loyal servants of the Sultan who gained knowledge of mining as time went on, given that ordinary servants could move up in the administrative apparatus of Ottoman provinces.[351] A *yasa-qdjı* could attain a very powerful position. In times of monetary depreciation, a *yasaqdjı* was also responsible for supervising mint operations, confiscating un-minted silver illegally held by miners, and enforcing the State's monetary and weight regulations. In a fifteenth-century act about the mines and metal found-ries of Zaplanina, the *yasaqdjı* supervised *yamaq*, miners, and *knez et urubār*.[352] The *yasaqdjı* enjoyed the right to punish the *amil* and his officers, when these acted contrary to mining laws. This officer also granted permissions for establishing ore-refining installations and supervised the buying and selling of ores by *ṣarrāf*.[353] The latter was a specialist in metal and monetary exchanges, who bought refined silver from cupellation factories, but was bounded by law to sell only to imperial mints.[354]

At the bottom of mining governance was the *yamak* mentioned above. The role of the *yamak* is not clear. Beldiceanu argues that they were village men appointed to be guardians of the common good in each village. Their existence went back to the times of Sultan Mehmed II.[355]

The *amil* was appointed by the Sultan. This was an important job requiring literacy and writing skills in Turkish language, since an *amil* certified all documents concerning the leasing, renting, mortgaging, and selling of mining shares. The *yarar adamlar* or *mu'temed adamlar* was an expert jury, composed of 'trustworthy men,' experts in mining law. They assisted the *urbarar* in conflicts over mine boundaries. It is possible that they were appointed by the *urbarar*. At the top of the mining governance was the Sultan, whose chief role was to create the laws and principles governing the Porte's usufructuary rights. The latter were exercised through taxation. As a general rule, the Sublime Porte imposed a one-fifth tax, known as *khums-i sher'I*,[356] although Islamic interpretations varied.[357]

As in other world mining regions, appointing mining officers was a task that no central power delegated to private citizens. But unlike what happened in all other world mining regions, the functions of Ottoman mining officers never led to the creation of autonomous bodies or tribunals governing over mining policy.

It is unclear the extent to which surveys by the *qāḍī* and *emîn* yielded an efficient administration of the mining industry. Nominally, they relied upon officers with steadiness and resolution, but one must speculate that not all bureaucrats were tempered for the job. As mentioned earlier, the law made no distinction between mines and other land economies; thus, mining incomes were aggregated to other taxable incomes belonging to a *timar* estate. Another problem is that little is known about liabilities of *timar* holders in the Balkans, as Kuran states, because the intention of compiling *defters* was to account for taxable land incomes.[358] The system opened no formal institutional channel for liabilities of *timar* holders with their mines to serve as feedbacks for mining policy.

Besides, one must confidently assume that mines existed within the *timar* system but also outside at least for short periods of time, since Sultan Mehmed

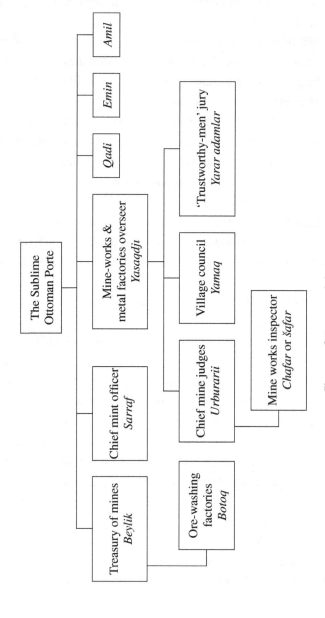

Fig. 3.15. Ottoman mining governance

II ordered a revision of the legal revision of certain *timar* estates that stood in dubious status in A.D. 1461.[359] It is not clear if this heavy fiscal policy left owners of mining rights with incentives to conceal mine revenues. That there were quotas of men that each *timar* holder had to provide to the Sultan depending upon the incomes of *timars,* leaves much room for speculating that *timariots* had good reasons for dissembling. Sultan Bâyezîd II established the following census quotas: 'timar-holders drawing 1,000 akçe incomes had to go to war themselves, those drawing 2,000 had to take along a young servant, those making 3,000 had to go with a man at arms plus a young servant, those with 6,000 with two men at arms and a tent, and an additional man at arms for every 3,000-akçe income.'[360]

Much remains unknown. How did *varaq* relate to *timar* holders? What was the relationship between *varaq* partnerships and Ottoman criminal law institutions? The Ottomans made 'original contributions' by developing comprehensive regulations of criminal law and procedure known as *qānūn*, and assembled in codes or *qānūnnāme*.[361] These coexisted with religious ruling and courts; thus, it remains to be known what areas of transgressions to mining regulations fell under 'secular' codes, and if they emphasized property and mining rights of individuals rather than the state. Setting a shaft on fire, fraudulent transactions with mining shares, negligence in mining works, missing payments to foremen and technical experts—these are areas that in one way or another all other medieval mining statutes addressed. None of these areas are mentioned in the mining regulations described here. Are we to conclude that a *varaq* accused of fraud was dealt with by *sharī'a* courts? Was a *varaq* exempted from the typical corporal punishment that religious courts delivered? Did a *varaq* enjoy the right of appeal? Systematic research is needed for finding correct answers to these questions, but one idea is clear from the sources discussed here. The Ottoman emphasis on centralization of fiscal resources made it difficult for individual *varaq* to be a step closer to enjoying private mining rights, comparable to those in other parts of Europe. While in Europe, signs of improvement of *argentifodina* firmly put private investors closer to enjoying mining rights with minimal feudal intervention, in the Ottoman Balkans signs of improvement of mining works put the state imperial bureaucracy closer to the benefits of mining. The timid progress of early capitalist forms of mining did not survive the Ottoman exploits of the underground wealth of the Balkans.

4

Capitalist Profits of Mining Corporations

THE QUESTION OF CAPITALIST PROFITS is a difficult matter. Certainly, mining corporations were the entrepreneurial agents *par excellence* of the medieval mining world without which mining could not thrive. But balance sheets of corporations are simply nonexistent. This fact should not preclude us from asking the question of whether or not mining corporations enjoyed the necessary conditions for generating profits. Examining this question requires us to clarify one observation beforehand. Capitalist profit is a matter of money but also a matter of legal, economic, and political preconditions guaranteeing that corporations enjoy a relatively stable and long-term investment climate. It is only in the examination of the sum of these relations that the essence of capitalist profits is to be found, even if mining history only allows to identify what Pierre Vilar once called 'the general feeling' of these relations.[1]

The advent of the shareholder model was a pivotal precondition to the emergence of capitalist profits. Defining legal rights and responsibilities of citizens in improving mines was a great leap forward, since capitalist profits cannot exist without law. At a time when the mining industry relied in most places upon unwritten customs and *una certa ereditarietà*,[2] the industry of Trento, Kutná Hora, Massa, and Iglesias was based upon standardized legal formulas deciding participation, wins, and losses in mining ventures. Mining contracts, then, required written law, which in turn depended and impinged upon prevailing legal practices and norms. Customary practices that allowed great lords to monopolize mine tithes by exploiting peasants and serfs at will were no longer viable if lords wanted to enjoy the rent of mines. A new institutional and legal instrument, the mining corporation, which appeared because of lords' inability to improve mines, effectively curtailed a lord's habit of 'selling' mines when he could not make them productive. The latter was a practice that lords disguised under their rights of investiture or sovereignty.[3]

A second economic pre-condition that was in the making was the erosion of old feudal lord-vassal contractual obligations. Nominally, a lord's inputs for making his mines productive were essentially his peasants and 'serfs,' a category which included various classes of semifree and unfree subjects.[4] But the advent of written contractual law governing relations among lords, miners, and 'public officials' changed a lord's legal basis for deciding upon matters related to mining works and labor. Confronted by a new institutional and legal initiative for the organization of mining, a lord's obligation to protect peasants and serfs in exchange for feudal services such as military service became legally obsolete once silver ores were discovered in the lord's lands. Indeed, the disappearance of military obligations as part of lord-vassal contractual relations took place in Trento earlier than anywhere else, as indicated by the legal formula of *rectum feodum* contained in all documents pertaining to agrarian taxes and grants of the *Codex*.[5]

A third pre-condition to the rise of capitalist profits is the fact that *societas* became legitimate holders of usufruct rights from mines. Absolute lordly and seigneurial jurisdiction over mining affairs was a thing of the past. In Trento, Bishop Wanga was forbidden from coercing *silbrarii* into the payment of the special *subsidium* by A.D. 1214. The Bishop's *gastaldia*, that tax-collecting institution typical of Trento, lost its jurisdiction over administration of mining works. The corporations formed by *Gewerken* in the mountains of Bohemia forced the King to reform its royal mining bureaucracy aiming at contributing to the success of private mining works. Neither *urburarii* nor *magistri*, the supreme public mining officers representing royal power, were above the *lex humana* embodied in *Constitutiones*.

Tools were considered movable mine property in all mining statutes. Bishop Wanga prohibited innkeepers and blacksmiths from accepting 'iron tools, measuring ropes, or any other mining instrument as security or pledge or payment from those who work in the mountain [*Arzentarie*], unless received by a chief officer of a mining society.'[6] Massa's statute contains an exhaustive list of mining tools, including the following: pickaxes; hammers of different types and sizes; *fornellus,* or fans used for mine ventilation; *bulge,* or leather sacks used

Table 4.1. Mining shares and aspects of mine geometry (m), by world mining region

World mining region	No. shares	Distance between shafts	Shaft depth[a]
Alps-Lombardy		15	20[b]
Carpathians-Saxony	32	6[c]	50[d]
Tuscany	32	15–20	10–100[e]
Sardinia	32	—	80–100; 200[f]
Asia Minor, Balkans	64, 66, 68	14	85.5–200

[a] Based upon archeological findings. [b] Refers to Faedo mine in Luserna, Trentino. [c] Distance separating second and third colonists' concessions, within the first colonist's seven *Lanei* claim area. [d] Refers to Jeroným mine. [e] Shafts discovered in Campiglia Marittima, Grosseto, and Serrabottini and Poggio Montierino. [f] Exceptional shaft length discovered at Montevecchio mine.

Sources: Aranguren et al., 'Serrabottini (Massa Marittima, GR)'; Beldiceanu, *Les Actes des Premiers Sultans*, vol. 2; Cruciani, 'The Montevecchio mining district'; Francovich and Dallai, 'Colline Metallifere (Toscane, Italie)'; Kaláb et al., 'Mine water movement in shallow medieval mine Jeroným'; Schumacher, 'The ore deposits of Jugoslavia and the development of its mining industry'; Willies, 'The mines at Campiglia Marittima, Livorno, Italy'; Zammatteo, 'A Luserna e Faedo sulle tracce di una storia mineraria millenaria.'

for transporting ore and water; ropes, needed for the infrastructure connecting a shaft portal to its deepest part; belts; metal rings; iron blades; caldrons; charcoal; *puntellus,* or wood sticks used for marking topographic points; and cattle and other beasts of transport.[7] Similar tools were mentioned in the statute of Iglesias.[8] Agricola's *De re metallica* contains a long list of tools, instruments, and supplies needed in typical mining and smelting sites, such as: different types of fans for ventilation machines; water wheels; wooden barrels; pipes; heels; bellows; horses, if and when employed; different types of hammers; cloths of different fibers; ladders of different sizes; ropes; iron hooks and trays, and cranks. These were by no means cheap inventories. In any case, they were part of the total capital expenditure of a corporation.

Fourth, the mining statutes reveal that corporations were agents determined to make economic gains from flooded mines. In Massa, the *societas foveae* established its own investment rules, independent from the governing council of the city. The same took place in Sardinia, where the *communitas foveae* retained its autonomous character even after the invasion of the island by the King of Aragon. In both cases, corporations kept the feudal power of generating mine rent under check, by the ways in which they handled credit relations among shareholders. Only in Ottoman jurisdictions did the functions and roles of public officers remain unaltered, at least nominally. The fact that the *emîn* and the *qāḍī* retained plenary powers over all mining affairs in the newly conquered Balkan territories suggests that capitalist profits, if and when generated, served the needs of the state and its ruling military class.

The pre-conditions for the rise of capitalist profits were formed by, and in turn formed, a gap between the old legal feudal understanding of mine exploitation and a new way of doing mining business. Silver-bearing ores were no free gift of Nature. The toil and trouble it required left very little room for lordly power to control over mining works. Corporations absorbed the costs of land-surveying techniques, which by the thirteenth century had spread throughout Europe. This is an instance that illustrates that corporations embodied the spirit of an early capitalism, by relying upon medieval scientific-technical revolutions and the material transformation of Europe. Citizens organized in corporations did what feudal lords could not do: absorb the science and techniques of their times and risk capital before mines yielded any return. The intervention of a professional and technical culture, with rights and responsibilities codified by written law, widened the gap between the typical feudal lords and corporations. Much in tune with the climate of the commercial revolution of the long thirteenth century studied by medievalist Robert Sabatino Lopez, mining absorbed the accounting methods then in vogue. Mine accounting required literacy and familiarity with the legal process, as well as of the functions and structure of the mining business. 'It should be noted that knowing how to keep good and orderly records teaches one how to draw contracts, how to do business, and how to obtain a profit.'[9] The advice, coming from Benedetto Cotrugli, a fifteenth-century merchant from Naples, had been part of the daily doings of mining corporations since the thirteenth century. Accounting techniques were indispensable to the efficient day-to-day operation of a corporation.[10] Commercial arithmetic, probably involving algorithms in some regions, abacus arithmetic, and calculations of metal recuperation rates, mattered.[11] It is possible that aspects of the double-entry bookkeeping were adapted for purposes of mining. The technique was theorized in Leonardo Fibonacci's *Liber Abaci* or 'The Book of Calculations,' published circa A.D. 1305.[12]

Did the pre-conditions for capitalist profits appear only because private citizens enjoying economic privileges and social advantages needed them? Citizenship status implied breaking off feudal loyalties and emancipation from

Table 4.2. Samminiato's assets: an example of a fourteenth-century mining portfolio

No. shares	Shafts and mine property
10 ½	Santa Piccal
2 ¾	La Communata
23 ¾	Nasella e Fiore
32	La Castellana
29	Galassa
?	Guardaroba & Bambola
?	*Ohiandili* ore-washing *piazza*[a]
22	*Canale d'Acqua* ore-washing *piazza*

[a] The ore-washing piazza, or *piazza da lavare vena*, was immovable property or real estate which could be sold or leased. Participation in a *piazza* was divided into thirty-two *trente*.

Source: Baudi di Vesme, *Historiae patriae*, vol. 17, *Codex Diplomaticus*, p. cxlii, p. cxcii, pp. 397–398.

military and ecclesiastical obligations, something that was already taking place in many jurisdictions of western Europe but that became codified in mining law in selected regions, as discussed earlier. Citizens with money embodied a different group of vassals, suddenly replacing lords and feudal officers in charge of the management and supervision of mines, something that in time led to usurpation of mining lands. Replacing lords and their tax officers was not only a legal and political affair but also a matter of money. We can only speculate that lords felt the loss of profit at the moment when shareholders profited from their investments. The profits of land improvements were distributed among lords, mining capitalists, and labor, but in uneven ways. The heaviest loss did not go to the corporation but was most likely shared by lords and miners who were outside the world of corporations. It is in relation to the economic losses of miners that it is important to remember that citizens with money were in the position of enforcing all of the vices of Latin western Europe, such as exclusion and marginalization of itinerants, foreigners, and Jews from mining sites, denying to these groups of people participation in the mining industry.

A property inventory of a 'rich Tuscan man' by the name Baron Betto de Samminiato (d. A.D. 1324), summarized in table 4.2, offers a glimpse of what a medieval metallic portfolio probably looked like. Samminiato invested in the

Iglesias mines. La Castellana belonged exclusively to him; he owned all thirty-two shares. Samminiato was an absentee investor, a structural feature of Iglesias' medieval economy, as described earlier. This Tuscan man also held majority shares in the 'Nasella e Fiore' and 'Galassa' shafts. We do not know how these shafts compared to one another in terms of income and cost. We know this much: Samminiato left in his will an amount of money to be used exclusively to pay for the restoration of the San Giovanni Chapel in Monte Barlao, Iglesias. His will shows unequivocal signs of wealth.[13]

Adam Smith had no idea that men like Samminiato were part of the medieval world that he described in *The Wealth of Nations*. In Smith's view, 'the problem of entails' was the only obstacle to land improvement in feudal Europe.[14] Entails protected lands 'from caprice or extravagance of one possessor' since lands belonged to a number of persons in succession. Such was the 'transitory evil,' the bad contribution of the proliferation of lordships everywhere. Western Europe had good geography but 'human institutions' that impaired the movement toward land improvement under the condition of perfect freedom. The fact that lords laid out their stocks, in the form of cattle, for example, for making food out of land at a reasonable profit, meant that land improvement was subordinated to the whims of landlords. Thus, lords acted as 'petty princes' who relied upon serfdom, attending 'to ornament [consumption] rather than profit.' What Smith failed to see is that mine improvement took place as part of the grand transformation of land that sustained the medieval commercial revolution and that it happened by private citizens forming corporations. Corporations, and not the petty feudal princes that Smith criticized, laid out stocks upon mines, creating the conditions for making profit.

Ore Prices and Incomes

Many argue that the economic returns of a medieval mining enterprise depended upon the ability to maintain equilibrium between product, by-product, and input markets.[15] Others insist that incomes were simply a function of the costs of production and ore prices. The difficulty lies in defining production and a corporation's incomes. The Marxist formula described earlier, if feudal, then pre-capitalist, then free gift of Nature, ironically developed by Marxists and not Marx himself, takes too much for granted.[16] Smith did no better either, since he was interested in how trade allowed nations to create wealth. Besides, it is most likely that the most insightful observations by Smith on nature he borrowed from the writings of Columella (first century A.D.), especially the idea of 'barrenness or fertility of the soil.'[17] There is a lack of records of metal outputs measured in kind and virtually no price data for unrefined, uncoined silver.[18] Evidence of medieval metal outputs has come down to us measured in quantities of money, and great discrepancies exist as to the precise meaning of figures. Historian John Nef provided figures of silver outputs in mines of Europe and America for the early modern period, attempting to revise the nineteenth-century classical work by German economist Adolf Soetbeer (A.D. 1814–1892).[19] In the last three decades, Blanchard, Munro, and Vázquez De Prada, working independently, added new data that offered a thorough examination of Nef's estimates.[20] Their accounts of silver production for famous mines, such as Kutná Hora, vary.[21] Blanchard estimates a total amount of 34.5 tons of silver, obtained from the mines of Saxony, Bohemia, Tuscany, and Sardinia in A.D. 1155–1200; nine tons in A.D. 1210–1300; and 15.77 tons in the first half of the fourteenth century. His estimates include no output for mines located in the Pyrenees, Islamic Andalusia, the Maghreb, or Massif Central in France. The same omission is found in Munro and Vázquez De Prada. None of these mining historians include metal outputs for the mines of Asia Minor or Turkey, and Central Asia.

Concerned with the same issues that interest us here, a German economist a century ago attempted to give a definite answer to the question of medieval silver prices. His calculations allow us to address some questions and entertain hypotheses on prices. Ulrich calculated the quantity of gold grains that a Tuscan miner could obtain per pound of silver at the Bruges trade fair.[22] The fair attracted merchants and goods 'from all these kingdoms,' according to Piero Tafur writing in A.D. 1438.[23] The *villa di Bruggia in Fiandra* was not unknown to Lombards or *Cahorsins*, as they were known in medieval Bruges, since it offered many commercial advantages, as economic historian Raymond De Roover discovered many decades ago. Commercial transactions, bills of exchange, and loans were the main affairs of Italian bankers in Bruges since at least the first Genoese cargo arrived at Bruges in A.D. 1278 'if not earlier.'[24]

Ulrich's numbers on silver and gold metal prices show a pattern that can be useful for making general observations about ore prices. The following graphic, adapted from Ulrich's results, illustrates a remarkable stability of the price of Tuscan silver.

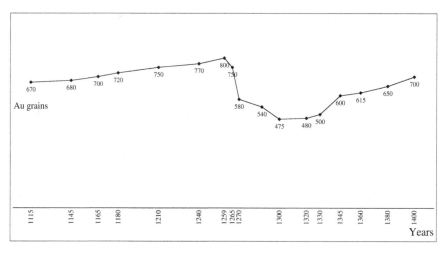

Fig. 4.1. Exchange value of one pound of Tuscan
silver in gold grains at Bruges, A.D. 1100–1400

Prices of Tuscan silver in Bruges reached a peak in A.D. 1259 and declined afterwards for almost a century, before starting to rise again until the early fifteenth century. This pattern is consistent with the growth of the mining industry of Tuscany, characterized by increasing productivity and standards of living. Possibly, incomes of *partiarii* grew concomitant to improvements to the mining fief. The income argument has a global side. Conditions hindering a capitalist growth of mining businesses in other regions worked to the advantage of Tuscan producers. Goslar silver commanded a much lower price in Bruges, lowering the prices of total stocks. By then, the Saxon industry was in decline.[25] Price per pound of silver ranged between 168 and 309 grains by A.D. 1300, much lower than the price for Tuscan silver. Fifty years later, the entire stock of Tuscan and Goslar ores commanded a higher price, 600 grains; at the end of the century, the stock was bought at 450 grains per pound of ore. When Bruges merchants bought silver in Venice, the price was lower: 304–309 grains of gold per pound of silver, *affinato di Venezia e della bolla di Papa*.[26] When Venetian silver was transported to Cyprus and Tana east of the Black Sea, it commanded a lower price—between 155 to 175 grains of gold per pound of silver. When they traveled to Bruges, ores commanded a slightly higher price—between 191 to 211 grains of gold.

Ulrich's numbers suggest three explanations. Bruges market received only a small amount of the silver available in the international markets, assuming that the commodity market prevailing at the time responded normally to what Smith called *effectual demand* and that the laws for forcing gold into circulation in A.D. 1399 disturbed the Bruges market, but only on a short-term basis.[27] Second, supply of silver from Balkan mines or Lombardy's Agordo mine lowered prices in Venice. Third, eastern markets were characterized by detrimental terms of trade for silver.[28] If so, this was an advantage that Europe enjoyed over other regions.

Let us approach the question of production costs from the side of money, since the evidence leaves us no other choice. Beldiceanu's remarkable study offers details about expenses in Ottoman mines. The cost of sinking a shaft varied significantly from one mine to the next. Costs ranged from one hundred akçe per *kulaç* in cases when miners cut through soft limestone to 2,500 akçe per *kulaç* in hard-limestone conditions.[29] In Janjevo, the cost of sinking a shaft started at 400 akçe per *kulaç* and could run as high as 600 akçe per *kulaç*. In Kratovo, the cost of sinking a shaft reached an astonishing sum of 1,200 akçe per *kulaç*.[30] Some shafts in Kratovo reached sixty *kulaç* in length, with running costs that ranged between 60,000 and 72,000 akçe. In Novo Brdo, mining works reached depths of eighty, ninety, and one hundred *kulaç*, the equivalent of 136.8 meters and 171 meters. The cost of shaft sinking at Novo Brdo varied between 7,500 and 20,000 akçe for each fifteen to twenty *kulaç*. This meant that before reaching the *tchah* or the point of contact with the ore vein, the cost of digging ranged between 40,000 and 100,000 akçe. At Trepča, the cost of shaft sinking varied between 5,000 and 48,000 akçe. Cost differences no doubt were transferred to the value of mining shares.

One must resist the temptation to conclude that longer and deeper shafts led to qualitative increases in technical improvements and low production costs— and thus higher incomes. The relation between technical improvements and low production costs on the one side, and higher incomes on the other, is by no means a direct and proportional relation. Higher incomes were a function of variations in the allocation of factors of production, which depended upon historical relations of unequal access to resources, crystallized in mining statutes. The playing field was highly uneven, long before the rise of capitalism.

In addition, debasements of the Ottoman silver akçe took place very frequently, so costs of sinking shafts and mine improvements were frequently inflated. Thus, plowing back into the subsoil became increasingly expensive as the sixteenth century progressed. Figure 4.2 shows that Ottoman mine lease values varied.

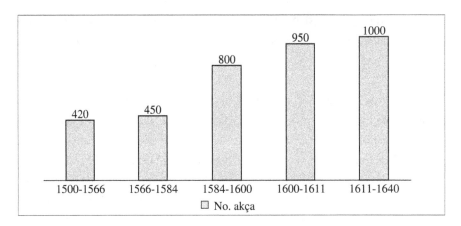

Fig. 4.2. Lease values of selected Ottoman mines, in Ag akçe, A.D. 1500–1640

The latter decreased dramatically from the values they had registered in the last decades of the fifteenth century. Only in Vilk and Laz mines in Serbia, tax-farmers headquartered in Novo Brdo, Serres, and Constantinople generated approximately 8,000,000 akçe in A.D. 1468. Three years later, tax-farmers from Kratovo generated 2,250,000 akçe with leases for the mines of Kratovo and Sidrekapsi.[31]

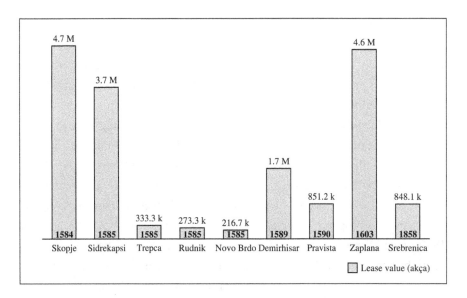

Fig. 4.3. Number of silver akçe struck from 100 Ag
dirhams in Ottoman mints, A.D. 1584–1858

Were silver currency debasements the independent variable? Did the Otto-man state lack capital for industrialization? Any observation about the debase-ments of the silver currency must consider that the 'Ottoman Empire was a gold zone,'[32] in the words of Braudel. Gold from central Africa, Sudan, and Abyssinia reached the Ottoman markets via Egypt and North Africa. When Spain flooded the Eastern currency markets with its *piaster* or pieces of eight, the Levant and the Ottoman state were 'overrun by silver coins minted in the *Zecca* of Venice.'[33] Ottoman mining industrialists had very little time to turn the table to their advantage. The rigid arrangement of factors of production, and not religion, played against the globalization of their businesses. The modest evi-dence studied here implies that any increase in mining incomes did not easily translate into savings for investments in the mining industry. Other independent variables, such as the opening of new mines in the Spanish territories of Potosí, Bolivia, and Zacatecas and Guanajuato in Mexico, were at work here.[34]

The Myth of a Miner's 'Perfect Liberty'

Time to turn to the difficult matter of the value of labor. Corporations replaced feudal lords in the economic hierarchy of medieval mining economy. Miners at the lowest stratum were left with no other option than bartering their 'liberty' for the opportunity to join a diverse group of free and semifree labor in mining fields. But this was only a general pattern that admitted of many exceptions. In Trento, ordinary miners enjoyed virtually no freedom. The *Codex* criminalized situations that probably occurred in mining sites at high frequency. In the first years of the thirteenth century, Bishop Wanga warned that any miner starting a fire 'fraudulently,' or instigating shaft flooding, or blocking a mine's por-tal with rocks, or vandalizing any land where *silbrarii* carried on their mining businesses 'with the intention of damaging works' would pay a fine equiva-lent to fifty pounds Verona Mark.[35] Miners were forbidden to carry weapons to mining fields, whether swords, light spears, small knives, or daggers.[36] Anyone destroying the property of *Werchi* or members of the *consilium Wercorum* of Trento faced draconian forms of punishment: the poor devil would have seen his right hand cut off.[37] Miners caught in Mons Arzentarie working on their own, and not hired by a *Wercorum*, were fined ten pounds Verona Mark.[38]

The most intriguing case, the *Constitutiones* statute of Bohemia, deserves a lengthy observation. *Constitutiones* gives the impression that miners enjoyed a better position than anywhere else. As noted earlier, Grozio portrayed the King as 'protector of the humble,' responsible for the 'common good.' The King was responsible, according to *Constitutiones*, for the well-being of 2,000 miners working in 200 extraction shafts of Kutná Hora. His duty was to protect the kingdom's subjects. The law guaranteed the right to work in the mines, a point of great significance considering the migration of seasonal miners from Saxon forests into the Carpathians and the subsequent urban boom of Bohemia.[39] Grozio's underlying idea: the common good binds together the Prince, the *urburarii*, colonists, and *Gewerken*—even against the will of this last group.[40] Despite the mobility that some groups of immigrant miners enjoyed, it is safe to conclude that most miners were alienated from the benefits of the silver-mining economy. A Carpathian miner could hardly subsist on the pay of one or two working-shifts. In the mid-sixteenth century in Bohemia, when shifts consisted of three periods of seven hours each, a miner could not sustain himself with the pay equivalent to one shift, according to Agricola.[41] Most certainly, increasing numbers of miners in all world mining regions lived in debt.

This alienation was *sine qua non* condition to the emergence of capitalist profits of the mining corporations described earlier. If a miner possessed no tools or ready cash or access to creditors, nor capacity to hire labor, nor legal citizenship status, he was excluded from the shareholding business. Migration created some economic opportunities in the short run; however, and from a continental viewpoint, migration altered in no significant way the alienation of ordinary peasants from the shareholding business once the mining industry was consolidated. In the Carpathians, privileges were no more granted on a hereditary basis, 'everything had to be conferred through royal acts.' Land and other assets were granted in exchange for military services, depending upon a ruler's ambition and foreign policy. King Andrew II of Hungary (r. A.D. 1204–1235) needed a large army, and to this purpose, ennobled men of the lower classes who became *servientes regis*, entitled to some property. 'After the shock of the Mongol invasion in 1241, Hungarian kings frequently bestowed noble status upon entire communities of free peasants in return for military service.'[42] In exchange, they provided military service—something that nobles of ancient origin could not do, or refused to do. The advantages gained by German miners were never fully settled.

Mountain geography renewed feudal quarrels to the detriment of miners occupying the lowest stratum of economic life. Croat horsemen, after dominating the Slavic agriculturalists of Slavonia, became landholders. They refused to abide by the Hungarian king's policy of ennobling peasants. Croatian nobility in Slavonia and Croatian hills retained possession of hereditary lands—and made it virtually impossible for 'foreigners,' including Germans, to acquire land south of the Petrova Gora divide.[43] Urbanization in the Balkans exacerbated old ethnic divisions, diminishing the opportunities for miners to move upwardly. 'In Bulgarian and Serbian cities, the indigenous element was very negligible, and the non-Turkish city population consisted mostly of Greeks, Jews, Armenians, Tsintsars, and foreigners (Ragusans, Germans).' Historian Vucinich concludes that the urban class was 'far more developed among the Greeks than among the Bulgarians and Serbs.' He continues, 'Jews, Armenians, and Tsintsars in the Balkans were almost exclusively engaged as money-lenders, merchants or artisans.'[44] City population included 'Muslim officials, prosperous landlords, military personnel, merchants, artisans, the *ulemâ* (the learned class), and the city poor.'[45]

An additional impediment to a poor miner's upward mobility was that Crusading soldiers returned to Eastern Europe at a bad time. The early Crusades relied upon soldiers of Frankish stock, and allowed Germans to travel far and acquire familiarity with general economic affairs of distant places. In Transylvania, German soldiers were called from Jerusalem and granted ample privileges in salt mines and gold-mining lands in the twelfth century. They were hired to guard Carpathian mountain passes and transport corridors.[46] 'Because the land was without people, Adolph sent messengers into all regions round about [. . .] to proclaim that all who were in want of land might come with their families and receive the best soil, a spacious country, rich in crops, abounding in fish and flesh and exceeding good pasture,' stated the *Chronica Slavorum* in A.D. 1143.[47]

In world mining regions with prosperous commercial cities, clashes between urban patricians and mountain peoples were inevitable, but not because towns arrived earlier at liberty and independence, as Adam Smith postulated.[48] By the first half of the fourteenth century, the mining settlement of Massa had 'a diversity of population': 'adventurers, technical experts, businessmen, metal traders, artisans of different ranks and specializations, and miners and smelters from Germanic towns.'[49] The propertied class of commercial city-states was not too happy. It perceived the growth of affluent rural settlements with disdain, as Balestracci states in the following words:

It was not by chance that around this time Tuscany's city people developed a new insult for rustics. They had always been called thieving, untrustworthy, lazy ingrates. Now, they became *baccalari*, or 'know-it-alls.' This epithet was the reaction of urban landowners to these presumptuous bumpkins who, having mastered something of the alphabet, now used it to resist those who had previously overawed them. Meo, Benedetto, and all the rest with their 'rhetoric learned on the handle of the hoe,' were the irritating reminder of changed times.[50]

Rural peoples and towns of Tuscany were favored by expansion of commercial agriculture and extractive production, as described earlier. The standard of living of miners in Tuscany was possibly higher than anywhere else. Miners possibly encountered literacy early, because schooling in several Tuscan communes was subsidized. 'At Santa Maria al Montem near Pisa, [subsidized schooling] was stipulated in the late 1300s "so that men have the wherewithal to allow their children to learn knowledge and virtue, that no one who has begun to learn letters grammar, or other discipline . . . may, or should be compelled, nor oppressed by any official of the commune, or by his emissary, to do any personal service, while he is studying."' A similar provision, Balestracci notes, existed in the Tuscan village of Castelfranco di Sopra, where 'the community paid a teacher "who knows to teach children and others who wish to stay in his school."'[51] A 'handful' of peasants kept personal account books in fifteenth-century Tuscany.[52] Well-to-do peasants and burghers had one common enemy: the feudal landlord.

In addition, town fortification and castle building in Tuscany, 'a phenomenon closely related to the organization of land clearance and the maintenance of coherent proprietorial power over wide areas,'[53] had positive spillover effects in the Tuscan hills. Mining settlements emulated the practice. Approximately forty *castelli minerari* or mining castles have been discovered in Tuscany.[54] In the Florentine plain, *incastellamento* took place between the eleventh and the thirteenth centuries. Research on the castles of Rocca San Silvestro, Cugnano, and Rocchette-Pannocchieschi by Italian archeologist Riccardo Francovich (A.D. 1946–2007) and others demonstrates how castles served as factories of production, from mining to smelting, and coinage operations.[55] In Rocca San Silvestro, the *castello minerario* became the central territorial and administrative unit of the mining economy, even when poor miners possibly occupied the lowest stratum of economic life, filling the lowest-paying jobs.

A miner's liberties in Iglesias were severely limited. Class structure was more rigid, after nearly two centuries of intensive mining and agrarian colonization.[56] The statute explicitly separated the *homo di buona fama* from the *popolo*, or *homini habitatori di Villa*.[57] Men of good reputation were exempted from *tormento* and *martoriato*, torture procedures which entailed public humiliation and corporal punishment.[58] The *popolo,* consisting of a diverse class of rural laborers, however, was not exempted from punishments. The *Breve* prohibited rural laborers from taking their animals to grazing lands adjacent to the mines.[59] It is difficult to estimate the proportion of miners caught violating these laws *in flagrante* out of the total number of miners that daily occupied Iglesias' mining sites. It required a tremendous policing effort by royal guards and other mining officers. The penalty against ore thefts—*furto di vena o piombo non smirato*—was severe: death by hanging.[60] Judicial decisions were firm and final; no court of appeals was allowed.[61]

In Ottoman mines, poor miners were far from enjoying the product of mines. Mining relied upon labor quotas. With time, certain regions developed a reputation connected to mining and metallurgy. In Janjevo, situated in the southern extremity of Mount Kopaonik, people 'enjoy a special reputation in the Peninsula as metal-workers, and, with their Vlach instinct for itinerant commerce, sell their cheap jewelry and church ornaments through all the countries between the Black Sea, the Aegean, and the Adriatic.'[62] Specialization was molded by broader Christian-Balkan traditions in contact with the Ottoman rulers.[63] Christian feudatories, who collaborated with the Ottomans, retained their estates and were granted further privileges. The Greek *archons* or elders, entered the Ottoman administrative system for the Balkans as part of an official aristocracy representing Turkish dignitaries but administering their own affairs. Christian tribal leaders in Serbia retained their positions. 'As a general rule, Christian peasants paid higher taxes than their Muslim counterparts.'[64]

There is no doubt that miners belonged to a dynamic but hierarchical society, far more complex than what statutes reveal. Historian Tenfelde described several decades ago the occasions that gave rise to public festivals in mining towns: findings of new deposits, a 'new shaft successfully sunk, a galley opened up or a seam found to be more productive than expected,' claim-staking, the granting of fiefs, inspection and measurement of loads, distribution of proceeds, personnel changes, and even the quarterly presentations of the accounts of the Mine Office, as in the Harz. In the twelfth century, Freiberg miners developed the *Erbbereiten*, a festival that celebrated the discovery of new deposits. Its activities included a miners' procession, with their musical band; the provision of food and drink for the miners and their families; and a banquet for the officials of the town.

Later in the fifteenth century, with the rise of the Habsburg Empire, other traditions took hold of old mining towns. In Catholic towns, miners' festivals coincided with the church's saint calendar—such as the St. Daniel, St. Procopius, and St. Barbara, 'especially honoured among miners.' After the Reformation, in some Protestant mining towns, the church celebrated a service that included a sermon 'in which work was glorified as service to God.'[65] In Špania Dolina, the famous Aušus services are still held today. Originating in the fifteenth century, the services still include 'miners' feast, miners' mass, miners' wedding and miners' funeral.'[66] It was the Erzgebirge that gave birth to the miner's garb, 'black is the shaft, black is the brow of the rock, black is your dress in which you descend'—a garb immortalized by the creator of the seven dwarfs from the Snow White story.[67]

In Ottoman towns, the cultural world of mining was much more diverse. Historian Vucinich states that the Ottoman society was a complex mosaic of Arabic traditions, with significant divergences between Sunni and Shia societies, Persian, Seljuḳ, and Byzantine cultural worlds, not immune to one another.[68] But here, the Christian labor force was never assimilated 'either to Islam or to the Turkish language,' both pivotal identities for social mobility. Non-Muslims were defined as infidels or *zimmis* and 'socially castigated and deprived of rights belonging to the ruling Muslim elite.' 'The peasant masses,' continues Vucinich, 'remained Christian, alien in language and culture as well as in religion, outside the cultural horizon of the Turks.'[69]

Women, 'Old People,' and Slaves: The Wretched of Mining History?

The inquiry of mining labor has a weighty problem: how to measure the value that certain nonstandard classes of person represented to mining corporations. On the question of women in mining, there is almost no reliable information the further back we explore the history of capitalist businesses. The *Codex Wangianus* made no mention of women, nor did *Ordinamenta. Constitutiones juris metallica* prohibited mining judges from relying upon women when gathering witnesses' accounts, as described earlier. The *Breve* of Iglesias explicitly mandated that minors, *maschio et femina*, be excluded from owning *trente*.[70] It prohibited notaries from registering shares on behalf of children of ten years of age or less. Notaries, however, could register *trente* on behalf of males and females as long as these were *persona grande*, over ten years of age.[71]

The mining statute of Iglesias offers a rich picture of gender relations in a medieval mining setting. Noble women could own mining shares, either by inheritance, or dowry, or donation. A woman enjoyed the right to claim her *trente* dowry—*domandare le suoi dote*—within two years after a husband's death. *Trente* dowries granted three years before the enactment of the *Breve* remained valid, and could not be *litata nè molestata*—harassed by prospectors, nor creditors, nor her children.[72] Women belonging to lower classes belonged to the complex social fabric of Iglesias. The *Breve* restricted the fish market to *de la piassa de la Corte a la pancha che è a pe' del palasso*; only there the *pescatori provinciali* could conduct their businesses. The law prohibited women from buying *pescii* or visiting the market on Saturdays, Sundays, and Mondays.[73] The same prohibition was extended against women's access to Iglesias' grain market on weekends.[74]

Women were mentioned under the category of *vinajouli*, or wine sellers, which had to observe regulations prohibiting wine adulteration.[75] Prostitution was probably part of the social fabric. The mining statute ordered that chaplains be removed if there was proof that they had 'intimate' affairs with women—*tenesse alcuna femina por amansa*.[76] Bigamy was forbidden, punished with a fine.[77] Men were fined if caught with women *contra la volontà del marito*.[78] Unlike *Constitutiones*, the mining statute allowed notaries to rely upon testimony by men and women alike, as long as notaries observed the regulations pertinent to the collection of eyewitness evidence.[79]

Evidence of women's labor in mining for the rest of the mining regions is almost nonexistent, except for the case of England, where the available evidence indicates that women were engaged in diverse smelting-related activities.[80] Iconographic evidence of women's labor in the mines of Europe is also scanty. The well-known engravings published in *De re metallica* by Agricola in the sixteenth century portray women preforming different roles and functions.[81] On one engraving, the artist depicted a woman shaking a sieve in a tub nearly full of water. The task takes place in the open field. A boy fills the sieves with the material that requires washing, while a man removes from another tub material that has passed through a sieve. A perfect gendered division of labor! A second drawing shows a wife seated at a table placed in a front corner of the drawing of a smelting laboratory scene. The woman eats what looks like a piece of cheese or bread. She is barefoot and appears as if she is enjoying a moment of repose while her husband works. Another drawing portrays a woman carrying a baby in her arms while men perform different tasks in a glass-making laboratory. There is only one engraving which has four women performing the task of ore sorting, separating the available metal in trays and discarding unwanted rocks or waste into buckets. Most likely, these women were experienced in the art of sorting metal from waste and required no supervision. Two men accompany the women in the drawing, who are performing the same task. Another drawing, however, shows a different ore sorting performed by men and a young child not older than ten years of age. Two men break up lumps of ore by using a broad hammer, to separate the 'more precious from the worthless.' The young child appears as if playing with a small hammer, with a dog resting by his side, while two men work attentively on their tasks. While the drawings represented Agricola's view of Germanic mining towns, it is possible that the role of women in mining was generally as Agricola described it, at least in prosperous mining towns.

Other than these engravings, it seems that along with Smith's *brewer, butcher, and baker*, men appeared as the main labor force of mining. In the East, however, some sources offer hints worthy of consideration. A work commissioned by Japan's Sumitomo family, owner of copper smelting factories, gives us some clues about the evolution of gender relations in Asian mining regions. The work depicted women and 'old people' performing ore sorting and cleaning tasks:

> There are high grade ores and low-grade ores with an admixture of plain rock. After crushing, very low-grade ore and plain rock are separated out and discarded. This is work for old people and women.[82]

The *Kodō Zuroku* further describes how women washed slags and ashes, as follows:

> The earthen slag remaining in the crucible used for melting copper is ground fine in a stone mortar, then washed with water in a pan. The particles of earth, being light, will be washed away, whereas the particles of copper, being heavy, will remain in the pan and be retrieved.[83]

Japan's *Kodō Zuroku* raises relevant questions about gender division of labor in the mines. How did 'women and old people' adapt to the rhythm of mining when it 'disbanded them of feudal retinues'?[84] Historians offer no details on gender in mining towns of medieval Europe. One can infer that certain conditions brought women into the orbit of the mining economy. Sixteenth-century treatises offer specific details about women's labor in the mines. Women were ore sorters and washers, according to Agricola. The job was done as part of the household economy. Any sudden change in a town's demographics increased the toll on women's livelihoods. Agricola stated:

> Mountains, too, slide down and men are crushed in their fall and perish, like when Rammelsberg sank down, so many men were crushed in the ruins that in one day about 400 women were robbed of their husbands.' Agricola continues: 'And eleven years ago, part of the mountain of Altenberg, which had been excavated, became loose and sank, and suddenly crushed six miners; it also swallowed up a hut and one mother and her little boy.[85]

Other sixteenth-century mining experts recognized the role of women in discovering useful applications of metals. In Biringuccio's *Pirotechnia* one reads:

> In addition to these useful effects, lead has power to serve men in many other ways; for the doctors also make use of it in many sicknesses. Women in particular are greatly indebted to it, for, with art, it disposes to a certain whiteness, which, giving them a mask, covers all their obvious and natural darkness, and in this way deceives the simple sight of men by making dark women white and hideous ones, if not beautiful, at least less ugly.[86]

Women, 'much more patient than men,' cut narrow gold strips to be used in spindle wheels, after men 'goldbeaters' flattened and hammered gold squares into leafs.[87] The gender division of labor in older mining towns probably adjusted itself to the tempo of montane extractive activities. It is possible that women's labor was mostly allocated to the household economy in winter, when a household's fuel demand increased. Women healers, a phenomenon of medieval Europe, probably played a role in all mining towns, although information is limited to south Italy.[88]

In regions where geography imposed a heavy toll on long-term habitation, women carried a heavier burden. It is possible that the use of female slaves, prevalent in the gold mines of Upper Egypt and salt mines of the Sahara, extended to silver mines of Morocco, other Islamic lands, and mountain regions outside the Latin West. Bernard Lewis, commenting on the work of fifteenth-century Persian writer Ibn Buṭlān, indicates that 'a proper ethnic division of labor for both male and female slaves' was suggested by this Persian authority. In Lewis's words:

> As guards of persons and property, he recommends Indians and Nubians; as laborers, servants, and eunuchs, Zanj; as soldiers, Turks and Slavs. On female slaves [Ibn Buṭlān] goes into somewhat greater detail, discussing their racial attributes, of both body and character, and the different functions for which they are best fitted.[89]

If the working conditions of the 'black slave gangs who toiled in the salt flats of *basra*' applied to Moroccan women miners, then, there is no question that women endured atrocious labor conditions. The entombment that Marx described of aboriginal labor in American mines was but an evolution of a structure integral to mining. In Morocco, slave gangs 'lived and worked in conditions of extreme misery.' Lewis continues: 'They were fed, we are told, on "a few handfuls" of flour, semolina, and dates.'[90] The times were different than those when Xenophon (c. 430–350 B.C.) advocated for the use of slaves to improve Athens mining revenues. 'Every husbandman knows how many yoke of oxen and servants are necessary to cultivate his farm, and if he employs more than he has occasion for, reckons himself so much a loser; but no dealer in the silver mines ever thought he had hands enow [enough?] to set to work.'[91] Xenophon's words were apt for a slave-based, agrarian Mediterranean society and surrounded by expansionist powers. 'And this is the only profession I know of where the undertakers are never envied, be their stock or profits ever so extraordinary, because their gains never interfere with those of their fellow traders.' Surely, Xenophon was more conservative than other ancient writers in the judgment of the utility of slavery to mining.[92] Diodorus of Sicily commented, 'these slaves that continue as so many prisoners in these mines, incredibly enrich their masters by their labours, yet toiling night and day in these golden prisons, many of them by being overworked, die underground.'[93] Unfortunately, the mining statutes discussed in this book do not shed much light on women, old people, and slave labor in the mines. If slave labor did occur, it is doubtful that it significantly increased mining's returns in thirteenth-century European world mining regions.

The forces that antagonized the old lordship-serfdom relations impacted gender relations. It is true that changes to the condition of *lacrimabili montanorum*,[94]

Fig. 4.4. Indian miners of Potosí, as depicted by engraver Theodor de Bry in *Indiae Occidentalis* (A.D. 1590). No Spanish *encomendero* appears in the engraving. Indians carry sacks of ore on their backs outside the mine, while others dig and cut through rockwalls using pickaxes. Bry, a man of prolific imagination, copied Renaissance drawings and styles popular among painters of his time. Gianni Dagli Orti / The Art Archive at Art Resource, NY.

or the suffering of mountain people, took a long time. In the Alps and Lombardy, labor relations likely took longer to escape from the lordship-serfdom economic spectrum. Lordship 'persisted tenaciously as an element of elite status and privilege,' stated medievalist Bisson.[95] Lordships still enjoyed economic advantages. Many Lombard communes tenaciously adhered to certain feudalization of property—a winning card against Venice's expansionist impetus.[96] In certain Alpine villages, the local nobility formed corporations and financed construction projects and government buildings, while relying upon serf labor. Nonetheless, the 'theology of inequality,' in the words of Bisson, ingrained in serfdom relations was open to attack by the rise of mobile forms of free mining labor.[97]

The speed at which gender relations changed is a question for further re-

Fig. 4.5. *The Mine,* by Jacopo Zucchi (A.D. 1540–1596). Burckhardt once remarked that Italians had a great enthusiasm for classical antiquity, and Jacopo Zucchi was no exception. He worked for Lorenzo the Magnificent, who entrusted much of his propaganda campaign to painters like Zucchi. The landscape background of the painting setting evokes enjoyment. Distinguished guests quietly stare at the mining works. In the foreground, a miner chained at the leg raises his eyes as if accepting his lot, while a silent spectator stares at us. The message is that the evils of slave labor in mines naturally descend upon the men who refuse to abide by the good government of the rulers of Florence. Scala / Art Resource, NY.

search. Material life of medieval Europe worked against women. From an early thirteenth-century treatise on medicine attributed to a woman physician, the 'inferiority of women' is set as the general scientific principle for the treatment of diseases:

When God, the creator of the universe, in the first beginning of the world, distinguished the individual natures of things according to their kind, He endowed the human race with a singular dignity. To it above the condition of all the rest of the animals. He gave freedom of reason and intellect. And wishing to ensure its perpetual generation, and arranging this by means of different sexes, before all else He provided for the propagation of future offsprings with prudent deliberation, and created male and female so that from them might emerge more fecund offspring. Nature tempered their generated complexions with a certain mixing, establishing the man's complexion hot and dry. But lest the male abound too much in either of these, [Nature] wished to restrain [him] from too much excess by the apposite frigidity and humidity of the woman. [Nature] attributed to the man the stronger qualities, i.e., heat and dryness, in as much as he is the stronger and worthier person, and to women weaker qualities, i.e., frigidity and humidity, in as much as the weaker should be dominated [by the stronger], so that the male might pour forth the product of his stronger qualities into the woman as into a field of nature set aside for him, [and the woman] might receive the seed into the womb of nature.[98]

The problem that lies in front of us is colossal. Historian Balestracci stated that, 'we still know very little about the people who worked in the fields.'[99] His questions about fifteenth-century Tuscan peasants are suitable for future studies about medieval miners:

How did they live? How did they think? What did they believe and fear? It is as if, once outside the city gates, society lost all its complexity and nuance [. . .] As one considers the many unanswered questions, it is apparent that the few things that are known have been generalized to encompass and homogenize the entire rural world [. . .] It is as if, once outside the city gates, society lost all its complexity and nuance.[100]

More research is needed to provide definite answers to these questions. The succinct description of mining statutes undertaken in this book suggests that the mining roots of capitalism were violent, and poor miners, including women, paid the highest price. The wage laborer that slowly emerged from the mining *feodum* had a predatory past; his alienation from the means of production was not eliminated with the displacement of feudal lord by corporations. Rather, alienation was reinforced and reinvented by new ways of digging underground wealth.

Ideological Foundations of the Business

Mining was catching up with the dominant legal and political culture of its times. The legal concepts of *universitas, multitudo, societas, collegium,* and *communitas* defined voluntary associations of individuals with collective will and means of 'exercising a common goal.' Through the exercise of a common goal, the medieval corporation demonstrated its will and consciousness of forming one legal person. Jurists in the Roman law tradition employed the term *universitas* as an object of law and applied it as an abstract idea to a wide range of 'universes.' They were not unfamiliar with this type of association, since its origins go back to the compilations of canonical and civil law that formed the core of the juridical culture of Europe before the advent of Aristotle's writings.[101] It was this juncture that gave legitimacy to the mining corporation. The dominant legal culture of the period served to legitimize the usurpation by the corporation of the mining rights of the feudal lord. But it was a propitious usurpation since a diversity of *corpus*, *communitas*, *collegium*, *consilium*, and *societas* flourished in every branch of industry and commerce between the twelfth and fourteenth centuries.

Generally speaking, 'development of the corporation meant the discovery of techniques by which the common purposes of a group of individuals could be advanced without recourse to a benevolent guardian,' in the words of historian Lewis.[102] Hence, a corporation had economic interests and enjoyed the capacity to advance its motives but, unlike a natural person, was not subjected to a guardian. A corporation was only subjected to its own individual members, if and when these were 'bound into unity by Jurisprudence.'[103] 'Unity of decision and consistency of action'[104] belonged only to individuals when they formed a corporation.

Sinibaldo, Count of Fieschi, after he became Pope Innocent IV (A.D. 1185–1254), employed the phrase *persona ficta* in A.D. 1243 to refer to a collegiate or cathedral church.[105] 'The corporation is a person, but it is a person by fiction and only fiction.'[106] Historians still argue over the meaning of Sinibaldo's words. Possibly, the words signified that, first, a corporation represented a collegiate body of a monarchy of the Church, and second, that it could commit no crime.[107] The fragile consensus reached by medieval jurisprudents and lawmakers was that a corporation was 'capable of proprietary rights; but it is incapable of knowing, intending, willing, acting.' Gierke continues: 'By action of its guardians it can acquire property, and, if it is to take the advantage of contracts, it must take the burden also.'[108]

Lawyers and lawmakers adapted Innocent's view and forced upon it an 'organic theory,' stating that 'the law does not create the corporate person, but finding it in existence invests it with certain legal capacity.'[109] A medieval mining corporation was not a juridical person in the modern sense of the word, as Blanch Nougués clarifies.[110] A Prince or city governing body could dissolve the corporation, but not punish it, given that its personality was given by law. The fact that it was a fictitious person meant that it enjoyed no natural right. Corporators assembled into a corporation, not the other way around. No corporation, in and by itself, appointed its members. The prince and sovereign citizens could punish corporators, but not the corporation. Mining corporations operated within the confines of private law, in contrast to the state. Thus, a prince exercised administrative control of the assets of the corporation, but never absolute jurisdiction over the medieval mining corporation. The risks of venturing into the mining business were absorbed by members of corporations.

Lack of evidence makes it difficult for us to have a complete picture of how corporations inhibited or suppressed competition, one of the most incisive questions that Armando Sapori raised many years ago. Nor can we know how corporations 'exempted themselves from societal prohibitions such as usury.'[111] What we know is that members of a corporation were subjected to punishment. But, could a prince, king, or emperor punish a corporation? Did medieval corporations enjoy rights of fictitious persons? No theoretical or legal principle directly identified a corporation as *persona ficta* or fictitious person.[112] The notion originated in sacerdotal law or *Jus Sacrum*, 'in which the principle that *in sacris simulata pro veris accipiuentur*, had long since been recognized, and legal fiction is, according to it, merely the idea of the sacrificial fiction—which was made use of in antiquity as a simple means of warding off the wrath of the Deity, and of enlightening it as to the conviction of the willing intention of the sacrificer—put into a general theoretical shape.'[113]

5

A 'Lengthy Digression':
Why Mining Lagged Elsewhere

WAS GEOGRAPHY AN IMPLACABLE factor for miners in other mountain ranges of the known world? Answers to this question require us to take a detour into the mining history of the mountains of the rest of the world.

England: An Industry Restrained by Royal Policy

Major silver discoveries took place in Bere Ferrers or Bere Ferris, a valley of the Tamar River in North Devon, southwest of Dartmoor, and at Combe Martin in the north after the mid-thirteenth century. The Bere Ferrers mine was located on a tiny peninsula formed by a 'gently undulating plateau rising from around 80–100 meters in the west to 150 meters in the east.' Metalliferous ores start on the eastern side, the steep side of the peninsula, and continue westwards. 'Only one of those lodes, often referred to as the "eastern cross-course" was worked in the medieval period.'[1] Earlier works at 'the Mine of Carlisle' in the north Pennines, Alston, were possibly exploited at a profit, although most of the evidence studied by Rippon and his colleagues comes from the Great Rolls of the Exchequer, otherwise known as the Pipe Rolls.[2] The Pipe Rolls, accounts of sheriffs from the reigns of Henry II to William IV dealing with feudal dues and judicial fees, revenues, and expenses, offer, however, no account of the organization of the mining industry. Other prospection works at *la Hole* in north Devon in the mid-thirteenth century were possibly abandoned due to lack of investment capital. Thus, we must make generalizations from the case of the

Bere Ferrers mine about the essential form and shape that the English mining industry took before the rise of capitalism.

Miners came to Bere Ferrers from 'the established lead mining districts across England and northeast Wales,' recruited not by private investors but by the Crown in A.D. 1292.[3] Here, the English Crown established a policy which worked in detriment of the capitalist impetus of mining: the Crown decided to 'manage the Devon mines directly, using its own officers and employing miners on contract.'[4] This meant that the Crown held the prerogative over silver, gold, and copper mines, a distinctive legal principle with no parallel in the world's mining regions discussed previously.[5] The right of prerogative meant that management of mines and allocation of mining resources were the Crown's prerogative and privilege.

The economic situation of England in the mid-thirteenth century was plagued by adversity. Real monetary and coinage pressures occupied the thoughts of English kings as well as the merchant class. Royal indebtedness, land market fluctuations, rising grain prices, loss of territory at the Battle of Bouvines in A.D. 1214, and expulsion of the Jews left no easy way out for English kings.[6] Conflicts with barons, monasteries, and creditors as well as merchants buying and selling Jewish bonds on land had devastating consequences for the English Crown. We are indebted to Michael Postan for throwing light on the economic problems of the English kingdom in this period. The burden of mortgages owed to Jewish creditors precipitated a massive change in ownership of land from small-scale landowners to Jewish bankers. These were times when ecclesiastical orders in England 'were heavily burdened with papal and royal imposts.' There was only one way out: extending regalian rights as a way of 'waging war' on barons and monasteries, while weakening the foundation of their power.

While industrialists formed voluntary *societas* for exploiting mines elsewhere, the *mercanti del re* or bankers of the King, with the incentive of codified mining law, became administrators of the silver mines of Birland in England.[7] In A.D. 1299, the Frescobaldi banking family was granted a mine concession, the *custodia e l'appalto* of the silver mine of Birland, which lasted for a very short period of time.[8] The contract was a loss to the bankers, possibly because of the bankers' inexperience with mining. The Frescobaldi rescinded from the concession a year later, when Thomas de Swaneseye took over the role of keeper of the mines and the Crown took over the mining operations.[9] The company spent much more money increasing the labor supply by hiring miners from other regions than in drainage and ore smelting infrastructure.[10] Mining works ceased in A.D. 1349.[11]

The opinion that the Exchequer's view was 'that occasional periods of loss were acceptable' fails to acknowledge the powerful force of banking.[12] The Exchequer was not free from Frescobaldi's agents. In A.D. 1300, the King granted custody and government of the Exchanges of Northumberland, located in Newcastle-on-Tyne, Devon in Exeter, Dublin, Kingston-upon-Hull, Bristol, and other counties to the Frescobaldi.[13] They became keepers of the Exchanges of London and Canterbury, an office which they zealously held, creating controversies with the Archbishop of Canterbury. Can this banking record be taken as evidence for arguing that the English Crown used the mines as securities? The question is open for debate, since it has a lot to do with the commercialization of feudal bonds in northern Europe. The banking record of the Frescobaldi suggests that the Crown used its mines as securities, at least in its financial dealings with the Italian bankers. During the decade starting in A.D. 1290, the Frescobaldi loaned high sums of money to the English Crown, including 1,000 Pounds to the Exchequer, 4,666 Pounds to the King, 2,000 Pounds to the King of France on behalf of the English king, and 1,680 Pounds paid to Spanish merchants on behalf of the English King, among other outstanding loans.[14] If the Crown used its mines as securities, as Rhodes argued and Sapori confirmed, this was by no means a financial policy exclusive to the English Crown.[15] Renaissance princes tended to view mining and other real estate assets in a similar fashion, as the work by Richard Ehrenberg demonstrated decades ago.[16] Impetus toward privatizing mining rights was not on the English horizon yet. King Edward II no doubt raged like a leopard, as did the Exchequer when confronted with the poor yields of the Birland mines.

The short period of time under which the mines belonged to private bankers yielded no institutional arrangement comparable to the mining legal institutions that emerged in other parts of Western Europe. The bankers managed the mines as an asset of the banking firm, something that possibly exacerbated rancor by magnates against foreign bankers since they were mentioned in Parliament rolls 'with some note of opprobrium,' 'in close connection with, "Lombards, Jews, Saracens, and secret spies,"' according to Smirke.[17] More importantly, the Frescobaldi's portfolio was diversified, and wool trade, finance, and the Exchequer presented lucrative opportunities to the Italians in England and northern Europe in general, as opposed to raw material production.

No radical change in the legal structure of mining claims took place under Crown control. While in Trento, Tuscany, Massa, and Bohemia key institutional and contractual arrangements emerged that directly impinged upon the central government's role in mining governance, the English case lagged behind but only in terms of the new business structures and institutional power that the medieval mining corporation entailed elsewhere. The Crown relied upon its administrative rationality and made unwise decisions concerning capital and labor in the mines.[18] At the peak of mining production at Bere Alston, there were only 700 miners, and many 'pump men, carpenters, smiths, chandlers, ore-washers, ore-roasters, refiners, charcoal-burners and carters.' The mine's silver output equaled 800 Pounds annually between A.D. 1292 and 1297. This number rose slightly to 1,773 Pounds in A.D. 1305, 'but thereafter output declined rapidly to only £70's worth of silver in 1347.'[19] However, royal prerogative offered no incentives for private investment or technological improvements. Miller and Hatcher assert that expansion of mining output between A.D. 1100 and 1350 was by no means continuous, nor dramatic. That mining was a seasonal occupation, rather than a full-time occupation exercised by specialists, contributed to the 'self-supplying motive' of England's mining districts. They state:

> Some mining, like manorial agriculture, was intended for the self-supply of land-lords on whose lands it was conducted: this was [. . .] the acknowledged purpose of some early monastic iron mines in Yorkshire; in 1268–69 iron from mines at Bolton went to Cockermouth castle (Cumberland) to make nails, plough parts and tyres for cartwheels; and as late as 1384 the keeper of Bamburgh castle (Northumberland) was instructed to mine enough coal for those dwelling in the castle, although any surplus was to be sold.[20]

Geography added other challenges. English mines were physically distant from the central arteries of international trade of continental Europe and the commercial cities with continental catchment areas—Bruges, Champagne, Cologne, Milan, Brescia, and others. England had other challenges. In the last decades of the twelfth century, England embarked upon the difficult task of expanding its rule to Wales and Ireland and at the same time consolidated territorial politics. Even when a high number of new towns and markets emerged in a century and a half after the Norman Conquest of A.D. 1066—an unprecedented urban feast—the commercial and political culture of cities remained tied to the economic life and culture of the more advanced towns of northern France and the

Low Countries. 'For at least three hundred years after 1066, French—or *roman*, as the language was called in French-—remained the vernacular of polite society,' states historian John Gilligham.[21] The consolidation of dynastic politics by Norman kings absorbed too much of their time, especially in the case of William the Conqueror, who had to confront the power intricacies of the 'shires and their courts, sheriffs and witts,' 'the mechanisms by which Anglo-Saxon kings could reach out to the localities.'[22] Territorial challenges were no small thing: powerful magnates in the north, compact lordships entrenched in rich lands, and increasing demands for improving agrarian and mining lands threatened the already fragile gains of the Crown. The main challenge of English kings was the consolidation of an administrative monarchy, which required claiming jurisdictional privileges in areas pertaining to industry. In contrast, the mining industry in Trento, Massa, Sardinia, and Bohemia benefited from the positive spillover effect that proximity to medieval banking and commercial cities created, as discussed previously. It also benefited from the rise of autonomous city-states that effectively challenged the power of central governments, urban aristocracy, and a feudal monarchy in the case of Kutná Hora. The resources of the countryside in these cases were in no way committed to military expansionist campaigns by central governments; the opposite is true, if judged by the cases of Massa and Iglesias, the cities that posed the most enduring political challenges to their governing powers, as mentioned earlier.

Inhabitants of the Tamar Valley contended with the disadvantages mentioned above. The valley in southwest England was far away from the busiest continental trade corridors, unlike Trento, Massa, Sardinia, and the Hungarian and Transylvanian mines. It lacked the demography of several towns located in world mining regions.[23] Some Lombardy cities had a population of as high as thirty thousand inhabitants in the mid-thirteenth century, while only four towns in England had a population size averaging ten thousand to eighty thousand inhabitants, and none located in the Tamar Valley.[24] Population of towns of the Tamar Valley barely exceeded two thousand inhabitants. Leaving the problems of quantitative comparisons aside, the numbers give a general idea of the low level of urbanization of the Tamar Valley. They also allow for speculation on the size of demand from the mining economy. It is possible that the low population levels of the Tamar Valley explain underinvestment in the mining economy.[25]

No large silver deposits were discovered in the twelfth or thirteenth centuries; fertility of soil mattered more, something that Smith described in his argument about the relationship between agriculture and opulence. The question of mining still stands: did geology strengthen the cause of 'sovereign lordships,'[26] allowing for the survival of feudalism in thirteenth-century England? The question opens an immense avenue for further research. Suffice to add here that feudalism had its wish in the mines of the Tamar Valley.

Islamic Andalusia: A Case of Good Geology in Bad Times

Andalusia stands over the Iberian Pyrite Belt, a metalliferous zone containing 'supergiant massive sulphide deposits' and extending from southwestern Spain to Atlantic Portugal.[27] The Belt erupted to the surface in the last millennia in the form of the Baetic Cordillera, stretching over a distance of 230 kilometers south of the peninsula. This zone contains impressive amounts of metals, in 'concentrations that range from small lenses with thousands of tons, to giant bodies with hundreds of million tons.'[28] Sulfides are concentrated in about ninety known deposits, 'estimated at more than 1.7 billion tons,' according to geologist Fernando Barriga. Only about 20 percent of this amount has been mined, with between 10 percent and 15 percent lost to erosion.[29]

Slag discoveries in localities in Cordova, Sierra Almagrera, and Sierra Morena in Spain and Aljustrel in Portugal support the abundant literary evidence of intense mining activities during the period of Islamic rule.[30] 'Andalusia abounds in mines of silver and quicksilver, which have not their equal anywhere in the world, either in the countries subject to the Moslems, or in those which the Infidels occupy,' according to Persian geographer Ali Al-Mas'ūdī (d. A.H. 345/A.D. 956).[31] Ceuta geographer Al-Idrīsī (A.H. 493–560/A.D. 1100–1165) praised the Hisin Ābal mine in Cordova, with shafts of 250 qāmas or fathoms 'exploited by thousands of people, divided in groups of miners and ore transporters.'[32] The mine was probably surrounded by silver mining works located in Belalcázar, Cerro Muriano, Dehesas de la Plata, Hornachuelos, Ingertal, and Mirabuenos.[33] Ibn Sa'īd Al-Maghrībī (d. A.H. 685/A.D. 1286), born in Granada, said that 'mines of all the known seven metals were to be found in the north and north-west of Andalus, in those countries which were in the hands of Infidels.' According to his description, 'silver is also very common; it may be produced near Tudmir, and in the mountains of Al-hamah, near Bejénah, and in the neighborhood of Kartash town belonging to the district of Cordova.'[34]

Mining also took place in the western fringe of the Atlas Mountains in North

Africa. The mountains are a 'mirror image' of Spain's Baetic Cordillera.[35] The Atlas range stretches for more than two thousand kilometers and connects the Mediterranean and the Atlantic sides of northern Africa.[36] Moroccan miners exploited surface veins, in depths of up to twenty-five meters in the case of the 'Awwām and 'Addana mines.[37] The mining works of Fāzāz, a name that designated the 'north-western extremity of the Moroccan Middle Atlas,' lasted until the twelfth century. The evidence comes from *al-Istibṣārfī 'aǧā'ib al-amṣ ar* (A.H. 585/A.D. 1191), written by an anonymous author who took care to mention silver mines in Warkanas, Zukandar, and Raqid in the valleys of Sous and Fāzāz. A sixteenth-century Spanish account of the kingdoms of North Africa described silver mines in Tarudant, Sous, as follows: *Ay muchos y buenos montes, críase algunos cavallos buenos, y muchos camellos, ay muchos y buenos pastos, y minas de plata, y otros metales en abundancia.* The chronicler stated that the mints and jewelry factories of the Moroccan kingdom were fed by abundant mines of silver, gold, and iron found in Teguriri. The writer based his account on the testimony of Juan De la Sierra, a captive man who worked in a gold mine in Teguriri. If Sierra made no exaggeration, the Xarife, preventing Christian invasion, had ordered the shutdown of the mine—*que si los Cristianos supiesen, que allí avia tãto oro no lo iriã a buscar a las Indias.*[38]

Arab geographer Ibn Khaldūn (A.H. 732–808/A.D. 1332–1406), *el gran historiador*,[39] described two types of silver mines in Morocco and the Maghreb: *grottas* and the mineral formations hidden deep in the subsoil of the earth.[40] Ibn Baṭṭūṭa also described the silver *grottas* of the Maghreb, while other Arab writers mentioned the 'famous Ma'din 'Awwām silver mine' in Morocco.[41] The mine is identified today with the locality of Djabal 'Awwām. These mining sites were located approximately ten kilometers west of the city of M'rirt and 120 kilometers southwest of Fez. The anonymous author of the *Kitāb al-Istibṣār* observed that 'Mu'tamid was a prisoner there [and] it was built of wood and the majority of its population consisted of Jewish merchants.'[42]

As in Latin Europe, the law regulated mining works. Islamic scholars or *muftī* recognized that mines located in lands conquered by war belonged to the caliphate. However, Andalusia was a different type of conquest.[43] In the opinion of Ibn Rušd al-Qurṭubī al-Mālikī al-Ŷadd (A.H. 450–520/A.D. 1058–1126), Andalusia represented land conquered by alliance rather than war. In Islamic lands conquered by war, people were treated as members of tribes. This meant that 'when a non-Arab became Muslim, he acquired political significance—if at all—by becoming the client or *mawlā* of a patron or a tribe,' according to Dennett. They were 'treated with scorn and contempt,' as 'dregs of society,' 'the mob,' 'the anonymous,' and 'the foolish.'[44] Such was not the legal case of Andalusians, at least nominally. If the Andalusian nobility and merchant class possessed mining claims before Islamic ruling, these owned by non-Muslims before Islamic conquest were legitimate.

This was a broad legal interpretation of mining rights that to some extent exempted Islamic rulers from creating a cohesive legal doctrine ruling the underground wealth of Andalusia. Different opinions flourished in the few *fatwā* or notarial documents written by *muftī* scholars regarding mining available today. Al-Wanšarīsī (A.H. 834–914/c. A.D. 1430–1508) stated that only when a mine owner died did mines legally revert to the Caliph; further, only the Caliph could grant them in concession to another individual.[45] This opinion seems to suggest that Andalusian mines eventually were destined to be owned by the Caliph. Ibn Rušd and Ibn al-Hāŷŷd (A.H. 458–529/A.D. 1066–1134) agreed that owners of mining shares enjoyed the right of selling, donating, and transferring their shares, but only under certain conditions.[46] For Ibn Rušd, donation of shares was valid if ores were not in sight at the time the donation took place.[47] Share sales were valid, with the exception of shares of unproductive mines, according to Ibn al-Hāŷŷd.[48] The person who leased a mining claim was responsible for mining operations until he cancelled his debt with the landowner.[49]

It is possible that miners enjoyed freedom of prospection; however, the right of prospection was subordinated to surface land rights. Compensation to landowners varied between a third and a fourth of total metal output, after deduction of expenses, in the opinion of Ibn al-Hāŷŷd. But this was no absolute formula, since compensation depended upon types of ores. If a man obtained a land lease, and afterwards extracted silver from lead or copper ores, and the ore value equaled ten dirhams for each *dinar* after assaying tests were done, this man was responsible for mining works and was forbidden from selling the mine back to the landowner.[50]

Another legal peculiarity of Andalusia was how *muftī* scholars interpreted the relationship between the Caliph and religious institutions, when the latter held mining claims.[51] The governing principle came from Tunisian scholar Ibn 'Arafa (A.H. 716–803/A.D. 1316–1401). Ibn 'Arafa stated that a claim granted by the Sultan to a religious institution was a concession of usufruct rights rather than property rights. Religious institutions enjoy absolute mining rights only when those rights were to be exercised in the exploitation of debris, ruins, and similar mine property.[52] This interpretation was far from capricious; religious property could constitute as much as a tenth of the total area of a Muslim district, as was the case in Naṣrid Granada (A.D. 1238–1492).[53] It is possible that in that kind of district, owners of mining claims profited from mixing their assets with those of religious institutions for tax evasion purposes.[54]

In the absence of a unifying mining statute, long-term investments in mines depended upon good relations with local authorities, whose stability came to depend, in turn, upon the vagaries of the Reconquista. By the mid-thirteenth century, local authorities in north and central Andalusia increasingly became part of Christian institutions.[55] Sales of rural property became frequent, and land transactions became cumbersome, as Christian populations migrated to Andalusia in the fifteenth century.[56] The long-term stability needed for capital to plow back its gains into the subsoil at a profit was not possible in Andalusia from the thirteenth-century onward.

In addition, the Reconquista created commercial interests difficult to align with the development of a capitalist mining industry. The slavery of Saracens, Turks, captive Moors, and many other groups fed the markets of Barcelona, Valencia, Palermo, Genoa, and other Mediterranean and North Atlantic cities.[57] These markets had little to contribute to mining, at a time when the most advanced mining industries in Europe relied upon free and salaried miners.

Was Geography to Blame?

When the Naṣrid Dynasty (A.D. 1238–1492) ascended to power, agriculture, public works, and war had exhausted precious state resources. Building much-needed hydraulic infrastructure absorbed great quantities of public and private money. The distinction that Spaniards make between *secano* or dry land and *regadío* or irrigated land is an old fact of peninsular life. If 'the palm groves of Elche were one of the sights of the country,' arid soil was to blame for it—no matter how lovely palm trees seem to the traveler's eye.[58]

Dry land covers nearly two-thirds of the peninsula's surface, which is affected by irregular rainfall patterns. Evaporation aggravates the situation.[59] Almost half of the surface land is composed of lowlands that receive inadequate amounts of river water. The Guadalquivir River in the southeast of the Meseta receives much water from numerous tributaries that carry melting snows from the Sierra Nevada, but only in summer. The Guadix-Baza and Granada rivers are relatively short, as are most mountain rivers in Andalusia. Coastal rivers flow north and west into the Atlantic and have no great length either. The Douro, Tagus, and Guadiana rivers have an extremely irregular supply of water, draining the Meseta toward the Atlantic.

This geography forced Islamic rulers to set their priorities straight: to invest in food production for the export market. To the majority of people, the region was no *Arabia feliz*, as Spaniards wittily put it. Millers used 'horse-driven mills or water-mills,' without which Andalusian wheat would have never become a leading commodity export.[60] In Granada, public and private money was used for building *sāḳiya* or *acequia*. The latter were irrigation channel networks, which, along with dikes and artificial ponds, provided water to cities surrounded by mountains with no fluvial access. Private investments earned good returns: water rights were fully privatized in *acequia* of Albolote.[61] This was hardly an exception. Surely, communities joined efforts to maintain hydraulic infrastructure, but they did so when compelled by chaotic environmental changes, such as famines, rising water levels, and wars. They did so when rulers ordered inhabitants of villages to provide labor, as in most *acequias*.[62] The Reconquista forced caliphs to implement policies that guaranteed protection of hydraulic infrastructure. Muslims in Granada built the Acequia Gorda del Genil and that of Aynadamar in peripheral lands or lands less vulnerable to attacks.[63]

Dry lands were reserved for cereal cultivation, but slopes and coastal arid soils benefited olive tree cultivation. *El verdadero país de los olivos*: such was Andalusia's fame.[64] 'Extraction methods were primitive, but the quantities of oil produced were sometimes in excess of local needs, and the surplus was exported to the rest of the Islamic world.'[65] Other commodities for the export market became part of the agrarian landscape. Starting in the ninth century, grapevines were cultivated almost in every *comarca* or village. The wine trade took off in Estribaciones del Gorbea, Montaña Alavesa, and Tierra de Ayala, villages with agrarian surpluses in no other commodity.[66] By the twelfth century, wine became an important commodity of Pamplona.[67] Wine consumption became so prevalent that a bishop reprimanded people for *costumbre de comer et beber a superfluidat et por ingurgitation ultra lo que la natura puede sostener et por esto cayen en ebriedat o en vomito*.[68]

Other geographic factors possibly increased the costs of mining. The population of Andalusia experienced several famines that forced it to rely on wheat imports from North Africa, itself a region in political turmoil. The most devastating famines took place in the villages of Tuy, Braga, Porto, and Viseu, in the Douro region northeast of the Meseta in the mid-eighth century.[69] Famines added to the pressure of investing in hydraulic infrastructure. People could not easily escape famines by migrating to faraway lands: Mediterranean Africa and northern Spain were not open frontiers. Islam took centuries to conquer the Berbers of North Africa and achieved only an incomplete colonization. The world it encountered in North Africa was not the one it encountered in Andalusia; it found no Roman mines there.[70] The Romans possessed no lead mines in the Molochath territory; a place that they came in contact with after the 'Jugurthine Civil Wars.'[71] If the Romans advanced as far as Mount Atlas, as Pliny insisted, they failed to leave the engineering feast they left elsewhere.[72] Besides, Islam found in North Africa a civilization in retreat, according to Lombard's history of Islam. Decades of raids and punitive expeditions by Berber nomads suffocated 'towns' economic aspirations.'[73]

By the thirteenth century, when private money was displacing feudal lords in other mining regions, Andalusia's mining was in decline. Geology was not the culprit but the ill development of mining laws in a land challenged by geography. The Christian advance that eventually led to the conquest of Granada in A.D. 1492 and the end of the Reconquista marked the beginning of the end for Andalusia's Islamic silver-mining industry.

China under the Liao State: The Burden of Forced Labor

It is today common to see China as the warehouse of precious metals of the medieval world. Credit goes to Gunder Frank for the wide appeal of this idea.[74] Unfortunately, neither historians nor archeologists have been able to rebuild the record of China's medieval silver production.[75] Geologists offer one explanation: eight hundred years ago, China did not possess rich silver deposits that could have triggered large, capital-intensive silver mining operations, at least not outside Yunnan. The veins where silver occurs in the Jehol Mountains are 'too limited in extent and too irregular in character to allow of their being worked with a profit upon a larger scale than that employed by the natives.'[76] The Jehol chain of mountains lies directly north of Beijing. Jehol forms 'a mass of very rugged mountains, bare except for scrub, that begins rising at the Great Wall,' 'arranged like the vertebrae of a quadruple.'[77] The range extends from the plateaus of Inner Mongolia to the easternmost fringe of the Manchurian Plain.

The silver content of galena ores found in Jehol is 'far from impressive.' What made this mountain famous were its iron and gold deposits and, more recently, rare minerals deposits.[78]

However, three medieval accounts identified prosperous silver mining works in the Jehol Mountains. The first account comes from *Chu-fan-chï*, a book which appeared in the mid-thirteenth century but is believed to be of tenth-century origin. Its author, Chau Ju-Kua, was a descendant of Emperor Tai-tsung, 'in the eighth generation through the Prince of Shang, a younger brother of the Emperor Chön-tsung (A.D. 998–1023).' He possibly held the post of inspector of foreign trade in Fujian.[79] Hirth and Rockhill, who translated the account, laudably praised the author: 'he deserves to be mentioned among the most prominent writers on the ethnography and trade of his time'; 'his notes compete successfully with those of Marco Polo and the early Arab and Christian travelers.'[80] Chau Ju-Kua praised the 'lands of the Arabs' for the abundance of mines and goods but said nothing of China.[81] This silence is expressive, given that a trade inspector would not overlook Chinese exports of silver.

The second medieval account comes from *Liao Shih*, a book compiled by a Mongol ruler. It epically narrates the history of the Liao state, founded by Yeh-lü Ta-shih (r. A.D. 1124–1143), ruler of the Kara-Khitan Khanate, or Western Liao state. The Khanate included former Manchuria, Mongolia, and northeastern China and was ruled by the Liao state for almost two hundred years. Founded by the nomad tribe of Ch'i-tan, the state relied upon extractive economies developed in the Jehol range.[82] About mining under the Liao state, the *Liao Shih* states:

> Mining and smelting began when T'ai-tsu first annexed the Shih-wei. Their territory produced copper, iron, gold, and silver, and their people were skilled in making copper and iron articles [. . .] since mining and smelting were conducted mostly in the eastern part of the country, an Office of the Ministry of Revenue was therefore established in the Eastern Capital and an Office of Money and Sill was created in Ch'ang-ch'un Prefecture.[83]

Supposedly, mines were located in the old grazing grounds of the Ch'i-tan, or modern Liaoning:

> Returning after his punitive campaign against Yu and Chi, T'ai-tsu encamped with his army at the foot of a mountain [where] silver and iron ore were found. He ordered the establishment of a smelting plant. During [the reign period] T'ai-p'ing

of Shêng-tsung, both at the Yin Mountains north of Huang River and at the source of the Liao River, gold and silver were discovered. Smelters were established for refining [the ore]. From this time down to T'ien-tsu the state depended throughout on these benefits.[84]

The account states that additional mines were located to the west, in the *jabal* or mountains of Al-Buttam, in the eastern fringe of the lands ruled by the Seljuk dynasty. The Liao state by then included the Qarā-Khitāy vassal countries of Bukhara, Samarkand, Kashgar, and Khotan. Mines were situated in the mountain slopes 'bathed by the Zarafshân River.'[85] It is possible that the Liao state took over the mines after its western expansion in A.D. 1130–1131, when Yeh-lü Ta-shih invaded northeast Transoxiana and forced Kashgar, today's Kashi in east Turkistan, into a tributary relationship with the Liao state. Mines are mentioned a century later, when 'in 1221, the native economy, weakened but not destroyed by the Mongol onslaught, continued to produce a variety of goods: among them, salt from the mountains, silver, and pearls.'[86]

More silver mines were presumably opened in Kiang-che in the Chekiang province and in Kien-ning and Nan-kien in the Fukien province in A.D. 1284 on the southeast coast of China. Mines were also worked at Shau-chow, in Kiangsi province, in A.D. 1286. Smelting factories were located near the Chu Kiang or Canton River, in Hunan, at So-shan district in A.D. 1316, according to the *Liao Shih*. The latter were opened by the successors of the Liao state, the Mongols. Exploration work took place in Mi-yün, 'thirty-five miles to the north of Peking,' in A.D. 1290.[87] Nothing further is known about this mining site aside from the amount of taxes collected by imperial officers.[88] A Mongol 'manager of the mines' showed up in the district in A.D. 1292.[89] Mongol mine administrators were posted at Ta-ming-fu at T'an-chow, in the central province of Hu-Kwang in A.D. 1274; Ki-chow in the northern Chihli province in A.D. 1279; Yün-yang-shan in Kiangsi in A.D. 1291; and Hwei-chow, or former Manchuria, in A.D. 1317. The latter managed a large mining complex: 'he had under him thirty-six silver mines' and had to 'look after the smelting of silver ore and convey the legal amount of silver to the revenue office.'[90] Unfortunately, the *Liao Shih* contains nothing about the rights or duties of Mongol administrators.

The third literary account is Marco Polo's *Il Milione* (c. A.D. 1300).[91] The Venetian traveler described silver mines in Siuen-te-chow and Yu-chow in the Siuenhaw Valley. Siuen-te-chow was 'the summer residence of the Kin [Qing]

Dynasty,' 'more than once besieged and taken by Chinghiz.'[92] Polo stated that 'in a mountain of the [Sindachu] province, there is a very good silver mine, from which much silver is got: the place is called Ydifu.'[93] Scottish geographer and Orientalist Henry Yule (A.D. 1820–1889) only identified Sindachu as a place with 'fine parks full of grand trees remain on the western side. It is still a large town and the capital of a *Fu*, about 25 m. [40 kilometers] south of the Gate on the Great Wall at Chang Kia Kau, which the Mongols and Russians call Kalgan.'[94]

The three literary accounts available to us today tell a story that geologists are reluctant to confirm. If medieval China had silver mines in route to becoming capitalist industries, success or failure of these industries depended upon freedom of mobility for labor, access to water and timber, and optimal resource allocation. There is only one problem. The cornerstone of the accumulation mode of medieval Asian empires was forced labor. A forced labor system guaranteed a constant labor supply but put obstacles upon the increasing returns of labor. Writing about the accumulation mode of the Mongol empire, Janet Abu-Lughod states without apprehension that 'this was not an economic system designed to create a surplus, nor could it be perpetuated indefinitely.'[95] Wittfogel, expert in medieval China, once stated that the *Liao Shih* was 'rather thin as historical record.' It is more plausible to argue that if and when silver mining flourished, it did so following what Wittfogel called 'the mode of production of tribal industry' distinctive of nomadic and pastoralist cultures. Wittfogel defined it as a mode of production 'in harmony with the tribesmen's principal occupations and modes of life.'[96]

Tribal industry was not exclusive to the Manchurian Plain, but here it took a dangerous turn because it relied upon limited specialization and capital. The work by Wittfogel allows us to conclude that mining benefitted from tribal family structure; thus, miners came from family groups put together, ranging from 'three hundred families in one case and as many as a thousand in another.' Wittfogel adds:

> An average family was expected to provide two male adults between the ages of fifteen and fifty as soldiers; and young boys could be used for industrial work before they were fit for military service. Therefore the actual number of workers in these settlements may easily have reached six hundred or two thousand respectively.[97]

In addition, population re-settlements and displacements determined the success or failure of the Liao state. Laborers included forced tribesmen and -women, free tribesmen, slaves, war prisoners, and convicts, including female convicts in copper mines. These were re-settled in mining sites, depending upon the specific needs of each mining site. Some social mobility probably took place among the free tribesmen occupying administrative functions and men employed as militia soldiers. Skilled artisans, when employed in the mines, belonged to a special group of workers with 'an honorary designation' known as 'the precious ones' and 'received bonuses for special achievements.'[98] Wittfogel states:

> Ch'i-tan rulers preserved the industrial level of the South of the Manchurian Plain [. . .] There was little of that division of labor that we associate with the ordinary use of the word "industry," [but] manufacture was sufficiently widespread and important in the economy of this people to justify the term.[99]

The geography of northeast China imposed certain obstacles to mining. A Chinese geographer once described Jehol as a region enclosed in a river triangle, covering an area of 250 miles from west to east, of 'little commercial activity.'[100] Uplands in Jehol's eastern side were 'the land of hunters.'[101] The eastern side has abundant water supplied by rivers that flow to the east. The Pei River flows southeast and runs parallel to the Great Wall before reaching the Gulf of Chihli. The Lwan River runs northwest to southeast and borders Jehol to the south before emptying in the same gulf. The San Kang Ho is the only commercially important river that affords communication into the western side of the Jehol, connecting Kalgan and Suanhua en route to Mongolia.

Agriculture flourished to the east, aided by moisture and continental climate.[102] Vegetation consisted of forests of Siberian larch and birch, favored by moisture and rain. To the west is the Jehol's dry side. This is the side that makes Eurasia 'a drainageless belt,' in the words of nineteenth-century archeologist Sir Marc Aurel Stein.[103] The lands between 'the Pamirs in the west and the Pacific watershed in the east' contain limited water supplies.[104] The Pamir side yields the 'succulent Pamir grass' praised by Kirghiz herders. Nature's formula here was abundance of Kirghiz grass and 'almost total absence of timber or of cultivation.'[105] The land was hostile to agricultural development other than pastoralism. Here, winters are long, with snowfall lasting from October through

April in the south, and September through May in the north. Summers are short. July and August are the months of heavy precipitation, with rainfall amounts of approximately twenty-four inches in the east and fifteen inches in the west.

Chinese emperors exacerbated the water asymmetries of the Jehol. The northern side of the mountains was once covered with forests rich in timber, but the obsession of the Northern Sung dynasty (A.D. 960–1127) with a naval industry put an end to Jehol's forests. A poem by Liu Zongyuan, who lived at the turn of the eighth century, describes the green cost of China's military expansion:

> The official guardians' axes have spread through a thousand hills,
> At the Works Department's order hacking rafter-beams and billets.
> Of ten trunks cut in the woodland's depths, only one gets hauled away.
> Ox-teams strain at their traces—till the paired yoke-shafts break.
> Great-girthed trees of towering height lie blocking the forest tracks,
> A tumbled confusion of limber, as flames on the hillside crackle.
> Not even the last remaining shrubs are safeguarded from destruction;
> Where once the mountain torrents leapt—nothing but rutted gullies.
> Timbers, not yet seasoned or used, left immature to rot;
> Proud summits and deep-sunk gorges now—brief hummocks of naked rock.[106]

The Mongols did no better: 'it is recorded that on one occasion an army of 17,000 men was sent to fell trees in Jehol.'[107] Chinese settlers, 'who needed wood for fuel and as building material, depleted the rich fauna these forests harbored.'[108] Severe deforestation created erosion of mountain valleys—something that did not prevent later the 'penetration of Jehol by a society based on intensive agricultural practices and water control.'[109]

A short-term reversal of fortune to the mining industry came when Chengzu (A.D. 1360–1398), first emperor of the Ming dynasty, opened several mines throughout the Empire. A tax bonanza, similar to the one enjoyed by the Ottomans in the Balkans, proved disastrous to the mining industry:

In 1403, Chengzu's first full year on the throne, the dynasty's receipts from silver mining reportedly rose to 80,185 taels (3,007 kilograms) from a previously recorded high of just over 29,830 taels (1,119 kilograms) in 1390. By 1409, those receipts had reached 272,262 taels (10,210 kilograms) and did not fall below 149,000 taels (5,587 kilograms) annually for the rest of Chengzu's reign. Shortly after the emperor's death in 1424, there was a sharp drop in receipt.[110]

Ming's fiscal policy, carved out of an economic system based upon forced labor, engendered any early capitalist impetus that the mining industry might have had. By A.D. 1430, mines controlled by the government 'declined significantly in productivity and were becoming increasingly expensive to operate.'[111] As the fifteenth century progressed, mining was increasingly undertaken by 'dubious characters who had neither the capital nor the organizing ability to carry it out properly.'[112] Successful mining enterprises were 'short-lived,' and the 'projects usually ended in armed rebellion by the miners'—for instance the miners' rebellion of A.D. 1444 in the border region between Kiangsi and Chekiang.[113] It took the powerful Ming government five years to suffocate the rebellion. The Ming government banned silver mining in this area. The road that led to the mines was cut off with stone and brick walls. The mines of Shang-jao in Kiangsi were sealed off.[114] In the first years of the sixteenth century, the eunuch official Liu Chin assigned quotas for silver production to Fukien, Szechuan, and Yunnan. Only Yunnan silver mines 'apparently went on being worked' until A.D. 1521, when they too were shut down by the government.

In A.D. 1559, the government opened the mining industry to private entrepreneurs, who delivered 40 percent of the metal output to the government. 'Before this policy had time to show the results the miners in the Chekiang-Kiangsi border again turned to large-scale banditry, and in 1566 attacked and seized the city of Wu-yüan in South Chihli.'[115] Mining was forbidden in the provinces of Chekiang, Kiangsi, and South Chihli—'orders were engraved in stone prohibiting anyone from entering the area.' The government published maps showing mountain passes, pathways, and possible transport corridors that needed to be under the blockade, to prevent miners from reaching the area. Moreover, the provincial government of Shantung published 'a list of all its gold, silver, copper, and tin mines, noting that all of them had been "firmly sealed off."'[116]

Did underdevelopment of the mining industry have anything to do with the silver bonanza triggered by the Acapulco-Manila galleon trade? This is a plausible scenario. Trade advantages gained by Ming China through the Acapulco-Manila galleon trade route were unprecedented.[117] Historian Henry Kamen summarizes these as follows:

With or without controls, the Manila trade was in its day "probably the most lucrative branch of international trade with the Orient." The cargo of silk in the Manila galleon was usually estimated as wroth between two and three million pesos on each shipment. The silver ship from Acapulco brought in return about two million pesos in an average year. The consequence of this inflow of Mexican silver was that during the first half of the seventeenth century Spanish coins became the effective international currency of Southeast Asia.[118]

No incentives for capitalist silver-mining businesses to flourish.

Southern France: Lands of 'Ferocious' Feudal Lords

Mountain ranges in southern France experienced a significant mining boom in the late twelfth through thirteenth century.[119] Especially in the Cévennes Mountains, running southwards from central France to the Languedoc region, mining works proliferated during the twelfth and thirteenth centuries. Mining works extended into the Spanish frontier or the Languedoc/Roussillon region, as well as the Hérault department and the Rhône-Alps.[120] The most intense activity took place in the town of Saint-Laurent-le-Minier. The town belongs to the mining district of Hièrle in Mont Lozère, the highest mountain of the Cévennes, where geology confirms the occurrence of copper-based silver deposits.[121]

Mining works southwest of Saint-Laurent-le-Minier, in operation since A.D. 1140, consisted of networks of underground tunnels extending for approximately 2.5 kilometers.[122] In A.D. 1164, powerful local lords heavily contested ownership of mines. Ermengarde, Viscount of Narbonne, and Raymond Trencavel, Viscount of Béziers, no doubt thought that mines were an asset for their ambitions of coining and minting money. This was a time when the hierarchical society characteristic of southern France was 'undergoing transformation,' as Marc Bloch described many decades ago.[123] Seigneurial custom, dictating the pace of relations between a lord and his men, refused to go away with the changes in land tenures and demesnes that took place over the twelfth and thirteenth centuries. Private holdings emerged, allodial plots of land appeared in many provinces, but seigneurial regime became 'more firmly and more widely entrenched than ever.'[124]

Thus, the *argentiers* that invested in the mines of Saint-Laurent-le-Minier unfortunately encountered 'rapacious feudal lords'[125] unwilling to relinquish seigneurial power over mines. The evidence comes from the Chart of Hièrle (A.D. 1227). In the thirteenth century, the lands of Hièrle belonged to the seigneurial domains of the Count of Toulouse, an administrative district of medieval Languedoc. Mines became exploitations of silver-bearing copper ores.[126] The Chart was granted by the Lord of Sauve, Pierre Bermont, a relative of the Count of Toulouse, and confirmed by Pierre's brother Trancafers and his *bayle* or bailiff, Pierre de Lèques.[127] The articles of the Chart reveal that mining achieved a level of sophistication comparable to other mining sites. Once miners spotted a vein, they sank prospection shafts for estimating profitability of mining works. The Chart stipulated that new mining claims had to build three shafts, one for prospection purposes and two for ore-extraction purposes until one shaft proves profitable, separated by five fathoms. A shaft or gallery that reached ten to twelve fathoms and showed no sign of production had to be denounced to the church or the owners of the mining claim. A mining concession was declared vacant if it showed no sign of improvement after one month, but the owner of a mining claim had fourteen days for reimbursing mining expenses.

Argentiers enjoyed freedom for exploiting silver and copper mines in Hièrle, and were exempted from paying the *taillage* and servicing 'forced loans' to the lord. The Chart recognized the principle of hereditability of mining claims in case of sudden death of the claim holder, but only if the 'deceased has parents, children, or legitimate heirs.'[128] *Argentiers* also enjoyed the right to settle among themselves mining disputes, except when a case has already been brought to the lord's court.

The Chart confirms that *argentiers* and their mining businesses were not outside the seigneurial orbit of power. The mining industry never seized administration of mining affairs from the Lord of Sauve. The lord's bailiff retained jurisdiction over matters pertaining to mining works as well as criminal law. The bailiff could bring a case against an *argentier* to the lord's court, in which case the *argentier* had the right to pay a bond guaranteeing his presence in the lord's court. His duties included estimating ore prospects when new shafts were opened near operating shafts. He also disposed of mining tools and equipment once mining property was seized. His responsibilities included punishing miners for abandoning mining sites and concealing discoveries of new veins.

It is still unclear if a bailiff exercised accounting tasks on behalf of the Lord of Anduze. One thing is clear: the bailiff represents a lord's coercive power. He was not like the *magister montium* of the Carpathians or the *gastaldione* of Trento. A lord's bailiff in Languedoc rarely reached the status of a professional judge. 'In his personal status,' stated Bloch, 'there was nothing to elevate him above those he governed.'[129] Le Roy Ladurie describes a *bayle* or bailiff as a 'simple steward' in the fourteenth century.[130] Nonetheless, a bailiff 'enjoyed the prestige which is always inseparable from the right to command.'[131] His role was that of a seigneurial sergeant, who could achieve knighthood status, but for the most part he belonged to a small world 'held together by the operation of the hereditary principle.'[132]

Mining works that proliferated in neighboring lands enjoyed the same fate. Exploitation rights for Ceilhes-et-Rocozels were monopolized by the Rocozels family by A.D. 1221. Silver and copper were extracted at Bouche-Payrol by the Cistercian Order of Sylvanès in Aveyron until A.D. 1250, and even afterwards, when in A.D. 1311 a royal representative of the French King Philip the Fair (A.D. 1268–1314) made an agreement with the Cistercian Order regarding mine revenues.[133] The Bishop of Vivarais administered the L'Argentière mines in A.D. 1146 and 1177. By A.D. 1208, a law was written regarding supervision of mining works in L'Argentière.[134] Ecclesiastical lords were also administrators of mining works in Melle in Deux-Sèvres, Brioude in Chazelle in Haute-Loire, Brionnais in Saône-et-Loire,[135] and Puy-Dabert in Charenton.[136] The mines of Brandes were worked on behalf of the lords of Dauphiné Viennois.[137]

Mining was also a seigneurial affair further to the west, in the works that proliferated in the northern slopes of the Pyrénées. Here, the mines of Argentera and Bielsa originated in *fueros* or population charts granted by the Crown of Aragon. In A.D. 1191, King Alfonso II (r. A.D. 1157–1196), ruler of Aragon, granted a *fuero* to fourteen miners of Bielsa and authorized them to build a castle and *villa y molinos*.[138] King Peter III of Aragon (A.D. 1239–1295) confirmed this privilege in A.D. 1277, and although the document emphasized the iron mines, there is mention of lead and silver in the region.[139] Silver mines in Benasque Valley in Huesca were exploited by Arnaldo de Benasque, after King Alfonso II granted him feudal grants in A.D. 1182. Little is known about this exploitation; only the text of the grant survived.[140]

Geography favored the strengthening of seigneurial power and worked against any capitalist development of mining. Changes in agrarian services in demesnes made lords increasingly dependent upon towns and cities for craft work.[141] The urban and demographic explosion that the region experienced up to the mid-fourteenth century had a lot to do with this process.[142] In Languedoc, there were the big centers of Toulouse, Carcassonne, Limoux, Béziers, and Narbonne and seventy-one small towns. In Provence, there were seven big cities and sixty-five *bourgs* by the end of the thirteenth century. These towns absorbed a large portion of the peasant labor, creating overlapping property arrangements and impinging upon rents and tithes. 'Five hundred *bastides* were founded in southern France between the early thirteenth century and the beginning of the Hundred Years War.'[143] Lords responded by strengthening seigneurial justice, a trend that continued after the crisis of A.D. 1348 when lords became 'legally empowered to take possession of uncultivated estates' in many provinces.[144] Justice remained seigneurial justice.

The most powerful symbol of the evolution of seigneurial power became the castle. Only prosperous lords enjoyed the conditions for acquiring castles, since it meant having at their disposal resources for granting fiefs, rents, and agrarian revenues to loyal vassals of lesser-rank for the service of *custodia* or guard. 'To retain the fidelity of other lineages and of equestrian fighting men, the ruler had to share his power with them: that is, to distribute his castles.'[145] With these words, Bisson described the importance of castles in the territorial history of the Mediterranean. A castle was, in sum, the center place for seigneurial admin-istration.[146] Between A.D. 1300 and 1400, 'the science of rendering a fortified place impregnable was matured.'[147] Ruins of military castles in the landscape of the Cévennes allowed for no other conclusion. Unlike the medieval walled cities of Tuscany, castles of the Cévennes were 'carved out of bosses of rock on natural platforms above ravines.'[148] Access was possible only by 'goat-path or by steps cut in stone': these were, in the words of Gould, 'nests built by the robbers for themselves.'[149] On the western side, moving along the Pyrenées, a high number of well-distributed castles were the sign of the strategic considerations that motivated the feudal lords of the region, albeit commercial interests cannot be ruled out.[150]

Nature saved mountain people no toil either. Massif altitudes are covered with snow for five to eight months every year. Rivers and streams form torrents that drain into the Loire, Garonne, and Rhône river basins. They cut across five different types of terrain: table-lands or Grands Causses, in the border between Aveyron and Lozère; the alluvium-yielding river valleys of the lower reaches of the rivers Lot, Tarn, and Loire around Le Puy; volcanic summits affording high and plentiful summer pastures; basalt soils, located at the lower slopes, 'excellent medium for rye cultivation'; and crystalline soils, including granite 'ramparts' and schist areas, offering 'a mediocre context for settlement and agriculture.'[151]

The heaviest rainfall occurs on the southeastern side of the Massif. Floods became a quasi-permanent condition. Average annual rainfall varied between 510 to 1,020 cubic millimeters and can reach 2,000 cubic millimeters per year. Recently, a team of scientists from the Groupe Hydrologie measured rain intensity and pattern for a period of ten years. The team discovered that 'during phases of high activity, rainfall had the very specific shape of a narrow rainy strip a few kilometers wide, parallel to the topographic crest, but located distinctly in front of it at a distance of approximately twenty kilometers.'[152] Rainfall pattern contributed to the growth of good pastures for goats—a problem for agriculture. With time, 'goats and sheep nibble away what is left of the bushes and herbs, gradually the whole soil has vanished and the bare rock has appeared; the flanks of the mountains are furrowed with deep channels and gorges, which in a rainy season are filled with wild torrents that formerly did not exist.'[153]

This problem, coupled with urban and demographic explosion, created harvest failures and food shortages. The response strengthened seigneurial power: lords sponsored intensification of forest use. Feudal lords turned into 'enlightened' lords, as food historian Conran states. Roger-Bernard III (A.D. 1243–1302), the Count of Foix, granted all people 'complete and unimpeded freedom to use the woods according to their needs,' 'far more extensive than any liberties, usages and customs granted further north.'[154] Peasants were encouraged to hunt. Monsieur Lannoy, a fourteenth-century Superintendent of Water and Forests, proclaimed to the populations of Montaigne Noir south of the Massif: 'Go into the forests, cut the trees, assart (break ground ready for sowing), burn charcoal, break the soil to plough, make ash, plaster, lime, graze your sheep and cattle, hunt slags, partridges, rabbits, boars and other wild animals, fish . . . to your heart's content.'[155]

It is possible that labor shortages ensued at mining sites. We know that Languedoc suffered famines starting in A.D. 1302 until A.D. 1348. In Montagne Noir, peasants 'attempted to survive eating anything and everything.' By the late fourteenth century, 'the population of the villages were so reduced by plagues and famines that the wilderness started to encroach into the villages and settlements'; 'deer, wild boar and other predators were so abundant that whole crops could be ravaged between dawn and dusk and the villagers had to stand guard at night.'[156] As late as A.D. 1586, a witness of a famine in the Languedoc countryside stated that 'even in Grabian, considering all these weeks when the local people have been forced to survive the famine and driven to looking for the decaying remains of dead livestock and to eat them with bread made from ferns, and looking for the shriveling figs that had dried on the trees, which they ate, and thanks to them survived the winter.'[157] Chestnut came to 'occupy the landlord's thoughts,' and it became 'the big business of the mountains.'[158]

Feudal lords did the best they could in mountains that tended themselves to the proliferation of conflicting lordships. Seigneurial administration seemed a sensible response, but it was incapable of standardizing the laws and methods of capitalist mining. A lord's mining policy in southern France was subordinated to the fortunes and misfortunes of seigneurial coinage.[159] One cannot assume that mining *universitas* or corporations were not in the making, but one can speculate that the business structure of claim holders in southern France was still backwards, when compared to mining businesses of other European regions. It was not where silver-mining was destined to prevail.

Japan's Silver Bonanzas: Soon Ripe, Soon Rotten?

There is virtual silence in the available sources on silver mines in medieval Japan or for the period starting roughly in A.D. 1185 and ending before the sixteenth century.[160] Historians have examined Japan's *ritsuryō* code, laws adapted from Chinese institutions between the seventh and eighth centuries of the modern era, medieval census figures, and diverse civil and criminal laws that appeared between the ninth and thirteenth centuries, looking for clues about medieval mining.[161] Their findings are unequivocal: there were mining operations before the thirteenth century, but no systematization of mining laws before the fifteenth century.[162] This situation, coupled with the rigid land-control system endemic to northeast Asia, condemned mining to a feudal path, despite the bountiful geological endowments of the region.

The two main geological zones of Japan are the Southwest and the Northeast, divided by 'Fossa Magna,' the fault that cuts across central Honshu from the Japan Sea coast to the Pacific coast.[163] The Southwest, containing the oldest formations, was intensely exploited before the thirteenth century and after the second half of the sixteenth century. The mountains of Polo's *Zipango* yielded silver in A.D. 670, on the island of Tsūshima.[164] A mining history account commissioned by Japan's Bureau of Mining states:

In 699 A.D. the mint was established, at which copper and silver coins were made. The zeal of the Emperor for mining industry was so intense that he took the initiative for the issuing of the mining law which is known to us in the famous code, "Taihōrei" issued in A.D. 701.[165]

The Taihōrei was an imperial code whose basis were the laws of the Tang dynasty of China 'modified in accordance with the ancient customs and traditional usages of the Japanese nation.'[166] The code contained criminal and civil laws; laws related to mine organization and administration, crafts and trade; and laws concerning religion and worship rituals. It states that people were free to prospect for copper and iron 'everywhere throughout the country, provided that the government had not the same interests in those districts, but even in the latter cases, mining was allowed to tax payers.' Freedom was restricted in the case of discovery of gold or silver ores.

In this early period, mines were subjected to taxation, according to the *Chu-fan-chï* cited earlier. Chau Ju-Kua stated that 'gold and silver are used in paying taxes to the government; these metals are found in Yüé-chóu, in the east of this country, and in another island.'[167] These operations lasted for more than two centuries. In the same work one reads about silver mines in the times of Tokugawa Iyeyasu (A.D. 1543–1616), the last Shogun of Japan:

> The demise of Hideyoshi was followed by the Regency of Tokugawa Iyeyasu who adopted the proposal of Ōkubo Iwami-no-Kami concerning the mining industry. He opened for the first time gold and silver mines in the Idzu Province, at the same time having a control of the Ōmori silver mine (Iwami). In July of 1601 A.D., the gold and silver mine of Aikawa (Sado), which was afterwards known as the Sado mine, was discovered. This mine became conspicuous for the production of an enormous quantity of gold and silver, which was also brought under the control of Ōkubo together with the Tsurushi silver mine and the gold placer of Nishimi-kawa. Before long these mines were developed to such an extent that they yielded an immense output of these valuable ores. It was during this year that gold and silver currency was in abundance.[168]

Historians and geologists have provided evidence on additional mines exploited after the fifteenth century. The Ikuno mines in the Hida Mountains or Japanese Alps were opened before the sixteenth century but were fully developed only after the sixteenth century. Ikuno mines are a spectacular geological treat of groups of rich metalliferous veins, located in the Hyogo Prefecture, in the Kansai region, to the south of the island of Honshū.[169] In the mid-sixteenth

Fig. 5.1. Workers in a copper-smelting factory owned by the Sumitomo family. The image at left illustrates the separation of silver and lead. The image to the right shows the separation of copper and lead, also called liquation. The technique, which required alloying copper with lead, was introduced to Japan by 'a barbarian [foreign] merchant who came to Sakai in Izumi province,' according to the *Kodō Zuroku*. The technique was still used in the early nineteenth century at the main Sumimoto copper factory, triggering environmental and economic problems that the country was forced to acknowledge in the twentieth century. Courtesy of National Diet Library, Tokyo, Japan.

century, Ikuno and Iwami mines generated 'approximately 200,000 kilograms of silver or about one-third of all the silver then being produced in the world.'[170]

In the sixteenth century, exploitation of ore deposits was undertaken 'as a result of the zealous plans of the warring *daimyos* for increasing their own resources'; 'gold and silver, as military funds and as rewards for warriors, gradually demonstrated their use as a measure of high monetary value.'[171] This distribution system could only develop in a place where warriors were rarely unemployed. According to Kobata, mines of gold and silver became an important financial pillar of the Tokugawa Bakufu's hegemony. 'At the end of the sixteenth century,' Kobata states, 'the amount of silver transported from the Ikuno silver mine in Hyogo Prefecture as tribute to Hideyoshi came to 10,000 kilograms; the silver taken as tribute to Ieyasu near the beginning of the seventeenth century from only one shaft of the Iwami silver mine (Shimane Prefecture) amounted to 12,000 kilograms; and finally about the same time, the production of silver of the Sado mine can be presumed to have reached between 60,000 and 90,000 kilograms per year.'[172]

The sixteenth-century bonanza, albeit significant, was not representative of the medieval state of mining. Capital was a centuries-long problem.[173] In A.D. 815, a limitation was put upon the use of gold and silver for ornaments. Years later, the same prohibition was extended to 'the use of foil and powder of gold and silver throughout all ranks of people.'[174] By this time, the mine of Tsūshima descended approximately 122 meters below the surface. A miner's worst nightmare was about to occur. 'It happened that in the summer of 864 A.D. [the mine] was buried by the heavy rain water [and] the contrivance of the drainage involved heavy expenses which were not supportable by the miners so that the tax levied was to be appropriated for the purpose of drainage.'[175]

Silver-mining sites were located in mountainous regions that lack the elongated valleys found in the Alps or the Carpathians. This means that 'provisions for miners had to be transported from distant places, [and] at the outbreak of famines, it was really a serious question how to keep a vast number of working men from starvation. Because of the famines of A.D. 1642–1643, the Karuizawa and Sado mines were abandoned. The Ikuno mine, according to official sources, escaped a similar fate by 'working the bonanza of Sanzensanbyakumai lode.'[176] In addition, the Chinese land and tax system adopted during the *ritsuryō* period favored the development of land institutions dependent upon patronage. By the eleventh century, 'land area outside the state sector expanded in the form of private estates (*shōen*) held by aristocrat bureaucrats in Kyoto, and to a lesser extent, by Buddhist temples and monasteries.'[177] This created a geographically de-centralized system, with estates scattered everywhere and lacking a central demesne. Nominally, this system favored the development of capitalist agriculture since it led to a vigorous commercialization of agrarian surpluses at the domestic and regional levels. But some historians agree that the system culminated in the strengthening of feudal relations and institutions—even if by 'feudal' one cannot assume West European notions of feudalism.[178] Various claimants of land incomes mediated between absentee proprietors and real land cultivators. On top of these claimants, there was 'a land steward on the aristocratic estate,' one of the outcomes of the first Samurai government in the twelfth century.[179]

Development of extractive economies before the tenth century coincided with a pattern of climatic change in Japan.[180] At the peak of Japan's warm period, which some say started in the seventh century and ran to the tenth century, tillers reclaimed lands and increased agricultural output.[181] In the following centuries, however, droughts, crop failures, and food shortages became common, which, coupled with soil depletion, limited crop yield per hectare.[182]

Starting in the twelfth century new unclaimed land became scarce. Military men rose to power, and after setting their headquarters at Kamakura in eastern Japan, demanded increasing amounts of tribute in a system that had started to collapse in the early fourteenth century.[183] 'Smallpox and measles struck repeatedly decimating village populations,' and keeping demographic stability in check. Population stood between five and seven million by A.D. 1150. The paddy agrarian culture kept the *Anopheles* mosquito thriving, a factor that probably contributed to keep population in check. In addition, 'sedition, banditry, piracy, and tax evasion' became the maladies of a fragile social order, according to historian Totman. A military-dominated government was the only outcome in the thirteenth century. Such a system recognized three categories of land and producers. In the words of Totman:

> Those whose tribute payments went to provincial and central warehouses to support the monarch, his (or her) household, and the governing apparatus; those whose payments went (whether via government warehouse or directly) to aristocratic officialdom as office stipend or merit reward; and those whose payments went directly to aristocrats—and increasingly to Buddhist monasteries and professional soldiers—as hereditary household income.[184]

Freedom to mining industrialists possibly ensued but was geared toward feeding 'top aristocrats, monastery and nunnery residents, local grandees, military men, and their families, followers, and menial attendants.'[185]

Japan's thirteenth century was a period of military campaigns and centralization of power. When 'the Mongols began serious preparations for an attack on Japan,'[186] Japanese rulers prepared the country against a foreign invasion. This situation left no option but to monopolize administration of resources in the hands of family members. God's 'divine winds' saved Japan from a devastating Mongol attack, but could not defend mountain villages from the 'disorder and disintegration' that characterized Japanese society from A.D. 1150–1350.[187] A new class of warriors had emerged from the twelfth century onwards, 'knit together by personal relationships of fidelity and loyalty.'[188] The period prepared Japan for Shogunates exercising nodal control,[189] when new lineages of military men supplanted the old *ritsuryō* elite.

Ottoman Anatolia: The Failure of an 'Intensely Mineralized' Region

Leon Dominian, while a student in Constantinople, observed how Asia Minor 'lent itself admirably' to societies based on 'recognition of the economic value of metals.'[190] Civilizations from Asia Minor to Armenia took hold of 'an intensely mineralized area.' 'The first metal-using ancestors of the human race,' Dominian remarked, settled in the valleys between the Tigris and Euphrates rivers.[191] The reputation of Anatolia, 'the greatest supplier of silver-bearing ores,' was geologically justified.[192] The Pontic mountain range bordering the south shore of the Black Sea consists of granite and various metamorphic rocks yielding limestone that bear testimony to the volcanic processes that continue to influence mountain building. Ore veins, hosted by volcanic-sedimentary rocks, consist of quartz, sphalerite, galena, and diverse sulfide minerals.[193]

The Pontic Mountains contain numerous lodes mined since antiquity.[194] Greek historians wrote about the 'numerous caves hollowed out of the solid rock in which the miners dwelt' in the Pontus region.[195] The famous Sandaraca Works at Pimolis were described by Strabo: 'The Sandaracurgium is a mountain hollowed out by vast excavations made by the miners [. . .] the mining work is always carried on at the public charge'; 'and the slaves are convicts.'[196] Miners exploited rare minerals, cinnabar, and sulfurous and arsenic deposits, yielding raw materials for the fabrication of pigments, textile dyes, and inputs for alchemical and medicinal substances.[197] Realgar, red arsenic sulfate, was mined from 'the mother lodes of arsenic-laden minerals' in the Halys River Valley.[198] Medieval travelers also wrote about the bountiful mines of the Pontic. Marco Polo described 'a mine rich in silver' located in Bayburt Maden.[199] A Seljuķ mint was located here in A.D. 1289–1291. Bayburt Maden was 'in various Muslim hands' until the arrival of modern mining companies, which have exploited so far deposits at Balia-Karaïdin in the Broussa Vilayet in Bayburt Maden, and Bulgar Maden in the former Konya Vilayet.[200] Today, geologists estimate that the mountains contain 'over 400 massive deposits' of copper, lead, and zinc minerals, making the Pontic 'one of the most important metallogenic provinces of the world.'[201]

Anatolia's second mining region was formed by the Taurus Mountains. The mountains form 'the western extension of the Himalayas.'[202] The range extends east-west, in the form of an inverted curve penetrating the Anatolian Plateau. The Taurus' heights exceed 2,000 meters, with exceptional peaks southeast of Lake Van that reach an astonishing 4,000 meters. Bolkardağ was the mining district of the middle Taurus, stretching east-west for twenty-five kilometers along the southern slopes of the range. The mines were located at the lowest elevations of the mountains, ranging from 1,950 meters to 3,000 meters. The region is 'deeply cut by several rivers, it is highly forested with pine trees' and 'attests to the availability of wood resources for mining and smelting operations.'[203] Turkish archeologist Yener describes Bolkardağ's mining landscape as follows:

> The valley of the mines is 25 kilometers long, about 40 kilometers from the strategic Cilician Gates, and adjacent to the major artery through the mountains from central Anatolia to the Mediterranean Sea. These are very important passes and countless historical documents note the traffic in trade through the Gates. Bolkardağ [. . .] [is] the source of some of the richest argentiferous lead ore deposits in the Near East and geologists in Turkey have reported ancient metalworking there for over a century.[204]

Recent archeological research has uncovered approximately eight hundred mining sites dating from the early Ottoman period.[205] Mines consisted of large caves of astonishing dimensions: twenty meters wide, fifteen meters high, and as much as four kilometers long.[206]

Another mining district was located in the eastern side of the Taurus, formed by the Kebban Maden Mountains. The mountains form a short range between the Euphrates River and the Kharput Valley. They form a mosaic of 'bare surfaces of grey,' the result of rocks formed by compact limestone, and argillaceous with chloritic slates.[207] Kebban Maden mines enjoyed a privileged geographic location, nested in the deep valley that cuts through the range and runs northwards for approximately thirteen kilometers along the Euphrates.

Armenian geologist Kharajian decades ago found 'countless pieces of evidence' of mining in the region: 'The surface of hills as well as here and there on the opposite side of the Euphrates are covered with innumerable heaps formed in attempts to open mines which have rarely been pushed more than two or three feet in the ground.'[208] He noticed small strings and lumps of galena in shafts driven through shale and limestone, remaining from nineteenth century mining works. Lower mines showed plentiful portions of 'nearly pure argentiferous sulphuret of lead, but it nowhere had the appearance of occurring in veins.'[209] In the upper mines, 'a sort of gossan mingled with threads of gypsum is excavated as ore'; the ore contained a maximum of 1½ ounces of silver in one hundred English pounds.[210] This side of Anatolia was under the jurisdiction of the Sulka-dar governorship. The governor had to keep Taurus mountain passes free of trouble. Taurus mountain geography, however, preferred to submit to instability rather than Ottoman wishes.

It is possible that miners exploited other deposits south of Armenia's Elburz (or Alborz) Mountains. This area coincides with the Upper Euphrates and the highlands of Ararat, Armenia's sacred mountain. It is a 'tableland buttressed by mountain ranges.'[211] Erzrum, or Arzan-al-Rum, or Erzerom, was the most important city, 'where the great caravans between Persia and Turkey recruited their stores.'[212] The city was best known for the 'severity of its winter'; thus, it gained the epithet 'the Siberia of the Ottomans.'[213] The Euphrates River makes the city a 'sort of peninsula,' according to Odoric of Pordenone (A.D. 1286–1331), a Christian European friar who spent three decades trying, to no avail, to convert Asia rulers to Christianity.[214] Limestone of different geological periods forms the basis of the surface. A more recent limestone, found in subordinate mountains interbedded with shales, is of 'softer features.'[215] The chalk of this limestone whitens the waters of Lake Van, south of Erzrum. Here, gold and copper ancient mines of Alaverdi-Kirovokan in Alaverdi district were exploited in 4,500 B.C.

The Shamlugh open pit belongs to this mining district and continues to be worked today. In the same district, the Akhtala deposit contains polymetallic and steeply dipping veins, hosted by magmatic formations that reach a breadth of 3.5 kilometers.[216] The Ottomans here exploited lead minerals, but nothing further is known about possible works anteceding those of the Ottomans. Gold and copper deposits in Kapan, southeast Armenia, are hosted by a 6,500-meter-thick pile of varied volcanic rocks.[217] In the nineteenth century, miners dug these volcanic rocks, exploiting copper deposits. Today, only the polymetallic Shahumyan de-posit is of much profit to the mining industry. It is possible that Ottoman miners exploited the Kapan deposit, but the available evidence is inconclusive. Friar Odoric noticed 'copper and crystal' mines in Ziganah, located between Trebi-zond and Erzrum, which gave the name to the pass known as Ziganah Dagh or the pass of the Pontic.[218] Nothing further is known about the mines. The fact that Odoric seemed to have 'a gullible ear for wild stories' leaves us with more questions than answers.[219]

An Implacable Geography

Anatolia belongs to the semi-arid zone that stretches from the Nile as far as the Maghreb to the Oxus River. The area, as Hodgson remarked, was once good for farming, but 'human species proved a devastatingly destructive phenomenon' here. Ottoman agrarian land patches depended upon 'gathering water' and on 'continuity of well-balanced human initiative.'[220] In the lands of today's Iraq, from the end of Sâsânian times, 'salinization and silting, deforestation and erosion, as well as shifts in land inclination (resulting in smaller areas of natural irrigation), possibly some marginal changes in rain levels at headwaters,' reduced overall agrarian productivity.[221]

Anatolia's societies turned to herding economies, responding to the general agricultural decline of this vast territory. 'Semi-nomadic forms of production' were the norm.[222] Sheep, goat, and camel herding became the dominant silvo-pastoralist activities in the Pontic.[223] Goats 'proved able to find forage in the most difficult conditions, but they found it by destroying all small plants that might have grown larger, notably the shoots of trees.'[224] The breeding of the Anatolian black goat gained preeminence very early, as indicated by prehistoric paintings of goats in caves in Kürtün and Suğla Göl.[225] Today, the black goat continues to be the basis of livestock production in the Taurus. The goat is 'resistant to ailments, not highly selective in terms of food, and has an ability to climb that allows it to reach practically all available grazing land.'[226]

Herding economies flourished with migration of diverse populations from Asia. The Yoruks or Yûrûks, a tribe that migrated from Central Asia, reintroduced camel husbandry in tenth-century Taurus. Tribesmen were masters of Tûlû camel breeding. In the survey by Wilson, one reads:

> The Armenians of the Bozûk, as the country round Yûzgat is called, are great camel breeders, and they and the Turkomans breed the fine Tûlû camels which are so much admired by the passing traveler, on the quays at Smyrna. The Tûlû is a cross between a Bactrian, two-humped, father, and a Syrian mother; he has one hump, like his mother, but in other respects, especially the fine head and abundant beard, follows his father. The Tûlû is invaluable in Anatolia as he works in mud and snow, which would soon kill the Syrian camel; he cannot, however, stand great heat, and

in the summer he is taken off to the plateau, and is replaced on the coast by the Syrian camel. The Armenians often make long journeys to Turkestân or Tiflis in search of good Bactrian stock; and in the breeding season the males are sent round from village to village, as stallions are in this country.[227]

The advantages brought by the use of the camel as a beast of burden did not go unnoticed by European travelers.[228] In the eastern side of Anatolia, the camel did not totally replace the horse, long-lasting evidence of Islam's Arabization of mountain cultures centuries earlier. The horse gained preeminence in the eastern side from Mesopotamia to Kurdistan. In the tenth century, if the account of a medieval Persian historian is accurate, there were between Lake Aral and Khorāsān three hundred thousand villages each capable of providing a horse and a rider.[229] There, mountain cultures had gradually changed from pastoralism to *race mobile et belliqueuse.*[230]

The most important Taurus feature was the Cilician Gates or Gülek Bogazi, a corridor that afforded communication between Anatolia and Syria since Byzantine times. Mamluk, Arab, and Italian merchants trading spices, dyes, and silk cloth crossed the Gate and its surrounding mines in a route that ran from Ere li across the middle Taurus, leading to cities beyond the Cilician plain.[231] A nineteenth-century geographer summarized the strategic significance of this trade route in the following:

The great highway between the east and the west passed through Taurus [. . .] From Taurus the road to the Anatolian plateau passes by an easy ascent to Sarishek Khan, on a branch of the Cydnus, where it is joined by a road from Adana constructed by Ibrahim Pacha. At Sarishek Khan the road enters a narrow gorge [. . .] After about five miles the road passes through the Cilician Gates, a narrow opening of 25 feet [approximately eight meters], where the stream rushes between perpendicular walls of rock, which break back in a succession of precipitous cliffs to the mountains on either side [. . .] At this place, the road again divides, one branch running up a narrow rocky valley to Pachamakji and Kiz, or Kilisseh Hissar to Nigdeh; the other by an easier route to Eregli [Ereğli, Konya]. All these roads were probably used at a remote period; the first is the direct road from the plain to Pteria (Boghaz Keui) by Mazaca (Kaisarîeh), and passes near the Bereketli Maden mines; the second, on which numerous rock-cuttings show the line of the ancient road, was the great thoroughfare, of which we have details in the Jerusalem and other itineraries, which connected Tarsus with Ancyra (Angora) and Constantinople; whilst the third, over which Ibrahim Pacha took his guns when he invaded Anatolia, passed

near the mines of Bûlghar Maden to Eregli, and thence continued onwards by
Konieh to Ladik, where it joined the great highway from Ephesus.[232]

By the fourteenth century, the Loulon fortress, near Ulukisla, still stood in the
doors of the Cilician Gate surrounded by a network of mine galleries, according
to a Persian traveler.[233] The heavy international traffic that crossed the middle
and eastern Taurus favored Ottoman trade but not silver-mining production.[234]
Profitable exploitation of the Bolkardağ mines depended upon Ottoman's military defense of borderlands, a factor that did not benefit the mining industry,
as will be seen later.[235] Life was hard in the Taurus. The eastern coastal strip of
the range offered only a narrow stretch of alluvial land, inviting a precarious
habitation conditioned to the 'danger from malaria.'[236] In this part of the range,
the Adana Valley offers a large plain of arable land. Here lies the Cilician plain,
formed by deposits from the Saros and Pyramos rivers. Malaria, however, kept
the populations of all western coastal plains under check. Historian John Mc-
Neill blamed malaria for the deserts into which the plains, 'so populated and
prosperous in the first century A.D. and again after 1945,' were transformed in
'intervening centuries.'[237] It was not until the last decades of the nineteenth
century that malaria rapidly declined. The general pattern of previous centuries
was that 'the most insalubrious regions' of the eastern Taurus were those which
'in ancient times gained a prominent place in history,' as Italian geographer Bodio
put it. He continued: 'localities flourishing for several centuries before the Christian era are now changed into pestilential and almost deserted countries.'[238]

The Ottoman mining industry relied upon a labor quota system, something difficult to envision today, but prevalent seven centuries ago in Asian raw-material
economies. Very little is known about this labor regime prior to the fifteenth century. It is possible that it evolved into something similar to a caste, whereby the
job of a miner passed from father to son, as part of a forced agreement, at least
in the opinion of Turkish sociologist Karpat.[239] Slaves were out of the question,
considering that neither Islam nor the Ottoman state relied upon 'a slave system of
production,' with the exception of large agricultural estates. There is no reliable data
on slave prices from medieval Anatolia or central Asia. It is possible that prices of
slaves in Egypt applied to Ottoman Anatolia, as Bernard Lewis delineates:

> Slave girls averaged twenty dinars (gold pieces), corresponding, at the rate of gold
> to silver current at that time, to 266 dirhams (silver pieces) [. . .] Black slaves seem

to have cost from two to three hundred dirhams; black eunuchs, at least two or three times as much. Female black slaves were sold at five hundred dirhams or so [. . .] White slaves, mainly for military purposes, were more expensive.[240]

Was scarcity of labor the independent variable? Most certainly, forced labor became cost-effective, and good for incomes of owners of mining shares, but bad for the development of a capitalist mining business. The tradition of forced labor in mining was finally abolished after the War of Liberation of A.D. 1921.[241] Wilson, who completed a military survey of Asia Minor commissioned by the Queen of England, noted the following about forced labor: 'The isolated villages are generally found near the mines, and it seems clear that in these cases the villagers were allowed to retain their language and religion on condition that they worked the mines for the Turks.'[242]

Floods and droughts repeatedly drove thousands out of their homes. In A.D. 1302, the flood of the Sangarius River carried an enormous volume of water and debris runoff 'that covered much of the substantial plain of the Ak Ova.' The river carried 'water, stones and silt for a month, sufficient for bringing the Sangarius and the Melas/Çark Su rivers into each other's beds.' Rivers today are 'three kilometers apart near Lake Sabanca and meet only after meandering for fifty kilometers northwards.'[243] Anatolia is a steppe, which meant that harvest success was almost entirely dependent upon rainfall. Anatolian rivers carry sufficient water, but only on a seasonal basis.[244] Thus, droughts were not uncommon. The Great Drought that started in A.D. 1591 and ended four years later was 'the longest for the past six centuries and by far the worst in the empire's history,' in the words of historian Sam White.[245] The extreme weather created by the Little Ice Age prolonged the crisis by bringing cold and snowy winters and ongoing 'El Niño episodes.' The climatic phenomenon affected thousands of villagers throughout Anatolia and the Mediterranean. 'Villagers from across Anatolia, Greater Syria, and the Balkans fled in search of food and safety; hundreds of thousands or perhaps millions of them perished of exposure, starvation, and disease.'[246] 'Inexorable want and famine invaded the land, followed by banditry, flight, and epidemics,' White states. 'The worst mortality came from animal diseases that preyed upon the exposed and starving herds.'[247]

Problems in agriculture came at unfortunate times. The heavy toll imposed upon Anatolia's lands by stock-herding economies was a bad omen. Rebellions and political crisis exploded everywhere in the last decade of the sixteenth century. The uncontrollable events, remarked historian Hess, 'excited the ignorant into believing that the Muslim year 1000 (A.D. 1591–92) would bring the end of the world.'[248]

In addition, a series of volcanoes along meridional lines in the eastern boundaries of the Ottoman state seriously challenged long-term peaceful habitation. Volcanic activity over time has led to a 'damming up of basins,' as in Lake Van.[249] The earthquake belt of the northeast Iranian plateau, with active reverse faults, made the area susceptible to earthquakes since at least the seventh century of the Common Era.[250] 'Not long ago,' wrote Ibn al-'Amid in A.D. 961, 'an earthquake in Ruyan caused two mountains to collide and tumble down; the debris of the collision blocked the course of the rivers that ran between, and the waters of the rivers receded and formed a lake.'[251] He was talking about the earthquake that shook the mountains northwest of Teheran in A.D. 958 'And to the east of the Tabas-e-Gilaki [now Tabas-e-Golshan], there is a strong mountain!' lamented Nasser Khosrau in A.D. 1052, distressed by the idea of more devastation to come from the mountain. He continued: 'Tun [Ferdows] used to be a large town, but when I visited it was in ruins.'[252] 'Four earthquakes devastated the Teheran region in a four-century period from 743 to 1117.'[253] In the summer of A.D. 1238, an earthquake damaged Gonabad and destroyed the Seljuk mosque of Qa'en. The natural dam, along with the ancient lake of the Dragon Valley, was destroyed by an earthquake that caused the 'rupture of the dam, the collapse of the blocks, and a huge longitudinal fissure running along the dam.'[254]

Silver mining enterprises found in Anatolia very little room for capitalist growth in the period under study in this book. Constant threats of military invasions in the east by the rulers of the Timurid Empire, and the Balkan and Mediterranean military campaigns, offered few incentives for innovating and investing in Anatolia's underground wealth. The Ottoman state was forced to rely upon silver mines in conquered Balkan territories.

The East of the Caucasus: Lands of Old 'Prominent Mines'

Silver mining flourished in the Persian Province of Khorāsān, the Samanid region of Transoxiana, and the Hindu Kush.[255] These are the lands of the most spectacular mountain heights, where mountains 'piled up one behind another' and 'mountain development assumes its grandest forms.'[256] Mountains here show incredible variation and deformation, formed by transcurrent movements and various types of folding.[257]

Khorāsān was the periphery of Persia beyond the Oxus River, north of the Hindu Kush Mountains. It was part of the Central Asian silk trade routes, 'hospitable to merchants' in the words of Janet Abu-Lughod.[258] To Persian geographer Ibn Ḥawqal (d. 380 A.H.), Khorāsān was part of Transoxiana or Maweralnahar, populated by 'people of probity and virtue, averse from evil, and fond of peace.'[259] The place was also a point of pilgrimage prior to the devastating intrusion of the Mongols. 'Find me a man who is pious and virtuous and I shall send him to Transoxiana to summon people to embrace Islam'—such were the words of the Governor of Khurāsān al-Ashras.[260]

Khorāsān contained the city of Núkân, part of Tûs or today's Tabaran. It was 'the Urva of the Vendidad, the eighth of the sixteen lands created by Ahura Mazda.'[261] Tûs was a vast region between the Binalud and Hezar Masjed mountains in the north. It included Taberan, Nogjan or Noqan, Radkan, and Torqbaz. Núkân, or Noghān was an extensive area to the east of Meshed, or today's Mashhad, 'stretching from near the walls of the modern city to the villages of Husaynāban and Mihrābad.'[262] Mining sites were most likely located in the mountain slopes of Mashhad, bordering the southern shores of the Caspian Sea, and running west and southwards into Herat, although the exact location is impossible to identify.[263]

Mining survived up to the eleventh century in certain areas north of the Atrek River.[264] A vast mining district probably extended into the Binalud Mountains bordering the Caspian Sea, and continued into the mountains south of the Atrek River in northeast Iran, up to the Elburz Mountains. The latter is a range stretching five hundred kilometers and dividing 'the Persian central plateau from the Caspian depression' and linking the Caucasus range with the Paropamisus in north Afghanistan.[265] Transoxiana mines, according to Ḥawqal, 'yield silver, and tin or lead abundantly; and they are better than the other mines, except those at Penjhir; but Maweralnahr affords the best copper and quicksilver, and other similar productions of mines; and the mines of sal ammoniac (used in tinning or soldering) in all Khorāsān are there.'[266]

The most 'prominent mines' of the Caucasus were those of Ghorband and Pandjhīr in the Bâmiyân Valley and Djariyana in the Hindu Kush of Afghanistan. The Bâmiyân area, 'exceptional site with wonderful colors,' was 'well known in ancient times as a restful and pilgrimage destination among the desert mountains.' This was the city of the giant Buddha statues, destroyed in A.D. 2001 by Taliban forces, 'but their cliffs, cross-hatched by huge faults, are still visible.'[267] Wounds inflicted by war, deeply seated in the landscape! The Band-e-Amir lakes, southwest of the Hindu Kush, a sacred place of Shiite Muslims, today offers a network of oases in the form of terraces.[268] The lakes, located in the Hazaratjat Massif at an elevation of 5,143 meters, run in an east-west orientation in the Hindu Kush. Today, nomad tribes of Taraki, Amarkhil, and Nurzaï share the grazing lands of Band-e-Amir. Kuchi nomad tribes travel to the area from Jalalabad from the end of May to the end of September. Shepherds still 'conduct their flocks to the water,' and 'waterfalls were exploited for their hydraulic energy until recently.'[269]

Pandjhīr also in Afghanistan lived its mining splendor in the ninth and tenth centuries. Known to the Arabs as Banjahîr or 'Five Hills,' the mine's output was thirty tons of silver during the silver rush, or 'twenty-five times as much as world silver production' in A.D. 1500, according to one account.[270] Sassanid rulers established a mint in the city, at the time when '10,000 miners inhabited the city,' according to Ibn Ḥawqal.[271] Drawing upon numismatic evidence, William Forslund believes that the silver-mining rush in Pandjhīr attracted Vikings from northern Europe, who reached Afghanistan through the Volga River.[272] They traded swords, furs, and slaves for silver. Vikings traveled through Caspian and Black Sea ports, using frequented routes of the Middle Ages that connected Baltic cities to the innermost provinces of China and India.[273] Gmelin, when he visited the Pandjhīr mine ruins in the early eighteenth century, noted:

> The ancients excavated the passages underground with incredible pains, and in numerous instances lost their lives by "caves" [. . .] the underground passages were so narrow that the workmen must have crawled and wriggled through them like worms, in order to get at the quartz, from which they picked the gold with the sharpened fangs of boars.[274]

These vast lands lacked any type of political centralization at the time of the rise of the Turkish dynasty founder of the Ottoman state. The Karakhanids, 'a people of Karluc Turkic stock who converted to Islam in the tenth century,' ruled over the mining district south of the Caspian Sea.[275] Khorāsān and Tûs were ruled by a Seljuḳ Sultan, Alp Arslan, from 455 A.H./ A.D. 1063 to 465 A.H. /A.D. 1073.[276] The decision to 'find a dwelling-place in Asia Minor'[277] by the Seljuk Turks left them with poor choices, from an industrialization perspective: to wage war, annex vassal states, sojourn for a while in conquered lands, and move forward to the west in successive military campaigns. It was from there that the Seljuk took over Anatolia and the greater part of former Byzantine and Armenian lands.

The Ghorband and Pandjhīr mines declined by the eleventh century.[278] Transoxiana and Hindu Kush mines experienced a crisis of production before the Seljuks made their way to these lands. The scanty evidence available today indicates that miners failed to reach deep ores. Shafts discovered in Pandjhīr decades ago were too shallow, compared to shafts in European mountains. Inefficient utilization of shafts did not go unnoticed by contemporaries. Syrian geographer Abu'l-Fidā (b. 672 A.H. / A.D. 1273) stated that 'more often, however, in underground mining, miners preferred to dig horizontal adits into the slopes of a mountain and follow the veins, rather than to sink shafts.' His description is worth quoting in full:

> The people of Pandhjīr made the mountain and the market-place like a sieve because of the many pits. They only follow veins leading to silver, and if they find a vein they dig continuously until they reach silver. A man may spend huge sums of money in digging, and he may find silver to such an extent that he and his descendant become rich, or his work may fail because he is overpowered by water or for other reasons. A man may pick a vein, and it is possible that another man picks the same vein in another position. Both start digging. The custom is that the miner who arrives first and intercepts the passage of the other miner wins the vein and its results. Because of this competition, they execute a work that devils cannot achieve [. . .] When one arrives first, the expenses of the other are wasted. If they arrive together, they share the vein and then they continue digging as long as the lamps are burning. If the lamps are extinguished and cannot be relit, they stop their progress because anyone who reaches that position would die immediately. [In this business] you will see that a man starts his day owning one million, and by nightfall he owns nothing. Or he may start poor in the morning, and by evening he becomes the owner of uncountable wealth.[279]

Much is yet to be discovered in the mountains east of the Caucasus. Researchers of the Moscow Institute for Oriental Studies have found here challenges that abound elsewhere, as the case of numismatist Nastich illustrates.[280] Mining towns described by Friar Odoric, Marco Polo, and numerous medieval travelers have disappeared, as Guy Le Strange warned some time ago.[281] Medieval castles built by Ghûrid rulers, governing the lands between Herât and Bâmiyân from the twelfth century up to the Mongol invasions, did not survive the centuries of military invasions and war that ensued.

The Rest of the Known World

Known to the Chinese chroniclers as *Hin-du-sz*, Indian mines figure in some medieval literary accounts.[282] An envoy sent by Chinghiz Khân in A.D. 1222, described 'rich silver mines' located in northwest India.[283] After his return from the 'West,' the envoy, Wu-ku-sun Chung tuan, stated about the lands of Hindustan:

> The people have thick beards, the hair of which is entangled like sheep's wool, and of different color, black, or yellow in different shades. Their faces are almost entirely covered by hair; and only the nose and their eyes can be seen. All their customs are very strange.' The *Mu-su-lu-man Hui-ho* (Mussulman) are very blood-thirsty and greedy. They tear flesh with the fingers and swallow it [. . .] There are further the Hui-ho of Yin-du (Hindustan), who are black and of good character [. . .] The people are all living in cities, there are no villages. The roofs of their houses are covered with clay. All the woodwork in the houses is carved. They use white glass for their windows and for vessels. The country is very rich in silver, pearls, cotton, hemp, etc.[284]

Persian historian Ali Al-Mas'ūdī (A.D. 896–956) included 'gold and silver mines' in his description of 'the strength of the kingdom of Gudjarāt.'[285]

India offered no ideal condition for the development of capitalist silver-mining industries, despite the development of advanced metallurgy in pre-historic and modern times. India was the land of zinc and copper. In Zawar, Rajasthan, northeast India, zinc was the main mined metal. According to Paul Craddock, here stands the earliest dated zinc mine of the world, and the earliest Indian lead-zinc ore beneficiation plant.[286] The territory originally extended from the Indus to Bundelkhand in the east, before 'Muslim invasions forced the Rajput southwards and they took refuge in the wild tracts of Rajasthan.'[287] The famous zinc and tin deposits in Mochia Magra and Ballaria, rediscovered in the late fourteenth century, were worked until 'the great famine' of 1812–1813.[288] 'The mines,' stated English Colonel James Tod (A.D. 1782–1835), 'were very productive in former times, and yielded several *lacs*[289] to the princes of Méwar.' He added:

The rich tin mines of Jawara produced at open time a considerable proportion of silver. Those of copper are abundant, as is also iron in the now alienated domain on the Chumbul; but lead least of all.[290]

Nothing further is known about these operations, except that 'the riches of the mines of Jawura were expended to rebuild the temples and palaces levelled by Alla' in the fourteenth century.[291]

India has a large 'copper belt,' an eighty-kilometer-long mineralized zone 'with Khetri at the north end, at an altitude of 350 meters and higher,' in the words of Lynn Willies.[292] The ores are formed in rocks containing garnet, chlorite, and quartz. The most spectacular mining operations along the belt took place before the twelfth century and after the sixteenth century. Silver outputs, if any, came from this mineralized zone, but evidence of galena mining is inconclusive. Neither gold nor silver attracted the Portuguese to the Indian subcontinent; it was, rather, species of all kinds traded in the ports located in the coasts of Malabar, Concan, and Coromandel.[293] A King of Calicut confirmed this point, in a letter addressed to the King of Portugal:

> Vasco da Gama, a gentleman of your household, came to my country, whereat I was pleased. My country is rich in cinnamon, cloves, ginger, pepper, and precious stones. That which I ask of you in exchange is gold, silver, corals and scarlet cloth.[294]

However, India's mining exploits did not compete with the achievements of European mining regions. Mining in Zawar endured technical difficulties. Geologist Bagghi states that miners worked on 'hard siliceous quarzitic ore bodies, where drilling today calls for the use of tungsten carbide bits.'[295] Discovered shafts at Mochia Magra were oval and not larger than 1.5 meters by 1.2 meters. 'Much of the drivages, as visible in old workings in Zawar, were just wide enough to crawl through.'[296] Bagghi further states that gun powder was unknown—fire-setting was still the principal technique used for rock breakage.[297]

Medieval miners abandoned mines 'as soon as water level was reached'; as 'no mechanical pump had been invented,' there were only 'few water-fall driven machines.'[298] This was a world where Hindu workers' resistance against Islamic conquerors took the form of 'guarding jealously their secrets concerning mining and metallurgy,' according to Biswas. This hypothesis no doubt leaves much room for doubt. Biswas cites the words of an English captain in A.D. 1831, who commented on the condition of the lead mines of Ajmer in Rajasthan:

> The system of restricting communication to the tortuous course of the vein, precludes the practicability of removing water; in as much as shafts, galleries, adits, and the usual concomitants found in similar cases in Europe, if not quite unknown, are altogether neglected. . . . While we wonder at the simplicity, the leading characteristic of their operations, we are compelled to acknowledge our surprise, that the results are so favorable.[299]

Mining operations suffered the devastating impacts of a clash of civilizations à la Huntington early in the eleventh century. These lands were the setting for global encounters among Hindu, Muslim, Mongol, and Christian cultures long before the Portuguese empire took hold of the region.[300] Empires of Hindustan and Delhi used their resources to either fight off, or pay tribute to Mongols, and to the great Tamerlane of Samarkand, the warrior who sought to unify Central Asian states in the late fourteenth century. Their resources were exhausted in defending ever-changing borders. Neither the Mongols, nor the Seljuḳ Turks, nor later Tamerlane, engaged in naval warfare, of the type that the Portuguese, the Dutch, and the English perfected in the Indian Ocean and the Atlantic Ocean from the sixteenth century onward. Their battlefields were the mountains and valleys of the Caucasus, the Hindu Kush, and northern India. The technological innovations that revolutionized the art of war by taking battles to the seas were not there yet.[301]

The military campaigns of Tamerlane offer striking examples of the negative effects of wars on extractive economies.[302] He commanded a devastating army, according to Castilian ambassador Ruy González de Clavijo; soldiers covered 'about twenty-seven miles, from the Caucasus to the shoes of the Caspian' in one campaign.[303] The Castilian, a firsthand witness traveling with Tamerlane, stated that the warrior 'looked down, with longing eyes, on the fertile plains of India.'[304] The rest is history. He entered India through Kabul, after crossing the defiles of the Hindu Kush with 62,000 men in A.D. 1398.[305] India, ruled by Mahmud as 'a disorganized empire, consisting of a Moslem army, and various Rajput states,' was ripe for the invasion, according to the same ambassador.

Clashes among different civilizations meant that Hinduism and Islam coexisted in India 'under considerable strain,' in the words of Biswas. 'What happened to eleventh- and twelfth-century Spain did not take place in Sind,' states

Biswas. He continues: 'The Hindu India was denied of political independence as well as the beneficial influence of Islamic scholars of science, such as those who flourished in Cordova, Spain. [. . .] In brief, the characters of Muslim influence that came to India and went to Europe were entirely different.'[306] Besides, none of the dynasties of northern India, from the Khwarizmi, to the Mongols, the Seljuk Turks, and the Afghan dynasties and, later, the Delhi Sultanate, succeeded in reaching the shores of the Mediterranean. This is a point that is difficult to ignore. This would have put Zawar and India's mining regions in contact with most advanced mining regions of the thirteenth century. The arrival of European empires further pushed the mining industry into decline. Tomé Pires made no mention of silver mines in his *Suma Oriental* (A.D. 1512–1515), the first Portuguese account of the lands of the 'Orient.' Rather, Pires' copious notes on Rajasthan emphasized the land's 'foodstuffs' and 'fortresses and strongholds.'[307] Lands torn apart by successive wars built no incentives for private money to plow back into the subsoil.

Beyond India, silver was found in the kingdom of Pegú, according to Portuguese explorer Vasco da Gama (A.D. 1460–1524).[308] Henry Yule identified Pegú as a kingdom that existed 'in the Delta of the Irawai, to the city which was its capital,' roughly coinciding with Burma's capital city.[309] According to Da Gama's journal:

> Peguo is Christian and has a Christian king. The inhabitants are as white as we [the Portuguese] are. [. . .] The King possesses an island about four days' sail, with a good wind, from the mainland. [. . .] The silver to be obtained here for ten cruzados is worth fifteen at Calecut.[310]

But Da Gama was interested in pillaging Pegú and not in learning how to produce ores. He reported, nonetheless, that 'much silver' was found in Bengal or 'Bemguala,' a kingdom with a 'Moorish King.'[311] Silver was also found at 'Ataprobama,' 'the largest island in the world,' otherwise known as Sumatra.[312] But finding the exact location of sources of freshly mined ores continues to be a difficult endeavor. Geologists have not yet mapped galena deposits, allowing for the conclusion that native silver was enough for supplying industrial and monetary needs. Certainly, high quantities of silver money circulated in islands and the mainland beyond India. Numismatist Robert Wicks listed all coin discoveries in Indonesia of recent decades; the impressive list gives the reader the idea of the heavy traffic of coins in the region. These discoveries bring much happiness to numismatists—and headaches to mining historians. None of the coin findings allow one to conclude much about the abundance or scarcity of domestic silver mines. In Indonesia, the 'sandalwood flower' was a type of coin struck by the Mataram state in the ninth century.[313] Wicks defined the 'sandalwood flower' as specimens of gold, silver, and electrum, normally weighing 2.4 grams.[314] He states that, despite the strong monetary economy of Java, 'the sources of the gold and silver used in early Java remain enigmatic.'[315] He states that, 'the flow of precious metals in this period of Southeast Asian history is still very poorly understood and it is unclear whether Java produced gold and silver sufficient for its monetary needs, received from some subordinate rulers elsewhere in the archipelago, or had to import both gold and silver from outside the region.'[316]

Sub-Saharan Africa was the land of gold, where mining lived its *belle époque* before the thirteenth century, later revived in the nineteenth century.[317] Its prominent role as a world mining region came to an end in the ninth century A.D., coinciding with the decline of the Egypt-Syria gold trade that had fed Byzantium's minting factories. East African towns used locally minted coins in late eighth century A.D.[318] Arab geographer Al-Ya'qūbī (d. A.H. 284/A.D. 897), author of *Kitāb al-buldān* or *The Book of Countries*, called *Ifriqiya* 'the country of mines,' perhaps referring to gold mines.[319] The reputation of Africa's gold mines continued, as Portuguese colonization of western and eastern Africa expanded after Da Gama's voyages. The Portuguese and the Genoese before them, under the auspices of the Castilian crown, attempted to find the sub-Saharan sources of African gold to no avail, as the work of Marxist historian Pierre Vilar illustrates.[320] Any gold mines discovered after the fifteenth century in Africa's eastern side became part of Portugal's booty. 'The [Portuguese] king is very powerful, and the owner of the gold mines of Sofala, the richest in that part of the world,' stated an African ambassador in A.D. 1504.[321] Elsewhere, Africa furnished salt mines in Taghaza, Bilma, and copper mines in Dar Fertit in the Nile-Congo watershed, the Limpopo Valley of the Tsonga territory, south Zimbabwe, and the lower Congo, among others.[322]

Evidence of a commercially viable silver-mining industry in Africa is almost nonexistent, even when evidence of silver-bearing deposits in the Atlas Mountains is mounting.[323] Until future archeological and historical research brings to light information on the place and role of Africa in the global development of the silver-mining industry, we must rely upon competent sources that claim that there is still debate as to 'whether the lead ores of ancient Egypt have silver content high enough for successful ancient exploitation.'[324] Ogden states that 'more research on lead ores within Egypt is clearly needed before galena or lead sources can be identified.'[325] No rich argentiferous galena deposit was known, with the exception of ancient mining works on the coast of the Red Sea. In the early twentieth century, Egyptologist MacIver conducted archeological research on the territory known as Rhodesia, to find out the date of what was known as the Rhodesian or Niekerk ruins. The ruins of the citadel of Dhlo-Dhlo nested the archeological site, yielding relics of silver objects. Studying the relation between these objects and the nature of Rhodesian soil, Randall-MacIver stated:

> The occurrence of silver is interesting because it has been so rarely found on Rhodesian sites. That the medieval Kaffirs of the Monomotapan Empire knew of the existence of silver in their country is proved by the curious history of the Portuguese hunt after silver-mines from 1572 onwards though the seventeenth century. The reigning Monomotapa, or ruler of a dominion which, according to the Portuguese writers, extended when they first entered the country over the greater part of South-East Africa, ceded in the year 1607 "all the mines, silver and other metals in the whole of his empire" to the King of Portugal in return for the latter's promised aid against the Monomotapa's rebellious subjects. And for many years the Portuguese were occupied in a vain search for the silver mines which were supposed to be situated on the Zambesi in the neighborhood of Tete. The natives showed them specimens, but either did not know of mines or would not tell them where they were situated.[326]

By the sixteenth century, Monomotapa belonged to a gold belt in southeastern Africa under Portuguese influence that included Zambesi, Kilwa, Mombasa, and Mozambique. Most probably, the mines of the Kaffirs yielded only gold, which the Portuguese exported to Goa.[327] Nothing attracted Europe's silver-hungry empires to these lands.

6

Capitalist Mining in West European Development

MARXIST SCHOLARS ASSERT THAT mining was pre-capitalist before the sixteenth century. They write liberally about what they call the 'feudal utility' of silver mining. The essence of this idea is that mines were fiefs, exploited by independent miners and serfs who paid rent in money, ores, or kind. This circumstance, the argument goes, was possible because feudal lords held legal claims over the mines and thus had the capacity to coercively extract surplus. The study of mining statutes undertaken in this book demonstrates that the Marxists' interpretation is open to attack. Mining was ahead of its feudal times. Feudal lords painfully learned the most enduring lesson of the moment, that a legal title to ore-yielding land made no mine. Capital did. The industry organized productive capital in a dynamic, hierarchical structure rooted in private entrepreneurs' investments in mining claims. This was no peaceful development; after all, European mining regions were not immune to their times.

No 'slow and comparatively simple evolution' into capitalist mining enterprises was possible.[1] But once the conditions were ripe, associations of private producers took over: *silbrarii* in the Central Alps and Lombardy, *universitas* and *communitas foveae* in Tuscany and Sardinia, and *Gewerken* in the Carpathians. Ownership of mining shares meant control over production and hence alienation of feudal lords and separation of miners from mining's productive assets. The *silbrarii* came from the aristocracy of Trento and put their liquid into Wanga's flooded mines. The *colonii principalii* of the Carpathians were German and Saxon miners who decades earlier obtained privileges for colonizing Carpathian and Transylvanian mining mountains. The mining law of the

Bohemian Kingdom legitimized the economic privileges of the *colonii princi-palii* by recognizing second- and third-class tenants of mining rights. In Tuscany and Iglesias, *communitas foveae* was an advanced corporation composed of urban merchants and rural aristocrats, men who exercised political power.

Neither kings nor popes could sanction these corporations. The fate of a corporation depended upon law and profits. Membership was a voluntary matter, not determined by birth. Corporations required neither sponsorship nor patronage by secular feudal lords for legitimizing their mining interests. These characteristics make of the mining corporation a significant capitalist structure in the midst of a feudal world. Moreover, a corporation's gains were not monopolized by the aristocracy or a militant feudal class, contrary to claims by Brenner and other Marxists. If anything, mining corporations were instrumental in encouraging competition for mining claims within and among rich aristocrats and merchants in world mining regions.

Were lords the victims of geography? Between the eighth and eleventh centuries, their improving of lands depended upon military might, abundant unimproved lands, and dependent vassals. Under these conditions, contractual obligations between lords and vassals for improvement of lands strengthened the basis of the power lords possessed. Lords enjoyed the rent of land and extracted surplus from peasants and serfs who worked the land and depended upon lords for protection. But this scenario was changing, and so were the contractual relations of *libellus*, *enfiteusis*, *conductio*, *precaria*, *praestaria*, and *beneficium* that we associate today with feudalism.[2] Demographic stability of Europe meant more people, a sustained effort toward improvements of lands, and diffusion and adaptation of water-drainage machines and techniques, all at a high price to lords. New groups of peoples reclaiming lands from marshes and river valleys claimed usufruct rights for the new and improved lands. Their claims for new forms of rent of land meant that *feodum* was less of a tangible thing and more about specific relations pertaining to incessant land improvement in a changing social hierarchy. Private citizens organized in corporations and enjoying the capacity to invest money in the *argentifodina* of kings and lords claimed much more than usufruct rights of mines: they claimed and forced a change in feudal institutional and contractual arrangements governing mining.

The situation was not catastrophic to lords, at least not in the short run. The emergence of codified mining laws and contracts provided an arena for defending lordly rights and jurisdiction and contesting claims by enemies. When

Wanga instructed his notary Ercetus to compile all notarized documents pertaining to the mines of Trent, his goal was to clear assets from legal controversy
—not always easy to achieve. A similar general feeling pervades in the abundant references made by Grozio to *res publica* or the common good in *Constitutiones*. He felt the need to remind the rest of his feudal society that much
was at stake in the appointment of a new royal bureaucracy for mining affairs.
The long list of responsibilities of the judges of the office of *urbura* indicates
that the lawyer author of *Constitutiones* was instructed not to leave a grey area
that could come back and legally hinder the King. The writers of the statutes
of Massa and Sardinia felt a greater sense of urgency when drafting the regulations pertaining to transactions with mining shares. They belonged to societies
for which notarized documents were essential for achieving commercial and
business success. The world around them reminded these lawyers that written
law was the much-needed offspring of an independent legal and political system—something good to have in the face of expansionist enemy powers, Volterra in the case of Massa and Pisa and Genoa in the case of Sardinia.

In other regions, the silver-mining business clashed with an implacable
geography bending to fragmentation of power. Feudal lords and investors in
Andalusia, China, France, Japan, and Ottoman Anatolia seized control of the
underground wealth of their lands under various forms of ownership of mining
stakes. Legal structures marking a distinction between private industrial producers and the state and defining the nature and function of private capital in
mines were slow to arrive. The capitalist takeoff of the silver-mining business
admitted very little legal atomization. Silver was unlike iron or tin. Iron mining
industries flourished almost everywhere, undisturbed by legal atomization, possibly because of the dispersed nature of iron deposits.[3] Tin mining, which pros-
pered in many regions, was open cast, and in many places 'did not need much
working capital,' at least in the early stages of production.[4] On the contrary,
silver mining required long-term and fixed investments and a legal structure
guaranteeing returns on invested capital.

The Legacy of the Latin West

Latin Western Europe was different than the rest of the world, but the dif-
ference lies not in culture nor politics. Mining mountains were colonized by
different types of *societas* very early after the disintegration of the Roman Em-

pire. Arab failures in establishing permanent settlements beyond the French Pyrenees, coupled with the fact that the largest crusading campaigns took place outside Europe, added impetus to the mining colonization mission of monastic orders.[5] The latter carried 'the cross and the plough' wherever they went.[6] The Cistercians, which spread everywhere, had but one 'chief characteristic': direct cultivation of land by *conversi* and *homines mercenari*, lay brothers and hired laborers.[7] Their motto: *ora et labora*, a succinct but eloquent phrase. Dominicans, Franciscans, and Orthodox monks did the same, advancing an early mining and agrarian colonization of mountain valleys. They built autonomous mining colonies which enjoyed autonomy from local feudal powers. The ideology behind it was 'the dignity of manual labor,' a mentality unique to Western monasticism.[8]

As ecclesiastical lands expanded through donations from lords and local princes seeking peace in the other life, autonomous mining colonies spread throughout the mountains of Europe. Desire for self-sufficiency, in an environment that left no other alternative, made of monastic orders early agents in the development and diffusion of land-improvement techniques and hydraulic machinery in Western Europe.[9] The colonizing force of monastic orders transformed European mountains into storages of mining experience by the eleventh century.[10] Mining 'made these mountains appear accessible to man and his horse, cart and wagon, much earlier than scientific evidence indicates.'[11] Remnants of abbeys' colonizing can still be seen in the forge on display in the Cistercian Abbey of Fontenay in Burgundy, today a UNESCO World Heritage Site.[12]

The rise of secular local powers rivaled the claims of monastic orders on the plentiful resources that formed the underground wealth of lands. Clashes between feudal lords and ecclesiastic orders meant that those with the means to exercise power usurped mining claims. That this development took shape after the tenth century A.D. is not a trivial point. The political map of Europe was divided, and kingdom boundaries were rarely secured. Charlemagne, 'who purported to govern vast stretches of Western Europe as "emperor" of the Holy Roman Empire,' could exercise real authority only over a small stretch of land.[13] And even there, he could not take his rules for granted. Thus, laws were still at a revolutionary stage, and no source of feudal law was taken for granted. Such a vacuum of a centralized political and legal power was filled at the local level with the rise of autonomous mining agents, supplying the nascent European economy with much-needed silver ores. The rise of free miners and free mining

towns in the heartlands of the Carolingian empire starting in the tenth century
A.D. is evidence of the undisturbed development that mining enjoyed. When
Carolingian and Ottonian dynasties secured imperial claims to the silver mines
of a 'unified' Latin West starting in A.D. 1158, there was already a vibrant mining industry with incentives to expand and grow everywhere. The need for easy
access to mined silver ores, which was fundamental for expanding markets as
well as the territorial basis of power of the empire, set the stage.[14] It is in this
period that a silver-based monetary economy linking the commercial cities of
Europe to the heartlands of the nascent Germanic empire was in ascent.[15] In
the historical process of 'Europeanization of Europe,'[16] borrowing the words of
Robert Barlett, mining enjoyed the upper hand.

Europe's demographic stability also benefited the development of capitalist
mining businesses. It meant increased commercialization, demand for silver
from the Eastern world, and increased supply of labor for 'the improvement
and cultivation of lands' à la Smith.[17] Population historians have emphasized
how cessation of external and internal waves of raids by Vikings, Arabs, and
the Magyars 'increased the capacity of the land to support humans.'[18] After the
eleventh century, when population 'was stationary, with local increases or de-
creases,' growth became a general characteristic.[19] In A.D. 1000–1250, 'approximately 25,000 people moved in the forests of Brie'; the number of towns in
northern France enclosed in medieval walls grew substantially.[20] In A.D. 1155,
eighty-three new towns appeared around Lorris and five hundred in Champagne after A.D. 1182. By A.D. 1035–1067, Flanders was heavily populated.
'The bishop of Rheims complimented Count Baudouin V on transformation of
unproductive land to fertile fields.' New towns grew rapidly in England, Davis
emphasized. 'In Taunton, England, the population rose rapidly from about 500
in 1205 to about 1300 in 1325.'[21] Population growth was not merely 'a second
safety-valve for Western Europe's rural population,' as one writer observed.[22] It
was also the condition that guaranteed a supply of free labor to the continent's
mining sites. A plus: surpluses built by the social labor of miners in the mountains found their markets in newly formed urban towns.

An additional demographic feature was high spatial mobility of rural populations. New evidence shows that populations in mining and commercial cities
were rarely stable. The image of mountain people living in the same valleys
generation after generation is a myth. The most voluminous evidence of mobility comes from surviving German census figures, meticulously dissected by

historian Steve Hochstadt. From his work, we learn that social classes were geographically mobile 'despite considerable hindrances to free movement.'[23] In sixteenth-century Jihlava, there were 1,104 migrants, 38 percent of which had moved 'over 100 miles,' according to Hochstadt. 'The typical *Bürger* class was composed of approximately equal parts of immigrants and natives.'[24] The pattern is discouraging to those insisting in rigid feudal relations: citizens were only a minority group among urban populations, reaching 15 percent of a town's population in the best cases. In Europe's flourishing towns, undocumented migrants were the norm.

The continent 'faces inward, away from the sea,' as Kellenbenz observed.[25] Its world mining regions enjoyed proximity to one another. No vast steppe separates European mountain ranges. Rivers and passes unite mountainous landscapes. A day's journey by the abbot Albert from Stade in Lower Saxony, Germany, to Rome in A.D. 1236 illustrates the advantage of mountain closeness:

> For Abbot Albert the route crossing the Harz Mountains was nothing to be afraid of. From Nuremberg he travelled to Schweinfurt, Meiningen and Gotha. He did not use a more comfortable road along the Leine river of the western rim of the Harz, but climbed the Harz via Nordhausen-Hasselfelde-Wernigerode [. . .] the problem of traversing the central plateau of the Harz mountains at a level of 500 meters, and coping with a height difference of 320 meters within two days cannot be exaggerated, considering the problems that the abbot confronted on the entire journey to Rome and back.[26]

The fact that mining 'made these mountains appear accessible to man and his horse, cart and wagon,' during the times of the abbot Albert was no doubt an incentive to embark upon the trip.[27]

No large geological or climatic phenomena affected long-term human habitation in European mountains. When these did happen, mountain peoples vigorously deepened land colonization. Gabriele Rosa shows how *societas* in north Bergamo paid for costly agrarian infrastructure in the Po Valley in response to flooding. By the early thirteenth century, the agrarian landscape of the Scalve Valley contained mills paid by Bergamo citizens. Urban merchants reclaimed Massa's lands before the mid-fourteenth century. Peasants intensively cultivated the hills surrounding Siena, partially responding to a growing demand for food from neighboring communes, affected by environmental crises.

The rise of a centralized Latin Christian Church played its part, too, in the

Fig. 6.1. Limestone statue of Saint Barbara, patron saint of miners. Veneration to the saint started in the seventh century A.D., according to most authoritative sources. According to legend, she was imprisoned in a tower by her father, Dioscorus, who hid her away from male suitors. While imprisoned, she converted to Christianity. Dioscorus brought her to the authorities, and she was sentenced to death. Her father carried out the sentence, but he was struck by lightning in punishment for his sin. Musée Départemental des Vosges, Epinal. Kharbine-Tapabor / The Art Archive at Art Resource, NY.

making of mining.[28] After all, 'the miner usually had a deep inclination for religion.'[29] Miners named shafts and levels 'following the saints of the calendar.'[30] 'Many, many hundreds of mines and tunnels of the Erzgebirge were named after religious personages' and symbols: 'Trust in God, Savior of the Whole World, Gift of God, Holy Trinity, Crown of Heaven, Easter Lamb.'[31] In the sixteenth century, miners' festivals in Catholic towns coincided with the saint calendar established by the Church. In Protestant towns, after the Reformation, the Catholic Church institutionalized a sermon 'in which work was glorified as service to God.'[32] In the Erzgebirge, 'every year on the Monday before Lent or Shrove Tuesday a miners' festival of thanksgiving was held.'[33] This mountain theology thrust some roots in mining fields. A peasant reported that 'a spirit haunts the silver mines of Brunswick; and another to be in the tin mine of Slackenwalde in his country of Bohemia.' Miners were not afraid of the spirit who 'in the shape of a monk, strikes the miners, sings and plays on the Bagpipes, and does many such tricks.'[34]

Martin Luther, himself the son of 'an active and skilled miner,' did much in his sermons to build 'a harmonious relation between theology and mining.'[35] 'I gladly see how the rich God bid grow His treasures beneath the surface, in order that he may prove, that he constantly cares for us, and let His mighty and skillful hand perceive,' stated Luther, according to a contemporaneous account.[36]

His poetic and oratory skills inspired one of his pastor friends, Johannes Mathesius, to write a hymn on miners entitled 'O Father, Son and Holy Ghost, thou God dost fix the miner's post.'[37] This at a time when 'allies of the devil,' as ignorant farmers saw Saxon and German miners, were opening new silver mines in Germany and Norway.[38]

These factors gave the mountains encircling the Mediterranean a providential role in the history of capitalist mining. It was there that corporations embodied the 'need to liberate individuals with power, prestige' and liquid capital from feudal bonds, in an era when exploitation of silver mines called for it.[39] Mining corporations restrained feudal takeovers of mines, while allowing sovereign individuals to carve out their version of the common good. What corporations did was to unify many individual wills into a single cause: to share liability and to enjoy the benefits of exploiting what became in time the underground wealth of the nations of Europe.

An 'Infertile' Crescent? The Legacy of the Islamic State

Was the Fertile Crescent 'partially infertile' long before the sixteenth century?[40] If so, did such a state determine the empire's mining legacy? Many have argued that the Ottoman state had a natural disadvantage when compared to the Latin West, that of underdevelopment of mining and extractive resource economies. According to historian Kaser, it was the exhaustion of raw materials, and not anything else, that 'turned the table against the East.'[41] This might be the case during the long sixteenth century, when Europe enjoyed access to the underground wealth of the Americas in the silver mines of Potosí, Zacatecas, and Guanajuato. But before the age of discoveries, the problem of the Fertile Crescent lay in a system of government that emphasized strong central authority over economy and society.[42]

In the early period of the Islamic state, mining colonization required tribalism, an amazing social force that Muslims turned to their advantage. Everywhere the Prophet found intertribal alliances and conflicts. Thus, emphasizing religious and communal bonds became an imperative of the nascent Islamic state. Tribes united by faith became the engine that made possible the rapid expansion of Islam in the Arabian Peninsula, North Africa, and Central Asia. The process by which 'tribalism ceded the high moral ground to a pan-tribal religious ideal'[43] was by no means easy. It required internecine wars and the adaptation of land and tax institutions from Byzantium, Persian Empire, and Central Asian nomadic cultures. The outcome was destined to astonish Latin Christendom: conquered lands expanded and were 'collectively at the disposal of the conquering tribesmen.' The early land institutions of the Islamic state required 'no distinction of public and private within the conquered land.'[44] The *iqtâ* institution was born, 'given by the Prophet'; it 'was quite simply a bestowal of property,' without any real obligation for its possessor.[45]

One must assume that 'the real state of affairs was far more complex,'[46] but by the tenth century, while different land laws and traditions were at a revolutionary stage in Latin Christendom, Islamic jurisprudence already enjoyed its classical period.[47] Two ideas became essential to the early Islamic thought: conquered land 'became the property of conquerors,' and the Caliph became the *walî* or trustee of property for the benefit of an undivided Muslim brotherhood.[48] These ideas became a coherent guiding colonizing principle for the nascent Ottoman state. While its predecessor was concerned with neutralizing tribalism, the Ottomans contended with much more powerful enemies bordering its outermost provinces. The Mongols in central Asia, European kingdoms in alliance with Rome, an invigorated Castilian kingdom after the Reconquista, and a Portuguese Crown expanding into Western Africa added a twist to the Muslim principles inherited by the Ottoman state. Expansion of the Muslim brotherhood required a class of conquerors; the *'askerî*, to be paid by the state; and resources for sustaining the organic renewal of this class. Enjoying usufruct rights from conquered lands guaranteed the economic foundations of the military class and loyalty to the Sultan, at least nominally.[49] Because *timar* grants guaranteed their incomes, the elitist military class added to the pressures of centralizing fiscal revenues.

Centralization of revenues thus became a method of conquest and the system of government of the Ottoman state. It acted as a potent force against the formation of self-governing, autonomous colonizing structures. The ideal view of territory that the Islamic state had, with one boundary dividing 'the abode of Islam' or *dār al-Islām* from 'the abode of war' or *dār-al-harb* 'governed by non-Muslims,'[50] provided no cohesion to project of the Ottoman state. Territories were defined by anticipated revenues, and boundaries were re-drawn many times in response to the fiscal needs of the state.

Geography facilitated the Ottoman system of government. The most productive Ottoman mines belonged to montane societies that barely resisted the centralized power of the state. These landscapes were colonized by different peoples that moved into the mountains with the threats of Byzantium and later crusading armies on their way to Jerusalem after the eleventh century.[51] Granting usufruct rights over these lands to non-Muslims and Muslims alike proved to be the best incentive for securing order in these lands while centralizing the revenues coming from the lands. Old associations by Teotonici, en route to self-governance, found no place in an Ottoman society built to sustain a centralized state. These were replaced by mining partnerships by *varaq*, which gained no juridical status of their own, unlike the *societas* of Latin Europe. They were recognized as partnerships,[52] based upon family or political affiliations operating within the boundaries of Islamic contract law. This by no means suggests lack of investments of time and money by Islamic partnerships. Historians have uncovered evidence of extraordinary technological achievements under the auspices of Islam. A few examples should suffice. Banū Mūsā described 'a machine for use in wells which kill those who descend in them' as follows:

> If a man uses this machine in any well, it will neither kill nor harm him. This machine is suitable for wells that kill and for dangerous pits. If a man has this machine, which we shall describe, with him, he can descend in any well immediately without fearing it and it will not harm him.[53]

The machine was used for ventilation.[54] According to the instructions written by Banū Mūsā, it required the construction of a pipe, 'from copper, reeds, skin or wood' or 'anything available from which pipes are made.' 'A skin is made like the skin of the blacksmiths with which they blow on the fire,' such as a bellows. A hole to the bellows for tightly fitting the pipe had to be built 'so that no wind or air enters the bellows at this place, and nothing can come out of it.' A hole was made in the bellows, and a valve was attached to it for air to enter through this hole. The pipe was then placed in the well, and 'we hold its end at the side of the man's nose and mouth, then blow continuously with the bellows'—'so the air which is suitable for the person who has descended into the well is adequate for the person's needs, and that foul, thick air which is in the well does not harm him, so he who descends into the well is safe.' The inventor of the machine confidently added the following words: 'And if he cannot see the descent because something is in the way, then the pipe should be inserted in the well for a period before the man descends, and the bellows used during that period to blow continuously in order to introduce good air, fit for life, until, after the discharge of the foul air a like quantity of good air has entered' the well.

On the topic of drainage works in the Zakandar mines in the Maghreb, Persian geographer Al-Kazwīnī (A.D. 1203–1283) stated:

> Here are the silver mines. Anyone who wishes can undertake processing them. There are underground mines in which many people are always working. When they descend 20 dhira's water appears. The Sultan installs water wheels and water is raised until the mud appears. Workers bring this mud up to the surface of the ground and wash it. He does this in order to take the fifth. . . . Water is raised in 3 stages, since it is 20 dhira's from the ground level to the surface of the water. He installs a wheel down in the mine on the water surface. Water is lifted and it is discharged into a large tank. Another wheel is installed on this tank. It lifts the water and pours it into another tank. On this tank a third wheel is installed. It lifts the water and discharges on to the surface of the ground to irrigate the farms and gardens. This operation cannot be undertaken except by a very rich person possessing thousands. He sits at the mouth of the mine and employs artisans and workers, who bring out the mud and wash it in front of him. When the work is done, the fifth of the Sultan is put aside and the rest is given to him. It may come to be smaller than his expenditure, and it may be [more]. This depends on the man's efforts.[55]

Leaving aside the many puzzling questions that historians of technology have raised about the history of hydraulic devices, it is likely that Ottoman water wheels compared favorably to the wheels employed throughout Western Europe.[56] But water was a problem for the Ottomans, just as it had been a central problem in earlier centuries. Areas under Ottoman control had severe shortages of freshwater resources, as in Central Asia and Syria, or abundant rainfall, as in the Balkans. This diversity offered tremendous trading opportunities, but made water policy a heavily localized enterprise with few possibilities of developing autonomous financial arrangements.[57] 'Water-related projects on a relatively large scale remained few and far between.'[58] In arid lands, the Ottomans relied upon native plants resistant to droughts, especially the four trees mentioned in the Qur'an—date palm, fig, olive, and pomegranate trees. In regions where nature 'took care of the delivery of water,' the state withdrew from investing in hydraulic machinery.[59] This was the case in the Balkans, endowed with abundant rainfall and a 'relatively rich supply of water.'[60] There, bridges, much needed for military success, and not water wheels, became the most important Ottoman water infrastructure.

Why did the accumulated experience of investments in time and money not lead to a capitalist industry? Here, geography was unforgiving, denying to the Ottoman Empire the key pre-conditions that Latin Europe enjoyed. Balkan mines were located in the periphery of the empire, distant from Constantinople. Communication was costly. Sending a letter from Massa to Montieri, which were separated by a landscape formed by hills of low elevation and stretching for just a few kilometers in Italy, was not the same as sending a letter from Constantinople to the Balkan hinterlands. The poor state of Roman roads and the mountainous routes crossing Macedonia did not help either. 'Six major postal routes' connecting Istanbul with distant Ottoman regions emerged only after the mid-sixteenth century.[61] Besides the high transaction costs of administering the state's territories, there was the problem of neighbors. Balkan mines were close to Venice, a city that was on the path to becoming the most powerful republic of the region. The city's 'capitalist aristocracy,' borrowing Robert Brenner's phrase, was determined to rise to power by exploiting the lands and resources surrounding the *Terrafirma*. Pressured by the hostile geography of Venetian lands, the capitalist aristocracy of Venice, wasting no time, secured access to mines in the Balkans as well as mines in eastern and central Lombardy.[62]

Demography in Ottoman territories added other challenges. Around A.D. 1000, the population of Anatolia and the Balkans was around 19 million, 6.5 million in the Balkans. The Empire's population between A.D. 1520 and 1535 was approximately 12.5 million at its peak.[63] Kaser describes at length why this number remained stable in the course of the millennium.[64] Mining elsewhere relied upon geographic mobility of labor and capital; however, population increases are a condition for an early capitalist start if geography affords the luxury of a stable climate for private money to plow back into the subsoil. In Anatolia and the Balkans, settlements flourished only where water and wood were abundant.[65] And even there, forced migrations and relocation of people were the dreadful standard set by the Ottomans. No long-term stable mining settlement was possible south of the Taurus, where the Syrian Desert begins, nor in the lands beyond the Caucasus, where the steppes begin to open the Caucasus to foreign invasions. Silver, thus, never figured among 'the four great products of eastern civilization—silk, porcelain, sandalwood, and black pepper.'[66]

Islam in the West had enjoyed no better fortune. Alas, mining progressed in Andalusia and Maghreb from the eleventh to the late twelfth centuries, feeding the mints striking the dinar. This 'silver kept the Umayyad court in luxury' and sustained an immodest Fatimid court in the East. Lombard states that 'it was Sudanese silver which maintained the brilliant Andalusian civilization of the eleventh century'[67]—as long as Spain's Meseta Central and coastal plains could afford protection from invading armies. Wars and pressing water challenges diminished the potential for exploiting Andalusia's geological endowments by the time the Naṣrid Dynasty (A.D. 1238–1492) came to power. The impetus of the Christian Reconquista, in lands plagued by hydrological challenges, put obstacles to an early capitalist growth of the mining industry.

In Maghreb, raids and punitive expeditions of Berber nomads had one deplorable outcome: 'civilization was in retreat,' according to Lombard. Towns experienced a 'de-Romanization and a resurgence of the distant Berber past.'[68] Lombard coined the phrase 'savage individualism' for explaining the circumstances that pushed for a return to Berber's tribal structure. Lacking a central authority, Berber societies functioned as 'separate mountain Republics,' or 'nomadic clans.'[69] Islam Berbers certainly reintegrated Northern Africa into the world economy, but mainly by exporting gold.[70] Their greatest achievement was to transform North Africa and the Maghreb into 'a storehouse of military power' and a 'supply of manpower' to Islam.[71]

In sum, mining mountains in the lands of Islam were colonized by forces that favored centralization. From an ideology that emphasized the ideal of an undivided religious brotherhood to a society and system of government that centralized revenues and power, the lands of Islam left no space for autonomous, self-governing agents to take the lead.

The Mongols: A Dubious Legacy

The recent attention paid by global history scholars to the rise and fall of the Mongols justifies our examination of what went wrong with the mining cities in Central Asia under Mongol rule. To the east of the rising Ottoman state was the Mongol empire, which had very little use for silver. One cannot identify a growth of native silver-mining industries in the lands dominated by the Mongols, comparable to that of silver-mining in the Latin West. If the Mongols had any use for silver, the expansionist logic of their empire contained too many internal disadvantages to the development of capitalist mining. Mongol military campaigns after A.D. 1227 extended Chinghiz Khân's empire into the Caucasus on the eastern shores of the Black Sea. The Empire was built upon 'a demonstrated willingness to slaughter whole cities,' aided by the fact 'that nomad power was at its peak of destructive potential,' according to Hodgson.[72] Tûs was invaded and ravaged incessantly by Mongol forces after A.D. 1219.[73] Even the great poet of the city, Firdawsi, 'drank to the dregs the bitterness of the Mongol cataclysm.'[74] The final blow to what was once a magnificent city was dealt by Mîrān Shāh, son of Tamerlane. In A.D. 1389, the Shāh 'turned the city into a desert'; 'the remnant which escaped from the wholesale massacre settled round the shrine, and Meshed from that date became the chief city of Khurāsān.'[75]

Khovarezm or Khwarezm was 'one of the most interesting and culturally fruitful areas in the Oxus basin.'[76] The entire region 'fell prey to the revenge of the Mongols'; surviving rulers saved their honor by making incursions and raiding campaigns against the West, but to no avail. Sultan Aladdin made alliances with Ayyubids of Syria, against the Khwarizmi rulers, and finally defeated them in the Battle of Yassi Çimen. Ghûr, situated in lands stretching from Herât to Bâmiyân, was ravaged by the Mongols in A.D. 1222, after a century of 'splendor under the Sâm dynasty.'[77] The valleys of the eastern side of the Elburz made possible several invasions by the Mongols in the thirteenth century.[78] Transoxiana and Hindu Kush mines lost their importance by the thirteenth century, coinciding with the arrival of the Mongols.[79] Despite the great military patronage that became the symbol of a world empire, the strength of the empire 'was largely used for destruction.'[80]

The destructive campaigns against industrial and commercial Eastern cities was, however, an organic component of the economy of the Mongols. The Mongols 'derived profits from trade across their domains,' according to Janet Abu-Lughod.[81] They had little use for immovable assets or fixed capital stocks other than the steppes. The world economy of the Mongols 'was not an economic system designed to create a surplus.'[82] In Robert Lamborn's words:

> Since the reduction of ores was carried on in mountain fastnesses, far from regions frequented by men of cultivation; and mining and metallurgy were not then, as they have become in modern times, subjects to which men of the highest mental capacity directed their attention [. . .] What in later days men such as Swedenborg, Humboldt, Le Play, Rivto, and Scheerer have studied and written upon with laborious care, was then left almost entirely to the hands of serfs and malefactors.[83]

Conquerors, stated the controversial economist and mining engineer Alexander Del Mar more than a century ago, found no use for mining knowledge.[84] The Mongols were no exception. They left nothing in writing about Transoxiana mines.[85] 'All that remains from the vast empire which Genghis founded is a granite tablet erected near the silver mines of Nertschinsk,' commented Del Mar.[86]

Central Asian mining development after the Mongols came a little too late. The age of discoveries by then had delivered a mortal blow to Central Asian mines. Across Turkestan lay the oldest and most frequented Silk Road. The Jungar route, in modern day Kazakhstan, connecting the Altai Mountains to the Tien Shan in eastern China, and the Terek-Davan Pass in the Altai range of the Tien Shan Mountains, were strategic routes for the empires of the east. These geographic features invited banditry, attacks, and above all, imperial invasions. 'By this road,' wrote Bretschneider, 'passed the hordes who at one time threatened to engulf the whole of Europe.'[87] 'By this way, finally, until the Dutch discovered the ocean route, went all the embassies from Europe to the great sovereigns of the East.'[88] With the discovery of silver deposits of Potosí in Bolivia and Zacatecas in Mexico in the sixteenth century, the contribution of the East to mining development declined. The East experienced a mining revival after the mid-seventeenth century, especially in Japan. In Central Asia, decades of war against the Seljuk Turks and Ottomans on the western side and the Mongols on the eastern side depleted the resources of the Khwarizmi Turks who had ruled Transoxiana, condemning the once-prosperous mines to extinction. The 'general prosperity' of Islam was a thing of the past.[89]

Time and Space of Capitalist Mining: A Final Word

Mining prospects fueled the expansionist impetus of ancient, medieval, and modern civilizations. 'Beyond the Strait [of Gibraltar], the Carthaginians founded Gades (Cadiz) and, a half-century earlier, had overthrown the Iberian state of Tartessos, which in all probability had spread across the Sierra Morena.'[90] 'Some thousand years before Christ a westward migration [to Sardinia] took place from Asia Minor which is comparable with the great discoveries of the fifteenth and sixteenth centuries. There was the same fever for the possession of the precious metals.'[91] The Romans dared not to cross the 'Pillars of Hercules,' as the straits of Gibraltar were known, and settled in Hispania, where abundant copper and gold mining works were about to happen.[92] There, and with the native Iberian cultures, they excavated and worked mines of copper, gold, and lead, building remarkable mine works. Celtic mining and metallurgy were an incentive for Roman generals to conquer and subdue Celtic tribes.[93]

The most spectacular expansion was that of Europe to the rest of the world in A.D. 1450–1650. In Central and South America, Europe found much-coveted silver-bearing ore deposits. In A.D. 1599, an employee of the German Fugger bank wrote a note to the patriarch in the headquarters in Augsburg:

> The Spaniards have conquered a new kingdom in India, called Old Mexico. It is inhabited by intelligent people who are to be instructed in the Christian faith. Very rich gold and silver mines exist there also.[94]

The banking employee knew nothing about American mines. All he knew was that a new geological bounty was waiting for the right entrepreneurs to embark upon a project of global investments in mining. The geology of the Sierra Madre Mountains of Mexico contained abundant silver and copper deposits. In the Peruvian Andes, Spaniards discovered high-grade sulphides with rich veins of native silver that in time changed the course of history.[95] But the geographic conditions leading to capital plowing its gains into the subsoil were slow to emerge. Compulsory minting of mined silver ores, royal monopolies of the silver trade, and slave and forced labor, among others, became part of European mining colonization in the Americas.[96] The latter were virtually absent in mining districts of Europe in which capitalist businesses rose to power. Mining capital in Europe experienced a dramatic financialization in this period. Capitalists invested their profits from industrial silver and copper mining into other industrial and banking ventures. The Fugger House built an impressive banking portfolio after it monopolized metal outputs from the mines of Tyrol, Hungary, and Spain. It financed Portuguese maritime expansion in the A.D. 1500s.[97] In the meantime, mining capital in Spanish America lagged behind. This duality, or the coexistence of a highly developed mining industry and capital in Europe and underdeveloped mining capital elsewhere, became an organic structure of world development in A.D. 1450–1650.

The enduring nature of this historical phenomenon requires further research and examination of the time and space of capitalist mining. Why did good starting points of time and space, Europe's geography in the long thirteenth century, become mining capital's accumulated advantages? When does geography turn its back on mining capital? What happens then? Do clashes between mining capital and labor follow? Do struggles within the class of mining capitalists become the normal state of affairs? We cannot answer these questions with the evidence studied in this book; however, we can advance some modest hypotheses for further inquiry. The rise of West European development that coincided with the emergence of capitalist mining was a unique historical event. European businesses exploiting the accumulated mining experience of Mediterranean societies had the upper hand. They deepened specialization in industrial metal-mining and related activities, as evidenced by the history of Italian mining and metal-trade houses in the Black Sea and beyond.[98] These businesses took advantage of a time when silver was an industrial raw material sought after by European and Eastern Asian clients alike.

The increasing speed at which production and trade of silver took place was matched domestically by the increasing speed at which privatization of mining claims took place. Such was the strongest and most enduring legacy of the capitalist mining business to West European development. The legacy is most remarkable, if one considers that it was accomplished without fully separating land from subsoil rights—a problem that the nation-state that rose after the Peace of Westphalia had to deal with. Rudolf Hübner, studying Germanic legal history, argued that private mining rights evolved in three stages. The first stage was the 'bare right of tribute—which might be designated as the first and oldest form in the evolution of the mining regality.' The second stage was donation of mining rights to landowners, 'which practice was justified by the king's claim of title to particular minerals.'[99] At this stage mineral deposits were defined in Germanic law as *iuris imperii*, a principle that meant that usufruct depended upon the crown's consent. 'This consent was given only to him who could formerly have exercised mining privileges without it: the landowner.'[100] The third stage, overlapping the second one, occurred when mining passed 'into the hands of the Territorial princes, who thenceforth conveyed to landholders the right of mining upon land they owned or held as tenants, just as the king had formerly granted them these rights directly.'[101] The evidence presented in this book indicates that in the time and space of mining coinciding with the rise of a European economy, landowners could not fulfill this condition.[102] A radical separation of mining profits from the landowner took place in Western Europe, in a process that led to shareholding mining corporations. It was a process that legitimized

Fig. 6.2. Silver mines of the world, A.D. 1450–1650. World mining regions of the long sixteenth century shifted to the Atlantic. Digging up the underground wealth hidden in the Sierra Madre and Andes mountains retarded the growth of capitalist mining businesses. Sixteenth-century mining investors failed to recognize the constraints imposed upon them by forced labor and capital scarcity. Trans-montane corridors connected the mining sites of Sierra Madre, but in uneven ways. The case of the Andes was similar. Human power remained central to mining production for most of the period, a structural-historical deficiency perpetuated by geography.

Der Bergknapp.

Jch treib alles Ertz Knappenwerck/
Jm Thal vnd auff Sanct Annen Berg/
Mit den Steigern/Knappen vnd Bubn
Jn Stollen/Schacht vnd den Ertzgrubn/
Mit graben/zimmern/böltzn vnd bauwn/
Mit eynfahren/brechen vnd hauwn/
Wird ich fündig vnd Silber bring/
So ist der Bergherr guter ding.

Fig. 6.3. *Der Bergknappe* (A.D. 1568), by Jost Amman, with verses by German burgher and poet Hans Sachs. The son of a famous scholar of Zurich, Jost Amman was a goldsmith, woodcutter, and engraver. This image comes from *Eygentliche Beschreibung aller Stände auff Erden*, best known as *Ständebuch* or *The Book of Trades*. The book was an autograph album, a literary genre that flourished in sixteenth-century Germany. No mine accountant, bookkeeper, or ore piles are shown in the drawing. Only a free miner or *Bergknappe* proudly stands in the foreground, while two miners work in two separate shafts in the background. bpk Berlin / Art Resource, NY.

no ownership of land in the hands of mining corporations. Mining corporations only required ownership of the interest-bearing capital that took the form of mining shares.

The new cycle of Western industrial development starting in A.D. 1450–1650 imposed a different set of requirements to mining businesses. Proximity to Mediterranean trade networks mattered, but proximity to Spain and Portugal mattered even more. With rich metal-buying clients seeking profits at the doorsteps of Lisbon and Seville, new European mining regions gained supremacy. The effects upon medieval capitalist mining businesses were unprecedented: the old capitalists of Lombardy, Tuscany, and Sardinia fell, and the new mining capitalists plowing capital into the mines of the Carpathians and the eastern Alps rose to power. The latter regions became Europe's world mining regions, consolidating a new time and space of capitalist mining.

In studying the time and space of capitalist mining, one condition, however, ought to be the guiding torch: that when good geology meets good geography,

Fig. 6.4. Miners in the snow (A.D. 1880), by Vincent van Gogh. Van Gogh
may have created this drawing of coal miners while at Borinage, near Mons,
Belgium, where he spent a short period of time. Although 'pretty rudimentary,'
as Antony Tudor said of Van Gogh's drawings of miners, this drawing shows that
coal miners carried the burden of modernizing northern Europe. By the beginning of
the eighteenth century, coal was an industrial raw material, and Belgian coal mines
experienced large-scale development afterwards. In the twentieth century, the coal-
mining industry relied upon migrant miners of Italian, Greek, Moroccan, Spanish, and
Turkish stock. Collection Kröller-Müller Museum, Otterlo, The Netherlands.

capitalist mining businesses flourish. The survey presented in this book shows
that the economic behavior of agents did not deviate much in medieval mining districts meeting this condition. Private citizens plowed capital back into
the underground wealth of nations. A common cohesive ethic was not needed
either, contrary to what Max Weber argued long ago. It is worth remember-
ing Rostow's warning against the tendency of sociologists of his time to make
John Calvin 'bear quite the weight' of the capitalist ethic. By the same token,
the Jewish-Christian tradition praised by David Landes provided, if anything,
an insufficient basis for the rise of capitalist mining. The ethic, if there was

one, that pushed miners into digging the underground wealth was carved from 'classical, Moslem, and Byzantine worlds.'[103] In the words of historian William McNeill:

> The speed and single-mindedness with which Europeans learned what more anciently civilized neighbors had to teach them perhaps permitted the European novices to carry further than their Asian contemporaries the effort at rationalization of human effort—an effort toward which their share in the Greek inheritance predisposed them. Roman law, Greek science and philosophy, and the ecclesiastical encouragement of reasoning about doctrine and the world all forwarded this development.[104]

Capital endowed these diverse cultural traditions that met in Europe with a new life. The whole of the ramifications of this breath of new life fall outside the limited scope of this book. How did investments in mining lay a foundation for European development of modern chemistry? The success and failure of the search for 'the Stone' that haunted alchemists were bound to an understanding of the Earth and its substances. Among the earliest pioneers was Ibn Umail (A.D. 900–960). Umail wrote that 'the silver water and the Starry Earth' allowed for an early diffusion of alchemical and astrological ideas attributed to ancient writers. One of these ancient writers was Hermes, who 'has the reputation of being the first alchemical writer.'[105] *Bermannus* (A.D. 1530), *De Animantibus Subterraneis* (A.D. 1549), and *De re metallica* (A.D. 1556) by Agricola were pioneering works for the development of *chymia,* or modern chemistry.[106] We will never know the full scope and amount of knowledge that European sciences distilled from centuries of mining and the practical experience of miners.

The relation between mining and global development continues to evolve. From the Alps in continental Europe to the mountains of Central Asia, geologists continue to map the vast mineral resources contained in the Earth's orogenic belts. As the science of tectonic plates progresses, more about the nature of ores will be revealed in the near future. Mountains, which Chinese geologist Xu Zhiqin called 'natural laboratories of continental dynamics,'[107] occupy the center of attention of mining capital today more than ever. Geologists currently study mineral deposits of 'archaean cratons' or fragments of old continents in the seabed floor 'that are more richly endowed with mineral deposits than younger terrains.'[108] Cratons contain a wide variety of mineral deposits. Licenses for exploration and mining of this vast landscape suggest that underground wealth is a concept that changes over time, and with these changes, new legal challenges emerge. What this new growth stage of mining indicates is that the relation between mining and technological progress will continue to be contentious, as that between mining capital and labor will be in its time. Will an advanced stage of capitalism require getting rid of the nation-state in order to put humankind closer to exploiting the wealth of the mid-ocean rises? The modest question explored in this book gives no safe ground for anticipating a description of the future of the capitalist mining business. We venture here one timid observation: that mining will continue to enjoy a supreme position in the next cycle of world industrial development, as it did in the cycle of industrial development of the long thirteenth century.

Much work remains to be done for a complete picture of the origins and evolution of capitalist mining. A mining engineer once described the tasks ahead for a full history of mining, with words that we are compelled to cite here:

> I may hope to have cut many a lode while opening the depth. Even if the vein again and again runs off in another direction due to a fault; nevertheless, I believe that I have not lost it while sinking through the barren rock. It is not a highly paying mine, which could give manifold returns. But it is workable, because prospecting in its field presents rare, and therefore, precious goods to be hauled.[109]

Our view today of mountains as storages of industrial wealth have come a long way from the old 'scientific' idea describing mountains as 'organs of the respiration of the globe' and 'metals, a production of putrefaction and disease [accounting] for their bad smell.'[110] The more we advance knowledge about the Earth's orogenic belts, the more incisive our questions concerning capital-labor relations in mining ought to be. In the past, saints went to the mountains. 'It was from a mountain that Buddha ascended into heaven,' says a Chinese proverb.[111] It was from a mountain that Jesus delivered his most famous sermon.[112] Before becoming prophet, Muhammad used to leave Mecca and climb the surrounding low mountains to devote himself to meditation and prayer, Muhammad Ibn Ishaq reminds us.[113] Mount Zion is 'where the ark and saints will be gathered,' according to Jewish sacred texts.[114] Today, capital goes to the mountains, searching for the raw materials that continue to accelerate capitalist development. Between the sacred and the profane, the eschatological and the scientific, there lies mining, an underground world, as a French geologist called it, waiting for us to finally give it its proper place in economic history.

APPENDIX A: GERMAN LOANWORDS
IN MINING STATUTES

Loanword	Code[a]	German word and code's definition
actufus	CW	*abteufen* Deepening or sinking a drainage adit; to deepen an adit perpendicular to another adit.
arialla	OM	*erzhältig, erzhalden* Installations for refining ores; abundance of ore; ore dump.
bareitare	CW BC	*bereiten, berechnen* To afford a charge or bill; to calculate expenses.
beistante, beistantaria	OM BC	*beistand* Patronage, sponsorship, creditor.
caroegus, carowegus	CW	*karren weg* Transport tunnel; minecart path.
claffter	CM	*klafter, klafterruthe* A fathom in length.
dorslagum, dorslago	CW BC	*dürchschläge* The point where several traverse shafts meet; orthogonal crossing; crosscut adit.
falumberg	CW	*fäule berg* A friable rock easily broken in small pieces.
gewerken, werhe, guerco, werke[b]	CW OM BC OL	*werk* Worker.

Loanword	Code[a]	German word and code's definition
hangundez	CM	*hängenden* Vein's hangingwall.
kenner	CW	*kennen* To be acquainted with charcoal use for ore smelting.
lachter	CM OM	*lachter, Berglachter* Old German unit of distance.
lenkhovar, lenhavar	OL	*lehenhäuer* An undertaker of a specific work related to mining; *varaq* in charge of renting pit units.
liegundez	CM	*liegenden* Vein's footwall; the rockwall that lies or is streched along the ore vein.
mulokh	OL	*mundloch* Orifice of a vein; a gallery opening exposed to sunlight, or to the foot of a mountain.
prant	OL	*brand* To catch fire or be inflamed; to burn large masses of rock.
raitungum, raitungus	CW	*rechnung* Account; to settle a bill.
rošt	OL	*röste, rost* Ore roasting that eliminates sulfur compounds, producing argentiferous galena; to make a heap or bed of ore, wood, and charcoal.
schichta, šihte	CM OL	*schicht* A work-shift.
silbrarius	CW	*silber* Silver.
siliffo, siliffare	BC	*schleifen* To cut or cross.
smelzer, ismuičar, smiačar	CW OL	*schmelzen* To smelt or melt metals; cupellation workers, in charge of liquifying ore mixture.

Loanword	Code[a]	German word and code's definition
stollo, stollone, ištolna, štovna, štona	CM OL	*stollen* Horizontal tunnel or gallery; adit; to drive an adit.
trente	OM BC	*trennen* Parts; to come off or separate; to unite itself.
truogara	BC	*trog* Pail or bucket; a bucket made of wood used in ore-washing and grinding processes.
xaffar, xafetum, xafetus, safiatores, scafiatore, scasia- tore, šafar	CW OM BC OL	*schaffen* To manage; administrator of mining works; foreman; factor of the mine.
xenkelochi, xenkationes, xencare, xencator	CW	*senken* To sink or lower an adit; a worker who sinks an adit.
xurfus	CW	*schurf* Exploratory excavation; to hammer a rock for finding the strike of an ore vein.
waffar, wassar	CW CM	*waschen* To wash; to clean; a worker who washes the ores.
wazzerseiger	CM	*wasserziehen* Lifting water from a shaft using buckets.
žaq	OL	*sack, sackerl* A carrier bag; a leather bag used for transporting ore rocks and materials outside the shafts.

[a] CW=*Codex Wangianus*; CM=*Constitutiones juris metallica*; OM=*Ordinamenta Massa*; BC=*Breve Chiesa*; OL=*Ottoman Laws*. [b] Other forms of the word in CW are *Werch, Werchi, Wercorum, Wercuss, Wercus*; *guercus* in OM; *guelco* and *guerco* in BC; *werke, werki, werhe, warak, vurhe, varaq*, and *gwark* in OL.

Sources: Beldiceanu, *Les Actes des Premiers Sultans*, vol. 1, p. 294, vol. 2, pp. 290–299, 303–307; Braunstein, 'Les statuts miniers de l'Europe médiévale'; Curzel, *Il Codice Vanga*, p. 27; Ebers, *The new and complete dictionary of German and English languages*; Marchese, 'Sopra alcuni vocaboli contenuti nel Breve di Villa di Chiesa di Sigerro'; Jánošíková, 'Mining business "Ius Regale"'; Jireček, *Codex juris Bohemici*, vol. 1, pp. 265–317; Mispoulet, *Le régime des mines à l'époque romaine*, p. 76, footnote 4; Poggi, *Discorsi economici, storici, e giuridici*, pp. 494–495; Vesme, *Historiae patriae*, pp. xxv, clii.

APPENDIX B: CARBON YIELD AND CHARCOAL CHARACTERISTICS

Tree	Habitat	Carbon yield (parts in 100) & charcoal characteristics[a]
Lignum vitae *Guaiacum officinale*	Caribbean Islands Central America Venezuela, Colombia	26.8 of carbon, 'greyish, resembles pit coal, compact, remarkably hard'
Mahogany *Swietenia mahogani*	Caribbean Islands	25.5, 'tinged with brown, spongy, firm'
Laburnum *L. vulgare*	Pennines Central Europe	24.6, 'velvet black, compact, remark-ably hard'
Chestnut *Castanea sativa*	Tuscany	23.3, 'glossy black, compact, firm'
Oak *Quercus pedunculata*	Harz Tuscany Jehol Dinaric Alps	22.7, 'black, close, very firm'
American black beech *Fagus grandifolia*	North America	21.4, 'fine black, compact, remarkably hard'
Walnut *Juglans regia*	East France Germany, England Caucasus, China Dinaric Alps	20.6, 'dull black, close, firm'
Holly *Ilex aquifolium*	Southern Pennines Scottish Highlands	19.9, 'dull black, loose, bulky'

Tree	Habitat	Carbon yield (parts in 100) & charcoal characteristics[a]
Beech *Fagus sylvatica*	Black Forest Harz, Carpathians Tuscany	19.9, 'dull black, spongy, very firm'
American sycamore *Platanus occidentalis*	North America	19.9, 'dull black, close, moderately firm'
Sycamore or Great Maple *Acer pseudoplatanus*	North America	19.7, 'fine black, bulky, moderately firm'
Elm *Ulmus campestris*	Harz	19.6, 'fine black, moderately firm'
Norway pine *Pinus resinosa*	North America	19.2, 'shining black, bulky, very soft'
Sallow or willow *Salix alba*	Tuscany	18.5, 'velvet black, bulky, loose and soft'
Ash *Fraxinus excelsior*	North America	17.9, 'shining black, spongy, moderately firm'
Birch *Betula alba*	Harz Jehol	17.5, 'velvet black, bulky, moderately firm'
Scotch pine *Pinus sylvestris*	Scottish Highlands	16.4, 'tinged with brown, bulky, pretty firm'

[a] Refers to color, nature, and compactness.

Sources: Adapted from Mushet, *Papers on iron and steel*, p. 51. See also Elwes and Henry, *The trees of Great Britain and Ireland,* vol. 6, p. 1525; Kerner von Marilaun, *The natural history of plants,* vol. 2, pp. 338, 433, 527, 559, 722; Rhind, *A history of the vegetable kingdom,* p. 437; Society for the Diffusion of Useful Knowledge, *A description and history of vegetable substances used in the arts and in domestic economy,* vol. 1, pp. 148, 163; Turner, *A new herbal,* 'Index V'; Ure, *A dictionary of arts, manufactures, and mines,* p. 370.

NOTES

Chapter 1. Mining the Underground Wealth of Nations

1. Smith, *The wealth of nations*, p. 606.
2. Ibid.
3. Ibid.
4. Ibid., pp. 607–608.
5. Ibid., p. 607.
6. Auty and Mikesell, *Sustainable development in mineral economies*; Badeeb et al., 'The evolution of the natural resource curse thesis: A critical literature survey'; Gilberthorpe and Papyrakis, 'The extractive industries and development.'
7. Smith, *The wealth of nations*, p. 160.
8. Marx, *Capital*, p. 158.
9. Brenner, 'The agrarian origins of European capitalism,' p. 34.
10. Aymard, *Dutch capitalism and world capitalism*; Braudel, *Civilization and capitalism*, 3 vols.; Chaudhury and Morineau, eds., *Merchants, companies, and trade: Europe and Asia in the early modern era*; Lee, ed., *The longue durée and world-systems analysis*; Overbeek, 'Cycles of hegemony and leadership in the core of the world system'; Wallerstein, *The modern world system*, vol. 1.
11. Marx, *Capital*, p. 158.
12. Ibid.
13. Bisson, 'Medieval lordship,' p. 749; Toch, 'Lords and peasants: A reappraisal of medieval economic relations.'
14. Kriedte, *Feudalismo tardío y capital mercantil*.
15. Cole and Wolf, *The hidden frontier: Ecology and ethnicity in an Alpine Valley*, pp. 78, 85.
16. Anderson, *Passages from antiquity to feudalism*, p. 199.
17. Ibid.
18. Kink, *Fontes Rerum Austriacarum*, p. 431, footnote 1.
19. Emperor Frederick Barbarossa (A.D. 1152–1190) declared as follows: *Mandamus igitur omnibus vobis et singulis sub obtentu gratie nostre precipientes, ut nullus vestrum se de*

predicta argentifodina intromittat nec aliquid iuris sine nostra licentia sibi in ea usurpet. By A.D. 1317, the principle was part of the legal custom and tradition of Alpine lands, *secundum jura et consuetudinem, quae in mineris hujusmodi observatur.* dMGH, *Monumenta Germaniae Historica, Legum Sectio, Constitutiones et Acta Publica*, pp. 465–466; Kink, *Fontes Rerum Austriacarum*, p. 433, footnote 4.

20. The grant referred to Pisa, Tuscany. Baudi di Vesme, *Historiae patriae*, p. cxxxii.
21. Jireček, *Codex juris Bohemici*, pp. 82, 284, 318, 320, 322, 324, 330.
22. Baudi di Vesme, *Historiae patriae*, p. 309.
23. Ibid., p. cxliii, 398.
24. Ibid., pp. 1084–1085.
25. Ibid., p. 283.
26. Kink, *Fontes Rerum Austriacarum*, p. 433.
27. Baudi di Vesme, *Historiae patriae*, p. 1077.
28. Ibid., p. 446.
29. Ibid., p. 788.
30. Ceccarelli, 'Renaissance machines in Italy: from Brunelleschi to Galilei'; Le Goff, *Intellectuals in the Middle Ages*; Lopez, *The commercial revolution of the Middle Ages, 950–1350*. On cultural change, see Noble and Engen, eds., *European transformations: The long twelfth century*.
31. I borrowed the phrase from Wallerstein, *The modern world-system*, vol. 1, p. 7.
32. Knorn et al., *Dissertatio historica de metallifodinarum*, p. 23.
33. Kink, *Fontes Rerum Austriacarum*, pp. 437, 450–451.
34. Baudi di Vesme, *Historiae patriae*, p. 265.
35. Ibid., p. 45.
36. Newbigin, *Geographical aspects of Balkan problems*, p. 1.
37. Ibid.
38. Isidore, *Isidore of Seville's Etymologies*, XIV.7.7.
39. For urbanization between the tenth and twelfth centuries, see Pounds, *An economic history of medieval Europe*, pp. 223–282.
40. Klápště, *Czech lands in medieval transformation*, p. 173.
41. Bini et al., 'Medieval phases of settlement at Benabbio castle, Apennine mountains,' p. 3060; Gamberini, 'La territorialità nel Basso Medioevo: un problema chiuso?' p. 1001; Mensing et al., 'Human and climatically induced environmental change in the Mediterranean,' p. 55.
42. Klápště, *Czech lands in medieval transformation*, p. 173.
43. Ferrante and Mattone, 'Le comunità rurali nella Sardegna medievale'; Pungetti, 'Anthropological approach to agricultural landscape history in Sardinia,' p. 47.
44. Stojsavljević et al., 'Serbian medieval towns and their tourist potentials,' p. 191.
45. Fumagalli, *Uomini e paesaggi medievali*; Provero, 'Le comunità rurali nel medioevo'; Lazzari, 'Comunità rurali nell'alto medioevo.' For a brief argument pertaining to the history of rural towns in England, see Dyer, 'How urban was medieval England?'
46. Stretch, *Prospecting, locating, and valuing mines*, p. 16.
47. Lamborn, *The metallurgy of silver and lead*, p. 63; see also Horák and Hejcman, '800 years of mining and smelting in Kutná Hora region (the Czech Republic),' p. 1594. Galena was known by multiple names in the medieval world: *galanza, ghiletta, gheletta,*

gliletta, chiletta, aguilecta, aguileta, aghilecta, aglecta, gileta, and *agecta* in the Mediterranean. French miners employed the term *alquifoux* to designate a pure lead sulphide. In Italy, galena was identified by the term *alchifoglio.* Arab miners used the word *kuḥl* for galena, as well as for antimony and other substances with certain medicinal and scientific applications. In ancient Chinese literature, the term *hei chhien yin* was used to designate 'black' lead silver. Baudi di Vesme, *Historiae patriae,* pp. clxxxvi–clxxxvii; Corriente, *Dictionary of Arabic and allied loanwords,* p. 86; Needham, ed., *Science and civilization in China,* vol. 5, p. 279.

48. Forbes, *Metallurgy in Antiquity,* p. 50.
49. Stretch, *Prospecting, locating, and valuing mines,* p. 20.
50. Hoover and Hoover, trans., *Georgius Agricola De Re Metallica,* p. 39.
51. Perini, *Dizionario geografico, statistico del Trentino,* p. 37.
52. Hoover and Hoover, trans., *Georgius Agricola De Re Metallica,* p. 129.
53. Zaitsev, 'The meaning of early medieval geometry,' p. 523, also pp. 527–535 for pre-Euclidian geometry.
54. Hoover and Hoover, trans., *Georgius Agricola De Re Metallica,* p. 129.
55. Rodolico, cur., *Ordinamenta super arte fossarum,* 'Item VIII,' pp. 68–69.
56. Korey, *The geometry of power, mathematical instruments, and Princely mechanical devices from around 1600,* p. 22; on Reinhold's contribution to astronomy, see Cunningham, 'Erasmus Reinhold at 500.'
57. Goguet, *The origins of laws, arts, and sciences, and their progress among the most ancient nations,* vol. 1, pp. 149–150.
58. Nriagu, 'Cupellation: the oldest quantitative chemical process,' p. 668; see also Blanchard, *Mining, metallurgy, and minting in the Middle Ages,* vol. 1; Greenaway, 'Thirty centuries of assaying,' p. 103; Hahn, 'Ore reduction in the Harz, II'; Thibodeau, 'The strange case of the earliest silver extraction by European colonists in the New World'; Vázquez De Prada, 'La coyuntura de la minería y de la metalurgia europeas (siglos XIII–XVIII).'
59. Nriagu, 'Tales told in lead.'
60. Gill, 'An outline of the chemistry of lead smelting,' p. 3.
61. Ibid.
62. Ibid.; Rippon et al., *Mining in a medieval landscape,* p. 89.
63. Rippon et al., *Mining in a medieval landscape,* p. 90.
64. Ibid.
65. Ibid.
66. Peter Claughton, personal communication, November 13, 2017.
67. Rippon et al., *Mining in a medieval landscape,* p. 98.
68. Martiñón-Torres et al., 'Some problems and potentials of the study of cupellation remains,' p. 60. Many thanks to Peter Claughton for calling my attention to the work by Marcos Martiñón-Torres. The rest of the paragraph, unless otherwise noted, comes from this work.
69. Galena's density and compact nature facilitated the separation of wanted metals from gangue, or the worthless minerals contained in an ore deposit. Oxidized lead, or PbO by its chemical name, was sometimes recycled for cleaning silver-bearing copper ores. Segers-Glocke and his colleagues illustrate the chemical reaction with the following equation: Ore + Charcoal+ (Fluxes) + Air $\leftrightarrow$ Metal + Slag + Dust/Gases (as CO, CO_2,

SO_2). Craddock, *Early metal mining and production*, p. 205; Cumming, ed., *Mining explained*, p. 127; Greenaway, 'Thirty centuries of assaying'; Segers-Glocke et al., eds., *Aspects of mining and smelting in the upper Harz Mountains*, p. 54.

70. Rippon et al., *Mining in a medieval landscape*, p. 98.

71. Other lead ores, besides galena, contain silver minerals. Cerussite, a lead carbonate ($PbCO_3$), and anglesite ($PbSO_4$), a lead sulphate, 'occur with native silver and silver ores in the oxidized portions of lead ore outcrops on the surface of the earth.' Cerussite resembles calcite, a soft and slightly colored crystal. Anglesite looks like the crystals of gypsum with a brilliant luster. According to Craddock, these oxidized lead ores 'may have been much more important in antiquity as sources of silver than has been generally believed.' Craddock, *Early metal mining and production*, p. 205; Forbes, *Metallurgy in Antiquity*, p. 181.

72. Hoffman, *An environmental history of medieval Europe*, pp. 196–203; Martín Gutiérrez, 'En los bosques andaluces: los carboneros a finales de la Edad Media'; Pastoreau, *Una historia simbólica de la Edad Media occidental*, pp. 89–106; Steane, *The archeology of medieval England and Wales*, pp. 222–223.

73. Ure, *A dictionary of arts, manufactures, and mines*, p. 370.

74. Blanchard, *Mining, metallurgy, and minting in the Middle Ages*, vol. 3, p. 76.

75. Wright, *A new and comprehensive gazetteer*, vol. 4, p. 558. For earlier mining activities in Saxon forests, see Häseler, *Das bergwerk in Rammelsberg bei Goslar*; Large and Walcher, 'The Rammelsberg massive sulphide Cu-Zn-Pb-Ba-deposit, Germany'; Mueller, 'The Rammelsberg share-hosted Cu-Zn-Pb sulfide and barite deposit, Germany'; *New York Times,* 'Frommer's Thuringia Forest'; Séguin, *The Black Forest: Its peoples and legends*; Thompson, 'Dutch and Flemish colonization of mediaeval Germany.'

76. Cosgel, 'Scattering and contracts in medieval agriculture.'

77. Blanchard, *Mining, metallurgy, and minting*, vol. 3, pp. 75–78.

78. Ibid., pp. 76–77.

79. Forbes, *Metallurgy in Antiquity*, p. 180.

80. Ibid.

81. Hall, *Lead ores*, p. 92.

82. King, 'Minerals explained 3: galena.'

83. I consulted the following works: Browne, 'Concerning damps in the mines of Hungary and their effects'; Kaláb et al., 'Mine water movement in shallow medieval Mine Jeroným (Czech Republic)'; Lambton, 'The qānāts of Yazd'; Munro, 'Industrial energy from water mills in the European economy'; Savery, *The Miner's Friend, or an engine to raise water by fire*; Sempat Assadourian, 'La bomba de fuego de Newcomen y otros artificios de desagüe'; Smith and Wolfe, *Technology and resource use in medieval Europe: Cathedrals, mills, and mines*; Squatriti, *Water and society in early medieval Italy*.

84. Arnoux, 'Innovation technique et genèse de l'enterprise: quelques réflexions à partir de l'exemple de la métallurgie européenne (XIIIe–XVIe siècles)'; Braunstein, 'De minerais au metal: la longue durée à l'épreuve des sources et des methods'; Long, 'The openness of knowledge: An ideal and its context in 16th-century writings on mining and metallurgy'; Tylecote, 'Roman lead working in Britain.'

85. Booth, *The historical library of Diodorus the Sicilian*, p. 321.

86. Matías Rodríguez, 'Ingeniería minera romana,' p. 168.

87. The expense of building drainage infrastructure was absorbed by the Imperial treasury. Domergue, *Minería y metalurgia en las antiguas civilizaciones mediterráneas*; Hirt, *Imperial mines and quarries in the Roman world: Organizational aspects*; Matías Rodríguez, 'Ingeniería minera romana,' pp. 167–168.

88. For a thorough description, see Hirt, *Imperial mines and quarries*, chap. 2.

89. Forbes, *Metallurgy in Antiquity*, pp. 53–54.

90. Costa, 'Notes on traditional hydraulics and agriculture in Oman'; Tengberg, 'Beginnings and early history of date palm garden cultivation in the Middle East.'

91. Macini and Mesini, 'The evolution of pumping systems through the early Renaissance,' p. 235.

92. Ibid.

93. Forbes, *Metallurgy in Antiquity*, p. 54.

94. A good example of ancient drainage is the *Galeria dos Alargamentos*, built in the open cast gold mine of Três Minas located in Aguiar, Portugal. Its 150-meter-long gallery continues to impress experts today for its effective design for the purpose of removing water. Matías Rodríguez, 'Ingeniería minera romana.'

95. Claughton, 'The medieval silver-lead miner, a preliminary study,' pp. 28–30; for general reference and photographs, see Gamble, *Cornish Mines: St Just to Redruth*.

96. Hirt, *Imperial mines and quarries*, p. 39.

97. I consulted the following works: Campopiano, 'Rural communities, land clearance, and water management in the Po Valley'; Corona et al., 'Millennium-long summer temperature variations in the European Alps'; Curtis and Campopiano, 'Medieval land reclamation and the creation of new societies: Comparing Holland and the Po Valley'; Garçon et al., 'Silver and lead in high-altitude lake sediments: Proxies for climate changes and human activities'; Squatriti, *Water and society in early medieval Italy*; Bundi, ed., *Alpine waters*.

98. Macini and Mesini, 'The evolution of pumping systems through the early Renaissance,' p. 234.

99. Magnusson and Squatriti, 'The technologies of water in medieval Italy,' p. 224.

100. Jireček, *Codex juris Bohemici*, p. 330.

101. Ibid.

102. Ehrenberg, *Capital and finance in the age of the Renaissance*.

103. Based upon the work by Gustav Schmoller, cited by Spufford, *Money and its Use in Medieval Europe*, p. 113.

104. Travaini, 'Mint organization in Italy: The twelfth and fourteenth centuries.'

105. Spufford, *Money and its Use in Medieval Europe*, p. 188.

106. Clark, 'The consumer revolution: a turning point in history?'; for a critique, see Flynn and Giráldez, eds., *Metals and monies in an emerging global economy*; Kovačević-Kojić, 'Les mines d'or et d'argent en Serbie et Bosnie,' pp. 194, 255; Porteous, *Coins in history*, p. 48; Shipton, 'The prices of the Athenian silver mines.'

107. Peter Claughton, personal communication, September 22, 2017. See also Munro, 'The medieval origins of the financial revolution'; Munro, 'Industrial energy from water mills in the European economy, 5th to 18th centuries'; Needham, ed., *Science and civ-*

ilization in China; Nef, 'Industrial Europe at the time of the Reformation'; Nef, 'Silver production in Central Europe, 1450–1618'; Rubino, 'Metallurgia e comunitá agro-operaie del Mezzogiorno d'Italia nell'etá della manifatture.'

108. Baron et al., 'Medieval lead making on Mont-Lozère Massif (Cévennes-France)'; Cederlund, 'Structures and vessels for transport in early Swedish iron production'; Craddock, 'From hearth to furnace: Evidences for the earliest metal smelting technologies in the eastern Mediterranean'; Echevarría Arsuaga, 'Explotación y mano de obra en las minas y salinas de al-Andalus'; Leroy et al., 'La sidérurgie dans l'est de la Gaule, l'organisation spatial de la production de l'Âge du fer au haut Moyen Âge'; Nagel, 'Norwegian mining in the early modern period'; Nisser, 'Industrial archaeology in the Nordic countries, viewed from Sweden'; Segers-Glocke et al., eds., *Aspects of mining and smelting in the upper Harz Mountains*; Thomasius, 'The influence of mining on woods and forestry in the Saxon Erzgebirge'; Wedepohl and Baumann, 'Isotope composition of medieval lead glasses reflecting early silver production in Central Europe.'

109. Abraham, 'Les mines d'argent antiques et médiévales du district minier de Kaymar'; Domergue, 'L'utilisation des photographies aériennes dans l'étude des mines d'or romaines à ciel ouvert du Nord-Ouest de l'Espagne'; Humbert, 'De l'utilité pour la géographie de l'observation et de la photographie aériennes obliques'; Humbert, '*Suelo y vuelo* au XVIIIe s., les surfaces fictives d'arbres dans le *Catastro de La Ensenada*'; Ruíz, 'Panorama de la arqueología medieval de los valles alto y medio del Vinalopó (Alicante).'

110. For a brief commentary on the scientific controversies about the use of slags, see Agrawal et al., 'Ancient copper workings: Some new C-14 dates'; see also Baron et al., 'Medieval lead making on Mont-Lozère Massif (Cévennes-France)'; Canto García and Cressier, eds., *Minas y metalurgia en al-Andalus y Magreb Occidental*, pp. 245–252.

111. Klappauf, in Segers-Glocke et al., eds., *Aspects of mining and smelting in the upper Harz Mountains*, p. 5.

112. Brockner and Hegerhorst, in Segers-Glocke et al., eds., *Aspects of mining and smelting in the upper Harz Mountains*, pp. 53–65.

113. Braunstein, 'Les statuts miniers de l'Europe médiévale,' p. 44.

114. I have borrowed the phrase from historian Sir John Elliot. See Elliot, 'Teaching history in the twenty-first century.'

115. Historians who mastered the study of medieval diaries include Braudel, *Civilization & Capitalism in 15th–18th century,* 3 vols.; Bretschneider, *Medieval researches from eastern Asiatic sources*; Chaudhuri, *Trade and civilisation in the Indian Ocean.*

116. Sidiqqi, *Indo-Persian historiography*, p. 5.

117. Gibb et al., *The encyclopedia of Islam*, vol. 1, p. 748.

118. Del Mar, *A history of the precious metals*, p. 319.

119. On Bū Ragrāg. Gibb et al., *The encyclopedia of Islam*, vol. 2, p. 874.

120. Gozalbes Busto and Gozalbes Cravioto, 'Al-Magrib al-Aqsà en los primeros geógrafos árabes orientales'; Ḥawqal, *Bibliotheca Geographorum Arabicorum.*

121. Calvo, 'Ibn Ḥawqal.'

122. García Moreno adds that there is still no complete list of al-Rāzī's writings, and the available works suggest that a different author participated in the writings. García Moreno, 'Teudemiro de Orihuela y la invasión islámica,' pp. 534–535.

123. Gibb et al., *The encyclopedia of Islam*, vol. 1, p. 748.

124. Ibid., p. 488.
125. Bryer, 'The question of Byzantine mines in the Pontos,' p. 139.
126. Marco Polo situated the mine near a castle identified by the name 'Paipurth' 'that you pass in going from Trebizond to Tauris' in Armenia. Bryer, 'The question of Byzantine mines in the Pontos,' p. 139; Yule, ed., *The book of Ser Marco Polo*, vol. 1, p. 47.
127. Moreno Nieto, *Discursos leídos ante la Real Academia de la Historia*, p. 39; Lee, trans., *The travels of Ibn Batūta*.
128. Bryer continues: 'The identification of any of these places with Argyropolis or Gümüşhane would in any case have been anomalous, for I propose the following sequence: that what Byzantines and Trapenzuntines called Tzanicha fell to the Ottomans in 1479, that silver and gold mines were not opened there until 1546, that a mint of Tzanicha operated thereafter until after 1574 and before 1595, and that a new town called Gümüşhane was built to serve the mines before 1598, and that the name Argyropolis was not concocted by local Greek schoolmasters as a Hellenisation of Gümüşhane until about 1846, when the silver mines were in their last gasp. There is no ancient or medieval Gümüşhane or Argyropolis.' Bryer, 'The question of Byzantine mines in the Pontos,' p. 140.
129. Gibb et al., *The Encyclopedia of Islam*, vol. 2, p. 1139; see also Pitarakis, 'Mines Anatoliennes exploitées par les Byzantins'; on the geology of the region, see Demir et al., 'Mineral chemical investigation on sulfide mineralization of the Istala deposit, Gümüşhane.'
130. Kink's edition of *Codex Wangianus* is included in his *Fontes Rerum Austriacarum*. The edition contains a lengthy preface paged in Roman numerals, an introduction to the *Codex*, and the historical legal documents of the Trent Bishopric organized by theme and identified by Arabic numerals. The documents pertaining to mining are grouped under a second part of *Codex*, dedicated exclusively to Bishop Frederick Wanga. Citations in this book to mining documents from Kink's edition will contain document and page numbers, following the original work.
131. Curzel, *Il Codice Vanga*; Curzel and Varanini, *La documentazione dei vescovi di Trento*.
132. Czaja, 'Mining and hydrological transformations in Upper Silesia from fifteenth to nineteenth centuries'; Jánošíková, 'Mining business pursuant to "Ius Regale Montanorum" in the 14th century'; Kaláb et al., 'Mine water movement in shallow medieval Mine Jeroným (Czech Republic)'; Kalus, *Die Fugger in der Slowakei*; Klápště, *The Czech lands in medieval transformation*; Majer, 'Changes in silver mining of the Bohemian lands in the 16th century and their economic consequences.'
133. Baudi di Vesme's *Historiae patriae* is a lengthy book divided into several parts. The two parts used in our study are as follows: 'Dell'industria del territorio di Villa di Chiesa,' a thorough explanation of the mining statute, paged in Roman numerals starting at lxxxv up to cclxxxiv; and 'Breve di Villa di Chiesa di Sigerro,' a lengthy transcription of the statute, paged in Hindu-Arabic numbers starting at four and reaching 246. Citations from this work done in this book reflect the numbering systems employed by Baudi di Vesme.
134. Tangheroni, *Pisa e il Mediterraneo: uomini, merci, idee dagli Etruschi ai Medici*; *Commercio, finanza, funzione pubblica: stranieri in Sicilia e Sardegna nei secoli XIII–XV*; Tangheroni and Mercuriali, *La città dell'argento: Iglesias dalle origini alla fine del Medioevo*.

135. Baudi di Vesme, 'Dell'industria dell miniere nel territorio di Villa,' pp. 66, 441.

136. King, *The finances of the Cistercian Order in the fourteenth century*, pp. 7–28, 12; see also Alfonso, 'Cistercians and feudalism'; Lekai, 'Medieval Cistercians and their social environment.'

137. Heer, *The Holy Roman Empire*, p. 49; see also Bernhardt, *Itinerant kingship and royal monasteries in early medieval Germany*; for references to mining activities by Cistercians, see Burton, *The Cistercians in the Middle Ages*; Burton, *The Monastic order in Yorkshire*; for a pictorial essay, see Gaud and Leroux-Dhuys, *Les abbayes Cisterciennes en France et en Europe*.

138. Toussaint Reinaud, *Muslim colonies in France, Northern Italy, and Switzerland*, p. 135.

139. Hodgson, *The venture of Islam*, vol. 2, p. 406.

140. For sources on the subject, see Rachewiltz, *The secret history of the Mongols*, vol. 3.

141. Robinson, *Empire and elites after the Muslim conquest*, chap. 2; Faroqhi et al., eds., *An economic and social history of the Ottoman empire*, p. 59.

142. Lindner, *Explorations in Ottoman prehistory*, pp. 15, 17.

143. Beldiceanu translated to French language the Ottoman administrative and fiscal laws contained in Manuscript No. 39 or *Fonds Turc anciens 39* at Bibliothèque Nationale, Paris. Beldiceanu, *Les Actes des Premiers Sultans*, 2 vols.

144. Babinger's edition was published in 1975 by Xerox University Microfilm, Ann Arbor, Michigan. The edition by Anhegger and İnalcik appeared in Ankara in 1956, published by Türk Tarih Kurumu Basımevi.

145. Cited in Kriedte, *Feudalismo tardío y capital mercantil*, p. 61.

146. Gunder Frank, *ReOrient: Global economy in the Asian age*, p. 55.

147. Braudel, *History of civilizations*.

148. Ehrenberg, *Capital and finance in the age of the Renaissance*; Spufford, *Money and its use in medieval Europe*; Von Stromer, 'Nuremberg in the international economics of the Middle Ages'; Wallerstein, *The modern world-system*, 1.

Chapter 2. World Mining Regions before the Rise of Modern Capitalism

1. The phrase comes from Townson, *Philosophy of mineralogy*, p. 35. For points in dispute about ore-deposition theories in geology, see Duff et al., *Holmes' principles of physical geology*, p. 724; Edwards and Atkinson, *Ore deposit geology and its influence on mineral exploration*; Guilbert and Park, *The geology of ore deposits*, pp. 13–24; Rodgers, 'Differences between mountain ranges,' p. 11; Rosenberg, ed., *The revolution in geology: From the Renaissance to the Enlightenment*; Schaer, 'Introduction: Comparative anatomy in geology,' pp. 8–9.

2. McKinsty, *Mining geology*; Shaer, 'Introduction'; Townson, *Philosophy of mineralogy*; Wilson, *A history of mountains: Geographical and mineralogical*.

3. Umlauft, *The Alps*, p. 236. I also consulted the following works: D'Achiardi, 'La miniera del Bottino nelle Alpi Apuane'; Garlandi et al., *Il patrimonio storico industriale della Lombardia: censimento regionale*; Giovanelli, *Intorno all'antica zecca Trentina e a due monumenti Reti: lettere tre*; Hoffman, 'The commerce of the German Alpine passes during the early Middle Ages'; Hunt and Murray, *A history of business in medieval Europe, 1200–1550*; Kellenbenz, *Precious metals in the age of expansion*; La

Salvia, *Iron making during the migration period: The case of the Lombards*; Marinelli, 'The regions of mixed populations in northern Italy'; Perini and Lurati, *Illustrazione del Tirolo italiano e della Svizzera italiana*; Rosa, *Delle leggi di Bergamo nel medio evo*; Saggioro, 'Insediamenti, proprietà ed economie nei territory di pianura tra Adda e Adige (VII–IX secolo)'; Scheuermann, *Die Fugger als montanindustrielle in Tirol und Kärnten*; Timberlake, 'Early leats and hushing remains: Suggestions and disputes of Roman mining and prospection for lead.'

4. Corniani Degli Algarotti, *Dello stabilimento delle miniere relative fabbriche nel distretto di Agordo*, p. 19.

5. Magdalino, *The empire of Manuel I Komenos*, p. 82.

6. Perini, *Dizionario geografico, statistico del Trentino*, p. 193.

7. Braunstein, 'Les enterprises minières en Venetia,' p. 531.

8. Allen, *A history of Verona*; Cipolla, 'Un fiorentino a Trento nel sec. XIV,' p. 193; Sforza, 'Italiani non Trentini nel Trentino,' pp. 65–67.

9. Cantù, *Illustrazione del Tirolo italiano*, p. 73; for historical geography of the region, see Dai Prà, 'La cartografia storica come interfaccia dialettica tra discipline e competenze territoriali.'

10. Baillie-Grohman, *The land in the mountains, being an account of Tyrol*, p. 32.

11. Cantù, *Illustrazione del Tirolo italiano*, p. 73.

12. Dai Prà, 'La cartografia storica come interfaccia dialettica tra discipline e competenze territoriali.'

13. Collatera and Primerano, *Un Vescovo la sua Cattedrale, il suo tesoro*, p. 22.

14. Algarotti, *Dello stabilimento delle miniere*, p. 19; Umlauft, *The Alps*, p. 63.

15. Baillie-Grohman, *The land in the mountains, being an account of Tyrol*, p. 259; on the Fugger, see Graulau, 'Finance, industry, and globalization in the early modern period'; Ehrenberg, *Capital and finance in the age of the Renaissance*; Kellenbenz, *Los Fugger en España y Portugal hasta 1560*. The German edition of Kellenbenz's work, entitled *Die Fugger in Spanien und Portugal bis 1560: ein Grossunternehmen des 16. Jahrhunderts* (München, 1990), contains a useful appendix of primary documents in Spanish, Portuguese, German, and Latin.

16. Hall, *Lead ores*, p. 79.

17. Baillie-Grohman, *The land in the mountains, being an account of Tyrol*, p. 259.

18. Ibid., pp. 260–261.

19. Ibid.; Perry, 'Report by Mr. Consul-General Perry on the trade and commerce of Venice for the year 1867,' p. 465.

20. Umlauft, *The Alps*, p. 283.

21. Harding, *Salt in prehistoric Europe*; Kern et al., *Kingdom of salt: 7000 years of Hallstat*.

22. Bright, *Travels from Vienna through Lower Hungary*, pp. 640–641; Harding, *Salt in pre-historic Europe*, p. 62.

23. Umlauft, *The Alps*, pp. 75–76.

24. Bernhardt, *Itinerant kingship and royal monasteries in early medieval Germany*.

25. Cibrario, *Della economia political dell medio evo*, p. 10.

26. Ibid.

27. Rosen, *The Third Horseman: Climate change and the Great Famine of the 14th century*.

28. Loudon, *An encyclopedia of agriculture*, p. 33.

29. Ibid.

30. Peattie, *Mountain geography*, p. 125.

31. Brill, 'Alpes (Alps).'

32. Perini, *Dizionario geografico, statistico del Trentino*, p. 194.

33. Lupi, *Memorie istoriche della città e chiesa di Bergamo*, vol. 1, p. 194.

34. Földváry, *Geology of the Carpathian region*, p. 11.

35. Pounds, *An historical geography of Europe*, p. 140.

36. Ibid., p. 140.

37. Földváry, *Geology of the Carpathian region*, p. 11.

38. Raju, *Via Francigena*; Spufford, *Power and profit: The merchant in medieval Europe*.

39. Umlauft, *The Alps*, p. 116.

40. Ibid.

41. Byse, 'Milton on the continent,' p. 18.

42. Still, this was not an easy pass. Between the Great St. Bernard and the Simplon Pass there is a glacier zone stretching for more than ninety kilometers featuring 140 different glaciers. 'Hardly at any point between the two passes does the crest sink lower than 8,529 feet [2,600 meters], and twenty-one peaks rise above 13,000 feet' [3,962 meters]. Umlauft, *The Alps*, p. 115; on the pass in the Middle Ages, see Todd, *The early Germans*.

43. Baillie-Grohman, *The land in the mountains, being an account of Tyrol*, p. 35.

44. Ibid., p. 36.

45. Harreld, *High Germans in the Low countries*, p. 38.

46. Smith, *A system of modern geography*, vol. 2, p. 348.

47. Umlauft, *The Alps*, p. 382.

48. Ibid., pp. 142, 405.

49. Hahn, 'Ore reduction in the Harz, II'; Segers-Glocke et al., eds., *Aspects of mining and smelting in the upper Harz Mountains*; Tizzoni and Cucini, *Il comprensorio minerario e metallurgico delle valli Brembana, Torta ed Averara*; Tizzoni et al., eds., *Alle origini della siderurgia lecchese*.

50. Fagan, *The Little Ice Age: How climate made history, 1300–1850*, p. 19.

51. Umlauft, *The Alps*, p. 237.

52. Ibid.

53. Hoffmann, 'The Fondaco dei Tedeschi: The medium of Venetian-German trade'; Lieber, 'Eastern business practices and medieval European commerce,' p. 230, footnote 2; Holtfrerich, *Frankfurt as a financial center*, p. 43.

54. A succinct bibliographic review is contained in Cencini, 'Physical processes and human activities in the evolution of the Po Delta'; see also Ceruti et al., *Il delta del Po: nature e civiltà*; Guidoboni, 'Human factors, extreme events, and floods in the Lower Po Plain.'

55. Del Mar, *A history of the precious metals*, p. 60.

56. Machiavelli, *The Florentine histories*, vol. 1, p. 70.

57. Guidoboni, 'Human factors, extreme events, and floods in the Lower Po Plain,' p. 293.

58. Ibid., p. 282.

59. Ibid., p. 286.

60. Porter states that 'medieval diplomas make frequent mention of woods which were evidently regarded as exceedingly valuable possessions.' Porter, *The construction of Lombard and Gothic vaults*, p. 19, footnote 1. The rest of this paragraph comes from this work.

61. Venetian merchants imported wood from the Dinaric Alps, after exhaustion of Istria's timber reserves. In A.D. 1470, the Venetian Council of Ten pondered the question of wood scarcity and considered replanting oak trees for naval purposes. Perini, *Dizionario geografico, statistico del Trentino*, p. 388; Spufford, *Power and profit*, p. 322. For a general social history to the Venetian forestry laws, see Appuhn, *A forest on the sea: Environmental expertise in the Renaissance*, chap. 3.

62. Jones, ed., *The new Cambridge medieval history*, p. 161; for a general description of metal armor factories, see Pyhrr et al., *Heroic armor of the Italian Renaissance: Filippo Negroli and his contemporaries*; Williams, 'The gilding of armour: Medieval and Renaissance techniques.'

63. Perini, *Dizionario geografico, statistico del Trentino*, p. 194.

64. I consulted the following works: Dickinson, 'Mitteldeutschland: The middle Elbe basin as a geographical unit'; Illés, *Visions and strategies in the Carpathian Area*; Mackenzie and Irby, *Across the Carpathians*; Moscheles, 'Natural regions of Czechoslovakia'; Sedlar, *East Central Europe in the Middle Ages*; Štefánik, 'Italian involvement in metal mining in the Central Slovakian region, from the thirteenth century to the reign of King Sigismund of Hungary.'

65. Mackenzie and Irby, *Across the Carpathians*, p. 1.

66. Piskorski, 'Medieval colonization in East Central Europe,' p. 29.

67. McKinsty et al., *Mining geology*, p. xvii.

68. For the geology of the Flysch Belt, see Földváry, *Geology of the Carpathian region*; Nagel and Sawinski, *UXL Encyclopedia of landforms and other geologic features*, p. xiii.

69. Cotta, *A treatise on ore deposits*, pp. 296–297.

70. Thompson, 'Early trade relations between the Germans and the Slavs'; Wischnitzer, 'Origins of the Jewish artisan class in Bohemia.'

71. Cotta, *A treatise on ore deposits*, p. 228; Jireček, *Codex juris Bohemici*, p. 284.

72. Blanchard, 'Medieval crafts, guilds, and industrial development,' p. 1.

73. Molenda, 'Mining towns in central-eastern Europe in feudal times,' p. 175.

74. Klápště, *The Czech lands in medieval transformation*, p. 455.

75. Cotta, *A treatise on ore deposits*, p. 297.

76. Paul, *Mining lore*, p. 201.

77. Madgearu, 'Salt trade and warfare in early medieval Transylvania,' p. 271.

78. Bakos, 'Au-porphyry mineralization in the mantle of the Štiavnica strato volcano,' p. 4.

79. Townson, *Travels in Hungary*, p. 289.

80. Malte-Brun, *A system of universal geography*, pp. 450–451.

81. Földváry, *Geology of the Carpathian region*, p. 98; see also Burchfiel and Bleahu, *Geology of Romania*, pp. 28–31; Cotta, *A treatise on ore deposits*, p. 272.

82. Kovacs and Fülöp, 'Baia Mare geological and mining park,' p. 29.

83. 'In ancient times, large masses were obtained from quarries in the Csétatye-rock, partly by the aid of fire.' Ibid.

84. Cotta, *A treatise on ore deposits*, p. 275.

85. Postan and Habakkuk, eds., *The Cambridge economic history of Europe*, pp. 33–42.

86. A nineteenth-century traveler completing a journey from Constantinople to England narrated a story that he gathered on his way through the Carpathians that speaks of German migrants in the region, as follows: 'The town of Hamlin, in Germany, was at one time

so infested with rats, that the citizens were nearly destroyed by them: on a particular
day, a certain trumpeter, (*tubicen quidam*), appeared before the gates, and the sound of
his instrument greatly attracted the citizens, who crowded out to hear him: after some
parley, he promised, for a specific reward, to charm all the rats with his music, and lead
them with him out of the town. This was readily agreed to: the trumpeter began to play,
and the rats followed him into the country, and never returned. When he claimed his
promised reward, the citizens, now freed from their annoyance, refused to give it, and
he departed very discontented. He availed himself, however, of his opportunity to be
revenged: he came back, when the elder people were all at prayers, and began to play
in the streets, and all the children who were left at home flocked out to hear him; these
he led after him, like rats, to a mountain called Koppen; the mountain opened, and they
all entered together, and never were seen again at Hamlin. This event the citizens of
Hamlin formed into an epoch, and some of their archives are dated, "*Anno post exitum
puerorum nostrorum.*" About the time these children disappeared in Germany, in 1284,
the Transylvanian Chronicles related that a number of strange children were found, on
St. Peter and St. Paul's day, wandering by themselves about the roads in that country, and
who seemed to have issued suddenly from the ground; they spoke an unknown tongue,
which was afterwards ascertained to be Saxon, and their descendants have continued to
speak it to this day. The certain inference was, that these were the very children whom
the trumpeter had enclosed in the mountain, and led by a subterraneous passage under
several countries, till they arrived at this remote place. Kircher affirms, that this man was
certainly Satan, to which one of his commentators assents, by saying that his hand is on
the descendants of these children to this day, as they are all inveterate heretics. To complete this extraordinary chain of evidence, the very tomb of this minstrel, who seemed
to have lived to a supernatural age, is pointed out at Pavia, in the church of St. Laurence,
where the following epitaph is to be seen: *Valentino Grævio, alias Backfort e Transylvania, Saxon: German: colonia orto, quem fidibus novo et inusitato artificio cunentem
audiens, ætas nostra ut alterum Orpheum admirata obstupuit, ob. an.* MDLXXVI.' Walsh,
Narrative of a journey from Constantinople to England, pp. 309–310.

87. Especially so in the lands comprising the Brandenburg Mark under the rule of Otto (A.D.
1128–1184), son of the first Margrave Albrecht the Bear. Carsten, 'Slavs in north-eastern
Germany.'

88. Schröcke, 'Mining and German settlement in Slovakia,' p. 128.

89. Ibid., p. 131.

90. Moník and Šlézar, 'An analysis of metalworking by-products from the medieval town of
Uničov,' p. 230.

91. Ibid.

92. Some mining settlements survived the waves of Mongol invasions. This was the case of
Rodna in Romania and Rogozno in Poland, both of which survived well into A.D. 1350.
Engel, *The realm of St. Stephen: History of medieval Hungary*, pp. 61–62.

93. Schröcke, 'Mining and German settlement in Slovakia,' p. 131.

94. Ibid.

95. Baedeker, *Southern Germany and Austria*, p. 331; Schröcke, 'Mining and German settlement in Slovakia,' p. 131.

96. Schröcke, 'Mining and German settlement in Slovakia,' p. 131.

97. Piskorski, 'Medieval colonization in East central Europe,' p. 30.

98. Ibid.

99. Brutzkus, 'Trade with eastern Europe,' p. 34; see also Bidlo, 'The Slavs in medieval history.'

100. For a general history of medieval trade routes, see Le Goff, *La Baja Edad Media*; Lieber, 'Eastern business practices and medieval European commerce'; Lopez, *The commercial revolution of the Middle Ages*; Matthew, *Atlas of Medieval Europe*; Pirenne, *Economic and social history of medieval Europe*; Schildhauer, *The Hansa: History and culture*; Smith, *Premodern trade in world history*.

101. Czaja, 'Mining and hydrological transformations in Upper Silesia,' p. 60; Reynolds, *Stronger than a hundred men: A history of the vertical water wheel*, p. 51.

102. Mutton, 'The Black Forest: Its human geography,' p. 134.

103. Chisholm, ed., *The Encyclopedia Britannica*, vol. 5, p. 383.

104. Martonne, 'The Carpathians: Physiographic features controlling human geography,' p. 425.

105. Johnson, 'The conquest of Rumania,' p. 441.

106. Madgearu, 'Salt trade and warfare in early medieval Transylvania,' p. 271.

107. Ibid.

108. Martonne, 'The Carpathians,' p. 433.

109. Cunliffe, *Europe between the oceans: Themes and variations, 9000 BC–AD 1000*, p. 41.

110. Sedlar, *East Central Europe in the Middle Ages*, p. 5.

111. De Puy, *The world-wide encyclopedia and gazetteer*, p. 4293.

112. Sedlar, *East Central Europe in the Middle Ages*, p. 9.

113. Ibid., p. 10.

114. Malte-Brun, *A system of universal geography*, p. 451.

115. Ibid., p. 422.

116. Matley, 'Transhumance in Bosnia and Herzegovina,' p. 232.

117. Martonne, 'The Carpathians,' p. 433.

118. Matley, 'Transhumance in Bosnia and Herzegovina,' p. 247.

119. Plesník, 'Man's influence on the timberline in the West Carpathian mountains,' p. 495.

120. Ibid., p. 494.

121. Ibid., p. 502; Society for the Diffusion of Useful Knowledge, *A description and history of vegetable substances*, p. 92.

122. Society for the Diffusion of Useful Knowledge, *A description and history of vegetable substances*, p. 94.

123. Ibid., p. 93.

124. Plesník, 'Man's influence on the timberline in the West Carpathian mountains,' p. 494.

125. Martonne, 'The Carpathians,' p. 431.

126. The mines of Kutná Hora used more than 60,000 cubic meters of wood every year in the sixteenth century. Prices of wood increased slightly beginning in A.D. 1470; by A.D. 1535 the increase became general. Kellenbenz, *The rise of the European economy*, p. 100.

127. Grzés and Szupryczyński, 'Large floods in the lower Vistula River.'

128. Born, *Travels through the Bannat of Temeswar, Transylvania, and Hungary in the year 1770*, p. 8.

129. Zavoianu, 'Romania's water resources and their uses,' p. 26.

130. Klápště, *The Czech lands in medieval transformation*, p. 457.

131. Ibid.

132. Czaja, 'Mining and hydrological transformations in Upper Silesia,' p. 59.

133. Later in the nineteenth century, miners discovered some of these networks in Upper Silesia. The miners found them so 'complicated that they were afraid of getting lost and refused to enter them.' Ibid.

134. Hoover and Hoover, trans., *Georgius Agricola De Re Metallica*, pp. 194–195; for biographical notes on Agricola, see Hannaway, 'Georgius Agricola as humanist'; Prescher, 'Dr. Georgius Agricola'; Rocke, 'Agricola, Paracelsus, and Chymia.'

135. Moník and Šlézar, 'An analysis of metalworking by-products from the medieval town of Uničov.'

136. Bandy and Bandy, trans., *De natura fossilium*.

137. Klápště, *The Czech lands in medieval transformation*, p. 455.

138. Anderson, *Passages from Antiquity to feudalism*; Aston and Philpin, eds., *The Brenner debate: Agrarian class structure and economic development in pre-industrial Europe*.

139. Klápště, *The Czech lands in medieval transformation*, p. 455.

140. Jervis, *The mineral resources of central Italy*, p. 71.

141. Suess, *The face of the earth*, p. 275. Geologists divide the Tuscan Sub-Apennines into ten minor ranges, depending upon rock formation. Here, we describe only the formations that form part of the Ore Hills. For more, see Carobbi and Rodolico, *I minerali della Toscana*; Comunità Montana Colline Metallifere, *Colline Metallifere*; Morini and Bruni, *The Regione Toscana project of geological mapping*; Preller, *Italian mountain geology*, pp. 2, 121–133.

142. Smith, *A system of modern geography*, vol. 2, p. 341.

143. I consulted the following works: Álvarez, *The mountains of Saint Francis: Discovering the geological events that shaped our Earth*; Melis et al., *Industria e commercio nella Toscana medievale*; Petrocchi, *Massa Marittima, arte e storia*; Preller, *Italian mountain geology*, parts 1–2; Rossi-Doria, 'The land tenure system and class in southern Italy'; Rubino, 'Metallurgia e comunitá agro-operaie del Mezzogiorno d'Italia nell'etá della manifatture'; Settia, 'Assetto del popolamento rurale e coppie toponimiche nell'Italia Padana'; Tizzoni et al., eds., *Alle origini della siderurgia lecchese: ricerche archaeometallurgiche ai Piani d'Erna*; Wyse, ed., *Four centuries of geological travel*; Zammatteo, 'A Luserna e Faedo sulle tracce di una storia mineraria millenaria.'

144. Cotta, *A treatise on ore deposits*, p. 350; Thomson, *Outlines of mineralogy, geology, and mineral analysis*, pp. 72–73.

145. Preller, *Italian mountain geology*, part 1, p. 105.

146. Cotta, *A treatise on ore deposits*, p. 352.

147. Ibid.

148. Jervis, 'Mineral resources of Tuscany,' p. 693.

149. Carobbi and Rodolico, *I minerali della Toscana*, p. 139.

150. Cotta, *A treatise on ore deposits*, p. 348.

151. Carobbi and Rodolico, *I minerali della Toscana*, p. 202.

152. Cotta, *A treatise on ore deposits*, pp. 352–353.

153. Cesaretti, *Memorie sacra e profane dell'antica diocesi di Populonia al presente diocesi*

di Massa Marittima, p. 93; p. 32, footnote c; p. 33, footnote c; Comparini, ed., *Memorie storiche di Massa Marittima*, pp. 54–59.

154. Geologists in the twentieth century mapped a deposit containing argentiferous galena, extending for over three kilometers in northwesterly direction, between Monte Valerio and Monte Calvi, close to Massetano and Boccheggiano. Beyschlag et al., *The deposits of the useful minerals and rocks*, p. 410; Carobbi and Rodolico, *I minerali della Toscana*, pp. 83, 87; Cumming, ed., *Mining explained*, p. 15.

155. Massetano ores occur in irregular masses, and contain aggregates of barite, celestine, argentiferous galena, marcasite, and blende, all useful raw materials. Carobbi and Rodolico, *I minerali della Toscana*, p. 89; Comparini, ed., *Memorie storiche di Massa Marittima*, pp. 54–59; Repetti, *Dizionario geografico, fisico, storico della Toscana*, vol. 1, p. 29; vol. 3, p. 149; Salvioli, *Manuale diritto italiano*, pp. 203–209; Targioni Tozetti, *Relazioni d'alcuni viaggi fatti in diverse parti della Toscana*, pp. 144–145; Terreni et al., *Viaggio pittorico della Toscana dell'Abate Francesco Fontani*, p. 249.

156. Smith, *A system of modern geography*, vol. 2, p. 345.

157. Osheim, 'Countrymen and the law in late-medieval Tuscany,' p. 317.

158. Fivaller De Velaz, *Memoria del olivo y su cultivo*, p. 11.

159. Smith, *A system of modern geography*, vol. 2, p. 358.

160. Herlihy, *Medieval and Renaissance Pistoia*, p. 48.

161. In A.D. 1569, the total cereal harvest, according to a local historian, was 350,000 staia of wheat and 180,000 staia of grains, and 112,000 staia of wheat were exported to Prato and Florence. This agricultural activity required extensive drainage works. Herlihy comments: 'Even the toponyms of Pistoia and its surrounding plain preserve the memory of a once water-logged terrain: Pantano (bog), Piscina (pond), Padule (marsh), Acqualunga (long water)'; 'one of Pistoia's gates, the Porta Guidi was also known as the Porta del Pantano, "Bog Gate," as if to warn the traveler of the kind of terrain that he faced in leaving the city.' Ibid., pp. 48–49.

162. 'In 1285, in an effort to monopolize the wine trade, the city imposed delivery quotas on those rural communes which sold wine commercially.' Ibid., p. 45.

163. The wine of Montepulciano was produced by the *mercatura di vino* or association of merchants. Repetti, *Dizionario geografico, fisico, storico della Toscana*, vol. 3, p. 490.

164. Wickham, *The mountains and the city: The Tuscan Apennines*, pp. 18–19.

165. Ibid., p. 21.

166. Ibid., p. 22.

167. Repetti, *Dizionario geografico, fisico, storico della Toscana*, vol. 3, p. 56.

168. Curzel and Varanini, *Codex Wangianus, i cartulari della Chiesa trentina*, p. 286; Schneller, *Quellen und forschungen zur geschichte, litteratur und sprache Osterreichs und seiner Kronländer*, p. 151.

169. Wickham, *The mountains and the city*, p. 22.

170. Herlihy, *Medieval and Renaissance Pistoia*, p. 37.

171. Repetti, *Dizionario geografico, fisico, storico della Toscana*, vol. 3, p. 163.

172. Ibid., pp. 96, 282.

173. Herlihy, *Medieval and Renaissance Pistoia*, p. 30.

174. Wickham, *The mountains and the city*, p. 21.

175. Ibid., p. 79; see also Evans, 'Transhumance in Europe,' p. 176.

176. Ibid., p. 25.

177. Ibid., p. 31.

178. Balestracci, *The Renaissance in the fields: Family memoirs of a fifteenth-century Tuscan peasant*, p. 76.

179. Wickham, 'Paludi e miniere nella Maremma Toscana, XI–XIII secoli,' p. 451.

180. Bouchier, ed., *Sardinia in ancient times*, p. 53, footnote 1; Cacciaglia, 'Nella miniera dell'*Inferno.*'

181. Alexander, 'The reclamation of Val-di-Chiana.'

182. Simonin, 'La Maremma Toscana souvenirs de voyage, II,' p. 912.

183. Herlihy, *Medieval and Renaissance Pistoia*, p. 44.

184. Repetti, *Dizionario geografico, fisico, storico della Toscana*, vol. 1, p. 724.

185. Ibid., p. 684.

186. Machiavelli, *The Florentine histories*, p. 70; Sarti et al., 'The growth and decline of Pisa (Tuscany, Italy) up to the Middle Ages,' p. 316.

187. Pignotti, *The history of Tuscany, from the earliest era*, 'Notice.'

188. Squatriti, *Water and society in early medieval Italy*.

189. Machiavelli stated: 'Dante and Giovanni Villani have demonstrated that the city of Fiesole, situated on the summit of a hill, marked out a plot of ground upon the plain that lies between the skirts of that hill and the river Arno, for the convenience of merchants, that their goods might be transported thither with less difficulty, and their markets be more frequented.' Machiavelli, *The Florentine histories*, p. 70.

190. Sarti et al., 'The growth and decline of Pisa (Tuscany, Italy) up to the Middle Ages,' p. 313.

191. Villani et al., *Croniche di Giovanni, Matteo e Filippo Villani*, p. 23.

192. Sarti et al., 'The growth and decline of Pisa (Tuscany, Italy) up to the Middle Ages,' p. 314.

193. Herlihy, *Medieval and Renaissance Pistoia*, p. 36.

194. Adams, 'Architecture for fish: The Sienese Dam on the Bruna River.'

195. Comunità Montana Colline Metallifere, *Colline Metallifere*.

196. Copper mining works started in the early fifteenth century, but they lacked the success that silver mining enjoyed two centuries earlier. Petrocchi, *Massa Marittima, arte e storia*, p. 341.

197. Castro, *Descrizione geologico-mineraria della zona argentifera del Sarrabus*, p. 7.

198. Repetti, *Dizionario geografico, fisico, storico della Toscana*, vol. 4, pp. 842–843.

199. De Roover, *The Medici bank: Its organization, management, operation, and decline*, pp. 44–51.

200. Repetti, *Dizionario geografico, fisico, storico della Toscana*, vol. 5, p. 627.

201. In comparison, production in the worst year was eighty-four silver pounds, and 5,354 lead pounds, at a cost of 31,096 *lire*. Repetti, *Dizionario geografico, fisico, storico della Toscana*, vol. 4, pp. 234–235.

202. Ehrenberg, *Capital and finance in the age of the Renaissance*; Schevill, *The Medici*; Spufford, *Power and profit*.

203. Petrocchi, *Massa Marittima, arte e storia*, p. 341.

204. I consulted the following works: Consorzio del Parco Geominerario Storico e Ambientale della Sardegna, *I Codici minerari europei a confronto*; Gabrielli, 'Greeks and

Arabs in the Central Mediterranean Area'; Waele and Forti, 'Mineralogy of mine caves in Sardinia.'

205. Isidore, *Isidore of Seville's Etymologies: Complete English translation*, XIV.6.36.
206. Ibid., XIII.13.4.
207. Levi, 'Sardinia: Isle of antithesis,' p. 631.
208. De Vargas, 'On the mines of Sardinia,' p. 147.
209. Flitch, *Mediterranean moods: Footnotes of travel in the islands of Mallorca, Menorca*, p. 293.
210. De Vargas, 'On the mines of Sardinia,' p. 147.
211. Some 200-meter-long medieval galleries found in this area yielded metallic veins as late as the twentieth century. Tangheroni and Mercuriali, *La città dell'argento*, p. 95.
212. Massala, *Sonetti storici sulla Sardegna*, p. 114.
213. See Benedetto, ed., *The New Westminster dictionary of Church history*, p. 307; Genovesi, 'Lo spostamento di popolazione e persone nelle regioni minerarie delle province occidentali in età imperiale,' p. 765; Hirt, *Imperial mines and quarries*, p. 82, fig. 21; Levi, 'Sardinia,' p. 631; Rowland, *The periphery in the center*, p. 171; Scrittori di Detta Enciclopedia, *Dizionario generale di scienze, lettere, arti, storia, geografia*, p. 591; Sella, 'Condizione minerarie dell'isola di Sardegna,' p. 524.
214. Bignami, 'The mines and mineral industries of Sardinia,' p. 934; United States Hydrographic Office, *Mediterranean pilot: The coast of France and Italy from Cape Cabère to Cape Spartivento*, p. 29.
215. Bignami, 'The mines and mineral industries of Sardinia,' p. 935.
216. The mile-long vein of *Argentiera de Nurra* contained a gray silver ore and barytes. Bignami, 'The mines and mineral industries of Sardinia,' p. 934.
217. Blanchard, *Mining, minting, and metallurgy in the Middle Ages*, vol. 3, p. 933.
218. Castro, *Descrizione geologico-mineraria della zona argentifera del Sarrabus*, pp. 39–52.
219. Ibid., p. 47.
220. Frulio, 'Catalan methods for construction in Sardinia.'
221. Achenza, 'The use of adobe in the traditional buildings of Sardinia,' pp. 101–102.
222. Burnham, *History and uses of limestone and marbles*, p. 198.
223. Rowland, *The periphery in the center*, pp. 168–169.
224. Peattie, *Mountain geography*, p. 217.
225. Rowland, *The periphery in the center*, pp. 159–166.
226. Ibid.
227. These were as follows: James II (r. A.D. 1323–1327), Alfonso IV (r. A.D. 1327–1336), Peter IV the Ceremonious (r. A.D. 1336–1387), and Peter's two sons, John I (r. A.D. 1387–1395) and Martin I (r. A.D. 1395–1410). Grierson and Travaini, *Medieval European coinage*, p. 292.
228. Giunta and Boscolo, 'Geronimo Zurita ed i problemi mediterranei della Corona d'Aragona'; Manca, 'Colonie iberiche in Italia nei secoli XIV e XV'; Olla Repetto, *Studi sulle istituzioni amministrative e giudiziarie della Sardegna nei secoli 14. e 15*; Tangheroni, *Pisa e il Mediterraneo*.
229. Giacomo Ortu, 'Famiglia e possesso contadino in contest feudale: il caso sardo.'
230. Pounds, *An historical geography of Europe*, p. 321.

231. Villani et al., *Croniche di Giovanni, Matteo e Filippo Villani*, p. 179.
232. Ibid., p. 267.
233. Abulafia, ed., *The New Cambridge medieval history*, vol. 5, p. 422; Baudi di Vesme, *Historiae patriae*, p. xv; Baudi di Vesme, 'Dell'industria dell miniere nel territorio di Villa,' p. 237; D'Oriano et al., *Argyrophleps nesos: l'isola dalle vene d'argento*; Rowland, *The periphery in the center*, pp. 159–166; Salvioli, *Manuale diritto italiano*, p. 395; Scrittori di Detta Enciclopedia, *Dizionario generale di scienze, lettere, arti, storia, geografia*, p. 591; Villani et al., *Croniche di Giovanni, Matteo e Filippo Villani*, p. 267.
234. Forci, 'Feudi e fuedatari in Trexenta (Sardegna meridionali)'; Orsi Lázaro, 'Estrategia, operaciones y logística en un conflicto mediterráneo.'
235. Volpe, 'Montieri: Costituzione politica, struttura sociale e attività economica d'una terra mineraria,' p. 373. The words come from the text of a grant given to Giovanni Klug of Freiberg, a German miner, for a silver mine in Villa di Chiesa. For a general economic history, see Tangheroni, *Commercio, finanza, funzione pubblica: stranieri in Sicilia e Sardegna nei secoli XIII–XV*.
236. Romero Tallafigo, 'Ordenanzas para la explotación de la plata en el Condado de Prades,' p. 327.
237. Brown, 'Cultural and genetic adaptations to malaria,' p. 317.
238. Bouchier, ed., *Sardinia in ancient times*, p. 52.
239. Brown, 'Cultural and genetic adaptations to malaria.'
240. Ibid., p. 319.
241. Bouchier, ed., *Sardinia in ancient times*, p. 51.
242. Scrittori di Detta Enciclopedia, *Dizionario generale di scienze, lettere, arti, storia, geografia*, p. 591.
243. Levi, 'Sardinia,' p. 631.
244. Bouchier, ed., *Sardinia in ancient times*, p. 51.
245. Levi, 'Sardinia,' p. 631.
246. Brown, 'Cultural and genetic adaptations to malaria,' p. 316; Vinelli, 'Water conservation in Sardinia,' p. 397.
247. Vinelli, 'Water conservation in Sardinia,' p. 396.
248. Bouchier, ed., *Sardinia in ancient times*, p. 52.
249. Vinelli, 'Water conservation in Sardinia,' p. 395.
250. Ibid.
251. Ibid., p. 396.
252. Ibid., p. 402.
253. Ibid., p. 396.
254. Cumming, ed., *Mining explained*, p. 123.
255. Bouchier, ed., *Sardinia in ancient times*, p. 55.
256. Ibid., p. 53.
257. Baudi di Vesme, *Historiae patriae*, p. 68.
258. Bouchier, ed., *Sardinia in ancient times*, p. 53.
259. Ibid., p. 57.
260. Brown, 'Cultural and genetic adaptations to malaria,' p. 316.
261. Ibid., p. 322.
262. Bouchier, ed., *Sardinia in ancient times*, p. 58.

263. Puddu et al., 'Spatial-explicit assessment of current and future conservation options for the endangered Corsican Red Deer (*Cervus elaphus corsicanus*) in Sardinia,' p. 2002.

264. Levi, 'Sardinia,' p. 630.

265. Ibid.

266. Grierson and Travaini, *Medieval European coinage*, p. 292.

267. Tangheroni and Mercuriali, *La città dell'argento*.

268. Grierson and Travaini, *Medieval European coinage*, pp. 292–293.

269. Taitz, *The Jews of medieval France*, pp. 221–223.

270. Baudi di Vesme, 'Dell'industria dell miniere nel territorio di Villa,' p. 413; Baudi di Vesme, *Historiae patriae*, p. 117.

271. Baudi di Vesme, *Historiae patriae*, pp. ccxxv, ccxxviii, 17. A similar prohibition was added to the mining statute of Massa in A.D. 1328. *Et dominus Capitaneus vel Judex qui contra fecerit, et persona que pro eo tenuerit, pro qualibet vice condampuetyr in libris C denariorum.* Baudi di Vesme, *Historiae patriae*, p. 262.

272. Corraine, 'Para *unha* lingua sarda da referencia,' p. 406. The author concludes that medieval Sardinians had no practical use for Latin, but used this 'foreign tongue' in their diplomatic and political relations with the Holy See, Pisa, and Genoa.

273. Kamen, *The Spanish Inquisition*; Liebman, *Réquiem por los olvidados: los judíos españoles en América*; Ruvinskis, *Persecución judía en México*; Schorsch, *Swimming the Christian Atlantic: Judeoconversos, Afroiberians, Amerindians*.

274. Moore, 'The races of the Balkan peninsula,' p. 484.

275. Stanoyevich, *Early Jugoslav literature (1000–1800)*, p. 32, footnote 11; Suess, *The face of the Earth*, p. 273. I also consulted the following works: Bojović, 'Le passé des territoires: Kosovo-Metohija (XIᵉ–XVIIᵉ siècle)'; Ciggaar, *East and West in the crusader states: Context, contracts, confrontations*; Ferluga, *Byzantium in the Balkans: Studies on the Byzantine administration and the Southern Slavs from the VIIth to the XIIIth centuries*; Krekić, 'Dubrovnik and Spain: Commercial and human contacts, fourteenth–sixteenth centuries'; Schumacher, 'The ore deposits of Jugoslavia and the development of its mining industry'; Waring, 'Kosovo.'

276. The peninsula was praised by Herodotus, Clement of Alexandria, Strabo, and even Aristotle for its metallic wealth. Davies, 'Ancient mines in southern Macedonia,' p. 145.

277. Unless indicated otherwise, description of ore deposits comes from Palinkaš, 'Metallogeny of the northwestern and central Dinarides and southern Tisia,' pp. 505–508.

278. Jurković, 'Bakovići: The biggest gold deposit of Bosnia and Herzegovina,' p. 2.

279. The Vareš deposits, northeast of Sarajevo, in Bosnia and Herzegovina, were famous in the early twentieth century for their iron content. Geologists estimate that the ores of Visoko yield between 55 and 65 percent pure iron. This number justified, in the view of a British consulate general in A.D. 1905, mining works in the region—since 'the native workman, whether Christian or Mohammedam, is abstemious, intelligent, and physically suited to work.' Board of Trade, *Iron ore deposits in foreign countries*, p. 15; see also Radosavljević et al., '(Pb-S)-bearing sphalerite from the Čumavići polymetallic ore deposit.'

280. Jurković, 'Barite, hematite, and cinnabar ore deposits in the Dusin area.'

281. Radosavljević et al., 'Polymetallic mineralization of the Boranja orefield.'

282. Radosavljević et al., 'Mineralogy and genetic features of the Cu-As-Ni-Sb-Pb mineralization from the Mlakva polymetallic deposit (Serbia).'

283. Beldiceanu, *Les Actes des Premiers Sultans*, 2; Davies, 'Ancient mines in southern Macedonia.'

284. Katić, 'The *Sancak* of Prizren in the late 15th and 16th century,' p. 115.

285. Kovačević-Kojić, 'Les mines d'or et d'argent en Serbie et Bosnie,' pp. 249–251.

286. Ibid., p. 249.

287. From 'Initiative for making the passage' (A.D. 1332), an anonymous text included in Elsie, *Early Albania: A reader of historical texts, 11th–17th centuries*, p. 29.

288. Kovačević-Kojić, 'Les mines d'or et d'argent en Serbie et Bosnie,' p. 250.

289. Beldiceanu, *Les Actes des Premiers Sultans*, vol. 2, p. 73, footnote 1.

290. Likely gold ducats. Ibid., p. 68, note 2.

291. Davies, 'Ancient mines in southern Macedonia,' p. 149.

292. Elsie, *Early Albania*, p. 165; Miller, 'Bosnia before the Turkish conquest,' p. 647.

293. İnalcik, 'Ottoman methods of conquest.'

294. According to 'old laws,' the Tsar collected customs 'from the river Drin to Neretva.' Petkov, *The voices of medieval Bulgaria*, p. 234.

295. Elsie, *Early Albania*, p. 63.

296. Davies, 'Ancient mines in southern Macedonia,' p. 148.

297. For a brief discussion of the role of Venetian merchants under Byzantine emperor Alexios Komnenos in A.D. 1082, see Armstrong, 'Merchants of Venice at Sparta in the 12th century.'

298. Petkov, *The voices of medieval Bulgaria*, p. 235.

299. Ibid., p. 237.

300. Fine, *The late medieval Balkans*, p. 283; Rădvan, *At Europe's borders: Medieval towns in the Romanian principalities*, p. 90.

301. Stanoyevich, *Early Jugoslav literature (1000–1800)*, pp. 32–33.

302. Saxons were included in a document concerning the mines of Bosnia in A.D. 1270 and in A.D. 1280 in connection to Ragusa. Beldiceanu, *Les Actes des Premiers Sultans*, vol. 2, p. 60.

303. Waring, 'Kosovo,' p. 59.

304. Rădvan, *At Europe's borders*, pp. 92–93. The rest of the paragraph comes from this work.

305. McNeill, *The rise of the West: A history of the human community*, p. 518.

306. Miller, 'Bosnia before the Turkish conquest,' p. 649.

307. Serbia grew 'under the mighty auspices of Stephen Dušan,' which 'threatened at one moment to swallow up Constantinople itself. Herzegovina's prince, Michael Višević, was addressed by the pope as 'the most excellent duke of the people of the Hum.' The territory became part of the Serbian state, before its annexation to Bosnia under the powerful *ban* of Bosnia, Stephen Kotromanić, in A.D. 1325. Bulgaria was possibly more affected by the 'Tartar menace' than Serbia. Ibid., pp. 657, 647; Petkov, *The voices of medieval Bulgaria*, p. 231.

308. Colin Heywood in Pinson, ed., *The Muslims of Bosnia-Herzegovina*, p. 25; see also Magdalino, *The empire of Manuel I Komenos*, chap. 2.

309. Pitcher, *An historical geography of the Ottoman Empire*, p. 47.

310. Crampton, *A short history of modern Bulgaria*, p. 7.

311. Ibid.

312. Sedlar, *East Central Europe in the Middle Ages*, p. 283.
313. İnalcik, 'Ottoman methods of conquest,' p. 116.
314. Upham, *History of the Ottoman Empire*, p. 90.
315. Káldy-Nagy, 'The first centuries of the Ottoman military organization,' p. 160.
316. Ibid.
317. İnalcik, 'Ottoman methods of conquest'; Káldy-Nagy, 'The first centuries of the Ottoman military organization'; Miljković, 'The timar system in the Serbian lands from 1450 to 1550.'
318. Miljković, 'The timar system in the Serbian lands from 1450 to 1550,' p. 40.
319. İnalcik, 'Ottoman methods of conquest,' p. 116.
320. Káldy-Nagy, 'The first centuries of the Ottoman military organization,' p. 150.
321. Miljković, 'The timar system in the Serbian lands from 1450 to 1550,' p. 38.
322. Ibid., p. 37.
323. Káldy-Nagy, 'The first centuries of the Ottoman military organization,' p. 150.
324. Colin Heywood in Pinson, ed., *The Muslims of Bosnia-Herzegovina*, p. 48, footnote 38.
325. Miljković, 'The timar system in the Serbian lands from 1450 to 1550,' p. 37.
326. Ibid., p. 41.
327. Schevill, *The history of the Balkan Peninsula*, p. 16.
328. İnalcik, 'Ottoman methods of conquest,' p. 107.
329. Sedlar, *East Central Europe in the Middle Ages*, p. 12.
330. Ibid., p. 335.
331. Buxton, 'Balkan geography and Balkan railways,' p. 219.
332. Elsie, *Early Albania*, p. 62.
333. Sedlar, *East Central Europe in the Middle Ages*, p. 334.
334. Pounds, *An historical geography of Europe*, p. 6; Schevill, *The history of the Balkan Peninsula*, p. 18.
335. Pinson, ed., *The Muslims of Bosnia-Herzegovina*, p. 24.
336. Ibid., p. 25.
337. Niox, *Les pays balkaniques*, p. 3.
338. Peattie, *Mountain geography*, p. 146.
339. Evans, 'Transhumance in Europe,' p. 174; Matley, 'Transhumance in Bosnia and Herzegovina,' p. 232.
340. Matley, 'Transhumance in Bosnia and Herzegovina,' p. 234.
341. Ibid., p. 236.
342. Gjeçov, *The Code of Lekë Dukagjini*, p. xiii. I am deeply grateful to Halit Daci, author of many works on Albanian military history, who presented me with a beautiful edition of the book.
343. Evans, 'Transhumance in Europe,' p. 173.
344. Schevill, *The history of the Balkan Peninsula*, p. 22.
345. Evans, 'Transhumance in Europe,' p. 173, footnote 3.
346. Chang, 'Pastoral transhumance in the Southern Balkans,' p. 687.
347. Kaser, *The Balkans and the Near East*, p. 66.
348. Borojević, 'Nutrition and environment in medieval Serbia,' p. 459.
349. Ibid.
350. Ibid.

351. Nerantzis, 'Pillars of power: Silver and steel in the Ottoman Empire,' p. 76.
352. Dimitriades, cited in Nerantzis, 'Pillars of power,' p. 79.
353. Kovačević-Kojić, 'Les mines d'or et d'argent en Serbie et Bosnie,' p. 251.

Chapter 3. Digging the Underground Wealth of Europe

1. For a general history, see Castagnetti, *Governo vescovile, feudalità, 'communitas' cittadina, Trento*; Frapporti, *Della storia e della condizione del Trentino nell'antico e nel medio evo*; Perini, *Dizionario geografico, statistico del Trentino*.
2. Kink, *Fontes Rerum Austriacarum*, p. 96.
3. When Emperor Conrad granted rights to Bishop Udalrich, the boundaries of the district of Trento were still in the making. It is possible that the northern frontier of the district was the Tinna or Tinnebach River, and the Bria or Breibach River, or the right and left sides of the Isarco River. By the thirteenth century, the eastern limits of the territory were halfway to the Village of Ossenigo on the right-hand side of the Adige River and the Belluno River to the left. The water mill fed by the Adige River belonged to the Bishopric of Trento, while Belluno village belonged to the Bishop of Verona. The southern boundaries were set north of Lake Garda, although the area remained contested for a while. Riva became part of the Trento's Bishopric very early, in A.D. 1124, when a bishop granted rights to the inhabitants of the village to build a castle near Lake Garda. The Ledro Valley, located between Lake Ampola and Lake Garda, was part of the Bishopric of Trento by A.D. 1159. On February 10, 1167, Emperor Frederick I granted the Church of Trento *dominion* of Garda castle and court. By A.D. 1190, the southwestern borders of the Bishopric went as far as Bagolino, a village in Val de Sabbia, in Brescia. Curzel and Varanini, *La documentazione dei vescovi di Trento*, pp. 125–127; Malfatti, 'I confini dei Principato de Trento,' p. 16, footnote 1; p. 17; Mor and Schmidinger, *I poteri temporali dei vescovi in Italia*, pp. 181–183.
4. Mor and Schmidinger, *I poteri temporali dei vescovi in Italia*, pp. 183–184.
5. Ibid.
6. Ibid.
7. Wanga was appointed in A.D. 1206, after Conrad's dismissal. Conrad's dismissal was in response to a long string of conflicts involving powerful families from Trent and other cities, ending in armed revolt in A.D. 1201. For the A.D. 1189 grant to Bishop Conrad, see Kink, *Fontes Rerum Austriacarum*, pp. 431–432, footnote 3; see also Castagnetti, *Governo vescovile, feudalità, 'communitas' cittadina, Trento*, pp. 95–167; Cole and Wolf, *The hidden frontier: Ecology and ethnicity in an Alpine Valley*, p. 75; Collatera and Primerano, *Un Vescovo la sua Cattedrale, il suo tesoro*, p. 31.
8. Collatera and Primerano, *Un Vescovo la sua Cattedrale, il suo tesoro*, p. 31; Kink, *Fontes Rerum Austriacarum*.
9. Curzel and Varanini, *La documentazione dei vescovi di Trento*, pp. 12, 70–83; Cantù, *Illustrazione del Tirolo italiano*, pp. 68–69, footnote 3.
10. Kink, *Fontes Rerum Austriacarum*, pp. 438–439.
11. The *libra* and the *solidus* were moneys of account. The Veronese *denarius*, a real coin made of fine silver, weighed approximately 1.5 grams. It was one of the many different *denarii* that circulated in the markets of continental Europe since the twelfth century.

The French *denarius* was called *deniers*; *dineros* in Spain; and *dinheros* in Portugal, all of varying weights and finesses. These were described universally by the name *denarii*. Beginning in the thirteenth century, the *denarii* of North and Central Italy were debased, depreciating at a greater rate than the rest, hence the distinction with the *pfennigs* or good silver-money minted in Cologne, Germany, the Low Countries, and England. Cipolla, 'Currency depreciation in medieval Europe,' p. 417; Spufford, *Money and its use in medieval Europe*, pp. 104–106.

12. Kink, *Fontes Rerum Austriacarum*, p. 438.
13. Menant, *Lombardia feudale: studi sull'aristocrazia padana nei secoli X–XIII*, pp. 277–287.
14. Curzel and Varanini, *La documentazione dei vescovi di Trento*, pp. 122–127; Kink, *Fontes Rerum Austriacarum*, p. 96; Sperges, *Tyrolische bergwerksgeschichte*, pp. 263–265.
15. Braunstein, 'Les statuts miniers de l'Europe médiévale,' p. 42.
16. Curzel and Varanini, *La documentazione dei vescovi di Trento*, pp. 122–127; Kink, *Fontes Rerum Austriacarum*, p. 96; Sperges, *Tyrolische bergwerksgeschichte*, pp. 263–265.
17. Kink, *Fontes Rerum Austriacarum*, doc. 236, p. 441.
18. Editions of the *Codex* contain different organizations of Wanga's first mining law. In the edition by Emanuele Curzel and Gian Maria Varanini, *Carta* is a long document containing twenty-three articles. In Kink's edition, *Carta* is divided in four short documents based upon subject. Franz Kirnbauer describes *Carta* as a typical medieval *Bergordnung* or mining ordinance, containing fourteen articles. See Curzel and Varanini, *La documentazione dei vescovi di Trento*, pp. 350–351; Kirnbauer, 'Die Bergordnung von Trient aus dem Jahre 1208 und ihre Beziehung zur Bergbautechnik'; Kink, *Fontes Rerum Austriacarum*, docs. 236, 237, 238, 239, pp. 441–449.
19. Braunstein, 'Les statuts miniers de l'Europe médiévale,' p. 42.
20. Kink, *Fontes Rerum Austriacarum*, p. 444.
21. Ibid., pp. 442, 444.
22. Ibid., p. 441.
23. Harreld, *High Germans in the Low Countries*, p. 43.
24. Kink, *Fontes Rerum Austriacarum*, pp. 22–24.
25. Collatera and Primerano, *Un Vescovo, la sua Cattedrale, il suo tesoro*, p. 22; Kink, *Fontes Rerum Austriacarum*, pp. 434–435.
26. Kink, *Fontes Rerum Austriacarum*, doc. 239, p. 448.
27. Braunstein speculates that *Werchi* challenged the *fictum* various times, considering that annual mine incomes changed with new vein discoveries. *Fictum* was the Italian name for that which was paid *ad fiscum*. Wanga was aware of the amounts of extracted ore in certain mining shafts, especially those with new drainage infrastructure supervised by his *Gastaldia*. Braunstein, 'Les statuts miniers de l'Europe médiévale.'
28. See, for example, Kirnbauer, 'Die Bergordnung von Trient aus dem Jahre 1208.'
29. Voltelini, *Giurisdizione signorile su terre e persone nel trentino medievale*, p. 46.
30. Malfatti explains the survival of Lombard institutions by arguing that Trento acquired its territorial identity, the one that made it one of the most important cities of medieval Europe, between the sixth and seventh centuries A.D., coinciding with the consolidation of Lombard legal and political culture. In Malfatti's words: *L'epoca longo barda dà il fondamento territoriale al Principato di cinque secoli dopo, del quale il Trentino odierno*

è appena due terze parti. Malfatti, 'I confini dei Principato de Trento,' p. 6; see also Drew, 'The Carolingian military frontier in Italy,' p. 439.

31. Cusin, *I primi due secoli del Principato Ecclesiastico*, p. 20; Reich, 'Toponomastica storica di Mezocorona,' pp. 70–71.

32. For a brief commentary on *fictum*, see Wiener, *Commentary to the Germanic Laws and medieval documents*, p. 183.

33. For a discussion, see Mor and Schmidinger, *I poteri temporali dei vescovi in Italia e in Germania.*

34. Voltelini, *Giurisdizione signorile*, pp. 49–50.

35. Curzel and Varanini, *Codex Wangianus, i cartulari della Chiesa trentina*, pp. 65–66.

36. Kink, *Fontes Rerum Austriacarum*, doc. 237, p. 443.

37. The *solidus* in Western Europe was a multiple of twelve silver *denarii*. Grierson and Travaini, *Medieval European coinage*, p. 466; Sperges, *Tyrolische bergwerksgeschichte*, pp. 263–264; Spufford, *Money and its use in medieval Europe*, pp. 225–239.

38. Kink, *Fontes Rerum Austriacarum*, doc. 239, p. 448.

39. Ibid., doc. 238, p. 446.

40. Cantù, *Illustrazione del Tirolo italiano*, p. 73.

41. Kink, *Fontes Rerum Austriacarum*, p. 435.

42. Ibid., doc. 239, p. 448.

43. Mor and Schmidinger, *I poteri temporali dei vescovi in Italia e in Germania*, pp. 195–197.

44. Ibid.

45. *Si vero dñs episcopus necessitate imminente ab ipsis subsidium aliquod exigeret, ipsi ei subvenire et amminiculari debeant.* Kink, *Fontes Rerum Austriacarum*, doc. 236, pp. 441–442.

46. On the medieval tallage in France, see Bloch, *French rural history*, pp. 82–83; on the practice in England, see Mitchell, *Taxation in medieval England*, the four chapters dedicated to the discussion of the tallage in the realms of kings John, Henry III, and Edward I.

47. Kink, *Fontes Rerum Austriacarum*, doc. 236, pp. 441–442. The talent or *talentum* was used as a weight unit, or money of account. The *libra* was 'the chief unit in the Roman weight system.' It was equivalent to 327.45 grams, 'though the precise figure is uncertain.' The word *libra* was used either as the local weight standard, or as money of account divided into twenty *solidi* each of twelve denari. The *solidus* or *solidi* in plural, was 'originally the standard gold coin of the late Roman Empire,' weighing twenty-four carats (4.55 grams) and of pure gold when it was introduced in A.D. 309. The *solidus* was often qualified by the name of an emperor. It was a money of account in certain parts of Italy, equivalent to four *taris* (2.78 grams gold). Grierson and Travaini, *Medieval European coinage*, pp. 466, 473; see also Riera Melís, 'Monedas y mercados en la Edad Media: el Mediterráneo Occidental,' for a discussion of bimetallism.

48. Braunstein, 'Gli statuti minerari nel Medioevo europeo.'

49. Kink, *Fontes Rerum Austriacarum*, doc. 236, p. 443.

50. Curzel, *Il Codice Vanga*, pp. 172–173, 184–187, 350–354.

51. Braunstein, 'Gli statuti minerari nel Medioevo.'

52. Kink, *Fontes Rerum Austriacarum*, doc. 239, p. 448.

53. For a discussion on the medieval origins of the majority-rule principle, see Lewis, *Medieval political ideas*, vol. 1, pp. 193–240.

54. Braunstein, 'Les statuts miniers de l'Europe médiévale,' p. 41.
55. A *pace* was a Roman unit of distance, consisting of five Roman feet. It was employed in continental Europe, with some regional variations. The ordinary pace of Germany was equivalent to five *Rheinfuss*, or 5.1486 English feet. Curzel and Varanini, *La documentazione dei vescovi di Trento*, pp. 350–351; Jackson, *Modern metrology*, p. 62; Kink, *Fontes Rerum Austriacarum*, doc. 239, p. 448.
56. Kink, *Fontes Rerum Austriacarum*, doc. 239, pp. 448–449.
57. Ibid., doc. 238, 239, pp. 445–449.
58. Ibid., doc. 239, p. 448.
59. Ibid., doc. 238, p. 446.
60. Malfatti, *Degli idiomi parlati anticamente nel Trentino*, p. 17, footnote 4.
61. Kink, *Fontes Rerum Austriacarum*, doc. 239, pp. 447–449.
62. Ibid., doc. 241, pp. 450–452.
63. Ibid., doc. 239, p. 448.
64. Kirnbauer, 'Die Bergordnung von Trient aus dem Jahre 1208 und ihre Beziehung zur Bergbautechnik.'
65. Kink, *Fontes Rerum Austriacarum*, doc. 241, pp. 450–451.
66. Ibid.
67. For a commentary on the ancient origins of royalty, Salvioli, *Manuale diritto italiano*, p. 395, footnote 1.
68. Kink, *Fontes Rerum Austriacarum*, doc. 240, 241, pp. 447–450.
69. Ibid., doc. 242, pp. 453–454.
70. Curzel and Varanini, *La documentazione dei vescovi di Trento*, p. 499.
71. Ibid., pp. 480–481.
72. Braunstein, 'Les statuts miniers de l'Europe médiévale,' p. 43.
73. Cibrario, *Della economia politica del medio evo*, p. 241.
74. De Roover, 'Introduction: Cardinal Cajetan on "Cambium" or exchange dealings,' p. 199; De Roover, 'Scholastic economics: Survival and lasting influence from the sixteenth century to Adam Smith.'
75. Cibrario, *Della economia politica del medio evo*, p. 241.
76. De Roover, 'Introduction,' p. 199.
77. Ibid., p. 200.
78. Kink, *Fontes Rerum Austriacarum*, p. 437.
79. Braunstein, 'Les statuts miniers de l'Europe médiévale'; Patetta, 'La "Lex Frisionum," studi sulla origine'; Paulinyi, 'Die anfänglichen Formen des Unternehmens im Edelerzbergbau'; Virnich, *De juris regalis metallorum origine ac progressu*, p. 39.
80. Paulinyi, 'Die anfänglichen Formen des Unternehmens im Edelerzbergbau,' pp. 264–265.
81. Ibid., pp. 266–268.
82. Cibrario, *Della economia politica del medio evo*, p. 2.
83. Braunstein, 'Les statuts miniers de l'Europe médiévale,' pp. 40–42, 48–50.
84. Cibrario, *Della economia politica del medio evo*, p. 5.
85. Ibid.
86. John Langdon in Aston, ed., *Landlords, peasants, and politics in medieval England*, p. 63.

87. Adam Smith stated that fixed capital consisted of 'machines,' 'profitable buildings which are the means of procuring a revenue not only to the proprietor but to the person who possesses them and pays a rent, such as shops, warehouses, farmhouses, etc.'; improvements of land, such as 'clearing, draining, enclosing, manuring, and reducing it into the condition most proper for tillage and culture'; and the 'acquired or useful abilities of all the inhabitants or members of the society.' Smith, *The wealth of nations*, pp. 334–335.

88. Cibrario, *Della economia politica dell medio evo*, p. 21.

89. Ibid., p. 285.

90. Ibid.

91. Anderson, *Passages from Antiquity to feudalism*; Aston and Philpin, eds., *The Brenner debate*.

92. The Prague *groschen* was minted at sixty to the local mark of silver. It was also used as money of account. Jireček, *Codex juris Bohemici*, p. 264; Spufford, *Money and its use in medieval Europe*, pp. 225–239.

93. Jireček, *Codex juris Bohemici*, pp. 82–84.

94. Ibid., pp. 114–119.

95. Mispoulet, *Le régime des mines à l'époque romaine et au Moyen Âge d'après les Tables d'Aljutrel*, pp. 73–74, 78–79; Kalus, *Die Fugger in der Slowakei*, p. 34.

96. Jánošíková, 'Mining business "Ius Regale"'; Jireček, *Codex juris Bohemici*, pp. 264–317; Schröcke, 'Mining settlement Slovakia'; Zycha, *Das Böhmische Bergrecht*.

97. Kalus, *Die Fugger in der Slowakei*, p. 34.

98. Klápště, *The Czech lands in medieval transformation*, pp. 453–455.

99. Jireček, *Codex juris Bohemici*, pp. 270–272.

100. *Per occupationem hoc modo jus acquiritur cum quis spe ductus montanorum in campo libero, in quo ubilibet et cuilibet est licitum laborare et metattum quaerere, spatium ad argenti fodinam occupat faciendam, statim hoc jure montanorum suum facit, et ad eo forte in eo jus acquirit, quod ab eo non poterit, dummodo Ibidem continue laboret, sine juris ordine amoveri.* Einaudi, *La rendita mineraria: origini e basi*, p. 14. A note on etymology is in order: some Saxon words denoting *happiness* and *prosperity* 'are derived from these terms, signifying *possession-property*.' Whiter, *Etymologicon universale*, p. 125.

101. Einaudi, *La rendita mineraria: origini e basi*, p. 14.

102. A striking resemblance to the 'minerals must be found first' principle that holds to this day in several countries. Stretch, *Prospecting, locating, and valuing mines*, p. 79.

103. Ibid., p. 22.

104. Hoover and Hoover, trans., *Georgius Agricola De Re Metallica*, p. 68.

105. Ibid., p. 80; Jireček, *Codex juris Bohemici*, pp. 322–324; see also Hoover and Hoover, trans., *Georgius Agricola De Re Metallica*, p. 80; Jánošíková, 'Mining business "Ius Regale,"' p. 166.

106. Jireček, *Codex juris Bohemici*, pp. 290, 292.

107. Jánošíková, 'Mining business "Ius Regale,"' p. 166.

108. The statute justified it for avoiding *quod vulgariter rumbawm dicitur*. Jireček, *Codex juris Bohemici*, p. 318.

109. Later, the German *Lachter* was equivalent to '6 2/3 feet in Prussia, and seven feet in

Saxony.' Hoover and Hoover, trans., *Georgius Agricola De Re Metallica*, p. 617; Jackson, *Modern metrology*, p. 31.

110. Jireček, *Codex juris Bohemici*, p. 116.

111. Ibid., p. 117.

112. The total area included one *laneum* to be worked on behalf of the king, and one on behalf of burghers: *Si quis autem novum montem invenerit, mensurentur ei septem lanei ex utraque parte, domino regi unus ex utraque parte, burgensibus unus.* Ibid., p. 115.

113. Klápště, *The Czech lands in medieval transformation*, p. 453.

114. Ibid., p. 456.

115. Sedlar, *East Central Europe in the Middle Ages*, p. 64.

116. Braunstein, 'Les statuts miniers de l'Europe médiévale,' p. 52.

117. The Latin text reads as follows: *Reprobamus unam detestabilem conspirationem, quam quidam ex metalli emptoribus contra nostram rempublicam retroactis temporibus sic frequentius injecerunt, ut quidquid primus ipsorum in emptione metalli a debito longe distans pretio exhibeat, tunc secundus superveniens tamquam exhibitionis illius ignarus exhibuit statim minus, et sic de aliis. Itaque veri emptores istorum versutia dubii effecti recesserunt nihil emendo. Ipsi autem venditores affecti tedio compellebantur ip sum venale metallum pro multo minori, quam valebat, pretio venundari, in non modicum nostrae urburae ac ttoius argentifodii praejudicium et gravamen.* Jireček, *Codex juris Bohemici*, p. 316.

118. Ibid., p. 312.

119. Ibid., pp. 288, 326.

120. Jireček, *Codex juris Bohemici*, p. 314.

121. Hübner et al., *A history of Germanic private law*, p. 294; Weber, 'Introduction to the study of Saxon settlement in Transylvania during the Middle Ages,' p. 53.

122. Klápště, *The Czech lands in medieval transformation*, p. 470.

123. Anderson, *Passages from antiquity to feudalism*, p. 147.

124. Hübner et al., *A history of Germanic private law*, p. 294.

125. Mayhew and Spufford, *Later medieval mints: Organization, administration, and techniques*; Spufford, *Power and profit*.

126. Hübner et al., *A history of Germanic private law*, p. 296.

127. Jireček, *Codex juris Bohemici*, p. 264, especially the document titled *Novae monetae per Wenceslaum II. Institutio*.

128. Jireček, *Codex juris Bohemici*, p. 264; Klápště, *The Czech lands in medieval transformation*.

129. Spufford, *Money and its use in medieval Europe*, p. 125. For conservative estimates, see Braunstein, 'Les statuts miniers de l'Europe médiévale,' pp. 51–52.

130. An exception was done for workers of foundries or *refectoribus bulgarum*. Jireček, *Codex juris Bohemici*, p. 294.

131. Hübner et al., *A history of Germanic private law*.

132. Braunstein, 'Les statuts miniers de l'Europe médiévale,' pp. 52–53.

133. The word *urbura* has Gothic roots denoting 'tax,' 'produce,' 'rent.' Jireček, *Codex juris Bohemici*, p. 284; Kluge, *An etymological dictionary of the German language*, p. 374.

134. Jireček, *Codex juris Bohemici*, p. 388.

135. Ibid., p. 272.

136. Ibid., p. 274.
137. Ibid., p. 284.
138. Ibid., p. 274.
139. Ibid., pp. 275–276.
140. Ibid., p. 408.
141. *Mulier autem ideo removetur, quia levis est animi et inconstans, sed in testibus magna desideratur constantia, nec debet se virorum testibus immiscere.* Ibid., p. 410.
142. *Impuberes autem ideo removentur, quia nullum est eorum animi judicium [. . .] Et dicuntur puberes a pube, id est, a pudicitia corporis, quae incipit primo in eis florere; puerperae autem sunt, quae in annis puerilibus pariunt.* Ibid.
143. Ibid.
144. The *denarii grosso* was first introduced in the second half of the thirteenth century in Italian cities north of Rome. Because of their large size, they were known as *grosso*, distinguishing them from the pre-existing *denarii*, which came to be called *piccoli,* or little one. The *denarius grosso* contained approximately two grams of fine silver, equivalent to between four and twenty-six *piccoli.* The large range of values of the *piccolo* makes it difficult to define with precision prices of salaries in amounts of silver. Grierson, *Monnaies du moyen âge;* Jireček, *Codex juris Bohemici,* p. 296; Spufford, *Money and its use in medieval Europe,* pp. 225–239.
145. The Code stated: *Nostri autem argentifodii ammonitio nos ammonet, unam odibilem consuetudinem, imo potius corruptelam circa magistros montium salubriter emendare, qui un magnum praejudicium totis argentifodii et non inmodicam nostrae reipublicae laesionem, in omni concessione aliquam partem seu frequentius octavam sibi retinent.* Jireček, *Codex juris Bohemici,* p. 288.
146. Ibid., p. 292.
147. *Ne propter defectum alimentorum necesse cogantur, rapere aliena.* Ibid., p. 294.
148. Ibid., pp. 272–278, 288, 298, 300–308.
149. Ibid., p. 288.
150. Ibid.
151. Ibid., p. 290.
152. Ibid., p. 302.
153. Ibid., p. 306.
154. Ibid., p. 304.
155. Ibid.
156. Simonin, *Underground life; or mines and miners,* p. 108.
157. Jireček, *Codex juris Bohemici,* p. 308.
158. De Roover stated: 'Bernardino [of Siena] is outspoken in his condemnation of monopolistic prices, that is, of "fraudulent and pernicious agreements" by which merchants drive up prices in order to increase their profits.' De Roover in another work stated: 'Price is a social phenomenon and is set not by the arbitrary decision of individuals, but *communiter,* that is, by the community. How? There are two possibilities: The price of a commodity can be fixed either by the public authorities for the common good, or by the estimation currently arrived at in the market (*secundum aestimationem fori occurrentis*). The first is the legal price; the second is called later the natural price. Citing Henricus Hostiensis (d. 1271), San Bernardino stresses the fact that the market price has to

be accepted by the producer and is fair whether he gains or loses, whether it is above or below cost.' There are discrepancies among economists about Aquinas' concept of just price (see note below). De Roover, 'Scholastic economics,' pp. 164–165; De Roover, 'The concept of the just price,' p. 422.

159. Monroe, *Early economic thought*; Schumpeter and Schumpeter, *History of economic analysis*.

160. De Roover, 'The concept of the just price,' p. 423.

161. Baldwin states that the just price was determined by the supply side, or the cost of production, although there was little explanation about how Roman judges defined the just price. Werner Stark (A.D. 1909–1985) raised questions about interpreting the Thomist argument as a supply- or demand-side viewpoint: the thought of the nineteenth century: 'To me personally this whole discussion looks rather pointless and useless. It is difficult if not impossible to squeeze a thinker of the thirteenth century into categories taken from the thought of the nineteenth century. Aquinas belonged to neither school and at the same time to both. He belonged to neither school because his explanation of value and price is sociological rather than economic: price is a compromise, one of the basic conventions of society, a piece of custom. And he belonged to both because the germs of both later opinions are contained in his works.' Baldwin, *The medieval theories of the just price*, pp. 27–29; Carpintero Benítez, *Justicia y ley natural: Tomás de Aquino y otros escolásticos*; De Roover, 'Monopoly theory,' pp. 496–497, esp. footnote 1; De Roover, 'Scholastic economics,' p. 169; Dempsey, 'Just price in a functional economy'; Johnson, 'Just price in an unjust world,' offers a supply-side interpretation of the just price; Stark, 'The contained economy: An interpretation of medieval economic thought,' p. 7.

162. Grozio was described by a cardinal contemporary, Matteo Rosso, as *magistrum Gocium de Urbe Veteri utriusque juris tam canonici quam civilis professorem*. Lampertico, *Sulla legislazione mineraria*, p. 57, footnote 1. Unfortunately, the authoritative *Cambridge history of medieval political philosophy* contains no entry about Grozio or his legal writings.

163. Jireček, *Codex juris Bohemici*, pp. 270–272, 310.

164. Ibid., p. 272.

165. Ibid.

166. Jireček, *Codex juris Bohemici*, p. 270.

167. Ibid., p. 274.

168. Ibid., p. 286.

169. A similar appropriation of Roman law emerged in other European kingdoms, especially England. The intention of such appropriation was to 'claim that a king was "emperor in his own realm" independent of papal or imperial authority'—a claim that became very handy for 'overriding private property rights in an emergency for the common good.' This was not the case in Bohemia's mining industry. Mining shares were considered private property that could not be alienated by the King. Jireček, *Codex juris Bohemici*, p. 394; King and Penman, eds., *England and Scotland in the fourteenth century*, p. 198.

170. Braunstein, 'Les statuts miniers de l'Europe médiévale,' p. 51.

171. Kalus, *Die Fugger in der Slowakei*, pp. 15–23.

172. Ibid., pp. 31–33.

173. Whiter, *Etymologicon universale*, pp. 107–108.

174. Kalus stated that their tasks were not specifically defined in the primary documents he studied. Kalus, *Die Fugger in der Slowakei*, pp. 15–23.

175. Weber, 'Introduction to the study of Saxon settlement in Transylvania during the Middle Ages,' p. 59.

176. Ibid., p. 52.

177. Ibid., p. 55; Jireček, *Codex juris Bohemici*, p. 284, esp. 'Item no. 16'; Sternberg, *Umrisse der Geschichte des Bergbaues und der Berggesetzgebung des Königreichs Böhmen*, pp. 59–64.

178. Anderson, *Passages from antiquity to feudalism*, p. 247.

179. Cibrario, *Della economia politica del medioevo*, p. 117.

180. Petrocchi, *Massa Marittima, arte e storia*, p. 18.

181. Simonin, 'De l'ancienne loi des mines de la République Italienne de Massa-Marittima (Toscane),' p. 3.

182. Nardi, ed., *Condizioni economiche dell'industria mineralogica in Toscana durante il medio evo*, p. 3.

183. Rodolico, cur., *Ordinamenta super arte fossarum*, 'Item X,' p. 69.

184. Braunstein, 'Les statuts miniers de l'Europe médiévale,' p. 45.

185. Rodolico, cur., *Ordinamenta super arte fossarum*, 'Item I,' p. 65. The rest of this paragraph comes from this work.

186. Ibid., 'Item XXXVII,' p. 80. The Sienese standard was the *libra*, equivalent to 240 *denarii* and 20 *solidi*.

187. Jackson, *Modern metrology*, p. 62; Petrocchi, *Massa Marittima, arte e storia*, p. 340; Simonin, 'De l'ancienne loi des mines de la République Italienne,' p. 4.

188. Based upon archeological findings in Serrabotini and Poggio Montierino, Massa Marittima. Aranguren et al., 'Serrabottini (Massa Marittima, GR): indagini archeologiche su un antico campo minerario,' p. 80.

189. Simonin discovered ruins of these constructions in the nineteenth century. Simonin, 'De l'ancienne loi des mines de la République Italienne,' p. 4.

190. Baudi di Vesme, *Historiae patriae*, p. cxlv.

191. Mispoulet argued that *trente* meant thirty, but Mispoulet was alone in his interpretation of the meaning of *trente* in Massa. Baudi di Vesme, considered the authority on the subject, argued that the number of shares was always divisible by four. Thirty-two was also 'more or less in agreement with customs and traditions in other parts of the world.' The number of *trente* for the Montieri mines was seventeen. The meaning is unclear. Baudi di Vesme, *Historiae patriae*, p. cv; Mispoulet, *Le régime des mines à l'époque romaine et au Moyen Âge d'après les Tables d'Aljutrel*, p. 35, footnote 2; Simonin, 'De l'ancienne loi des mines de la République Italienne,' p. 4.

192. Rodolico, cur., *Ordinamenta super arte fossarum*, 'Item LXI,' p. 91.

193. Ibid., 'Item XVII,' pp. 72–73.

194. Ibid., 'Item XIIII,' pp. 71–72.

195. Baudi di Vesme, *Historiae patriae*, p. cxi.

196. Baudi di Vesme, 'Dell'industria dell miniere nel territorio di Villa,' p. 198.

197. Rodolico, cur., *Ordinamenta super arte fossarum*, p. 77.

198. Baudi di Vesme, *Historiae patriae*, p. cxcvii.

199. Braunstein, 'Les statuts miniers de l'Europe médiévale,' p. 45.
200. A similar provision was in place in other parts of Europe. Emperor Henry of Germany (A.D. 1211–1242) in A.D. 1224 imposed a ban on the export of silver, *sentenia de argento vendendo*, after a desperate petition by the Prince Bishop of Worms. Volpe, 'Montieri: constituzione politica, struttura sociale e attività economica d'una terra mineraria,' p. 365, footnote 4.
201. Boggi, 'Silver altar, Pistoia Cathedral'; Herlihy, *Medieval and Renaissance Pistoia*.
202. Stuard, 'Dowry increase and increment in medieval Ragusa.'
203. Rodolico, cur., *Ordinamenta super arte fossarum*, 'Item XXXVIII,' p. 80.
204. *Ei si non poterit solvere dictam penam, amputetur ei una manus*. Rodolico, cur., *Ordinamenta super arte fossarum*, 'Item LXXXII,' p. 98.
205. Castro, *Descrizione geologico-mineraria della zona argentifera del Sarrabus*, p. 8; Rodolico, cur., *Ordinamenta super arte fossarum*, 'Item LXXIIII,' 'Item LXXXII,' 'Item LXXXIIII,' pp. 96, 98–99.
206. Castro, *Descrizione geologico-mineraria della zona argentifera del Sarrabus*, p. 7.
207. Braunstein, 'Les statuts miniers de l'Europe médiévale,' pp. 45–46.
208. Rodolico, cur., *Ordinamenta super arte fossarum*, 'Item XI,' pp. 70–71.
209. Ibid., 'Item V,' pp. 66–68.
210. Ibid., p. 67.
211. According to Simonin, following Ulrich, the Volterra pound was equivalent to 7.82 Francs in the A.D. 1890s and 3.26 Francs in A.D. 1300. Ibid., 'Item VI,' 'Item VII,' pp. 68–69; Simonin, 'De l'ancienne loi des mines de la République Italienne,' p. 9, footnote 1.
212. Rodolico, cur., *Ordinamenta super arte fossarum*, 'Item V,' pp. 67–68.
213. Ibid., 'Item LIIII,' p. 87.
214. Petrocchi, *Massa Marittima, arte e storia*, p. 339; Simonin, 'De l'ancienne loi des mines de la République Italienne,' p. 11.
215. Rodolico, cur., *Ordinamenta super arte fossarum*, p. 21.
216. Simonin, 'De l'ancienne loi des mines de la République Italienne,' p. 5.
217. Ibid.
218. Curzel and Varanini, *La documentazione dei vescovi di Trento*, pp. 350–354; Rodolico, cur., *Ordinamenta super arte fossarum*, 'Item LXXXV,' p. 98.
219. Rodolico, cur., *Ordinamenta super arte fossarum*, 'Item XLI,' 'Item XLIIII,' 'Item LXVI,' pp. 83–85.
220. Ibid., 'Item LXXXV,' p. 99.
221. Braunstein, 'Les statuts miniers de l'Europe médiévale,' p. 46.
222. Petrocchi, *Massa Marittima, arte e storia*, p. 336.
223. De Roover, 'Introduction'; De Roover, *Business, banking, and economic thought in late medieval and early modern Europe*. For transcriptions and translations of fourteenth-century accounting documents, including examples of double-entry bookkeeping, see Lopez and Raymond, trans., *Medieval trade in the Mediterranean world, illustrative documents*, pp. 361–374.
224. Ibid., p. 375.
225. Petrocchi, *Massa Marittima, arte e storia*, p. 9.
226. Castro, *Descrizione geologico-mineraria della zona argentifera del Sarrabus*, p. 7; Pet-

rocchi, *Massa Marittima, arte e storia*, p. 338; Rodolico, cur., *Ordinamenta super arte fossarum*, 'Item LXXIII,' p. 96.

227. Rodolico, cur., *Ordinamenta super arte fossarum*, 'Item XL,' pp. 81–83.

228. Baudi di Vesme, *Historiae patriae*, p. cxix.

229. Simonin, 'De l'ancienne loi des mines de la République Italienne de Massa-Marittima (Toscane)'; Rodolico, cur., *Ordinamenta super arte fossarum*, 'Item XX,' p. 73. For a general description of medieval surveying instruments, see Glick, 'Levels and levelers: Surveying irrigation canals in medieval Valencia'; Price, 'Medieval land surveying and topographical maps.' For a description of the quadrant and compass used for measuring mines in the sixteenth century, see Korey, *The geometry of power, mathematical instruments, and Princely mechanical devices from around 1600*, pp. 17–18, 22–25.

230. Rodolico, cur., *Ordinamenta super arte fossarum*, 'Item I,' 'Item XX,' pp. 65, 73. On the history of land surveying instruments applied to mining, see Hoover and Hoover, trans., *Georgius Agricola De Re Metallica*, book 5.

231. Potamian stated that a letter written in A.D. 1269 by Pierre de Maricourt, a member of the engineering corps of the French army, 'the Gallic friend' of Roger Bacon, was 'of 3,500 words, the greatest landmark in the domain of magnetic philosophy' in Western Europe. Arnold, *The letter of Petrus Peregrinus on the magnet*, p. ix.

232. The unit of measurement was *bigongius*, a unit of volume used in the period. Rodolico, cur., *Ordinamenta super arte fossarum*, 'Item LXXVI,' pp. 96–97.

233. Ibid., pp. 22, 98.

234. Based upon eighteenth-century accounts. Targioni Tozetti, *Relazione a'alcuni viaggi fatti in diverse parti della Toscana*, p. 143.

235. Cesaretti, *Memorie sacra e profane dell'antica diocesi di Populonia al presente diocesi di Massa Marittima*, p. 32, footnote c; p. 33, footnote c; and p. 92.

236. The text of the Papal Bull reads as follows: *Sana petitio tunc nobis exhibita continebat, quod cum Potestas, Capitaneous, Priore, & Consiliarii Communis Massanii, ad Bona tua & Ecclesiae Massanae per iniuriam manus avidas extendentes, Te, ac Ecclesiam tuam Argenti Fodinis, & aliis redditibus, contra Justitiam spoliassent, Palatium de Monte Regio, Accesam, Montis S. Laurentii Marsilianae, Portus Baratuli, & Valli Castra, & quaedam alia bona ad Te, & dictam Ecclesiam pertinentia temeritate propria occupando.* Comparini, ed., *Memorie storiche di Massa Marittima*, pp. 54–59.

237. Lopez and Raymond, trans., *Medieval trade in the Mediterranean world, illustrative documents*, doc. 49, p. 122.

238. Ibid., p. 122.

239. The earliest feudal grant that mentions the mines of Iglesias was dated A.D. 1131, when Gonnario II of Turris granted to Pisa's Santa Maria Church half of the Argentiera mine located in Nurra, Sardinia—*medietatem montis qui dicitur Argentei*. Rowland states that 'Comita III of Arborea donated to San Lorenzo and to the commune of Genoa the church of S. Petrus de Claro and a village (curia) with all of their appurtenances, 100 serfs, 2,000 sheep and other animals, numerous lands, fishing rights and "half of the mountains in which silver is found in all my kingdom."' Tenneant mentions the grant to the Genoese, but under Comita II of Arborea, accompanied by the Latin text that mentions the silver mines—*medietatem moncium in quibus inventibur vena argenti in toto regno meo*. He also mentions a letter by the 'Comita d'Arborea' granting to Iglesias

jurisdiction over half of a mine in Turris. Silver mines appeared again in A.D. 1253, in a contract concerning the hiring of German technical mining experts in *la Nurra*. In A.D. 1282 the Donoratico Count donated in a *podestà* mining rights to *Bartolommeo detto Bacciameo del fu Gherardo Guinizelli* for mines located in Villa di Chiesa. Two years later, Ugolino, the new Donoratico Count, granted another *podestà* to Guidone. It is possible the old Breve was written in this period, a time when Pisa dominated Villa di Chiesa's mining industry as well as its *zecca*. These grants suggest that money from Pisa and Genoa came to the mines of Chiesa long before the emergence of *Breve*. Baudi di Vesme, 'Dell'industria dell miniere nel territorio di Villa,' p. 234, footnote 6; p. 235; Dyson and Rowland, *Archaeology and history in Sardinia, from the Stone Age to the Middle Ages*, pp. 106, 172–174; Forbes, *Studies in ancient technology*, p. 226; Gallin and Tykot, 'Metallurgy at Nuraghe Santa Barbara (Bauladu)'; Rowland, *The periphery in the center*, p. 160; Tennant, *Sardinia and its resources*, p. 4; Vargas-Bedemar, *Sulle miniere della Sardegna*, p. 5.

240. Grierson and Travaini, *Medieval European coinage*, p. 292.

241. Baudi di Vesme, 'Dell'industria dell miniere nel territorio di Villa'; Tennant, *Sardinia and its resources*, p. 4.

242. Mattone and Ferrante, 'Le comunità rurale nella Sardegna medievale.' The first written document mentioning the *Breve* is dated 16 September 1304. The document states that the *Anziani del Popolo Pisano*, a council of senior citizens of Pisa, nominated four citizens who were responsible for revising the *Breve Ville Ecclesie de Sigerro*. The statute is also mentioned in Pisa's *Breve del Commune e del Popolo di Pisa* in A.D. 1313. In the summer A.D. 1327, a reform to the statute enacted under Pisa rule was ordered by King Alfonso IV (A.D. 1299–1336) of Aragon. The new *Breve* was confirmed in A.D. 1358 by King Pedro of Aragon, Alfonso's successor. Baudi di Vesme, *Historiae patriae*, pp. 325–326. For a general history of Sardinia, see Giunta and Boscolo, 'Geronimo Zurita ed i problemi mediterranei della Corona d'Aragona'; Manca, 'Colonie iberiche in Italia nei secoli XIV e XV'; Olla Repetto, *Studi sulle istituzioni amministrative e giudiziarie della Sardegna nei secoli 14. e 15*; Tangheroni, *Pisa e il Mediterraneo*.

243. Baudi di Vesme, 'Dell'industria dell miniere nel territorio di Villa,' p. 375.

244. Sella, *Relazione del Deputato Sella alla commissione d'inchiesta*, p. 6.

245. Baudi di Vesme, *Historiae patriae*, p. cxxxiv; Tangheroni and Mercuriali, *La cittá dell'argento*, p. 116.

246. In Iglesias, wine, chestnuts, figs, raisin grapes, and other food commodities were exempted from dogana tax. The dogana tax on galena was two *denarii*. This sum was a fixed amount paid for the weighing of galena with the *Camerlingo*. Baudi di Vesme, *Historiae patriae*, pp. xxxiii, cclxviii; Tangheroni and Mercuriali, *La cittá dell'argento*, p. 116.

247. Sella, *Relazione del Deputato Sella alla commissione d'inchiesta*, p. 7.

248. Baudi di Vesme, *Historiae patriae*, p. cxxxv.

249. Ibid.

250. For a concise explanation of Sardinian marks and controversies on the subject, see Grierson and Travaini, *Medieval European coinage,* p. 448.

251. Ibid.

252. Ibid.

253. Ibid., p. cxxxvi.

254. Ibid.

255. The noun *parzonavilii* was used in other cities of Tuscany. In Florence and Siena, the form of the word was *parsonavoli*. In Massa, *parzonaoli* appeared by the late thirteenth century. The forms of the noun in Sardinia's *Breve* are *parsonavili, parsonaveli,* and *parsonavoli*. Baudi di Vesme, *Historiae patriae*, p. cvii.

256. Ibid., p. cv.

257. A reference to dowries occurs in a section on sales of land, vineyards, furnaces, and inherited property. Ibid., pp. 158–159.

258. Ibid., p. cxi.

259. Ehrenberg, *Capital and finance in the age of the Renaissance*; Graulau, 'Finance, industry, and globalization in the early modern period'; Kalus, *Die Fugger in der Slowakei*; Strieder, *Jacob Fugger the Rich*.

260. Postan, *Essays on medieval agriculture*, pp. 107–149.

261. Baudi di Vesme, 'Dell'industria dell miniere nel territorio di Villa,' p. 256, footnote 7.

262. Baudi di Vesme, *Historiae patriae*, p. cxi.

263. Scrittori di Detta Enciclopedia, *Dizionario generale di scienze*, p. 591.

264. Baudi di Vesme, *Historiae patriae*, p. cxi.

265. Ibid., p. xxv.

266. Ehrenberg, *Capital and finance in the age of the Renaissance*, p. 22.

267. Baudi di Vesme, *Historiae patriae*, pp. cvi–cvii.

268. Ehrenberg, *Capital and finance in the age of the Renaissance*, pp. 38–39.

269. Baudi di Vesme, *Historiae patriae*, p. 361; for a different estimate, see Tangheroni and Mercuriali, *La cittá dell'argento*, p. 116, footnote 87.

270. Baudi di Vesme, *Historiae patriae*, pp. cv–cvi.

271. Ibid., p. cvii.

272. Ibid., p. cxvi.

273. Braunstein, 'Les statuts miniers de l'Europe médiévale,' pp. 48–50.

274. Baudi di Vesme, *Historiae patriae*, p. cxc.

275. Ibid., p. cxix.

276. Baudi di Vesme, 'Dell'industria dell miniere nel territorio di Villa,' p. 219.

277. Sella, *Relazione del Deputato Sella alla commissione d'inchiesta*, pp. 6–7.

278. Production was astonishingly high: two to three silver ounces per *cantaro* of ore in the mines of Santa Lucia, Grotta, Gambara, Guspini, Arbus, Saffraiga and Montevecchio; one to two silver ounces in the Pula, San Rocco, San Vito, Domusnoas, Fonni, Iglesias, and Decimuputzu mines. Ores containing sulfur had sixty-seven parts of silver for each one hundred parts and sixteen pounds per *cantaro* of ore—a rich endowment that was exploited in the nineteenth and early twentieth centuries. Vargas-Bedemar, *Sulle miniere della Sardegna*, pp. 11–12.

279. Estimates vary because there were different cantaro units used throughout Mediterranean regions. Some historians state that the unit was equivalent to 104 pounds in Iglesias, and it reached an equivalent of 750 pounds in other places. The Genoese *cantaro*, prevalent in most Mediterranean markets, was equivalent to 127 pounds. Tangheroni and Mercuriali, *La cittá dell'argento*, p. 111; Jackson, *Modern metrology*, p. 231; Lopez

and Raymond, trans., *Medieval trade in the Mediterranean world, illustrative documents*, p. 353, footnote 43.

280. Especially in the growing field of medicine. In the words of Agricola, 'Of tin, bismuth, and lead,' lead alone is used in medicine. 'It cools and for that reason mortars and pestles are made from it and if liquids are rubbed in these so that there is a union with the lead solutions are produced that are more cooling. Sheets of lead are advantageously spread beneath the loins of athletes who, because of frequent exercises are harassed by dreams of beautiful women and discharge semen. Having been bound around the testes it drives away such dreams. Burnt lead has mixed properties and cures ulcers. A cooling lotion is made from it. It is most useful in filling ulcers and preventing scars. It can be used to advantage on both hard and cancerous ulcers, sometimes by itself, sometimes mixed with other drugs which prevent scars, for example, the drug made from *cadmia*.' Bandy and Bandy, trans., *Georgius Agricola, De natura fossilium*, p. 181.

281. Baudi di Vesme, *Historiae patriae*, p. 191.

282. This provision was already in place in the *Breve* of Pisa in A.D. 1318. Baudi di Vesme, 'Dell'industria dell miniere nel territorio di Villa,' p. 377; Baudi di Vesme, *Historiae patriae*, p. 355.

283. Baudi di Vesme, *Historiae patriae*, pp. cxvi–cxvii.

284. Baudi di Vesme, 'Dell'industria dell miniere nel territorio di Villa,' pp. 378–379.

285. Ibid.

286. Baudi di Vesme, *Historiae patriae*, p. 89; Sella, *Relazione del Deputato Sella alla commissione d'inchiesta*, p. 7.

287. Baudi di Vesme, 'Dell'industria dell miniere nel territorio di Villa,' p. 384, footnote 3; p. 394.

288. Sella, *Relazione del Deputato Sella alla commissione d'inchiesta*, p. 7.

289. Baudi di Vesme, *Historiae patriae*, p. 312.

290. Ibid., p. 185.

291. Ibid., p. cxxiii.

292. Ibid., p. cxxiii.

293. Braunstein, 'Les statuts miniers de l'Europe médiévale,' pp. 45–46.

294. Cost did not exceed twenty-five pounds *alfonisini minuti*. Baudi di Vesme, *Historiae patriae*, p. 63.

295. Braunstein, 'Les statuts miniers de l'Europe médiévale.'

296. Rowland, *The periphery in the center*, p. 170.

297. Ibid., p. 171.

298. Sella, *Relazione del Deputato Sella alla commissione d'inchiesta*, p. 7.

299. Baudi di Vesme, *Historiae patriae*, p. 191.

300. Tangheroni and Mercuriali, *La città dell'argento*, p. 93.

301. It is also possible that the Ottomans borrowed mining principles from Byzantium. The Justinian *Institutes* established mining rights to 'private citizens' and the payment of the one-tenth tax in the sixth century A.D. Bryer, 'The question of Byzantine mines in the Pontos'; Ferluga, *Byzantium in the Balkans*; Sandars, trans., *Institutes of Justinian*, for general reference; Vryonis, 'The question of Byzantine mines.'

302. These privileges did not last forever. Historian Burr stated that 'this clause only ap-

peared in the Prizren and Rakovica texts'; 'its omission by the later copyists is understandable, since its provisions were by their time obsolete, but its absence from the Athos and Struga texts is surprising.' Burr, 'The Code of Stephan Dušan,' pp. 520–521.

303. Rădvan, *At Europe's borders*, p. 91.
304. The word comes from the German *Schacht*. The law applied the term *chahat* for describing the way in which excavation of a pit proceeded. Deepening the *kuyu* for reaching the mineral was known as *paun*. Beldiceanu, *Les Actes des Premiers Sultans*, vol. 2, pp. 68, 303.
305. Beldiceanu, *Les Actes des Premiers Sultans*, vol. 2, pp. 77–78.
306. Ibid., pp. 77–78.
307. Creasy, *History of the Ottoman Turks*, p. 127.
308. Beldiceanu, *Les Actes des Premiers Sultans*, vol. 2, p. 75, footnote 4.
309. Ágoston et al., *Encyclopedia of the Ottoman Empire*, p. 595.
310. Ibid., p. 68.
311. Historian Mark Bartusis offers an excellent discussion of the historiography of the Byzantine *pronoia* in the Balkans. The latter refers to a 'kind of grant from the emperor to soldiers, lords, the powerful and bishops.' None of the sources discussed by Bartusis mention one single *pronoia* dealing with mining lands. Bartusis, *Land and privilege in Byzantium: The institution of pronoia*, p. 2; Beldiceanu, *Les Actes des Premiers Sultans*, vol. 2, pp. 289, 306–307.
312. It appears in many forms—*gwark, werke, werki, werhe, warak,* and *vurhe*. Beldiceanu, *Les Actes des Premiers Sultans*, vol. 2, p. 90; Dvornik, *The Slavs in European history,* p. 146; Sedlar, *East Central Europe in the Middle Ages*, pp. 115–116; Stojković, 'Saxon miners in Serbian medieval laws and written texts.'
313. Beldiceanu, *Les Actes des Premiers Sultans*, vol. 2, p. 92.
314. Ibid., pp. 93–94.
315. Ibid., p. 65.
316. Beldiceanu states that the Arab noun *ṣāḥib*, which appears frequently in the Turkish-language documents, identified a 'partner, associate, owner, or proprietor.' The same applies to the word *Issi*, a Turkish noun that means owner but also master. When preceded by the noun *kuyu*, it meant 'possessor.' Ibid., p. 89.
317. For general reference, see Aksan and Goffman, eds., *The early modern Ottomans: Remapping the empire*; Piterberg, 'The formation of an Ottoman Egyptian elite in the 18th century.'
318. Beldiceanu, *Les Actes des Premiers Sultans*, vol. 2, pp. 89, 92.
319. Ibid., p. 88.
320. Evans, 'Antiquarian researches in Illyricum, Parts III–IV,' pp. 57, 14; Talbert, *Rome's world: The Peutinger map reconsidered.*
321. Evans, 'Antiquarian researches in Illyricum, Parts III–IV,' p. 98.
322. Udovitch, *Partnership and profit in medieval Islam*, p. 18.
323. Ibid.
324. Beldiceanu, *Les Actes des Premiers Sultans*, vol. 2, p. 91.
325. Ibid., p. 88.
326. Ibid., p. 91.
327. Beldiceanu, *Les Actes des Premiers Sultans*, vol. 1, pp. 297–298.

328. Beldiceanu, *Les Actes des Premiers Sultans*, vol. 2, p. 96.

329. Ibid., p. 78.

330. Tezcan, 'Ottoman monetary crisis of 1585 revisited,' p. 461.

331. Vent and Milne, 'The standardization of mine accounting,' pp. 60–61.

332. Galleries were also known by the Arabic noun *naqbat*. Beldiceanu, *Les Actes des Premiers Sultans*, vol. 2, pp. 69, 296.

333. Beldiceanu, *Les Actes des Premiers Sultans*, vol. 2, p. 70.

334. Ibid., pp. 110–111, 289.

335. Ibid., p. 303.

336. Ibid., p. 112.

337. Ibid., pp. 290, 298.

338. Simonin, *Underground life; or mines and miners*, p. 144.

339. Kovačević-Kojić, 'Les mines d'or et d'argent en Serbie et Bosnie.'

340. Spremić, 'I tributi veneziani nel Levante nel XV secolo.'

341. Trading privileges granted to Venetian merchants in A.D. 1422 for trading silver and gold from Bosnia were limited to trading posts of the Adriatic. They did not include the hinterlands, where the mines were located. This was the case of the trading privileges granted by King Tvrtko II in A.D. 1422. Kovačević-Kojić, 'Les mines d'or et d'argent en Serbie et Bosnie,' pp. 251, 255.

342. İnalcik, 'Ottoman methods of conquest,' p. 110.

343. Ergene, *Local court, provincial society, and justice in the Ottoman Empire*, pp. 24–25; Faroqhi et al., eds., *An economic and social history of the Ottoman Empire*, p. 133.

344. İnalcik, 'Ottoman methods of conquest.'

345. Ergene, *Local court, provincial society, and justice in the Ottoman Empire*, p. 24.

346. For sixteenth-century evolution of the institution of *qāḍī*, see Shaham, ed., *Law, custom, and statute in the Muslim world*, pp. 87–110.

347. Kuran, 'The absence of the corporation in Islamic law,' p. 796.

348. Faroqhi et al., eds., *An economic and social history of the Ottoman Empire*, p. 133.

349. Ibid., p. 106.

350. Beldiceanu, *Les Actes des Premiers Sultans*, vol. 1, p. 171.

351. İnalcik, 'Ottoman methods of conquest.'

352. Beldiceanu, *Les Actes des Premiers Sultans*, vol. 2, p. 75.

353. Ibid., p. 75, footnote 9.

354. It is not easy to establish one sole duty for the *ṣarrāf*. Different documents define different responsibilities. In some documents, he was a supplier of refined gold, silver, and copper to official mints. In others, this officer appeared as the trusted expert investigating circulation of 'unauthorized' silver currencies. Beldiceanu, *Les Actes des Premiers Sultans*, vol. 1, p. 169.

355. Beldiceanu, *Les Actes des Premiers Sultans*, vol. 2, p. 171.

356. The origins of the tax are attributed to the words of 'Abdallāh b. 'Umar b. al-Khaṭṭāb (d. A.H. 73/A.D. 693), brother-in-law of the Prophet, as follows: 'After subtracting *the fifth* which I have dispatched for the purpose for which it was intended, I have decided that I should immobilize the lands with its inhabitants, imposing on them for it the *kharāj* and on their necks the *jizya* [*jizya* here clearly means poll tax], this *jizya* [*jizya* here clearly means the sum of the land and the poll taxes] being a *fay'* to the profit of the Muslim

fighters and of those who come after them.' According to Dennett, 'Umar quoted the Koran, Sūrah 59_{6-10}, the key sentences of which are: "Whatever God has given as spoil to his apostle from the people of the towns,—that belongs to God, to his apostle, to those of kinship, to the orphans, to the poor, and to the wayfarer, that it be not taken successively by the rich among you," and "those who come after them say, O Lord, forgive us and our brothers who preceded us in the faith and do not place in our hearts spite against whose who believe."' Coşgel, 'The economics of Ottoman taxation'; Dennett, *Conversion and the poll tax in early Islam*, pp. 20–21; Darling, *Revenue raising and legitimacy: Tax collection and finance administration in the Ottoman Empire*; Gibb et al., eds., *The encyclopedia of Islam*, vol. 5, p. 974.

357. In *Al-Muwatta*, considered 'the first formulation of Islamic law,' metals were considered as any other land produce, but paid the one-tenth. The book was compiled by Abu 'Abdullah Mālik Ibn Anas al-Asbahī al-Madini (d. A.H. 93/A.D. 712). Mālik, considered one of the greatest Imaans, was among the first compilers of Islamic legal principles. Mālik stated: 'In my opinion, and Allah knows best, nothing is taken from what comes out of mines until what comes out of them reaches a value of twenty gold dinars or two hundred silver dirhams. When it reaches that amount there is *zakat* to pay on it where it is on the spot. *Zakat* is levied on anything over that according to how much there is, as long as there continues to be a supply from the mine. If the vein runs out and then after a while more becomes obtainable, the new supply is dealt with in the same way as the first, and payment of *zakat* on it is begun as it was begun on the original supply. Mines are dealt with like crops, and the same procedure is applied to both. *Zakat* is deducted from what comes out without waiting for a year, just as a tenth is taken from a crop at the time it is harvested without waiting for a year to elapse over it.' The fifth appears again in *Kitāb Al-Amwāl*, or *The Book of Revenue*, a compilation of 'the oral traditions of Islam, the revelations of Allah on authority, taxation, distribution, charity, and a Muslim's responsibilities to Muslim communities.' The author, Abū 'Ubayd Al-Qāsim Ibn Sallām al-Khuzā'ī (d. A.H. 224/A.D. 838), was a legal scholar from Khorāsān. Ibn Sallām argued that the fifth was the *zakāt*, a tax required of Muslims: 'Yaḥyā ibn 'Abd Allāh ibn Bukayr related to me from Mālik ibn Anas from Ibn Shihāb from Sa'id ibn al-Musayyab and Abū Salama ibn 'Abd al-Raḥmān from Abū Hurayra from the Prophet (pbuh), who said: "A fifth is charged on precious minerals" [. . .] al-Qabliyya is a well known area towards Far [. . .] these minerals are subject only to *zakāt* till this day. [. . .] In traditions other than that of Mālik it is stated that he granted him the mines of al-Qabliyya consisting of the parts called Ghawrī and Jilsī. [. . .] Al-Ghawrī is what is in the territory of Tihāma, while al-Jisī is the area that falls in Nejd.' Yet, in another book, *Kitâb Futûḥ al-Buldân*, or *Origins of the Islamic State*, taxation depended upon locality. The author was Abu-l 'Abbâs Aḥmad ibn-Jâbir al-Balâdhuri (d. A.H. 279/A.D. 892). Al Balâdhuri stated: 'The Prophet gave out as fief to Bilâl a piece of land having a mountain and mines. The sons of Bilâl sold a part of it to 'Umar ibn-Abd-al-'Aziz in which one mineral (or he may have said two) appeared. The sons of Bilâl thereupon said: "What we sold thee is not the minerals but the tillable land." Then they brought forth a statement written for them by the Prophet on a palm leaf which 'Umar kissed and with which he rubbed his eye saying to his steward: "Find out what the income and the expenses are, retain what thou hast expended, and give them back the bal-

ance." The Prophet assigned as fief to Bilâil Ibn-al-Ḥârith certain mines in the Furu'
district. On this, all our learned men agree. Nor do I know of any disagreement among
our followers regarding the fact that in the case of mines the *zakât* is one-fourth of
the tithe. It is reported that az-Zuhri often repeated that in the case of mines *zakât* is
binding. It is moreover reported that he said that the *zakât* is one-fifth. That is what the
people of al-'Irâḳ say who at present impose on the mines of al-Furu, Najrân, dhu-l-
Warwah, Wâdi-l-ḳura and others [. . .] in accordance with the view of Sufyân ath-Thauri,
abu-Ḥanîfah, abu-Yûssuf and the school of al-'Irâḳ.' Bewley, *Al-Muwatta of Iman Malik
Ibn Anas*, pp. xxvii, 17; Khûri Hitti et al., eds., *The origins of the Islamic State*, pp.
28–29; Nyazee, *The Book of Revenue*, pp. 323–324, footnote 142.
358. Káldy-Nagy, 'The first centuries of the Ottoman military organization,' p. 159.
359. Ibid., p. 151.
360. Ibid., p. 152.
361. Baer, 'The transition from traditional to Western criminal law in Turkey and Egypt,' p.
139.

Chapter 4. Capitalist Profits of Mining Corporations

1. Vilar, *Iniciación al vocabulario del análisis histórico*.
2. Voltelini, *Giurisdizione signorile*, p. 35.
3. For examples of how lords claimed back fiefs from vassals, see Albertoni, *Vassalli, feudi, feudalismo*, pp. 161–163.
4. For a discussion of serfdom as slavery, see Hammer, *A large-scale slave society of the early Middle Ages*; for a different interpretation of serfs' rights and privileges, see Bloch, *Feudal society*; for a more recent interpretation following Bloch's perspective, see Scott, 'South-West German serfdom reconsidered.'
5. For an excellent discussion, see Reynolds, *Fiefs and vassals: The medieval evidence reinterpreted*.
6. Kink, *Fontes Rerum Austriacarum*, p. 446.
7. Baudi di Vesme, *Historiae patriae*, pp. 249–250, 254.
8. Gibb et al., eds., *The encyclopedia of Islam*, vol. 5, p. 968; Wulff, 'The qanats of Iran.'
9. Lopez and Raymond, trans., *Medieval trade in the Mediterranean world, illustrative documents*, p. 375.
10. Hoover and Hoover, trans., *Georgius Agricola De Re Metallica*, pp. 141–142.
11. Swetz, *Capitalism and arithmetic, the new math of the 15th century*, p. 27.
12. Sigler, trans., *Fibonacci's Liber Abaci*.
13. Baudi di Vesme, *Historiae patriae*, p. cxliii.
14. Smith, *The wealth of nations*, pp. 414–416. The rest of this paragraph comes from this work.
15. Blanchard, *Mining, metallurgy, and minting in the Middle Ages*, vol. 3.
16. In Marx's time, anthropology was still an infant field of knowledge, and neither Prescott nor Morgan, the two giants whose work greatly informed Marx's understanding of extractivism and colonization, had yet completed their masterworks. Marx's critique of the thesis of Kovalesky, the Russian historian who wrote extensively on agrarian and primitive societies, still awaits to be published in full in the English language, to give us

a more complete view of Marx's late ideas about agrarian societies. García Linera, *La potencia plebeya*, pp. 23–28.

17. For the influence of Roman and Greek authors on Adam Smith's work, see Pack, *Aristotle, Adam Smith, and Karl Marx*; see also De Roover, 'Scholastic economics.'

18. Vázquez de Prada, 'La coyuntura de la minería y de la metalurgia europeas (siglos XIII–XVIII).'

19. Nef, 'Industrial Europe at the time of the Reformation'; Nef, 'Silver production in central Europe, 1450–1618'; Soetbeer, *Litteraturnachweis über Geld- und Munzwesen*.

20. Blanchard, *Mining, metallurgy, and minting in the Middle Ages*, vols. 1–2; Munro, 'The medieval origins of the financial revolution'; Munro, *Bullion flows and monetary policies in England and the Low countries*.

21. Valentín Vázquez De Prada states that the amount of silver obtained from Kutná Hora in the late thirteenth century is undetermined, although it played a fundamental role up to the first decades of the fourteenth century. Ian Blanchard estimates an average annual output of two tons of silver for the period A.D. 1298–1350. Blanchard, *Mining, metallurgy, and minting in the Middle Ages*, vol. 3, pp. 927–930. Braunstein, 'Les statuts miniers de l'Europe médiévale,' pp. 50–52; Vázquez De Prada, 'La coyuntura de la minería y de la metalurgia europeas (siglos XIII–XVIII).'

22. In A.D. 1271, the value of the Tuscan florin was 'officially brought to 29 soldi' and this rate of exchange remained unaltered for the florin-pound used on international exchange. The Tuscan florin continuously rose, in comparison with the pound of *piccoli*, 'not so much on account of the depreciation of silver, as for the continual devaluation of the current money (used in the way paper money is used today) by the constant adding of cheap alloy.' The gold florin coined in A.D. 1252 was equal to twenty-four carats and weighed 3.53 grams; one gold florin, measured in silver pounds, equaled twenty soldi, each one subdivided into twelve denari. This was the initial rate of exchange between gold and silver. At the time when Ulrich made the calculations, one pound of silver ore was worth 440 grains of gold. Harreld, *High Germans in the Low countries*, pp. 19–21; Nardi, ed., *Condizioni economiche dell'industria mineralogica in Toscana durante il medio evo*, pp. 14–15.

23. Spufford, *Power and profit*, p. 319.

24. De Roover, *Money, banking, and credit in medieval Bruges*, p. 50.

25. Boyce, *The mines of the Upper Harz*; Häseler, *Das bergwerk in Rammeslberg bei Goslar*; Segers-Glocke et al., eds., *Aspects of mining and smelting in the upper Harz Mountains*.

26. Nardi, ed., *Condizioni economiche dell'industria mineralogica in Toscana durante il medio evo*, p. 20.

27. De Roover, *Money, banking, and credit in medieval Bruges*, pp. 77–78.

28. For Genoese trade in Black Sea ports and cities, see Oberländer-Târnoveanu, 'The coinage of the Genoese settlements of the Western Black Sea shore and on the Danube'; Rogers, 'To and from: Aspects of Mediterranean trade and consumption in the 15th and 16th centuries.'

29. Beldiceanu, *Les Actes des Premiers Sultans*, vol. 2, p. 67, footnote 5; pp. 78–79.

30. Ibid., p. 78.

31. Faroqhi et al., eds., *An economic and social history of the Ottoman empire*, p. 59.

32. Braudel, *Civilization and capitalism*, vol. 2, p. 204.

33. Ibid.

34. Álvarez Nogal, *Los banqueros de Felipe IV y los metales preciosos americanos*; Bethencourt and Ramada Curto, eds., *Portuguese Oceanic Expansion, 1400–1800*; Vilar, *A history of gold and money, 1450–1920*.

35. Kink, *Fontes Rerum Austriacarum*, p. 438.

36. *Inhibemus eciam omnibus tam laboratoribus quam aliis deferre ensem, lanceam, cultellum cum puncta, & omnia alia fraudulenta arma in aliquo Dorslago, qui fiat in aliqua putea, vel laborerio, in banno decem librarum.* Baudi di Vesme, *Historiae patriae*, p. xxxv.

37. Kink, *Fontes Rerum Austriacarum*, p. 438.

38. Ibid., docs. 280–281, pp. 503–504.

39. Molenda, 'Mining towns in central-eastern Europe in feudal times'; Klápště, *The Czech lands in medieval transformation*.

40. Jireček, *Codex juris Bohemici*, p. 268.

41. Hoover and Hoover, trans., *Georgius Agricola De Re Metallica*, p. 99.

42. Sedlar, *East Central Europe in the Middle Ages*, p. 63.

43. Ibid., p. 64.

44. Vucinich, 'The nature of Balkan society under Ottoman rule,' p. 605.

45. Ibid., p. 604.

46. Weber, 'Introduction to the study of Saxon settlement in Transylvania during the Middle Ages.'

47. Ibid., p. 53.

48. Smith, *The wealth of nations*, book 3, chaps. 1–2.

49. Braunstein, 'Les statuts miniers de l'Europe médiévale,' p. 48.

50. Balestracci, *The Renaissance in the fields*, p. 5.

51. Balestracci continues: 'Just as some customs and tastes trickled down from the upper classes to the lower ones, so too did the taste and the practical necessity for writing spread to rural populations.' Tuscan peasants 'perched between the oral and literate worlds.' Ibid., pp. 3–5.

52. Balestracci defines the accounting method as follows: 'When both contracting parties could not read and write, they turned to such people. The grocer Pasquino di Giacomo records that he "made this writing upon request of the two parties because they don't know how to write." A certain Giovanni d'Ugolino recorded that he wrote "this at their request because they do not know how to write," where they refer of Bendetto and another peasant from the Arbia valley. Another example of the same procedure is Astorre Andrea degli Amadori, who recorded Benedetto's purchase of a pig from another peasant, paying his mother, who could only scribble her cross.' Ibid., p. 9.

53. Wickham, *The mountains and the city*, p. 37.

54. Belli et al., *Archeologia de un Castello Minerario, Il sito di Cugnano*; Cicali, 'Le monete del castello minerario di Rocca S. Silvestro'; Francovich and Farinelli, 'Potere e attività minerarie nella Toscana altomedievale.'

55. Bianchi and Francovich, 'L'archeologia dell'elevato come archeologia'; Bruttini et al., 'Un insediamento a vocazione mineraria: il caso di Cugnano nelle Colline Metallifere'; Campana and Francovich, 'Landscape archaeology in Tuscany: Cultural resource management, remotely sensed techniques, GIS based data integration and interpretation'; Cicali, 'Le monete del castello minerario di Rocca S. Silvestro'; Francovich and Farinelli, 'Potere a attività minerarie nella Toscana altomedievale.'

56. Ferrante and Mattone, 'Le comunità rurali nella Sardegna medievale.'
57. As in regulations concerning sacramental oath. Baudi di Vesme, *Historiae patriae*, p. 38.
58. Ibid., p. 88.
59. Ibid., pp. 67–68.
60. Ibid., p. 94.
61. Ibid., p. 30.
62. Evans, 'Antiquarian researches in Illyricum, Parts III–IV,' p. 62.
63. Vucinich, 'The nature of Balkan society under Ottoman rule,' p. 602.
64. Ibid., p. 604.
65. Kalus, *Die Fugger in der Slowakei*, p. 380.
66. Kysel, 'Representative list of the intangible cultural heritage of Slovakia.'
67. Paul, *Mining lore*, p. 163.
68. Vucinich, 'The nature of Balkan society under Ottoman rule,' p. 601.
69. Ibid., p. 606.
70. Baudi di Vesme, *Historiae patriae*, p. 192.
71. Ibid., p. 193.
72. Ibid., p. 163.
73. Ibid., p. 80.
74. *Che nessuna femina possa entrare in de la paissa del grano* [. . .]. Ibid., p. 112.
75. Ibid., p. 107.
76. Ibid., p. 79.
77. Ibid., p. 112.
78. Ibid., p. 92.
79. Ibid., p. 101.
80. Rippon et al., *Mining in a medieval landscape, the royal silver mines of the Tamar Valley*, pp. 85–86.
81. Hoover and Hoover, trans., *Georgius Agricola De Re Metallica*, pp. 268, 270, 292, 553, 591. The rest of this paragraph comes from this work.
82. Tsuna, *Kodō Zuroku*, p. 32.
83. Ibid., p. 52.
84. Mandel, *An introduction to Marxist economic theory*, p. 46.
85. Hoover and Hoover, trans., *Georgius Agricola De Re Metallica*, p. 216.
86. Smith and Gnudi, eds., *The Pirotechnia of Vannoccio Biringuccio*, p. 55.
87. Ibid., p. 382.
88. Prioreschi, *Medieval medicine*.
89. Lewis, *Race and slavery in the Middle East: An historical enquiry*, p. 56.
90. Ibid., p. 56.
91. Spelman et al., trans., *The whole works of Xenophon*, pp. 684–685.
92. The discourse of Xenophon is worth citing at length: 'A master of a family indeed, when he is well provided with furniture, and household goods, buys no more, but no man was ever so overstocked with silver, as not to desire a farther increase. [. . .] No one ever pretended from tradition, or the earliest accounts of time, to determine when these mines first began to be wrought, which is a proof of their antiquity; and yet as ancient as they are, the heaps of rubbish which have been dug out of them, and lie above ground, bear

no proportion with the vast quantities which still remain below, nor does there appear any sensible decay, or diminution in our mines; but as we dig on we still discover fresh veins of silver-ore in all parts, and when we had most labourers at work in the mines, we found that we had still business for more hands than were employed. Nor do I find that the adventurers in the mines retrench the number of their workmen, but purchase as many new slaves as they can get; for their gain are greater, or less, in proportion to the number of hands they employ. And this is the only profession I know of where the undertakers are never envied, be their stock or profits ever so extraordinary, because their gains never interfere with those of their fellow traders.' Ibid., pp. 681, 684–685.

93. Booth, *The historical library of Diodorus the Sicilian*, p. 321. For Roman mines in the Iberian peninsula, see Boone and Worman, 'Rural settlement and soil erosion from the late Roman period through the medieval Islamic period in the lower Alentejo of Portugal'; Domergue, *Minería y metalurgia en las antiguas civilizaciones mediterráneas*; Hirt, *Imperial mines and quarries*; for useful observations from the case of mercury mines, see Matilla Tascón, *Historia de las minas de Almadén, desde la época romana hasta el año 1645*.
94. Jireček, *Codex juris Bohemici*, p. 276.
95. Bisson, 'Medieval lordship,' p. 746.
96. Menant, *Lombardia feudale*.
97. Bisson, 'Medieval lordship,' p. 746.
98. Cited in Prioreschi, *Medieval medicine*, p. 228.
99. Balestracci, *The Renaissance in the fields*, pp. xxii, xviii.
100. Ibid., pp. 23–25.
101. For a thorough history, see Michaud-Quantin, *Universitas Expressions du mouvement communitaire dans le moyen-âge latin*.
102. Lewis, *Medieval political ideas*, vol. 1, p. 202.
103. Gierke, *Political theories of the Middle Ages*, p. 72.
104. Lewis, *Medieval political ideas*, vol. 1, p. 202.
105. Gierke, *Political theories of the Middle Ages*, p. xix. For Roman canonists and their discussion of *persona ficta*, see Blanch Nougués, *Régimen jurídico de las fundaciones en derecho romano*, pp. 51–58.
106. Gierke, *Political theories of the Middle Ages*, p. xix.
107. I consulted the following works: Canning, 'Ideas of the State in thirteenth and fourteenth century commentators on the Roman Law'; Carpintero Benítez, *Justicia y ley natural*; Pulszky, *The theory of law and civil society*; Tierney, *Foundations of the Conciliar theory, the contribution of the medieval cannonists*; Ullmann, 'The development of the medieval idea of sovereignty.'
108. Gierke, *Political theories of the Middle Ages*, p. xx.
109. Freund, *The legal nature of corporations*, pp. 12–13.
110. Blanch Nougués, *Régimen jurídico de las fundaciones en derecho romano*, pp. 51–54.
111. Sapori, *The Italian merchant in the Middle Ages*, p. xviii.
112. Gierke, *Political theories of the Middle Ages*, p. xviii; Tierney, *Foundations of the Conciliar theory*, p. 92.
113. Pulszky, *The theory of law and civil society*, pp. 480–485. Also, Gierke, *Political theo-*

ries of the Middle Ages, pp. 67–73; Pennington and Eichbauer, eds., *Law as profession and practice in medieval Europe*, pp. 49–72; Tierney, *Foundations of the Conciliar theory*, pp. 91–94.

Chapter 5. A 'Lengthy Digression'

1. Rippon et al., *Mining in a medieval landscape*, p. 6.
2. Ibid.
3. Ibid., p. 54.
4. Ibid., p. 54.
5. 'Prior to that both silver and gold could, like lead, be worked as a right in common.' Common law, in the words of an English historian, referred to 'a collection of customs and maxims, which derive their binding power, and the force of laws, from long and immemorial usage, coupled with the express sanction, or the tacit consent, of the legislature.' According to common law, 'if gold or silver were found in any mine of base metal, or as some supposed, if the value of the gold or silver found therein exceeded that of the base metal, the whole would become a royal mine; but as this law impeded the working of mines by subjects, lest, if they contained any gold or silver, they should be claimed by the king, a statute in this reign declared, that no mines on that account should be claimed as royal mines, but the king, or the person claiming for him, should pay for the base metal a certain price.' Crabb, *A history of English law*, pp. 571–572; Rippon et al., *Mining in a medieval landscape*, p. 16; see also Birrell, 'Common rights in the medieval forest'; Birrell, 'Peasant craftsmen in the medieval forest.'
6. Abrahams, 'The expulsion of the Jews from England in 1290'; Postan, *The medieval economy and society: An economic history of Britain, 1100–1500*; Postan and Hatcher, 'Agrarian class structure and economic development in pre-industrial Europe.'
7. Sapori, *La compagnia dei Frescobaldi in Inghilterra*, p. 19.
8. Rippon et al., *Mining in a medieval landscape*, p. 60. In A.D. 1297, tinners were 'hired' to solve problems of shaft flooding in the king's mines of Devon in the last years of the thirteenth century. Two years earlier, royal commissioners recruited miners in Cheshire, Derbyshire, Shropshire, Gloucestershire, and Somerset for working the king's mines in Devon. Miller and Hatcher, *Medieval England: Towns, commerce, and crafts*, p. 71.
9. Sapori, *La compagnia dei Frescobaldi in Inghilterra*, p. 20, footnote 55.
10. Miller and Hatcher, *Medieval England*, p.68.
11. Rippon et al., *Mining in a medieval landscape*, pp. 62–63.
12. Ibid., p. 63.
13. The concession was conditioned to the bankers covering all expenses and working under the general supervision by clerks appointed by the Treasurer. Sapori, *La compagnia dei Frescobaldi in Inghilterra*, p. 21.
14. Sapori, *La compagnia dei Frescobaldi in Inghilterra*, pp. 10–14.
15. Ibid., p. 19.
16. Ehrenberg, *Capital and finance in the age of the Renaissance*.
17. Smirke, 'Original documents: Indenture under which the silver mines of Byrland, Devon, were worked,' p. 130.
18. Miller and Hatcher, *Medieval England*, p .68.

19. Ibid.
20. Ibid., p. 65.
21. Gillingham, 'A historian of the twelfth-century Renaissance,' p. 59.
22. Green, 'King Henry I and Northern England,' p. 38.
23. Britnell, 'The towns of England and northern Italy in the early fourteenth century.'
24. The four towns are York, Winchester, Norwich, and Bristol. Ibid., p. 22.
25. I borrow the argument from Bruce Campbell, who used it to explain the low levels of agrarian production in the fourteenth century. See Campbell, 'The agrarian problem in the early fourteenth century.'
26. Carpenter, 'The second century of English feudalism'; Milsom, *The legal framework of English feudalism*; Reynolds, *Fiefs and vassals*; Stenton, *The first century of English feudalism*.
27. In writing this section, I consulted the following works: Cara Barrionueva, 'Notas para el estudio de la minería almeriense anterior al siglo XIX'; Cardoso, *Diccionario geografico, ou noticia historica de todas as cidades, villas, lugares, e aldeas*; Carvalho, *Cidades medievais portuguesas, uma introdução ao seu estudo*; Cortijo Ocaña, 'La Crónica del moro Rasis y la Crónica sarracina: dos testimonios desconocidos'; Cressier et al., *Genèse de la ville islamique en al-Andalus et au Maghreb occidental*; Duarte, 'A actividade mineira em Portugal durante a Idade Média'; Dória, 'Evolução dos fluidos asociados a procesos mineralizantes: aplicação à região aurífera de Vila Pouca de Aguiar'; Dunlop, 'Sources of gold and silver in Islam according to al-Hamdānī (10th century)'; Estow, 'The economic development of the Order of Calatrava, 1158–1366'; Fagnan, *Extraits inédits relatifs au Maghreb (géographie et histoire)*; Ferreira Vieira, 'Christian religious landscapes and earlier archeological evidence in the Trás-os-Montes and Alto Douro Region (Portugal)'; Grañeda Miñón, 'Los lingotes andalusíes de plata de Hornachuelos (Córdoba)'; Hall, 'Early West African metallurgies: New data and old orthodoxy'; Jiménez Alcázar, 'Tierra, propiedad y paisaje agrario en la frontera de Granada: el núcleo medieval de Coy (Lorca, Murcia)'; Jiménez Mata, *La Granada islámica: contribución a su estudio geográfico-político-administrativo a través de la toponimia*; Lightfoot and Miller, 'Sijilmasa: The rise and fall of a walled oasis in medieval Morocco'; Marques, 'A origem do concelho de Ribeira de Pena (1331)'; Melechen, 'Loans and Jewish-Christian relations in the Archdiocese of Toledo'; Molina and Jiménez Mata, 'La propiedad de la tierra en la Vega de Granada a finales del siglo XV: el caso del Alitaje'; Neiva et al., 'Antimony quartz and antimony-gold quartz veins from northern Portugal'; Oliveira Marques, *Ensáios de história medieval portuguesa*; Palacios García et al., eds., *VII Congreso internacional sobre patrimonio geológico y minero*; Pérez Macías, 'Cerro Salomón y la minería hispano-musulmana en Garb Al-Andalus'; Puche Riart, 'La minería visigótica y musulmana en la Península Ibérica'; Quintana Frías, 'Minería y territorio durante el Califato de Córdoba'; Sociedad Anónima Hullera Vasco-Leonesa et al., eds., *Jornadas sobre minería y tecnología en la Edad Media peninsular*; Serrano-Piedecasas Fernández, 'El primer siglo de la Meseta bajo el dominio islámico, la restructuración del poder'; Sijpesteijn et al., *From al-Andalus to Khurasan: Documents from the medieval Muslim world*; Tobaruela, 'Una aproximación a la minería y la metalurgia andalusí en la depresión de Vera (Almería)'; Torres Lázaro, 'Obreros, monederos y casas de moneda, Reino de Castilla, siglos XIII–XV'; Vega Martín, 'Alternancias epigráficas en las monedas almorávides.'

28. Barriga et al., 'Introduction to the Iberian Pyrite Belt,' p. 2.

29. Ibid.

30. Ruins of Roman mining works are still visible in Riotinto, Huelva, and Romanera, San Platón, Descamisada, Campanario, São Domingos, and Aljustrel in Portugal. Bustamante Álvarez et al., 'Sigillatas claras de Ajustrel,' p. 164; Hall, *Lead ores*, p. 96; Martínez Frías, 'Sulphide and sulphosalt mineralogy and paragenesis from the Sierra Almagrera,' pp. 272, 274–275; Sáez et al., 'Geological constraints of massive sulphide genesis in the Iberian Pyrite Belt,' pp. 438, 442.

31. Brett, ed., *The history of the Mohammedan dynasties by Pascual de Gayangos*, vol. 1, p. 89.

32. Canto García and Cressier, eds., *Minas y metalurgia en al-Andalus y Magreb occidental*, p. 7; Oman, 'Al-Idrīsī.'

33. Martín Civantos, 'Cerro del Toro y minería Kura de Ilbira'; Piqueras Haba, 'Cartografía islámica, Sharq Al-Andalus'; Conde, *D⁻h⁻ikr 'al-'Andalus*.

34. Brett, ed., *The history of the Mohammedan dynasties by Pascual de Gayangos*, vol. 1, p. 89.

35. Ollier and Pain, *The origin of mountains*, p. 95.

36. Schaer, 'Evolution and structure of the High Atlas of Morocco,' p. 107. I have also consulted the following works: Canto García and Cressier, eds., *Minas y metalurgia en al-Andalus y Magreb occidental*; Choulet et al., 'Non-sulfide zinc deposits of the Moroccan High Atlas'; Grant, 'Walking with Berber nomads'; Hay, *Morocco and the Moors: Western Barbary*; Piqueras Haba, 'Cartografía islámica, Sharq Al-Andalus, siglos X–XII, Al-Idrisi y los precursores'; Rosenberger, 'Tāmdult: citè minière et caravanière pré-saharienne (IXᵉ–XIVᵉ s.)'; Rosenberger, 'Autour d'une grande mine d'argent du Moyen Âge marocain: le Jebel Aouam'; Gimlette, 'Morocco, on the high road in the Atlas Mountains.'

37. Gibb et al., *The encyclopedia of Islam*, vol. 2, pp. 873–874. The rest of this paragraph comes from this work.

38. Khaled Bem Romdhane, cited in Canto García and Cressier, eds., *Minas y metalurgia en al-Andalus y Magreb occidental*, p. 7; Torres, *Relación del origen y suceso de los Xarifes y del estado de los reinos de Marruecos, Fez, y Tarudante*, pp. 83, 281.

39. Moreno Nieto, *Discursos leídos ante la Real Academia de la Historia*, p. 9.

40. Khaldûn, *The Muqaddimah, an introduction to history*.

41. Gibb et al., *The encyclopedia of Islam*, vol. 2, p. 874.

42. Other Arab and Persian geographers commented on the mines of the Maghreb. Ibn Jurdādbih (d. A.H. 280/A.D. 893) wrote about the mines of Ŷabal 'Aūn, which were in the jurisdiction of the city of Wazaqūr, and Ŷabal 'Awn, nearby the Tayārāyārā city. Twelfth-century Arab geographer Ibn Faqīh al-Hamadānī, relying upon writings by Ibn Jurdādbih, commented upon silver mines located in the city of Dar'a. A mine in the Todgha Valley was exploited in the ninth century, during the times of the Idrīsid dynasty of Morocco (A.D. 784–974). Tazalaght, in Souss-Massa-Drâa, at an elevation of 1,800 meters above mean sea level, was also noticed by medieval travelers, as well as Maġġānat al-Ma'ādin, north of Tébessa. Gibb et al., *The encyclopedia of Islam*, vol. 2, p. 874; Gozalbes Busto and Gozalbes Cravioto, 'Al-Magrib al-Aqsà en los primeros geógrafos árabes orientales.'

43. Serrano Ruano, 'Minas en colecciones de feutas y casos jurídicos,' pp. 191–194.

44. Dennett, *Conversion and the poll tax in early Islam*, p. 39.

45. Martín Civantos, 'Alquife, un Castillo con vocación minera en el Zenete (Granada),' p. 336.

46. Gibb et al., *The encyclopedia of Islam*, vol. 2, pp. 866–867; Serrano Ruano, 'Minas en colecciones de feutas y casos jurídicos,' p. 196.

47. In this case, sixteen partners participated in the exploitation of the mine. No further details are known. The claimant was the person who received the donation of the mining share. He argued that a donated share was an indivisible asset. A document served as proof of a share donation, signed by two witnesses, 'who had never seen the mine, nor had any idea where the mine was located, nor had they been present at the mining site at the moment of demarcation of mining shares.' The original owner of the mining share argued that donation of the share never occurred. Rather, a sale took place first and foremost, and a donation occurred as a way of bidding for participation in the sale of the mine. According to Ibn al-Ḥāŷŷd, mine ownership in Cordova granted exclusive rights of extraction and exploitation because the custom dictated that rights of exploitation belonged to the mine owner in perpetuity. With this argument, Ibn al-Ḥāŷŷd expressed that Cordova's mines were unlike the mines commented upon by jurist Mālik. Mālik had observed elsewhere that the sale of mines situated in river basins (*al-girān*) was illegal because such a sale involved 'risk,' including the risk of death of the beneficiary of the concession, in which case the mining concession was ceded to another person. Hallaq, *Authority, continuity and change in Islamic thought*, pp. 24–56; Serrano Ruano, 'Minas en colecciones de feutas y casos jurídicos,' pp. 196–197.

48. In cases of fraudulent sales, the buyer enjoyed full compensation rights; the seller was responsible for returning the total amount of money paid for the claim. Ibn al-Ḥāŷŷd stated that selling anticipations of metal outputs was illicit because the sale entailed appropriation of property which did not belong to the seller at the moment of exchange. The goal of this principle, according to Serrano Ruano, was to keep bimetallic ratios in balance. Serrano Ruano, 'Minas en colecciones de feutas y casos jurídicos,' p. 197, footnote 39.

49. Ibid., p. 198, footnote 40.

50. Once the time period for rescinding the mine sale expired, the silver that the buyer obtained from the mined ores belonged to the seller. The seller in this circumstance retained the right to stop a buyer from processing ores. Ibid., p. 198, footnotes 41–42.

51. Ibid., p. 199.

52. There is a *fatwā* by Ibn 'Arafa dealing with mine tax payments. The mine in question was a special type of concession done by a Sultan through the enactment of a document known as *zahīr*, possibly Sultan Abū I-'Abbās (r. A.H. 772–796/A.D. 1370–1394). The Sultan was concerned with tax evasion by the owner of the concession. Ibn 'Arafa wrote the legal opinion deciding the mining case. He sided with the Sultan, arguing that taxes were owed by the owner of the concession, and that this principle applied to mines located in lands under the jursidiciton of religious orders. Ibid., p. 192.

53. Domínguez Rojas, 'La economía del reino nazarí a través de las fetuas,' p. 83.

54. Ibid., p. 83.

55. The small number of *fatwā* that exist concerning mining does not compare with the high number of legal documents that have survived concerning agriculture, cattle ranching, and trade. It is possible that mining controversies occurred frequently and for this reason escaped the jurists' radar. If so, how frequent was frequent? It is impossible to know with certainty. Serrano Ruano, 'Minas en colecciones de feutas y casos jurídicos,' pp. 189–190.

56. Sales contracts were done in diverse gold and silver dinars: 'the *dīnār dhahabī* of 22 carat gold'; 'the *dīnār fiḍḍī* or *mithqāl* worth 10 dineros' or silver dirhams; the '*dīnār* '*aynī* or of copper worth 40 silver *dīnārs*'; and the '*fals* or *fulus* of copper.' Domínguez Rojas, 'La economía del reino nazarí,' p. 84; Sijpesteijn et al., *From al-Andalus to Khurasan*, pp. 3–12, 25–26, 32. For examples of land-sale contracts, see Jiménez Mata, *La Granada islámica*; Molina López and Jiménez Mata, 'La propiedad de la tierra en la Vega de Granada.'

57. I consulted the following works: Echevarría Arsuaga, 'Esclavos musulmanes en los Hospitales de cautivos de la Orden Militar de Santiago'; González Arévalo, 'Cautiverio y esclavitud en el Reino de Granada'; Soto Company, '¿Una oferta sin demanda? La esclavitud rural en Mallorca antes de la peste negra.'

58. Gibb et al., *The encyclopedia of Islam*, vol. 1, p. 492.

59. Abrahão et al., 'Implementing irrigation: Water balances and irrigation quality in the Lerma basin.'

60. Gibb et al., *The encyclopedia of Islam*, vol. 1, pp. 491–492.

61. Jiménez Puertas and Martínez Vázquez, 'La organización social de un espacio andalusí, reflexiones en torno a la Vega de Granada,' p. 168.

62. Domínguez Rojas, 'La economía del reino nazarí a través de las fetuas,' p. 89.

63. Jiménez Puertas and Martínez Vázquez, 'La organización social de un espacio andalusí, reflexiones en torno a la Vega de Granada,' pp. 164–168.

64. Coinciding with Columella's advice on *De Re Rustica* in the first century A.D., farmers in Hispania preferred to plant olive trees close to the seashore. Farming experts recommended planting the olive tree at an approximate distance of 'twenty leagues from sea coasts.' Fivaller De Velaz, *Memoria del olivo y su cultivo*, p. 9.

65. Gibb et al., *The encyclopedia of Islam*, vol. 1, p. 492.

66. García Fernández, 'Viñedo y vino en Álava durante la Edad Media,' p. 1353.

67. Ibid.

68. The sermon on the *sexto peccado mortal* or gluttony aimed at instilling fear of wine among believers: *et por esto cayen en ebriedat o en vomito empero si el hombre se embriagasse una o dos vegadas et non continuadamente tal embriagadura non seria peccado mortal sy non venial.* It was a fourteenth-century sermon. Ibid., p. 1352.

69. Serrano-Piedecasas Fernández, 'El primer siglo de la Meseta bajo el dominio islámico; la restructuración del poder,' p. 905.

70. Domergue, *Minería y metalurgia en las antiguas civilizaciones mediterráneas y europeas*; Hirt, *Imperial mines and quarries*.

71. Smith, ed., *A dictionary of Greek and Roman geography*, p. 318.

72. Ibid., p. 319.

73. Lombard, *The golden age of Islam*, pp. 59–61.

74. Gunder Frank, *ReOrient*.

75. And even figures for sixteenth-century Yunnan mines are 'difficult to come by,' in the opinion of financial historian Huang. Yang states that 'although available documents cannot produce a map of silver production in Yunnan, we can assume silver mining was ongoing on the grounds that silver has always been listed as local product.' Huang, *Taxation and governmental finance in sixteenth-century Ming China*, pp. 242–243; Yang, 'Horses, silver, and cowries: Yunnan in global perspective,' p. 301.

76. Read, 'Mineral production and resources of China, II,' p. 617.

77. White, 'Jehol, mostly a wilderness, is land of paupers, bandits,' p. 5; Wilson, *A history of mountains: Geographical and mineralogical*, p. 547.

78. Some galena occurs in Baijiazi and Hongtoushan in Liaoning, the latter a massive sulphide copper-zinc deposit. Galena here is of infrequent occurrence. A richer galena is found in Changba and the Dengjiashan deposit, both in Gansu west of Inner Mongolia. The veins of galena are contained in quartz veins that cut across the slate, limestone, and dolomite formations of the Yin Shan system. Lee, 'Some rare-element mineral deposits in mainland China,' pp. 7–8.

79. Hirth and Rockhill, trans., *Chau Ju-kua: His work on the Chinese and Arab trade in the XII and XIII centuries*, pp. 35, 43.

80. Ibid., preface.

81. Ibid., pp. 23, 26–27.

82. Wittfogel, *History of Chinese society Liao, 907–1125*, p. 115.

83. Ibid., pp. 150–151, footnote 23.

84. Ibid., p. 143.

85. Ibid., p. 115.

86. Ibid., pp. 660–661.

87. Edkins, *Banking and prices in China*, p. 236.

88. According to the records studied by Edkins, the Yuen dynasty collected from silver mining the following tax amounts: 462 *ting*, 34 taels, and 5 *ts'ien* from Kian-si; 75.0.0 taels from Chihli and Shantung; and 6,289.2.0 taels from Kiang-chê. The Kian-si figures probably included the following taxes: Hu-kwang, 1,809 taels; Yünnan, 735 *ting*, 34 *liang*, 3 *ts'ien*, and 36,784.3 taels. The tael or *liang* and the *ting* represented units of silver currency. The tael was equivalent to thirty-seven grams of silver; the *ting* was equivalent to fifty taels. The *ts'ien* was a large copper and iron coin. Brook, *The troubled empire: China in the Yuan and Ming dynasties*, pp. 120–121; Edkins, *Banking and prices in China*, p. 236.

89. Edkins, *Banking and prices in China*, p. 236.

90. Ibid.

91. Most certainly, the accuracy of the account, which Polo dictated to cell mate Rustichello, is questionable, a point discussed at length elsewhere. For a succinct discussion of the topic, see Hunn, *First globalization: The Eurasian exchange*, p. 17; Jackson, 'Marco Polo and his "Travels"'; Larner, *Marco Polo and the discovery of the world*; Letts, 'Marco Polo: Discussion'; Palladius, 'Elucidations of Marco Polo's travels in North-China, drawn from Chinese sources'; Rockhill, 'Tibet.'

92. Yule, trans., *The book of Ser Marco Polo*, p. 276.

93. Ibid.

94. Ibid., p. 295.

95. Abu-Lughod, *Before European hegemony: The world-system A.D. 1250–1350*, p. 155.

96. Wittfogel, *History of Chinese society: Liao, 907–1125*, p. 141.

97. Wittfogel observed about copper mines: 'During the T'ang dynasty the copper mines of P'ing-yang County are reported to have had 280 such pits. Ore from these pits was smelted in two furnaces and yielded when minted twenty strings of cash daily or seven thousand strings annually, a much higher productivity than is recorded for the one mint of the Liao empire on which numerical data are available.' Ibid., p. 146.

98. Ibid., p. 147.

99. A tribal industry did not exclude specialization. Wittfogel states: 'It seems legitimate therefore to assume that the Ch'i-tan men also were capable of producing the military equipment of their soldiers within the framework of their tribal industry. Whether this industry remained undifferentiated or was delegated, at least in part, to certain artisan groups is not explained by the texts of the *Liao Shih*. It is probable, however, that certain crafts requiring a high degree of technical skill were entrusted to specialists. The making of iron implements and artifacts in Inner Asia long before the time of the Liao Empire must have led to the establishment of professional smiths at a relatively early date. Specialization must have occurred among the Shih-wei and His who were famous for their skill in working metal and in making carts. Specialization of some sort probably existed in most of the Ch'i-tan tribes in such crafts as metal work. But if iron was known and used by the early inhabitants of the Shira Muren region it was not necessarily smelted. Yet, we may ask to what extent did the newly established industries penetrate the cultural orbit of Ch'i-tan society? To what extent did they replace the products of pastoral craftsmen? The *Liao Shih* notes certain industrial innovations that were introduced by A-pao-chi's father and uncle prior to the establishment of the empire. His father, "the first to establish iron smelteries," began the casting of metal implements. His father's younger brother, Shu-lan, was interested in weaving. Such reports indicate a relatively primitive industry for the preceding periods, but we do not know whether the Ch'i-tan lacked all knowledge of metal work in those times or whether they engaged in crude metal work with little specialization.' Ibid., pp. 141-142.

100. Chen, *Chinese migrations, with special reference to labor conditions*, p. 26.

101. Cosmo, *Ancient China and its enemies: The rise of Nomadic power in East Asian history*, p. 17.

102. Ibid.

103. Stein, *Serindia*, vol. 1, p. viii.

104. Ibid.

105. Curzon, *The Pamirs and the source of the Oxus*, p. 18.

106. Cited in Elvin, *The retreat of the elephants: An environmental history of China*, p. 19.

107. Tuan, *A historical geography of China*, p. 41.

108. Forêt, *Mapping Chengde: The Qing landscape enterprise*, p. 91.

109. Ibid., p. 90.

110. Atwell, 'Time, money, and the weather: Ming China,' p. 86; see also Atwell, 'Ming observers of Ming decline.'

111. Atwell, 'Time, money, and the weather,' p. 91.

112. Huang, *Taxation and governmental finance in sixteenth-century Ming China*, p. 242.

113. Ibid.

114. Atwell, 'Time, money, and the weather,' pp. 86, 90.

115. Huang, *Taxation and governmental finance in sixteenth-century Ming China*, pp. 242-243.

116. Ibid.

117. Flynn, 'China and the Spanish Empire'; Giráldez, *The age of trade: The Manila galleons and the dawn of the global economy*; Ollé, *La empresa de China: de la armada invencible al galeón de Manila*; Schurz, *The Manila galleon*; Yuste López, *Emporios transpacíficos: comerciantes mexicanos en Manila*.

118. Kamen, *Empire: How Spain became a world power, 1492–1763*, p. 292.

119. Bailly-Maître and Benoît, 'Les mines d'argent de la France médiévale,' pp. 26–27; Baron et al., 'Medieval lead making on Mont-Lozère Massif (Cévennes-France)'; Benoît and Cailleaux, eds., *Moines & métallurgie dans la France médiévale*; Braunstein and Benoît, eds., *Mines, carrières et métallurgie dans la France médiévale*.

120. I consulted the following works: Bonami, 'Dans la Haute Vallée de L'Orb: les mines de Ceilhes-et-Rocozels au Moyen Âge'; Dumoulin, 'Les mines métallifères du département de la Loire'; Durant, 'Elements for a cultural history of wood in southern France (X–XVI centuries)'; Fluck and Bruno, 'Le paysage minier des sites métalliques des Vosges et de la Forêt-Noire'; Mugueta, 'Explotación minera en el Reino de Navarra: la mina de plata de Urrobi'; Porée, Études *historiques sur le Gévaudan*; Scoville, *The persecution of Huguenots and French economic development, 1680–1720*; Serrano Larráyoz, '*Item perrexil, mostarda, lechugas et raunos*, notas sobre la alimentación de mineros alemanes en Pamplona a finales del siglo XIV (1392).'

121. Geology confirms the occurrence of lead deposits in the Cévennes containing argentiferous galena, blende, pyrite, chalcopyrite, and antimony. Galena occurs with sphalerite and tetrahedrite. South of Auvergne, ores occur in limestone and dolomites, and veins contain galena, blende, anglesite, calamine, and other minerals. Hall, *Lead ores*, p. 82.

122. French archeologists, applying radiocarbon-dating techniques to slags discovered in Mont Lozère, estimate that mining took place in A.D. 1025–1210 and A.D. 1195–1280. Baron et al., 'Medieval lead making on Mont Lòzere Massif,' p. 245.

123. Bloch, *French rural history*, p. 70.

124. Ibid., p. 77.

125. Hilton, *English and French towns in feudal society*, p. 35.

126. Bailly-Maître, 'L'argent au Moyen Âge.'

127. Bailly-Maître, 'Pour une historie des mines au Moyen Âge,' p. 70.

128. Ibid.

129. Bloch, *French rural history*, pp. 191–192.

130. Le Roy Ladurie, *The peasants of Languedoc*, p. 38.

131. Bloch, *French rural history*, p. 192.

132. Ibid.

133. Bailly-Maître and Benoît, 'Les mines d'argent de la France médiévale,' p. 28.

134. Ibid., p. 26.

135. In Brionnais, a contract between Prior of Anzyle-Duc in Saône-et-Loire, from the dependency of Saint-Martin d'Autun, and Duke Hugh of Burgundy allowed both parties to operate 'in equal parts' the village's silver mines in A.D. 1277. Nothing further is known about these mines.

136. As late as A.D. 1234, the Cistercian Order of Noirlac made an agreement with the lord ruling Charenton over the mine of Puy-Dabert, supposedly discovered by the monks.

137. Many thanks to Peter Claughton for sharing details about the history of the mine.

138. De Asso y Del Río, *Historia de la economía política de Aragón*, p. 137; López Dueso, 'La Edad Media,' pp. 103–104; see also Abraham, 'Les mines d'argent antiques et médiévales du district minier de Kaymar.'

139. López Dueso, 'La Edad Media,' p. 113.

140. The text of a grant for the silver mines of Toulon in A.D. 1180 illustrates the heavy bur-

den of feudal taxation: 'In the year of the Incarnation of the Lord 1180, an agreement was made between Raymond Berenger, by the grace of God, Count of Provence, and William, Lord of Marseiller, about the silver mines of Toulon, viz., that the miners should have whatever they find as their own property together with the silver mined, wherever they find it, near Toulon; and purchases and sales of any lead and silver whatsoever ought to be divided in three parts, of which the Count will have one, William, Lord of Marseilles, another, and the miners another. But the taxes ought to be divided into two parts; the Count will have half, and William, Lord of Marseilles half; and all the said taxes ought to be collected and shared by the said miners. And it should be known that the said Count promised to defend Toulon with its territory as far as has been shown, and also all those coming and going, on land and sea, to the silver mine, or wherever they are in Provence on business with the said mine. Besides, it should be known that wherever lead or silver is taken from the said mine, it should be taken to Toulon; and all this just as was written above, William, Lord of Marseilles confirmed by oath in his own and his brother's name with one knight. And the Count swore the same with two knights.' Halsall, 'Medieval source book: Agreement on the exploitation of a silver mine, 1180'; Subías Pérez et al., 'Explotaciones mineras del entorno del Hospital de Benasque: geología y encuadre histórico,' p. 239.

141. Bloch, *French rural history*, p. 72.
142. Le Roy Ladurie, *The peasants of Languedoc*, p. 11.
143. Ibid.
144. Bloch, *French rural history*, p. 115.
145. Bisson, 'Mediterranean territorial power in the twelfth century.'
146. Evergates, ed., *Feudal society in medieval France*.
147. Gould, *The deserts of southern France*, p. 113.
148. Ibid., p. 111.
149. Gould, *A book of the Cévennes*, p. 50.
150. Bisson, *Medieval France and her Pyrenean neighbors*, p. 259.
151. Jones, *Politics in the rural society: The southern Massif Central*, pp. 8–9.
152. Rainfall patterns were studied in A.D. 1971–1979. Tourasse and Obled, 'Dynamique des épisodes pluvieux intenses sur le Sud-Est du Massif Central, aspects météorologiques et applications hydrologiques.'
153. Umlauft, *The Alps*, pp. 400–401.
154. Conran, '*La Ceuillette*: Foraging for edible wild plants in southern France,' p. 80.
155. Ibid., p. 81.
156. Ibid., pp. 83, 80.
157. Ibid., p. 84.
158. Le Roy Ladurie, *The peasants of Languedoc*, p. 67.
159. For an excellent summary of the state of lordly coinages in medieval Languedoc, see Bisson, 'Coinages and royal monetary policy in Languedoc during the reign of Saint Louis.'
160. I have employed the starting date of A.D. 1185, following the work by Asakawa. I borrowed the periodization of medieval political rule from the work by Yamamura, as follows: Heian period (A.D. 794–1185), with the capital city in Kyoto or Heian; Kamakura period (A.D. 1185–1333), or the rise of the earliest Samurais and their locating the cen-

ter of power at Kamakura; and, the period of Ashikaga hegemony (A.D. 1333–1573), characterized by consolidation of the first government established by the Samurai class. Asakawa, 'Some of the contributions of feudal Japan to the new Japan'; Yamamura, 'The development of *Za* in medieval Japan.'

161. Totman, *Pre-industrial Korea and Japan in environmental perspective*, p. 66.

162. I consulted the following works: Bishop, 'The historical geography of early Japan'; Chassigneux, 'Rica de oro et Rica de plata'; Habashi, 'The beginnings of mining and metallurgical education in Japan'; Juleff, 'Technology and evolution: A root and branch view of Asian iron from first millennium B.C. Sri Lanka to Japanese steel'; *Japan Weekly Mail*, 'Trade of Nagasaki for 1903'; Keiji and Yamamura, 'Shaping the process of unification: Technological progress in sixteenth and seventeenth century Japan'; Ludwin and Smits, 'Folklore and earthquakes: Native American oral traditions from Cascadia compared with written traditions from Japan'; Narita, 'Geology and ore deposits of the Onikobe-Hosokura district, northeastern Honshu, Japan'; Naumann, 'The physical geography of Japan, with remarks on the people.'

163. Imai, *Geological studies of the mineral deposits in Japan*, p. 1.

164. Del Mar, *A history of the precious metals*, p. 310.

165. Bureau of Mining of Japan, *Mining in Japan, past and present*, p. 3

166. Kuwasaburo et al., *History of the empire of Japan*, p. 87.

167. Friedrich Hirth and William Rockhill, who translated and annotated the document, stated the following: 'The text [. . .] is certainly corrupt here in two places. The character yüé in Yüé-chóu is clearly an error for au, as Ōshu was the part of Japan where gold was first discovered in A.D. 749. Ōshu is now divided into several provinces, but it is probable that the Handa mine in the province of Iwashiro is the one referred to. [. . .] The other error [. . .] is writing "another island", instead of "Tui-tau" in Japanese Tsushima, on which island silver was found in B.C. 675, and where mines were worked for a long period subsequently.' Hirth and Rockhill, trans., *Chau Ju-kua*, pp. 171, 175, footnote 22.

168. The famous Kamioca mine was discovered in A.D. 1589. Kanamori Nagachika (A.D. 1524–1608), a general under Hideyoshi and lord of Hida, 'ordered his vassal Modzumi Sōtei to make researches for useful ores in his estate.' The mine became Japan's largest lead and zinc producer, with an astonishing production record of forty-four million tons of crude ore, containing zinc, lead, copper, and silver. The Sado mine, in northwest Sado island facing the Japan Sea, was discovered in A.D. 1542. It was 'the largest mine in Japan in total production of gold and silver.' However, it was abandoned in A.D. 1664, 'owing to the water trouble at the Waremabu bonanza.' In A.D. 1607, 'the productive capacity of the mines of Sado and Idzu became exceedingly diminished, in all probability on account of water, so that thirty-six mining experts selected from Ōmori mine and the mines of Idzu were sent to the Sado mine to reform the operation, but in spite of all these efforts the mine was frequently swamped by gushing out of water in the rainy season.' Bureau of Mining of Japan, *Mining in Japan, past and present*, pp. 8–16; Imai, *Geological studies of the mineral deposits in Japan and East Asia*, pp. 54, 172–174; Schnell, *The rousing drum: Ritual practice in a Japanese community*, p. 48.

169. Veins here form what geologist Chōsajo calls 'deposit districts.' They contain tin, tungsten, copper, zinc, lead, and silver in three main groups, known as Tasei, Kanagase, and

Aokusa. Chōsajo, *Outlines of the geology of Japan*, pp. 137–138. The description that follows in this paragraph comes from this work.

170. Keiji and Yamamura, 'Shaping the process of unification,' p. 82.

171. *Daimyos* were lords of warring provinces. Kobata, 'The production and uses of gold and silver in sixteenth- and seventeenth-century Japan,' p. 245.

172. Ibid., pp. 247–248.

173. Yamamura, 'The development of *Za* in medieval Japan.'

174. Bureau of Mining of Japan, *Mining in Japan, past and present*, p. 6

175. Ibid., p. 6.

176. Ibid., p. 16.

177. Saito, 'Land, labor, and market forces in Tokugawa Japan,' p. 170.

178. For a thorough discussion of the problem of using the term feudalism in relation to medieval Japan, see Hall, 'Feudalism in Japan: A reassessment.'

179. Saito, 'Land, labor, and market forces in Tokugawa Japan,' pp. 170–171.

180. For a commentary about evidence and controversies on the subject, see Kawahata et al., 'Climate change and its influence on human society in western Japan during the Holocene,' p. 103.

181. Tanaka and Yoshino, 'Re-examination of the climatic change in central Japan'; Totman, *Pre-industrial Korea and Japan in environmental perspective*, p. 66.

182. Totman, *Pre-industrial Korea and Japan in environmental perspective*, p. 91.

183. Ibid., p. 66.

184. Ibid., p. 72.

185. Ibid., p. 84.

186. Ethan Segal in Friday, ed., *Japan emerging: Premodern history to 1850*, p. 210.

187. Ibid.

188. Asakawa, 'Some of the contributions of feudal Japan to the new Japan,' p. 5.

189. Philip Brown in Friday, ed., *Japan emerging*.

190. Dominian, 'Mining in the Asiatic Near East,' p. 309.

191. Ibid.

192. Eyuboglu et al., 'The Eastern Black Sea type volcanogenic massive sulfide deposits,' p. 29. In addition to the works cited in this section, I consulted the following works: Kurter, 'Glaciers of Turkey'; Lydon, 'Goulimine (also Goulimime)'; MacDonald, 'The ancient mine-workings of Laureion'; Nerantzis, 'Pillars of power: Silver and steel in the Ottoman Empire'; Ramsay, 'Cilicia, Tarsus, and the Great Taurus Pass.'

193. Demir et al., 'Mineral chemical investigation on sulfide mineralization of the Istala deposit, Gümüşhane,' p. 316; Gökçe and Bozkaya, 'Lead and sulfur isotope evidence for the origin of the Inler Yaylası lead-zinc deposits,' p. 91.

194. Hall, *Lead ores*, p. 99.

195. Del Mar, *A history of the precious metals*, p. 27.

196. Strabo added: 'Beside the severity of the labour, the atmosphere of the mines is filled with poisonous odours, which commonly prove fatal to the workmen'; 'the works are frequently suspended from the difficulty of obtaining labourers whose full number is two hundred, which is being continually diminished by disease and accident.' Sandaracurgium was located in the ancient city of Pimolis. Pimolis is generally thought to have been located 150 kilometers northwest of Sivas, on the river bank of Kizil-Irmak, coin-

ciding with the Osmanjik town. Forbes located Sandaracurgium in the realgar mines of the Pontic. Del Mar, *A history of the precious metals*, p. 27; Forbes, *Studies in ancient technology*, p. 144; Royal Geographical Society, *Dictionary of geographical knowledge*, p. 716.

197. Mayor, *The poison king: The life and legend of Mithradates*, p. 71.

198. Ibid., p. 121.

199. Forbes, *Metallurgy in Antiquity*, p. 190.

200. Bryer, 'The question of Byzantine mines in the Pontos,' p. 139; Hall, *Lead ores*, p. 99.

201. Creasy, *History of the Ottoman Turks*, p. 319; Eyuboglu et al., 'The Eastern Black Sea type volcanogenic massive sulfide deposits,' p. 29; Gökçe and Bozkaya, 'Lead and sulfur isotope evidence for the origin of the Inler Yaylası lead-zinc deposits,' p. 91.

202. Geray and Özden, 'Silvopastoralism in Turkey's mountainous Mediterranean region,' p. 128.

203. Eyuboglu et al., 'The Eastern Black Sea type volcanogenic massive sulfide deposits,' p. 39.

204. Yener, 'The archaeometry of silver in Anatolia: The Bolkardağ mining district,' p. 470.

205. Mango, 'Tracking Byzantine silver and copper metalware,' p. 222.

206. Yener, 'The archaeometry of silver in Anatolia,' pp. 470–471.

207. Kharajian, *Regional geology and mining of Armenia*, p. 59.

208. Ibid., p. 60.

209. Ibid.

210. Smyth, 'Geological features of the country round the mines of the Taurus,' p. 520.

211. Kharajian, *Regional geology and mining of Armenia*, p. 17.

212. Yule, *Cathay and the way thither: Medieval notices of China*, vol. 1, p. 46.

213. Ibid., p. 46, footnote 2.

214. Ibid., p. 46, footnote 3.

215. Kharajian, *Regional geology and mining of Armenia*, p. 20.

216. Mederer et al., 'Base and precious metal mineralization in Middle Jurassic rocks of the Lesser Caucasus,' p. 196.

217. Ibid., p. 193.

218. In his wanderings in Asia after A.D. 1316, the Franciscan friar visited 'Constantinople, Trebizond, Erzerum, Tabriz, Soltania; Kashan, Yezd, Perspeolis, Shiraz, Kurdistan, and Baghdad; the Persian Gulf, Hormuz, Tana, perhaps Surat; Malabar, Pandarani, Cranganor, Kulam, Ceylon, and Mailapoor; Sumatra, Java, Southern or Eastern Borneo, Champa, and Canton; Fokien, Fuchen, across the mountains to Hagcheufu and Nanking'; the Great Canal at Yangcheufu, Cambalec or Peking, 'where he spent 3 years'; Ortu or medieval Tenduc, Shensi, Lhassa in Tibet; returning to Europe through Kabul, Khrasan, 'and the south Caspian, to Tabriz, and finally Venice.' Ibid., pp. 6–7, 45.

219. Suárez, *Early mapping of Southeast Asia*, p. 77.

220. Hodgson, *The venture of Islam*, vol. 2, p. 388.

221. Ibid., p. 389.

222. Geray and Özden, 'Silvopastoralism in Turkey's mountainous Mediterranean region,' p. 129.

223. Gibb et al., *The Encyclopedia of Islam*, vol. 1, p. 463.

224. Hodgson, *The venture of Islam*, vol. 2, p. 389.

225. Geray and Özden, 'Silvopastoralism in Turkey's mountainous Mediterranean region'; Solecki, 'Cave art in Kürtün Ini, a Taurus Mountain site in Turkey,' pp. 87–88.

226. Geray and Özden, 'Silvopastoralism in Turkey's mountainous Mediterranean region,' p. 129.

227. Wilson, 'Notes on the physical and historical geography of Asia Minor, made during the journeys in 1879–82,' pp. 312–313.

228. Some men had the extravagant idea of bringing camels to the mines of the Americas for the same purpose, after camels were introduced in the Canary Islands. The Tûlû and Bactrian camels made it to the Americas—a chapter in the history of the Columbian exchange that remains to be studied. They were used in Santiago de Cuba for transporting copper ores. There is a fascinating account of the advantages and problems of employing camels, written by U.S. Navy Lieutenant David D. Porter. Porter stated: 'I met a gentleman in Jamaica, who had charge of some camels, working the copper mines in "St. Jago de Cuba"; he informed me that they were very useful until the "chiqua" got into their feet, and after that they were given up. As the "chiqua," it is to be hoped, does not exist in Texas, there is no danger of their being afflicted by them. The same gentleman informed me that in every other respect they suited admirably, and stood the climate.' Porter, 'Letter of Lieutenant Porter, United States Navy, to Secretary of War, May 28, 1856,' pp. 130–131.

229. Tchikhatchev, *Asie Mineure: Description physique de cette contree*, p. 660.

230. Ibid., p. 659.

231. Har-El, *Struggle for domination in the Middle East*, pp. 36–39.

232. Wilson, 'Notes on the physical and historical geography of Asia Minor, made during the journeys in 1879–82,' pp. 318–319.

233. Pitarakis, 'Mines Anatoliennes exploitées par les Byzantins: recherché récentes.' The Persian writer was Ibn Faḍlallāh al-Umari (d. A.D. 1349).

234. For a general summary of Ottoman military campaigns in the plains of Cilicia, see Har-El, *Struggle for domination in the Middle East*. Toynbee describes many military campaigns affecting trade and traffic passing through the Cilician gates. See Toynbee, *The treatment of Armenians in the Ottoman Empire*.

235. Pitarakis, 'Mines Anatoliennes exploitées par les Byzantins: recherché récentes.'

236. Bodio, 'A map showing the mortality from malarial fever in Italy during the three years 1890–91–92,' p. 132.

237. McNeill, *The mountains of the Mediterranean world*, p. 87.

238. Bodio, 'A map showing the mortality from malarial fever in Italy during the three years 1890–91–92,' p. 132.

239. Karpat, *Social change and politics in Turkey: A structural-historical analysis*, p. 155.

240. Lewis, *Race and slavery in the Middle East*, p. 13.

241. Karpat, *Social change and politics in Turkey*, p. 155.

242. Wilson, 'Notes on the physical and historical geography of Asia Minor, made during the journeys in 1879–82,' p. 312.

243. Lindner, *Explorations in Ottoman prehistory*, p. 109.

244. Faroqhi, *Approaching Ottoman history: An introduction to the sources*, p. 84.

245. White, *The climate of rebellion in the early modern Ottoman empire*, pp. 140–141.

246. White, 'Little Ice Age crisis of the Ottoman Empire,' p. 77.

247. White, *The climate of rebellion in the early modern Ottoman empire*, pp. 158–159.

248. Hess, *The forgotten frontier: A history of the sixteenth-century Ibero-African frontier*, p. 107.

249. Gibb et al., *The Encyclopedia of Islam*, vol. 1, p. 465.

250. The most recent volcanoes are Aghri-dagh, at 5,172 meters, Alagöz Dagh, at 4,094 meters, and Sübḥān Dagh, at 4,434 meters. Berberian and Yates, 'Patterns of historical earthquake rupture in the Iranian Plateau,' p. 123.

251. Ibid., pp. 124–125.

252. Ibid., pp. 128, 130.

253. Ibid., p. 125.

254. Bourrouilh-Le et al., 'Band-e-Amir Lakes and Dragon Valley (Bamiyan),' p. 124.

255. Lombard, 'Les bases monétaires d'une suprématie économique, l'or Musulmandu VIIe au XIe siècle,' p. 146. I also consulted the following works: Abu-Jaber and Kimberley, 'Origin of ultramafic-hosted vein magnesite deposits'; Al-Alijani, 'Effect of the Zagros Mountains on the spatial distribution of precipitation'; Amcoff, 'Distribution of silver in massive sulfide ores'; Borsuk and Sholpo, 'Correlation of endogenous processes in the Alpine cycle of the Caucasus'; Freeman, *The historical geography of Europe*; Harvey and Press, 'Issues in the history of mining and metallurgy'; McKinsty, *Mining geology*; Nweeya, *Persia: The land of the Magi*.

256. Kharajian, *Regional geology and mining of Armenia*, p. 17.

257. Rodgers, 'Differences between mountain ranges,' p. 15.

258. Abu-Lughod, *Before European hegemony*, p. 157.

259. Ouseley, *The Oriental geography of Ebn Haukal*, p. 233.

260. Governor of Khurāsān al-Ashras, 110 A.H. Dennett, *Conversion and the poll tax in early Islam*, p. 120.

261. Center for Iranian Studies, *Encyclopedia of Islam*, p. 1116.

262. Ibid.

263. Le Strange, *The lands of the eastern Caliphate: Mesopotamia, Persia, and Central Asia*.

264. Khorāsān contained the city of Núkân, which was part of Tûs, or Tús [today's Tabaran], which was 'the Urva of the Vendidad, the eighth of the sixteen lands created by Ahura Mazda.' Tûs was a vast region between the Binalud and Hezar-Masjed mountains in the north. It included Taberan, Nogjan or Noqan, Radkan, and Torqbaz. Núkân, or Noghān, was an extensive area to the east of Meshed, or today's Mashhad, 'stretching from near the walls of the modern city to the villages of Husaynāban and Mihrābad.' Center for Iranian Studies, *Encyclopedia of Islam*, p. 1116.

265. Center for Iranian Studies, *Encyclopedia Iranica*, vol. 1, Fasc. 8, pp. 810–821; Gibb et al., *The Encyclopedia of Islam*, vol. 1, p. 358; Le Strange, *The geographical part of the Nuzhat-al-qulūb*.

266. Ouseley, *The Oriental geography of Ebn Haukal*, p. 233.

267. Bourrouilh-Le et al., 'Band-e-Amir Lakes and Dragon Valley (Bamiyan),' p. 121.

268. Ibid., p. 126.

269. Ibid.

270. Bolin, cited in Forslund, *Visbys roller i ett växande handelsnätverk*, p. 20.

271. Le Strange, *The lands of the eastern Caliphate*, p. 350.

272. Forslund, *Visbys roller i ett växande handelsnätverk*, p. 20.

273. Holtfrerich, *Frankfurt as a financial centre*, p. 39.

274. Del Mar, *A history of the precious metals*, p. 316.

275. Beckwith, *Empires of the Silk Road*, p. 167.

276. Gibb et al., *The Encyclopedia of Islam*, vol. 8, p. 941. There were various branches of the Seljuks: the Seljuks of Persia and Iraq (A.H. 429–552/A.D. 1038–1157), to which Alp Arslan belonged; the Seljuks of Kirmān (A.H. 440–582/A.D. 1048–1186); those of Western Persia and Iraq (A.H. 511–590/A.D. 1118–1194); the group of Syria (A.H. 471–511/A.D. 1078–1117); and Rūm (c. A.H. 483–707/A.D. 1081–1307).

277. Creasy, *History of the Ottoman Turks*, p. 2.

278. About the specific location of the mines, Minorsky states: 'The mention of Indian coins *jītal* suggests an area on, or off, the high road to India (Bāmiyān-Chārīkār-Kābul); the 'jītal (jaytal?) was a copper coin usually taken for one-sixty-fourth of a silver tanga.' Minorsky, 'Some early documents in Persian,' p. 87, footnote 1; see also Le Strange, *The lands of the eastern Caliphate*, p. 334.

279. Gibb et al., *The encyclopedia of Islam*, vol. 5, p. 968.

280. Nastich, 'Almaty-town and mint dating back to the 13th century.'

281. Le Strange, *The lands of the eastern Caliphate*, p. 414.

282. Bretschneider, *Medieval researches from eastern Asiatic Sources*, vol. 2, pp. 25–26. I consulted the following works: Bagchi and Ghose, 'History of mining in India—*circa* 1400–1800, and technology status'; Balfour, *The encyclopedia of India and Eastern and Southern Asia*; Birrell, 'The medieval English forest'; Carver et al., *Wasperton: A Roman, British, and Anglo-Saxon community in Central England*; Chalmers, *Caledonia, or an account, historic and topographic of North Britain*; Claughton, 'The medieval silver-lead miner, a preliminary study'; Collis et al., 'The prehistoric and medieval field archaeology of Crownhill Down, Dartmoor, England'; Cross, *A history of England and greater Britain*; Gale and Stos-Gale, 'Ancient Egyptian silver'; Harrell, 'The oldest surviving topographical map from ancient Egypt'; Herbert, *Red gold of Africa: Copper in precolonial history and culture*; Hunt, *The lead miners of the North Pennines in the eighteenth and nineteenth centuries*; Huson, *The rise of the Demidov family and the Russian iron industry in the eighteenth century*; Krüger, 'Copper mining and metallurgy in prehistoric and the more recent past'; Kumar Biswas, 'Non-gem minerals in pre modern India'; Lindren, *Mineral deposits*; Mackenzie and Ross, *An historical, topographical, and descriptive view of the County Palatine of Durham*; Schmidt and Avery, 'More evidence for an advanced prehistoric iron technology in Africa'; Wade, *British history, chronologically arranged, comprehending a classified analysis of events and occurrences in Church and State*; Worth, *Historical notes concerning the progress of mining skill in Devon and Cornwall*; Wright, *Geology and mineral resources of West Africa*.

283. The account, entitled *Pei Shi Ki*, or *Notes on an embassy to the North (1222)*, appears in Bretschneider, *Medieval researches from eastern Asiatic Sources*, vol. 1, pp. 25–34.

284. Ibid., p. 30.

285. Gibb et al., *The Encyclopedia of Islam*, vol. 2, pp. 1123–1124.

286. Zawar's ore reserves are truly impressive: thirty-six million tons, containing 1.96 percent lead, and 4.68 percent zinc. Craddock, *2000 years of zinc and brass*; Kohad, 'Monitoring environmental impact of ore beneficiation processing at Zawar mines,' p. 134.

287. Naravane, *The Rajputs of Rajputana (a glimpse of medieval Rajasthan)*, p. 11.
288. Bagchi and Ghose, 'History of mining in India—circa 1400–1800, and technology status,' p. 29.
289. Lac or lakh is an Indian unit equal to one hundred thousand, used in reference to sums of rupees. Soukhanov, *Microsoft Encarta college dictionary*, p. 807.
290. Tod, *Annals and antiquities of Rajast'han*, pp. 117–118.
291. Ibid., p. 222.
292. Willies, 'Ancient and post-medieval mining sites in the Khetri copper belt and Kolar gold field,' p. 289.
293. Velho et al., *A journal of the first voyage of Vasco Da Gama*, p. 58.
294. Ibid., p. 75.
295. Bagchi and Ghose, 'History of mining in India—circa 1400–1800,' p. 29.
296. Ibid., pp. 27–28.
297. Ibid., p. 29.
298. Kumar Biswas, 'Minerals and metals in medieval India,' p. 294.
299. Ibid.
300. Bethencourt and Ramada Curto, eds., *Portuguese oceanic expansion, 1400–1800*; Jayasuriya, *The Portuguese in the East: A cultural history*.
301. Hess, *The forgotten frontier*, p. 11.
302. Abu-Lughod, *Before European hegemony*, p. 145.
303. Markham, trans., *Narrative of the embassy of Ruy González de Clavijo to the court of Timour*, p. xliii.
304. Ibid., p. xlv.
305. The audacity of the campaign deserves to be noted. In the words of González de Clavijo: 'He ordered his army to be lowered down the rocky walls, by ropes, from ledge to ledge. The sovereign [Timour] himself was lowered down on a stage of planks, secured together by iron rings, and the operation was five times repeated. The whole party was now on foot, except Timour himself, whose horse had also been lowered down; and this put them on equal terms with the mountaineers, who were, however, so amazed at the unexpected appearance of the invaders, that they abandoned their stronghold, sued for mercy, and humbly submitted to the authority of the mighty "lord of the conjunctions." Timour continued his march to Cabul [Kabul] and prepared for the invasion of India.' The translator of the text added the following note about the meaning of the title, "lord of the grand conjunctions": 'The easterns believe that in all the great conjunctions of the planets, there is a great revolution in the world. Thus Abraham, Moses, Zoroaster, Christ, and Mohammed, came into the world as a great conjunction. Layomurs, Solomon, Alexander, Zengis, and Timour, were each in their turn, *Sahib Keraun*, or "masters of the conjunctions," and of all the great events during their respective reigns.' Markham attributed the note to D'Herbelot. Ibid., p. xlvii, footnote 1.
306. Kumar Biswas, 'Minerals and metals in medieval India,' p. 287.
307. Pires, *Suma Oriental*, vol. 1, p. 32.
308. Fonseca and Ribeiro da Cunha, *De Vasco a Cabral: Oriente e Ocidente nas navegações oceânicas*.
309. Yule, *A glossary of colloquial Anglo-Indian words*, p. 693.
310. Velho et al., *A journal of the first voyage of Vasco Da Gama*, pp. 100–101.

311. Ibid.

312. Ibid., pp. 213–214; Yule, *A glossary of colloquial Anglo-Indian words*, p. 867.

313. Christie, 'Money and its uses in the Javanese states of the ninth to fifteenth centuries AD'; Wicks, 'Monetary developments in Java between the ninth and sixteenth centuries.'

314. Wicks, 'Monetary developments in Java between the ninth and sixteenth centuries,' p. 45.

315. Ibid., p. 47.

316. Ibid.

317. On Egypt, see Blanchard, 'Egyptian specie markets and the international gold crisis of the early fifteenth century.'

318. The earliest discovered coins come from stratified deposits at Shanga. These are small silver coins, weighing between 0.1 and 0.3 grams, 'with a name and a short statement such as "Muhammad/billah yāthīq,"' indicates Horton. Horton states: 'The coins were made in coin flans, a method described by Hamdani in the Yemen, examples of which have actually been found in excavations at Banbhore, the possible site for Daybul in Sindh. These eighth-ninth century coins from the Lamu archipelago develop into the silver and copper coinage of the Swahili towns. This series is best known from the Matambwe hoard, excavated in 1984 on Pemba island; it had been buried after 1066, the date of the latest Fatimid dinar found with the hoard. The locally made coins were of silver and contain the names of local rulers with rhyming couplets on their reverse, a practice found on both Fatimid coins and coins of the Amirs of Sindh. Copper coins were also made in East Africa. They are more commonly found with similar couplets and continued to be made until the fifteenth century. The evidence suggests that while the East African coinage was made for local rulers, it was influenced by coining practices around the Indian Ocean, including those of Sindh. It may not be coincidental that the traditional first land fall of the "Debuli" in the Lamu archipelago is also where the first evidence can be found for numismatic connections with the Indus delta.' Horton, 'Artisans, communities, and commodities: medieval exchanges between Northwestern India and East Africa,' pp. 75–76; see also Lombard, 'Les bases monétaires d'une suprématie économique, l'or Musulmandu VIIe au XIe siècle,' pp. 144, 149.

319. Lombard, 'Les bases monétaires d'une suprématie économique, l'or Musulmandu VIIe au XIe siècle,' p. 149.

320. Vilar, *A history of gold and money, 1450–1920.*

321. Velho et al., *A journal of the first voyage of Vasco Da Gama*, p. 233.

322. Herbert, *Red gold of Africa*; for a general introduction, see Oliver and Atmore, *Medieval Africa, 1250–1800.*

323. Many thanks to Peter Claughton for the information about the congress held in 2016 at Aix-Marselle Universite, Aix-en-provence, France, on the theme *Les métaux précieux en Méditerranée médiévale*, which included a paper on silver deposits of North Africa. Publication of conference proceedings had not occurred at the time of writing this work.

324. Ogden, 'Metals,' p. 170.

325. Ibid.

326. Randall-MacIver, *Medieval Rhodesia*, pp. 48–49.

327. Richards, 'Mughal State: Finance and the premodern world economy,' p. 302.

Chapter 6. Capitalist Mining in West European Development

1. Lewis, *The Stannaries*, p. 176.
2. Reynolds, *Fiefs and vassals*, p. 186.
3. I consulted the following works: Braunstein, 'Le fer et la production de fer en Europe, de 500 à 1500'; Díez de Salazar, 'La industria del hierro en Guipúzcoa (siglos XIII–XVI)'; Evans and Rydén, *Baltic iron in the Atlantic world in the eighteenth century*; Gardner, *Ironwork: From the earliest times to the end of the medieval period*; Halbout et al., 'Corpus des objets domestiques et des armes en fer de Normandie, du Ier au XVe siècle'; Hartwell, 'A cycle of economic change in Imperial China: Coal and iron in Northeast China'; Martín Civantos, 'Alquife, un castillo con vocación minera en el Zenete'; Vázquez De Prada, 'La coyuntura de la minería y de la metalurgia europeas (siglos XIII–XVIII)'; Wagner, 'The administration of the iron industry in eleventh-century China.'
4. Kellenbenz, *The rise of continental Europe*, p. 110.
5. 'We are probably justified in regarding this tribute as historically connected with the mining tax of Roman law, which,—in accord, on this point, with the original Germanic view—, recognized no other holder of mining privileges than the landowner and no other fiscal right of the crown in the mine than the tithe.' Hübner et al., *A history of Germanic private law*, p. 41.
6. Heer, *The Holy Roman Empire*, p. 49; King, *The finances of the Cistercian Order in the fourteenth century*.
7. Donkin, *The Cistercians: Studies in the geography of medieval England and Wales*, p. 16.
8. Reynolds, *Stronger than a hundred men*, p. 109.
9. Ibid., pp. 109, 112.
10. These included 'burial in the monastic precincts, a special chapel in the church being assigned for that purpose, the monastery assumed the arms of the ducal family, and the monks acknowledged the foundation as the result of the bounty of the ducal family in the inscription on the front of the church.' Parker Mason, 'The beginnings of the Cistercian Order,' p. 183; Thompson, 'The Cistercian Order and colonization of mediaeval Germany.'
11. Ibid.
12. Gaud and Leroux-Dhuys, *Les abbayes Cisterciennes en France et en Europe*.
13. Kuran, 'The absence of the corporation in Islamic law,' pp. 790–791.
14. Successful monetary and weight reforms undertaken by Charlemagne leave no doubt of the nexus between land conquest and mining. In the early years of the ninth century A.D., Charlemagne centralized ore-smelting factories located in the mining sites of the Harz Mountains. The dispersion of the heavyweight silver *denarius* throughout the *regnum Francorum* was dictated by location of mints, which in turn was based upon sites where successful mining works were in full swing. By the tenth century A.D., there were mints at Meppen, Widenbrück, Magdeburg, Bremen, Gittelde, and Odenhausen. In A.D. 1135, only three cities had mints in the lands stretching between the Alps and the Apennines; seventy years later, the number had grown to twelve. Around Freiberg, there were twenty-five mints by A.D. 1197, from only nine in A.D. 1130, reaching to almost forty by A.D. 1250. Thirty-seven mints appeared north of Rome by A.D. 1200, from only four mints in A.D. 1130. Old mints in northeast France and north Germany experienced 'a revival,'

according to Peter Spufford, as new 'semi-independent rulers' rose to power in Germany and France and 'usurped' coinage and minting rights. In the Italian peninsula, silver coins were struck at the mints of Bonaria, in southwest Cagliari, and that of Cagliari in mid-fourteenth century A.D.; Capua, north of Naples, in the ninth and tenth centuries A.D.; Castelsardo or *Castel Genovese*, near Sassari in northwest Sardinia, starting in A.D. 1401; Catania in Sicily in A.D. 1356; Chieti in Abruzzo in the last years of the fifteenth century A.D.; Cittaducale in Lazio in A.D. 1309; among others. This astonishingly high number of mints does not take into account the phenomenon of 'wandering mints' or mints that moved from city to city, more characteristic of later medival mints according to Spufford. Bachrach, *Charlemagne's early campaigns (768–777)*, pp. 52–54; Grierson and Travaini, *Medieval European coinage*, pp. 2–9, 25–27; Leyser, 'Ottonian government,' p. 743; Miskimin, 'Two reforms of Charlemagne? Weights and measures in the Middle Ages'; Segers-Glocke et al., eds., *Aspects of mining and smelting in the Upper Harz Mountains (up to the 13th/14th century)*, pp. 53–65; Spufford, 'The mint buildings of medieval Europe,' p. 1060; *Money and its uses in medieval Europe*, pp. 187–191; Steuer, 'Settlements in the southern Black Forest: Castels and mining (dominance through commerce),' p. 113.

15. Charlemagne secured control over the silver mines of Melle, in northern France, and sought the rich silver deposits of the Harz Mountains. This was part of a grand strategy aimed at building the economic basis for the conquest and annexation of tribes of Saxons, Avars, Slavs, and Arab and Greek populations inhabiting resource-rich Mediterranean islands. Military campaigns expanded beyond the Frankish lands at the heart of Europe into the lands of the Saxons near the Alps and the Slavic lands into the Carpathians. Moreover, the dispersion of the heavyweight silver *denarius* throughout the *regnum Francorum* is the best evidence of this point. Such a dispersion was dictated by location of mints, which in turn was based upon feudal lands where successful mining works took place outside the imperial radar. When Charlemagne attempted centralizing ore-smelting processes, he could only do so by granting privileges and exemptions to miners and smelters. Bachrach, *Charlemagne's early campaigns (768–777)*, p. 54; Blanchard, *Mining, metallurgy, and minting in the Middle Ages*, vol. 2, pp. 688–689.

16. Robert Barlett, cited in Gillingham, 'A historian of the twelfth-century Renaissance and the transformation of English society,' p. 45.

17. Smith, *The wealth of nations*, p. 410.

18. Davis, 'Regulation of human population in northern France,' p. 250.

19. Ibid.

20. Ibid., p. 251.

21. Ibid.

22. Lewis, 'The closing of the medieval frontier,' p. 481.

23. Hochstadt, 'Migration in preindustrial Germany,' p. 200.

24. Ibid., p. 199.

25. Kellenbenz, *The rise of the European economy*, p. 3.

26. Witthöf, in Segers-Glocke et al., eds., *Aspects of mining and smelting in the upper Harz Mountains*, p. 107.

27. Ibid.

28. Kalus, *Die Fugger in der Slowakei*.

29. Paul, *Mining lore*, p. 174.
30. Simonin, *Underground life; or mines and miners*, p. 105.
31. Paul, *Mining lore*, p. 174.
32. Kalus, *Die Fugger in der Slowakei*, p. 380.
33. Paul, *Mining lore*, p. 174.
34. Browne, *An account of several travels through a great part of Germany, in four journeys*, p. 120.
35. Paul, *Mining lore*, p. 49.
36. Cited in Paul, *Mining lore*, p. 133.
37. Ibid., p. 119.
38. Ibid., p. 49, footnote 18.
39. Nederman, 'Sovereignty, war and the corporation: Hegel on the medieval foundations of the modern State,' p. 502.
40. The phrase comes from Kaser, *The Balkans and the Near East*, p. 66.
41. Ibid., p. 66.
42. Bulut, 'Reconsideration of economic views of a classical empire and a nation-state during the mercantilist ages,' p. 793.
43. Kuran, 'The absence of the corporation in Islamic law,' p. 796.
44. Hodgson, *The venture of Islam*, vol. 2, p. 402.
45. With the exception of the obligation 'incumbent on every Muslim under the form of *zakâh*, the poor-rate (which, however was used for other ends, too).' Lokkegaard, 'Islamic taxation in the classical period,' pp. 15–16.
46. Ibid., pp. 55–56.
47. Gerber, 'The Muslim law of partnerships in Ottoman court records'; Kuran, 'The absence of the corporation in Islamic law'; for a brief description of the early Islamic legal corpus, see Udovitch, *Partnership and profit in medieval Islam*, pp. 12–15.
48. Lokkegaard, 'Islamic taxation in the classical period.'
49. Hess, *The forgotten frontier*, p. 161.
50. Ibid., p. 797.
51. Madgearu, 'Salt trade and warfare in medieval Transylvania.'
52. Kuran, 'The absence of the corporation in Islamic law.'
53. Gibb et al., *The encyclopedia of Islam*, vol. 5, p. 969; Hill, trans., *Kitāb al-Ḥiyal: The book of knowledge of ingenious mechanical devices*, p. 240.
54. Hill, trans., *Kitāb al-Ḥiyal*, pp. 240–241. The rest of this paragraph comes from this work.
55. Gibb et al., *The encyclopedia of Islam*, vol. 5, p. 969.
56. Reynolds, *Stronger than a hundred men*, p. 97.
57. Al-Asad, 'Landscape and hardscape: Historical problems and contemporary solutions to the scarcity of water in the Islamic world,' pp. 315–316.
58. Ibid., p. 319.
59. Ibid., p. 318.
60. Denny, 'Art, infrastructure, and devotion: Ottoman water infrastructure,' p. 186.
61. Akkach, *Letters of a Sufi scholar: The correspondence of 'Abd al-Ghanī al-Nābulusī*, p. 19.
62. For a general history of Venetian mining interests, see Corniani Degli Algarotti, *Dello stabilimento delle miniere relative fabbriche nel distretto di Agordo*.

63. Kaser, *The Balkans and the Near East*, p. 188.

64. Ibid., pp. 187–189.

65. Ibid., p. 59.

66. Chaudhuri, *Trade and civilization in the Indian Ocean*, p. 39.

67. Lombard, *The golden age of Islam*, p. 61.

68. Lombard describes how Berber tribes ceased to use the urban languages of Latin or Punic and returned progressively to Berber. Berber was a Semitic language, which derived from an ancient Libyan tongue and rested mainly upon oral tradition. Ibid., pp. 59–61.

69. Ibid.

70. Vilar, *A history of gold and money*.

71. Lombard, *The golden age of Islam*, p. 60.

72. Hodgson continues: 'there are fashions in atrocities, and it became the fashion for a time in the fourteenth and fifteenth centuries to display this willingness graphically by building great towers of severed human heads, cemented in a rough masonry, which gleamed afar at night with the flickering decomposition products of the organic materials.' Hodgson, *The venture of Islam*, vol. 2, p. 405. I also consulted the following works: Abu-Lughod, *Before European hegemony*; Gunder Frank and Gills, eds., *The world system: Five hundred years of five thousand?*; Rachewiltz, *The secret history of the Mongols*, vol. 3; Weatherford, *Genghis Khan and the making of the modern world*.

73. Center for Iranian Studies, *Encyclopedia of Islam*, p. 1115.

74. Ibid., p. 1116.

75. Ibid., p. 1118.

76. Lindner, *Explorations in Ottoman prehistory*, pp. 31–32.

77. Le Strange, *The lands of the eastern Caliphate*, pp. 416–417.

78. The words of a Taoist monk traveling through the Hindu Kush and summoned to the court of Chinghiz Khân in the first decades of the thirteenth century inspire fear: 'I left this place (Samarkand) on the thirteenth of the first month (February 23), and after three days travelling to the south-east, passed *Tie men kuan* (the Iron Gate). [. . .] We crossed the mountain in a south-eastern direction, and found them very high. Masses of rocks were lying scattered about. The escort themselves pulled the carts, and took two days to pass to the other side of the mountains. We proceeded along a river to the south, and our soldiers entered the mountains to the north to pursue the robbers [. . .] From Kieshuang-na (Kash), going southwest 200 *li* the way leads through mountains with difficult passages. There are no people or villages, and little water or vegetation. Then going 300 *li* south-east the Iron gates are reached. It is a narrow defile formed by two parallel mountains, which rise on each side perpendicularly and have the color of iron. There are in the defile folding gates strengthened with iron and furnished with many iron bells hung up. Because of these circumstances and of the strength and difficulty of this pass, it has received the name of Iron gate.' Bretschneider, *Medieval researches from eastern Asiatic sources*, vol. 1, pp. 80, 83–84.

79. Center for Iranian Studies, *Encyclopedia Iranica*, vol. 1, Fasc. 8, pp. 810–821; Nastich, 'Almaty-town and mint dating back to the 13th century'; Tsang Woo, 'Silver-mining and smelting in Mongolia.'

80. Hodgson, *The venture of Islam*, vol. 2, p. 402.

81. Abu-Lughod, *Before European hegemony*, p. 157.

82. Ibid., p. 155.

83. Lamborn, *The metallurgy of silver and lead*, p. 11.

84. Del Mar, *A history of the precious metals*, p. 317.

85. Sedlar, *East Central Europe in the Middle Ages*, p. 5.

86. Del Mar, *A history of the precious metals*, p. 319; for a biographcial sketch of Del Mar, see Mundell, 'Comment on academic exclusion: The case of Alexander Del Mar.'

87. Bretschneider, *Medieval researches from eastern Asiatic sources*, vol. 1, pp. 84–85.

88. Ibid.

89. This 'warrior mode of distribution of power' was not exclusive to the Mongols. Historian Laura Da Graça identified it also in medieval Castile, and medieval Islamic State. Braudel, *A history of civilizations*, p. 75; Da Graça, 'Feudal dynamics and Runciman's competitive selection practices in late medieval Castile,' p. 345.

90. Pounds, *An historical geography of Europe*, p. 41.

91. Flitch, *Mediterranean moods*, p. 291.

92. Kamen, *Empire*, p. 5.

93. Bonfante, ed., *The barbarians of ancient Europe: Realities and interactions*; Cauuet, 'Celtic gold mines in West Central Gaul'; James, *Europe's barbarians, B.C. 200–600*.

94. Klarwill, *The Fugger news-letters*, p. 237.

95. Brading and Cross, 'Colonial silver mining: Mexico and Peru.'

96. Craig and Robert, eds., *In quest of mineral wealth: Aboriginal and colonial mining and metallurgy*, pp. 119–135; Graulau, 'Ownership of mines and taxation in Castilian laws'; Mentz, coord., *Sultepec en el siglo XIX*, p. 26; for a commentary on the same subject, see Humboldt, *Political essay on the Kingdom of New Spain*, vol. 3, pp. 109–110; Solórzano y Pereira, *Política Indiana*, p. 285; Suárez et al., *Historia general de España*, p. 181.

97. Álvarez Nogal, *Los banqueros de Felipe IV y los metales preciosos americanos*; Graulau, 'Finance, industry, and globalization in the early modern period'; Kalus, *Die Fugger in der Slowakei*; Kellenbenz, *Los Fugger en España y Portugal hasta 1560*; 'The gold mining activities of the Fuggers and the cementation privilege.'

98. Balard, 'Gênes et la mer Noire,' pp. 32–33; Di Cosmo, 'Black Sea emporia and the Mongol Empire,' p. 85; Lopez, 'Majorcans and Genoese on the North Sea route in the thirteenth century,' p. 1166, for the Genoese in Cadiz; Oberländer-Târnoveanu, 'The coinage of the Genoese settlements of the Western Black Sea shore and on the Danube'; Rogers, 'To and from.'

99. Hübner et al., *A history of Germanic private law*, p. 291.

100. '[T]he main cause of this change may have been the fact that the land-lords early endeavored to free themselves from the payment of the mining tithe, and for this purpose turned to the crown, which, in the privileges it granted them, assured them the entire produce of the mines, including the tither. There resulted from this an idea that the king had full power to dispose of unmined metals; an idea which it was also attempted to support by citations from Roman legal sources.' Ibid., pp. 291–292.

101. Ibid., p. 292.

102. Einaudi, *La rendita mineraria: origini e basi*, p. 73.

103. McNeill, *The rise of the West*, p. 558.

104. Ibid.

105. Rocke, 'Agricola, Paracelsus and Chymia.'

106. Ibid.

107. Xu Zhiqin, in Zhiqin et al., *Orogenic belts*, p. vii.

108. De Wit and Thiart, 'Metallogenic fingerprints of Archaean cratons,' p. 59.

109. Paul, *Mining lore*, p. 9.

110. Cuvier, *A discourse on the revolutions of the surface of the globe*, p. 30; see also Schaer, 'Introduction,' p. 4.

111. Peattie, *Mountain geography*, p. 4.

112. Green, ed., *Dictionary of Jesus and the Gospels*, p. 324.

113. Cited in Powells, *The African and Middle Eastern World, 600–1500*, p. 26.

114. Birmingham, *Word and worship workbook*, p. 563.

BIBLIOGRAPHY

Abraham, Philippe, 'Les mines d'argent antiques et médiévales du district minier de Kaymar (Nord-Ouest de l'Aveyron),' *Gallia* 57 (2000), pp. 123–127.

Abrahams, B. Lionel, 'The expulsion of the Jews from England in 1290,' *The Jewish Quarterly Review* 7 (1894), pp. 75–100.

Abrahão, Raphael, et al., 'Implementing irrigation: Water balances and irrigation quality in the Lerma basin,' *Agricultural Water Management* 102 (2011), pp. 97–104.

Abu-Jaber, Nizar S., and Michael M. Kimberley, 'Origin of ultramafic-hosted vein magnesite deposits,' *Ore Geology Reviews* 7 (1992), pp. 155–191.

Abu-Lughod, Janet L., *Before European hegemony: The world system A.D. 1250–1350* (New York, 1989).

Abulafia, David, ed., *The new Cambridge medieval history*, vol. 5, *c.1198–1300* (Cambridge, England, 1999).

Achenza, Maddalena, 'The use of adobe in the traditional buildings of Sardinia,' in *Proceedings of the first International Congress on construction history*, vol. 2, comp. Santiago Huerta Fernández, pp. 101–111 (Madrid, 2003).

Adams, Nicholas, 'Architecture for fish: the Sienese Dam on the Bruna River—structures and designs, 1468–ca. 1530,' *Technology and Culture* 25 (1984), pp. 768–797.

Adas, Michael, *Technology and European overseas enterprise: Diffusion, adaptation, and adoption* (Belgium, 1996).

Ágoston, Gábor, et al., *Encyclopedia of the Ottoman Empire* (New York, 2009).

Agoston-Nikolova, Elka, ed., *Shoreless bridges: Southeast European writing in diaspora* (Amsterdam, 2010).

Agrawal, Dharampal P., et al., 'Ancient copper workings: Some new C-14 dates,' *Indian Journal of the History of Science* 11 (1976), pp. 133–136.

Akkach, Samer, *Letters of a Sufi scholar: The correspondence of 'Abd al-Ghanī al-Nābulusī (1641–1731)* (Leiden, 2010).

Aksan, Virginia H., and Daniel Goffman, eds., *The early modern Ottomans: Remapping the empire* (Cambridge, England, 2007).

Al-Alijani, Bohloul, 'Effect of the Zagros Mountains on the spatial distribution of precipitation,' *Journal of Mountain Science* 5 (2008), pp. 218–231.

Al-Asad, Mohammad, 'Landscape and hardscape: Historical problems and contemporary solutions to the scarcity of water in the Islamic world,' in *Rivers of paradise: Water in Islamic art and culture*, ed. Sheila Blair and Jonathan Bloom, pp. 314–335 (New Haven, 2009).

Albertoni, Giuseppe, *Vassalli, feudi, feudalesimo* (Roma, 2015).

Alexander, David, 'The reclamation of Val-di-Chiana,' *Annals of the Association of American Geographers* 74 (1984), pp. 527–550.

Alfonso, Isabel, 'Cistercians and feudalism,' *Past and Present* 133 (1991), pp. 3–30.

Allen, Alice M., *A history of Verona*, ed. Edward Armstrong (London, 1910).

Allen, David E., *The naturalist in Britain: A social history* (London, 1976).

Allen, Martin, 'The volume of the English currency, 1158–1470,' *Economic History Review* 54 (2001), pp. 595–611.

Álvarez, Walter, *The mountains of Saint Francis: Discovering the geological events that shaped our Earth* (New York, 2009).

Álvarez Burgos, Fernando, et al., *Catálogo general de la moneda medieval hispano-cristiana desde el siglo IX al XVI* (Madrid, 1980).

Álvarez Nogal, Carlos, *Los banqueros de Felipe IV y los metales preciosos americanos* (Madrid, 1997).

Amcoff, Orjan, 'Distribution of silver in massive sulfide ores,' *Mineralium Deposita* 19 (1984), pp. 63–69.

Amstutz, Gerhard C., and A. J. Bernard, eds., *Ores in sediments* (Berlin, 1973).

Anderson, Perry, *Passages from antiquity to feudalism* (London, 2013).

Andrade, Amélia A., 'A estratégia Dionisina na fronteira noroeste,' *História, Rev. da Faculdade de Letras II* 15 (1998), pp. 163–176.

Appuhn, Karl, *A forest on the sea: Environmental expertise in the Renaissance* (Maryland, 2009).

Aranguren, Biancamaria, et al., 'Serrabottini (Massa Marittima, GR): indagini archeologiche su un antico campo minerario,' *Archeologia Medievale* 34 (2007), pp. 79–94.

Archetype International Research Team, 'The medieval Bosnian fortress Čajangrad: Preliminary report and archeological project proposal' (2010–2011), pp. 1–22 [online] https://www.academia.edu/5668851/Cajangrad_-_2013, accessed March 11, 2014.

Armstrong, Pamela, 'Merchants of Venice at Sparta in the 12th century,' *British School at Athens Studies* 16 (2009), pp. 313–321.

Arnold, Benjamin, *Power and property in medieval Germany, c. 900–1300* (Oxford, 2004).

Arnold, Brother, *The letter of Petrus Peregrinus on the magnet, A.D. 1269* (New York, 1904).

Arnoux, M., 'Innovation technique et genèse de l'enterprise: quelques réflexions à partir de l'exemple de la métallurgie européenne (XIIIe–XVIe siècles),' *Histoire, économie et société* 20 (2001), pp. 447–454.

Asakawa, Kan'ichi, 'Some of the contributions of feudal Japan to the new Japan,' *Journal of Race Development* 3 (1912), pp. 1–32.

Aston, Trevor H., ed., *Landlords, peasants, and politics in medieval England* (Cambridge, 1987).

Aston, Trevor H., and C. H. E. Philpin, eds., *The Brenner debate: Agrarian class structure and economic development in pre-industrial Europe* (New York, 1985).

Atwell, William S., 'Ming observers of Ming decline: Some Chinese views on the "seventeenth-century crisis" in comparative perspective,' *Journal of the Royal Asiatic Society of Great Britain and Ireland* 2 (1988), pp. 316–348.

Atwell, William S., 'Time, money, and the weather: Ming China and the "Great Depression" of the mid-fifteenth century,' *Journal of Asian Studies* 61 (2002), pp. 83–113.

Austen, Ralph A., 'On comparing pre-industrial African and European economies,' *African Economic History* 19 (1990–1991), pp. 21–24.

Auty, Richard M., and Raymond F. Mikesell, *Sustainable development in mineral economies* (Oxford, 1998).

Aymard, Maurice, *Dutch capitalism and world capitalism* (Cambridge, England, 1982).

Aymard, Maurice, 'From feudalism to capitalism in Italy: The case that doesn't fit,' *Review Fernand Braudel Center* 6 (1982), pp. 131–208.

Bachrach, Bernard, *Charlemagne's early campaigns (768–777): A diplomatic and military analysis* (Leiden, 2013).

Badeeb, Ramez A., et al., 'The evolution of the natural resource curse thesis: A critical literature survey,' *Resources Policy* 51 (2017), pp. 123–134.

Baedeker, Karl, *Northern Germany as far as the Bavarian and Austrian frontiers* (Leipzig, 1893).

Baer, Gabriel, 'The transition from traditional to Western criminal law in Turkey and Egypt,' *Studia Islamica* 45 (1977), pp. 139–158.

Bagchi, S., and A. K. Ghose, 'History of mining in India—circa 1400–1800, and technology status,' *Indian Journal of History of Science* 15 (1980), pp. 25–29.

Baillie-Grohman, William A., *The land in the mountains, being an account of the past & present of Tyrol* (London, 1907).

Bailly-Maître, Marie C., and Paul Benoît, 'Les mines d'argent de la France médiévale,' in *Actes des Congrés de la Société des Historiens Médiévistes de l'Enseignement Supérieur Public, 28e Congrés*, ed. Claude Gauvard, pp. 17–45 (Clermont-Ferrand, 1997).

Bakos, František, 'Au-porphyry mineralization in the mantle of the Štiavnica stratovolcano,' *Mineralia Slovaca* 42 (2010), pp. 1–14.

Balard, Michel, 'Gênes et la mer Noire (XIIIe–XVe siècles),' *Revue Historique* 270 (1983), pp. 31–54.

Baldwin, John W., *The medieval theories of the just price: Romanists, Canonists, and theologians in the twelfth and thirteenth centuries* (Philadelphia, 1959).

Balestracci, Duccio, *The Renaissance in the fields: Family memoirs of a fifteenth-century Tuscan peasant*, trans. Paolo Squatriti and Betsy Merideth (Pennsylvania, 1999).

Balfour, Edward, *The encyclopedia of India and Eastern and Southern Asia* (London, 1885).

Bandy, Mark C., and Jean A. Bandy, trans., *Georgius Agricola, De natura fossilium* (New York, 1955).

Baron, Sandrine, et al., 'Medieval lead making on Mont-Lozère Massif (Cévennes-France): Tracing ore sources using Pb isotopes,' *Applied Geochemistry* 21 (2006), pp. 241–252.

Barriga, Fernando J. A. S., et al., 'Introduction to the Iberian Pyrite Belt,' in *Geology and VMS deposits of the Iberian Pyrite Belt, SEG Neves Corvo Field Conference*, Guidebook Series Vol. 27, ed. Fernando J. A. S. Barriga and Delfim De Carvalho, pp. 1–20 (Colorado, 1997).

Barthélemy, Dominique, and Stephen D. White, 'Debate, the feudal revolution,' *Past and Present* 152 (1996), pp. 196–223.

Bartusis, Mark C., *Land and privilege in Byzantium: The institution of the pronoia* (Cambridge, England, 2012).

Baudi di Vesme, Carlo, 'Dell'industria dell miniere nel territorio di Villa di Chiesa,' *Memorie della Reale Accademia delle Scienze di Torino* 2 (1871), pp. 225–461.

Baudi di Vesme, Carlo, *Historiae patriae*, vol. 17, *Codex Diplomaticus* (Torino, 1877).

Beckwith, Christopher, *Empires of the Silk Road: A history of central Eurasia from the Bronze Age to the present* (New Jersey, 2009).

Beer, Max, *Early British economics from the XIII to the middle of the XVIII century* (London, 1938).

Beldiceanu, Nicoară, *Les Actes des Premiers Sultans conservés dans les manuscrits Turcs de la Bibliothèque Nationale a Paris*, vols. 1–2 (Paris, 1964).

Belli, Maddalena, et al., *Archeologia de un castello minerario, Il sito di Cugnano* (Florence, 2005).

Belluzzo, Giuseppe, *La politica mineraria della Repubblica Veneta* (Roma, 1927).

Benedetto, Robert, ed., *The New Westminster dictionary of Church history*, vol. 1 (Louisville, Kentucky, 1989).

Bennett, Henry S., *Life on the English manor: A study of peasant conditions, 1150–1400* (Cambridge, England, 1999).

Benoît, Paul, and Denis Cailleaux, eds., *Moines & métallurgie dans la France médiévale* (Paris, 1991).

Benson, Elizabeth, et al., eds., *Pre-Columbian metallurgy of South America: A conference at Dumbarton Oaks* (Washington, D.C., 1979).

Berberian, Manuel, and Robert S. Yates, 'Patterns of historical earthquake rupture in the Iranian Plateau,' *Bulletin of the Seismological Society of America* 89 (1999), pp. 120–139.

Bernhardt, John W., *Itinerant kingship and royal monasteries in early medieval Germany, c. 936–1075* (Cambridge, England, 2002).

Berrío De Montalvo, Luis, ed., *Informes para obtener plata y azogue en el Mundo Hispánico*, introd. Manuel Castillo Martos (Granada, 2009).

Berza, Tudor, et al., 'Upper Cretaceous magmatic series and associated mineralization in the Carpathian-Balkan orogen,' *Resource Geology* 48 (1998), pp. 291–306.

Bessom, Thomas, *Of summits and sacrifices: An ethnohistoric study of Inka religious practices* (Austin, 2010).

Bethencourt, Francisco, and Diogo Ramada Curto, eds., *Portuguese Oceanic Expansion, 1400–1800* (Cambridge, England, 2007).

Bewley, Aisha A., *Al-Muwatta of Imam Malik ibn Anas, the first formulation of Islamic law* (New York, 2010).

Beyschlag, Franz H. A., et al., *The deposits of the useful minerals and rocks: Their origin, form, and content* (London, 1914–1916).

Bianchi, Giovanna, and Riccardo Francovich, 'L'archeologia dell'elevato come archeologia,' *Arqueología de la Arquitectura* 1 (2002), pp. 101–112.

Bidlo, Jaroslav, 'The Slavs in medieval history,' *Slavonic and East European Review* 9 (1930), pp. 34–55.

Bignami, Enrico, 'The mines and mineral industries of Sardinia,' *The Engineering Magazine* September (1904), pp. 933–951.

Bingley, William, *Travels in North Europe, from modern writers with remarks and observa-

tions exhibiting a connected view of the geography and present state of that division of the globe (London, 1822).

Bini, Monica, et al., 'Medieval phases of settlement at Benabbio castle, Apennine mountains, Italy: Evidence from Ground Penetrating Radar survey,' *Journal of Archaeological Science* 37 (2010), pp. 3059–3067.

Birmingham, Mary, *Word and worship workbook* (Mahaw, New Jersey, 1999).

Birrell, Jean R., 'Common rights in the medieval forest: Disputes and conflicts in the thirteenth century,' *Past and Present* 117 (1987), pp. 22–49.

Birrell, Jean R., 'The medieval English forest,' *Journal of Forest History* 24 (1980), pp. 8–85.

Birrell, Jean R., 'Peasant craftsmen in the medieval forest,' *Agricultural History Review* 17 (1969), pp. 1–107.

Bishop, Carl W., 'The historical geography of early Japan,' *Geographical Review* 13 (1923), pp. 40–63.

Bisson, Thomas N., 'Coinages and royal monetary policy in Languedoc during the reign of Saint Louis,' *Speculum* 32 (1957), pp. 443–469.

Bisson, Thomas N., *The crisis of the twelfth century: Power, lordship, and the origins of European government* (Princeton, 2009).

Bisson, Thomas N., 'Medieval lordship,' *Speculum* 70 (1995), pp. 743–759.

Bisson, Thomas N., 'Mediterranean territorial power in the twelfth century,' *Proceedings of the American Philosophical Society* 123 (1979), pp. 143–150.

Blanch Nougués, José M., *Régimen jurídico de las fundaciones en derecho romano* (Madrid, 2007).

Blanchard, Ian, 'Egyptian specie markets and the international gold crisis of the early fifteenth century,' in *Money, markets, and trade in late medieval Europe*, vol. 1, ed. Martin Elbl et al., pp. 383–410 (Leiden, 2007).

Blanchard, Ian, *The international economy in the 'age of discoveries,' 1470–1570: Antwerp and the English merchants' world* (Stuttgart, 2009).

Blanchard, Ian, *International lead production in the 'Age of the Saigerprozess,' 1460–1560* (Stuttgart, 1995).

Blanchard, Ian, 'Medieval crafts, guilds, and industrial development' (2006) [online] http://ianblanchard.com/CEU/, accessed February 12, 2013.

Blanchard, Ian, 'The miner and the agricultural community in late medieval England,' *Agricultural History Review* 20 (1972), pp. 93–106.

Blanchard, Ian, *Mining, metallurgy, and minting in the Middle Ages*, vol. 1, *Asiatic supremacy, 425–1125* (Stuttgart, 2001).

Blanchard, Ian, *Mining, metallurgy, and minting in the Middle Ages*, vol. 2, *Afro-European supremacy, 1125–1225* (Stuttgart, 2001).

Blanchard, Ian, *Mining, metallurgy, and minting in the Middle Ages*, vol. 3, *Continuing Afro-European supremacy, 1250–1450* (Stuttgart, 2005).

Bloch, Marc, *Feudal society: The growth of ties of dependence*, trans. L. A. Manyon (London, 1961).

Bloch, Marc, *French rural history: An essay on its basic characteristics*, foreword B. Lyon, trans. J. Sondheimer (Berkeley, 1966).

Bloch, Marc, *Land and work in medieval Europe: Selected papers*, trans. J. E. Anderson (New York, 2015).

Board of Trade, *Iron ore deposits in foreign countries* (London, 1905).

Bodio, Luigi, 'A map showing the mortality from malarial fever in Italy during the three years 1890–91–92,' *The Scottish Geographical Magazine* 11 (1895), pp. 31–133.

Boggi, Flavio, 'Silver altar, Pistoia Cathedral,' *Encyclopedia of Medieval Pilgrimage* (Leiden, 2013) [online] http://referenceworks.brillonline.com/entries/encyclopedia-of-medieval-pilgrimage/silver-altar-pistoia-cathedral-SIM_000190, accessed March 14, 2013.

Bojović, Boško I., 'Le passé des territoires: Kosovo-Metohija (XIᵉ–XVIIᵉ siècle),' *Balkan Studies* 38 (1997), pp. 31–61.

Bonami, Charles, 'Dans la Haute Vallée de L'Orb: Les mines de Ceilhes-et-Rocozels au Moyen Âge,' in *Mines et mineurs en Languedoc-Rousillon et régions voisines de l'Antiquité à nos jours*, ed. Fédération Historique du Languedoc Méditerranéen et du Rousillon, pp. 93–105 (Montpellier, 1977).

Bonfante, Larissa, ed., *The barbarians of ancient Europe: Realities and interactions* (Cambridge, England, 2011).

Boone, James L., and F. Scott Worman, 'Rural settlement and soil erosion from the late Roman period through the medieval Islamic period in the lower Alentejo of Portugal,' *Journal of Field Archaeology* 32 (2007), pp. 115–132.

Booth, George, trans., *The historical library of Diodorus the Sicilian in fifteen books*, vol. 1 (London, 1814).

Born, Ignaz V., *Travels through the Bannat of Temeswar, Transylvania, and Hungary in the year 1770* (London, 1777).

Borojević, Ksenija, 'Nutrition and environment in medieval Serbia: charred cereal, weed and fruit remains from the fortress of Ras,' *Vegetation History and Archeobotany* 14 (2005), pp. 453–464.

Borsuk, A. Magdalena, and Viktor N. Sholpo, 'Correlation of endogenous processes in the Alpine cycle of the Caucasus,' in *Profiles of orogenic belts*, ed. Nicholas Rast and Frances M. Delany, pp. 97–144 (Washington, D.C., 1983).

Bouchier, Edmund S., ed., *Sardinia in ancient times* (Oxford, 1917).

Bourrouilh-Le Jan, Françoise G., et al., 'Band-e-Amir Lakes and Dragon Valley (Bamiyan): Myths and seismicity in Afghanistan,' in *Myth and Geology*, ed. Luiggi Piccardi and W. Bruce Masse, pp. 121–132 (London, 2007).

Bowsky, William M., *A medieval Italian commune: Siena under the Nine, 1287–1355* (Berkeley, 1981).

Boyce, Helen, *The mines of the Upper Harz* (Menasha, Wisconsin, 1920).

Brading, David A., and Harry E. Cross, 'Colonial silver mining: Mexico and Peru,' *Hispanic American Historical Review* 52 (1972), pp. 545–579.

Bralia, A., et al., 'A revaluation of the Co/Ni ratio in pyrite as geochemical tool in ore genesis problems,' *Mineralium Deposita* 14 (1979), pp. 353–374.

Braudel, Fernand, *Civilization and Capitalism in 15th–18th century*, 3 vols., trans. S. Reynolds (Berkeley, 1992).

Braudel, Fernand, *A history of civilizations*, trans. R. Mayne (New York, 1994).

Braudel, Fernand, *The Mediterranean and the Mediterranean world in the age of Philip II*, vol. 1, trans. S. Reynolds (New York, 1973).

Braunstein, Philippe, 'De minerais au metal: la longue durée à l'épreuve des sources et des methods,' in *Au-delà de l'écrit: les hommes et leurs vécus matériels au Moyen Âge à la lu-*

mière des sciences et des techniques, ed. René Noël, Isabelle Paquay, Jean-Pierre Sosson, pp. 135–150 (Belgium, 2003).

Braunstein, Philippe, 'Gli statuti minerari nel Medioevo europeo,' in *Archeologia delle attività estrattive e metallurgiche*, ed. Riccardo Francovich, pp. 277–301 (Florence, 1993).

Braunstein, Philippe, 'Innovations in mining and metal production in Europe in the late Middle Ages,' *Journal of European Economic History* 12 (1983), pp. 573–591.

Braunstein, Philippe, 'Le fer et la production de fer en Europe, de 500 à 1500,' *Annales: Économies, Sociétés, Civilisations* 27 (1972), pp. 407–414.

Braunstein, Philippe, 'Les enterprises minières en Vénétie au XVe siècle,' *Mélanges d'Archéologie et d'Histoire de l'Ecole française de Rome* 77 (1965), pp. 529–607.

Braunstein, Philippe, 'Les statuts miniers de l'Europe médiévale,' *Comptes-rendus des séances de l'Académie des Inscriptions et Belles-Lettres* 136 (1992), pp. 35–56.

Braunstein, Philippe, and Paul Benoît, eds., *Mines, carrières et métallurgie dans la France médiévale* (Paris, 1983).

Brenner, Robert, 'The agrarian roots of European capitalism,' *Past and Present* 97 (1982), pp. 16–103.

Brenner, Robert, 'The Low Countries in the transition to capitalism,' *Journal of Agrarian Change* 1 (2001), pp. 169–241.

Brenner, Robert, 'The world economy at the turn of the millennium, toward boom or crisis?' *Review of International Political Economy* 8 (2001), pp. 6–44.

Bretschneider, Emil, *Medieval researches from eastern Asiatic sources: Fragments towards the knowledge of the geography and history of Central and Western Asia from the 13th to the 17th century*, Vols. 1–2 (Hoboken, 2000).

Brett, Michael, ed., *The history of the Mohammedan dynasties in Spain by Ahmed Ibn Mohammed Al-Makkarí, Translated by Pascual de Gayangos (1840)*, vol. 1 (London, 2002).

Bright, Richard, *Travels from Vienna through Lower Hungary* (Edinburgh, 1818).

Brill, 'Alpes (Alps),' *Brill's New Pauly: Encyclopedia of the ancient world* (Leiden, 2002–2010) [online] http://referenceworks.brillonline.com/entries/brill-s-new-pauly/alpes-alps-e11 6320, accessed March 14, 2013.

Britnell, R. H., 'The towns of England and northern Italy in the early fourteenth century,' *Economic History Review* 44 (1991), pp. 21–35.

Brook, Timothy, *The troubled empire: China in the Yuan and Ming dynasties* (Cambridge, Massachusetts, 2010).

Brown, Brockden Charles. 'A sketch of the state of Peru, at the close of the eighteenth century,' *The American Register, or General Repository of history, politics, and science,* vol. 5 (1809), pp. 348–367.

Brown, Edward, *An account of several travels through a great part of Germany, in four journeys* (London, 1677) [online] http://find.galegroup.com/mome/infomark.do?&source =gale&prodId=MOME&userGroupName=lehman_main&tabID=T001&docId=U104 137113&type=multipage&contentSet=MOMEArticles&version=1.0&docLevel=FASCI MILE, accessed December 17, 2013.

Brown, J. G., 'Miner's life in the German Harz,' *Quarterly Journal of Economics* 6 (1892), pp. 474–478.

Brown, Peter J., 'Cultural and genetic adaptations to malaria: Problems of comparison,' *Human Ecology* 14 (1986), pp. 311–322.

Browne, Edward, 'Concerning damps in the mines of Hungary and their effects,' *Philosophical Transactions* 48 (1669), p. 965.

Bruttini, Jacopo, et al., 'Un insediamento a vocazione mineraria: il caso di Cugnano nelle Colline Metallifere,' *The Journal of Fasti online* 179 (2010), pp. 1–10.

Brutzkus, J., 'Trade with eastern Europe, 800–1200,' *Economic History Review* 13 (1943), pp. 31–41.

Bryer, Anthony A. M., 'Byzantine agricultural implements: The evidence of medieval illustrations of Hesiod's "Works and Days,"' *Annual of the British School at Athens* 81 (1986), pp. 45–80.

Bryer, Anthony A. M., 'The question of Byzantine mines in the Pontos: Chalybian iron, Chaldian silver, Koloneian alum, and the mummy of Cheriana,' *Anatolian Studies* 32 (1982), pp. 133–150.

Buechler, Rose Marie, 'Technical aid to Upper Peru: the Nordenflycht expedition,' *Journal of Latin American Studies* 5 (1973), pp. 37–77.

Bulut, Mehmet, 'Reconsideration of economic views of a classical empire and a nation-state during the mercantilist ages,' *American Journal of Economics and Sociology* 68 (2009), pp. 791–828.

Bundi, Ulrich, ed., *Alpine waters* (Dübendorf, Switzerland, 2010).

Burchfiel, B. Clark, and Marcian Bleahu, *Geology of Romania* (Boulder, Colorado, 1976).

Bureau of Mining of Japan, *Mining in Japan, past and present* (Japan, 1909).

Burnham, Sarah M., *History and uses of limestones and marbles* (Boston, 1883).

Burns, James H., ed., *The Cambridge history of medieval political thought, c.350–c.1450* (Cambridge, England, 1988).

Burr, Michael, 'The Code of Stephan Dušan,' *Slavonic and East European Review* 28 (1950), pp. 516–539.

Burton, Janet E., *The Cistercians in the Middle Ages* (Rochester, 2011).

Burton, Janet E., *The Monastic order in Yorkshire, 1069–1215* (Cambridge, England, 1999).

Bustamante Álvarez, Macarena, et al., '*Sigillatas* claras de Ajustrel: a crise do século II d.C. nas minas do Sudoeste ibérico,' *Revista Portuguesa de Arqueologia* 11 (2008), pp. 163–181.

Butlin, Robin A., 'Proto-industrial regions of Europe, with a brief European contextual perspective,' in *The early-modern world-system in geographical perspective*, ed. Hans J. Nitez, pp. 136–150 (Stuttgart, 1993).

Buxton, Noel, 'Balkan geography and Balkan railways,' *Geographical Journal* 32 (1908), pp. 217–234.

Byres, Terence J., 'Differentiation of the peasantry under feudalism and the transition to capitalism: in defense of Rodney Hilton,' *Journal of Agrarian Change* 6 (2006), pp. 17–68.

Byse, Fanny, 'Milton on the continent,' *Modern Language Quarterly* 3 (1900), pp. 16–19.

Cacciaglia, Norberto, 'Nella miniera dell'*Inferno* (considerazioni sul c. VII e sulle '*Malebolge*'),' *Lingüística e Letteratura* 27 (2002), pp. 39–58.

Caferro, William, *Contesting the Renaissance* (Sussex, 2011).

Calvo, Emilia, 'Ibn Ḥawqal,' in *Encyclopedia of the history of science, technology and medicine in non-Western cultures*, ed. Helain Selin, pp. 1103–1104 (Frankfurt, 2008).

Campana, Stefano, and Riccardo Francovich, 'Landscape archaeology in Tuscany: Cultural resource management, remotely sensed techniques, GIS based data integration and interpretation,' in *The reconstruction of archaeological landscapes through digital technologies*, ed. Mauricio Forte, pp. 15–28 (Oxford, 2003).

Campbell, Bruce M. S., 'The agrarian problem in the early fourteenth century,' *Past and Present* 188 (2005), pp. 3–70.

Campopiano, Michele, 'Rural communities, land clearance, and water management in the Po Valley in the central and late Middle Ages,' *Journal of Medieval History* 39 (2013), pp. 377–393.

Cancik, Hubert, et al., 'Mineral resources,' *Brill's New Pauly: Encyclopedia of the ancient world* (Leiden, 2002–2010) [online] http://referenceworks.brillonline.com/entries/brill-s-new-pauly/mineral-resources-e218370, accessed March 14, 2013.

Canning, Joseph P., 'Ideas of the State in thirteenth and fourteenth century commentators on the Roman Law,' *Transactions of the Royal Historical Society* 33 (1983), pp. 1–27.

Canto García, Alberto, and Patrice Cressier, eds., *Minas y metalurgia en al-Andalus y Magreb Occidental: explotación y poblamiento* (Madrid, 2008).

Cantù, Cesare, *Illustrazione del Tirolo italiano e della Svizzera italiana* (Milano, 1859).

Cara Barrionuevo, Lorenzo, 'Notas para el estudio de la minería almeriense anterior al siglo XIX,' *Boletín del instituto de Estudios Almerienses* 6 (1986), pp. 11–24.

Carande, Ramón, *Carlos V y sus banqueros*, 3 vols. (Madrid, 1945).

Cardoso, Luiz, *Diccionario geografico, ou noticia historica de todas as cidades, villas, lugares, e aldeas, rios, ribeiras, e serras dos reynos de Portugal*, vol. 1 (Lisboa, 1747–1751).

Carobbi, Guido, and Francesco Rodolico, *I minerali della Toscana: saggio di mineralogía regionale* (Florence, 1976).

Carpenter, David A., 'The second century of English feudalism,' *Past and Present* 168 (2000), pp. 30–71.

Carpintero Benítez, Francisco, *Justicia y ley natural: Tomás de Aquino y otros escolásticos* (Madrid, 2004).

Carsten, Francis L., 'Slavs in North-Eastern Germany,' *Economic History Review* 11 (1941), pp. 61–76.

Carvalho, Sérgio Luís, *Cidades medievais portuguesas, uma introdução ao seu estudo* (Lisboa, 1989).

Carver, Martin O. H., et al., *Wasperton: A Roman, British, and Anglo-Saxon community in Central England* (New York, 2009).

Castagnetti, Andrea, *Governo vescovile, feudalità, 'communitas' cittadina, e qualifica capitaneale a Trento fra XII e XIII secolo* (Verona, 2001).

Castellanos, Manuel P., *História de Marruecos* (Tangier, 1898).

Castro, Calogero, *Descrizione geologico-mineraria della zona argentifera del Sarrabus (Sardegna)* (Rome, 1890).

Cauuet, Béatrice, 'Celtic gold mines in West Central Gaul,' in *Prehistoric gold in Europe, mines, metallurgy, and manufacture*, ed. Giulio Morteani and Jeremy P. Northover, pp. 219–240 (Dordrecht, 1995).

Cavaciocchi, Simoneta, cur., *Le interazioni fra economia e ambiente biologico nell'Europa preindustriale, secc. XIII–XVIII* (Florence, 2010).

Ceccarelli, Marco, 'Renaissance machines in Italy: From Bruneleschi to Galilei through Francesco di Giorgio and Leonardo,' *Mechanism and Machine Theory* 43 (2008), pp. 1530–1542.

Cederlund, Carl O., 'Structures and vessels for transport in early Swedish iron production,' *Archaeonautica* 14 (1998), pp. 265–272.

Cencini, Carlo, 'Physical processes and human activities in the evolution of the Po Delta, Italy,' *Journal of Coastal Research* 14 (1998), pp. 774–793.

Center for Iranian Studies, *Encyclopedia Iranica* (New York, 2012) [online] http://www .iranicaonline.org, accessed February 10, 2014.

Ceruti, Gianluigi, et al., *Il delta del Po: nature e civiltà* (Padova, 1983).

Cesaretti, Agostino, *Memorie sacra e profane dell'antica diocesi di Populonia al presente diocesi di Massa Marittima* (Florence, 1784).

Chadbourne, Paul A., *Lectures on natural history: Its relation to intellect, taste, wealth, and religion* (New York, 1860).

Chalmers, George, *Caledonia, or an account, historic and topographic of North Britain; from the most ancient to present times* (London, 1824).

Chancellor, Masters and Scholars of the University of Cambridge, *The Encyclopedia Britannica*, vol. 7 (Cambridge, England, 1910–1911).

Chang, Claudia, 'Pastoral transhumance in the southern Balkans as a social ideology: Ethnoarcheological research in northern Greece,' *American Anthropologist* 95 (1993), pp. 687–703.

Charvátová, Kateřina, 'The economy of the Cistercians in Bohemia,' *Cîteaux: commentarii cistercienses* 47 (1996), pp. 183–192.

Chase-Dunn, Christopher K., and Eugene N. Anderson, *Historical evolution of world-systems* (New York, 2005).

Chassigneux, Edmond, 'Rica de oro et rica de plata,' *T'oung Pao* 30 (1933), pp. 37–84.

Chaudhuri, Kirti N., *Trade and civilisation in the Indian Ocean: An economic history from the rise of Islam to 1750* (Cambridge, England, 1985).

Chaudhury, Sushil, and Michel Morineau, eds., *Merchants, companies, and trade: Europe and Asia in the early modern era* (Cambridge, England, 1999).

Chayanov, Aleksander V., *Theory of peasant economy*, introd. Theodor Shahin (Madison, Wisconsin, 1986).

Chen, Da, *Chinese migrations, with special reference to labor conditions* (Washington, D.C., 1998).

Chetrit, Yossef, 'Tarudant,' *Encyclopedia of Jews in the Islamic World* (Leiden, 2013) [online] http://referenceworks.brillonline.com/entries/encyclopedia-of-jews-in-the-islamic-world /tarudant-SIM_0021020, accessed March 7, 2013.

Chirot, Daniel, and Thomas D. Hall, 'World-system theory,' *Annual Review of Sociology* 8 (1982), pp. 81–106.

Chisholm, Hugh, ed., *The Encyclopedia Britannica*, vols. 5–13 (New York, 1910).

Chōsajo, Chishitsu, *Outlines of the geology of Japan* (Tokyo, 1902).

Choulet, Flavien, et al., 'Non-sulfide zinc deposits of the Moroccan High Atlas: Multi-scale characterization and origin,' *Ore Geology Reviews* 56 (2014), pp. 115–140.

Christie, Jan W., 'Money and its uses in the Javanese states of the ninth to the fifteenth centuries A.D.,' *Journal of the Economic and Social History of the Orient* 39 (1996), pp. 243–286.

Cibrario, Luigi, *Della economia politica del medio evo*, vol. 2 (Torino, 1861).

Cicali, Cristina, 'Le monete del castello minerario di Rocca S. Silvestro,' *Bolletino di Numismatica* 44–45 (2005), p. 81.

Ciggaar, Krijna N., et al., *East and West in the crusader states: Context, contracts, confrontations* (Leuven, 2003).

Cipolla, Carlo M., 'Currency depreciation in medieval Europe,' *Economic History Review* 15 (1963), pp. 413–422.

Cipolla, Carlo M., 'Un fiorentino a Trento nel sec. XIV,' *Archivio Trentino* 22 (1907), pp. 193–195.

Clark, Gregory, 'The consumer revolution: A turning point in human history or statistical artifact?' Paper, Department of Economics, University of California, Davis, July 4, 2010.

Claughton, Peter F., 'The medieval silver-lead miner, a preliminary study,' *Bulletin of the Peak District Mines Historical Society* 12 (1993), pp. 28–30.

Claughton, Peter F., and Paul Rondelez, 'Early silver mining in Western Europe: An Irish perspective,' *Journal of the Mining Heritage Trust of Ireland* 13 (2013), pp. 1–8.

Cohen, Saul B., *Geopolitics of the world system* (Lanham, Maryland, 2003).

Cole, John W., and Eric R. Wolf, *The hidden frontier: Ecology and ethnicity in an Alpine valley* (New York, 1974).

Collatera, Marco, and Domenica Primerano, *Un vescovo, la sua cattedrale, il suo tesoro: la committenza artistica di Federico Vanga (1207–1218)* (Trento, 2012).

Collis, John R., et al., 'The prehistoric and medieval field archaeology of Crownhill Down, Dartmoor, England,' *Journal of Field Archeology* 11 (1984), pp. 1–12.

Comparini, Olinto, ed., *Memorie storiche di Massa Marittima compilate dal Prof. Stefano Galli Da Modigliana*, Parte Seconda (Massa Marittima, 1873).

Comunità Montana Colline Metallifere, *Colline Metallifere* (Florence, 2003).

Conde, José Antonio, trans., *Descripción de España de Xerif Aledris conocido por el Nubiense* (Madrid, 1799).

Conran, Caroline, 'La *Ceuillette*: Foraging for edible wild plants in southern France,' in *Wild food: Proceedings of the Oxford Symposium on Food and Cookery, 2004*, ed. Richard Hosking, pp. 79–92 (Devon, 2006).

Consorzio del Parco Geominerario Storico e Ambientale della Sardegna, *I Codici minerari europei a confronto* (Iglesias, Sardinia, 2008).

Corniani Degli Algarotti, C. Marco A., *Dello stabilimento delle miniere relative fabbriche nel distretto di Agordo: trattato storico, mineralogico, disciplinare* (Venezia, 1823).

Corona, C., et al., 'Millennium-long summer temperature variations in the European Alps as reconstructed from tree rings,' *Climate Past* 6 (2010), pp. 379–400.

Corraine, Diego, 'Para *unha* lingua sarda da referencia,' in *Estudios de sociolingüística románica*, ed. Francisco Fernández Rei and Antón Santamarina, pp. 425–448 (Compostela, 1999).

Corriente, Federico, *Dictionary of Arabic and allied loanwords: Spanish, Portuguese, Catalan, Galician, and kindred dialects* (Leiden, 2008).

Cortese, Ennio, ed., *La proprietà e la proprietà* (Milano, 1988).

Cortijo Ocaña, Antonio, 'La Crónica del moro Rasis y la Crónica sarracina: dos testimonios desconocidos,' *La crónica: A journal of medieval Hispanic languages* 25 (1997), pp. 5–30.

Coşgel, Metin M., 'The economics of Ottoman taxation,' working paper 2004–02, Department of Economics, University of Connecticut (Storrs, Connecticut, 2004).

Coşgel, Metin M., 'Scattering and contracts in medieval agriculture,' *Journal of Economic History* 50 (1990), pp. 663–668.

Cosmo, Nicola, *Ancient China and its enemies: The rise of nomadic power in East Asian history* (Cambridge, England, 2004).

Costa, Paolo M., 'Notes on traditional hydraulics and agriculture in Oman,' *World Archaeology* 11 (1983), pp. 273–295.

Cotta, Bernhard V., *A treatise on ore deposits*, trans. Frederick Prime (New York, 1870).

Coureas, Nicholas, 'Cyprus and Ragusa (Dubrovnik), 1280–1450,' *Mediterranean Historical Review* 17 (2002), pp. 1–13.

Coutinho, Mauricio C., 'Economia de minas e economía da mineração em Celso Furtado,' *Nova Economia Belo Horizonte* 18 (2008), pp. 361–378.

Crabb, George, *A history of English law* (Burlington, 1831).

Craddock, Paul T., *2000 years of zinc and brass* (London, 1998).

Craddock, Paul T., *Early metal mining and production* (Edinburgh, 1995).

Craddock, Paul T., 'From hearth to furnace: Evidences for the earliest metal smelting technologies in the eastern Mediterranean,' *Paléorient* 26 (2000), pp. 151–165.

Craig, Alan K., and Robert C. West, eds., *In quest of mineral wealth: Aboriginal and colonial mining and metallurgy in Spanish America* (Baton Rouge, Louisiana, 1994).

Crampton, R. J., *A short history of modern Bulgaria* (Cambridge, England, 1987).

Creasy, Edward S., *History of the Ottoman Turks: From the beginning of their empire to the present time, chiefly founded on von Hammer*, vol. 1 (London, 1854).

Cressier, Patrice, et al., *Genèse de la ville islamique en al-Andalus et au Maghreb occidental* (Madrid, 1998).

Crone, Hugh D., *Paracelsus, the man who defied medicine* (Melbourne, 2004).

Cross, Arthur L., *A history of England and greater Britain* (New York, 1914).

Cruciani, Gabriele, 'The Montevecchio mining district: industrial archeology in SW Sardinia, Italy,' *Journal of the Society for Industrial Archeology* 27 (2001), pp. 17–35.

Cruz Coelho, Maria H., et al., *Portugal em definição de fronteiras, 1096–1325: do condado portucalense à crise do século XIV*, vol. 3 (Lisboa, 1996).

Cumming, John, ed., *Mining explained: A layman's guide* (Toronto, 2012).

Cunliffe, Barry, *Europe between the oceans: Themes and variations, 9000 BC–AD 1000* (New Haven, 2008).

Cunningham, Clifford J., 'Erasmus Reinhold at 500,' *Mercury* 40 (2011), p. 8.

Curtis, Daniele, and Michele Campopiano, 'Medieval land reclamation and the creation of new societies: Comparing Holland and the Po Valley, c. 800–c. 1500,' *Journal of Historical Geography* 30 (2013), pp. 1–16.

Curzel, Emanuele, *Il Codice Vanga: un principe vescovo e il suo governo* (Trento, 2007).

Curzel, Emanuele, and Gian M. Varanini, *Codex Wangianus, i cartulari della Chiesa trentina (secoli XIII–XIV)*, T. I, coll. Donatella Frioli (Bologna, 2007).

Curzel, Emanuele, and Gian M. Varanini, *La documentazione dei vescovi di Trento (XI secolo-1218)* (Bologna, 2011).

Curzon, George, *The Pamirs and the source of the Oxus* (London, 1896).

Cusin, Fabio, *I primi due secoli del Principato Ecclesiastico* (Urbino, 1938).

Cuvier, B. Georges, *A discourse on the revolutions of the surface of the globe, and the changes thereby produced in the animal kingdom* (Philadelphia, 1831).

Cuvier, B. Georges, *Essay on the theory of the Earth, with mineralogical notes* (New York, 1818).

Czaja, Stanisław, 'Mining and hydrological transformations in Upper Silesia from fifteenth to nineteenth centuries,' *Geographical Journal* 167 (2001), pp. 57–71.

Da Graça, Laura, 'Feudal dynamics and Runciman's competitive selection practices in late medieval Castile: An essay on differing processes of social differentiation in a pre-capitalist context,' *Journal of Agrarian Change* 3 (2003), pp. 333–366.

D'Achiardi, Giovanni, 'La miniera del Bottino nelle Alpi Apuane,' *Memoria Soc. Lunig. "G. Cappellini" Storia Nat. Reg.* 1 (1920), pp. 132–140.

Dábax, Hélène, *La féodalité languedocienne, XIe–XIIe siècles* (Toulouse, 2003).

Dai Prà, Elena, 'La cartografia storica come interfaccia dialettica tra discipline e competenze territoriali, progetti ed esperienze in Trentino,' in *Atti 14a Conferenza Nazionale ASITA*, ed. Federazione Italiana delle Associazioni Scientifiche per le Informazioni Territoriali e Ambientali, pp. 713–718 (Brescia, 2010).

Damian, Gheorghe S., 'The genesis of the base metal ore deposit, from Herja,' *Studia Universitatis Babeş-Bolyai, Geologia*, 48 (2003), pp. 85–100.

Darby, Henry C., 'The face of Europe on the eve of the great discoveries,' in *The New Cambridge Modern History*, ed. George R. Potter, pp. 20–49 (Cambridge, England, 1961).

Darling, Linda T., *Revenue-raising and legitimacy: Tax collection and finance administration in the Ottoman Empire, 1560–1660* (Leiden, 1996).

Davies, Kenneth G., *The emergence of international business*, vol. 5, *The Royal African Mining Company* (London, 1999).

Davies, Rees R., *Lordships and society in the March of Wales* (Oxford, 1978).

Davis, David E., 'Regulation of human population in northern France and adjacent lands in the Middle Ages,' *Human Ecology* 14 (1986), pp. 245–267.

Day, Joan, 'The continental origins of Bristol brass,' *Industrial Archaeology Review* 7 (1984), pp. 32–56.

De Asso y Del Río, Ignacio J., *Historia de la economía política de Aragón* (Zaragoza, 1798).

De Castro, Calogero, *Memoria descriptiva della carta geologica d'Italia*, vol. 5, *Descrizione geologico-mineraria della zona argentifera del Sarrabus* (Roma, 1890).

De Puy, William H., ed., *The world-wide encyclopedia and gazetteer*, vol. 6 (New York, 1908).

De Roover, Raymond, *Business, banking, and economic thought in late medieval and early modern Europe* (Chicago, 1974).

De Roover, Raymond, 'The concept of the just price: Theory and economic policy,' *Journal of Economic History* 18 (1958), pp. 418–434.

De Roover, Raymond, 'Introduction: Cardinal Cajetan on "Cambium" or exchange dealings,' *Journal of Markets and Morality* 2007 (10), pp. 197–208.

De Roover, Raymond, *The Medici Bank: Its organization, management, operations, and decline* (New York, 1948).

De Roover, Raymond, *Money, banking, and credit in medieval Bruges, Italian merchant bankers, Lombard and money-changers: A study in the origins of banking* (Cambridge, Massachusetts, 1948).

De Roover, Raymond, 'Monopoly theory prior to Adam Smith: A revision,' *Quarterly Journal of Economics* 65 (1951), pp. 492–524.

De Roover, Raymond, 'Scholastic economics: Survival and lasting influence from the sixteenth century to Adam Smith,' *Quarterly Journal of Economics* 69 (1955), pp. 161–190.

De Soto, Hernando, *The mystery of capital: Why capitalism triumphs in the West and fails everywhere else* (New York, 2000).

De Vargas, Count, 'X. On the mines of Sardinia: by the Count De Vargas, President of the Italian Academy, &,' *A Journal of natural philosophy, chemistry, and the arts*, October (1810), pp. 147–148.

De Wit, Maarten, and Christien Thiart, 'Metallogenic fingerprints of Archaean cratons,' in *Mineral deposits and Earth evolution*, ed. Iain McDonald, et al., pp. 59–70 (London, 2005).

Dean, Dennis R., *James Hutton and the history of geology* (Cornell, 1992).

Del Mar, Alexander, *A history of the precious metals: From the earliest times to the present* (New York, 1902).

Demir, Yilmar, et al., 'Mineral chemical investigation on sulfide mineralization of the Istala deposit, Gümüşhane, NE-Turkey,' *Ore Geology Reviews* 53 (2013), pp. 306–317.

Dempsey, Bernard W., 'Just price in a functional economy,' *American Economic Review* 25 (1935), pp. 471–486.

Denecke, Dietrich, 'Mining regions and metal trade in early modern Europe,' in *The early-modern world-system in geographical perspective*, ed. Hans J. Nitez, pp. 162–171 (Stuttgart, 1993).

Denemark, Robert A., et al., eds., *World system history: The social science of long-term change* (London, 2000).

Dennett, Daniel C., *Conversion and the poll tax in early Islam* (New York, 1973).

Denny, Walter B., 'Art, infrastructure, and devotion: Ottoman water infrastructure,' in *Rivers of paradise: Water in Islamic art and culture*, ed. Sheila Blair and Jonathan Bloom, pp. 184–211 (New Haven, 2009).

Dessì, Vincenzo, 'Ripostiglio di monete medioevali,' *Archivio storico Sardo* 3 (1907), pp. 3–47.

Deustua Pimentel, Carlos, 'La expedición mineralogista del Barón Nordenflicht al Perú,' *Mercurio Peruano* 38 (1957), pp. 510–519.

Devezas, Tessaleno, and George Modelski, 'The Portuguese as system-builders in the fifteenth and sixteenth centuries: A case study on the role of technology in the evolution of the world system,' *Globalization* 3 (2006), pp. 507–523.

Di Cosmo, Nicolo, 'Black Sea emporia and the Mongol Empire: A reassessment of the *Pax Mongolica*,' *Journal of the Economic and Social History of the Orient* 53 (2010), pp. 83–108.

Dickinson, Edward, 'Altitude and whiteness: Germanizing the Alps and Alpinizing the Germans, 1875–1935,' *German Studies Review* 33 (2010), pp. 579–602.

Dickinson, Robert E., 'Mitteldeutschland: The middle Elbe basin as a geographical unit,' *Geographical Journal* 103 (1944), pp. 211–225.

Diderot, Denis, and D'Alembert, eds., *Encyclopédie, ou dictionnaire raisonné des sciences, des arts et des métiers, etc. (1768)*, University of Chicago Press, ARTFL Encyclopédie Project (Chicago, 2011) [online] http://encyclopedie.uchicago.edu/, accessed February 20, 2014.

Díez de Salazar, Luis M., 'La industria del hierro en Guipúzcoa (siglos XIII–XVI), aportación al estudio de la industria urbana,' in *La ciudad hispánica durante los siglos XIII al XVI,* vol. 1, ed. Emilio Sáez, et al., pp. 251–276 (Madrid, 1981).

Dill, William A., 'Inland fisheries of Europe' (No. 52), *Food and Agriculture Organization* (Rome, 1993).

Dillon, Paddy, *Walking in the north Pennines: An Area of Outstanding Natural Beauty* (Cumbria, England, 2009).

Dionisi, Giovanni J., and Lodovico A. Muratori, *Dell'origine e dei progressi della zecca in Verona* (Verona, 1776).

dMGH [Digital Monumenta Germaniae Historica], *Monumenta Germaniae Historica, Legum Sectio, Constitutiones et Acta Publica Imperatorum et Regum, T. I* (1893), ed. Societas Aperiendis Fontibus (Munich, 2010) [online] http://www.mgh.de/publikationen/leges /constitutiones-et-acta-publica-imperatorum-et-regum/, accessed June 22, 2016.

Domergue, Claude, 'L'utilisation des photographies aériennes dans l'étude des mines d'or romaines à ciel ouvert du Nord-Ouest de l'Espagne,' *Mélanges de la Casa de Velázquez* 17 (1981), pp. 579.

Domergue, Claude, *Minería y metalurgia en las antiguas civilizaciones mediterráneas y europeas* (Madrid, 1989).

Domínguez Ortíz, Antonio, *Política y hacienda de Felipe IV* (Madrid, 1960).

Domínguez Rojas, Salud M., 'La economía del reino nazarí a través de las fetuas recogidas en el *Mi'yār* de Al-Wanšarīsī,' *Anaquel de Estudios Árabes* 17 (2006), pp. 77–107.

Dominian, Leon, 'Mining in the Asiatic Near East,' *Engineering and mining journal* 109 (1920), pp. 309–313.

Donkin, Robin A., *The Cistercians: Studies in the geography of medieval England and Wales* (Toronto, 1978).

Dorfman, Robert, 'Thomas Robert Malthus and David Ricardo,' *Journal of Economic Perspectives* 3 (1989), pp. 153–164.

Dória, Maria A., 'Evolução dos fluidos associados a procesos mineralizantes: aplicação à região aurífera de Vila Pouca de Aguiar,' in *Repósitorio aberto Universidade do Porto* (Lisboa, 1999) [online] http://hdl.handle.net/10216/10044, accessed January 12, 2014.

D'Oriano, Rubens, et al., *Argyrophleps nesos: l'isola dalle vene d'argento: esploratori, mercanti e coloni in Sardegna tra il 14. e il 6. sec. a.C.* (Modena, 2001).

Drew, Katherine F., 'The Carolingian military frontier in Italy,' *Traditio* 20 (1964), pp. 437–447.

Duarte, Luís M., 'A actividade mineira em Portugal durante a Idade Média,' *Revista da Faculdade de Letras* 12 (1995), pp. 75–112.

Duby, George, *Rural economy and country life in the medieval West* (Columbia, 1968).

Duff, Peter M. D., et al., *Holmes' principles of physical geology* (London, 1998).

Dumoulin, François, 'Les mines métallifères du département de la Loire,' *Revue archéologique du Centre de la France* 43 (2004), pp. 271–276.

Dunlop, Douglas M., 'Sources of gold and silver in Islam according to al-Hamdānī (10th century),' *Studia Islamica* 8 (1957), pp. 9–59.

Durant, Aline, 'Elements for a cultural history of wood in southern France (X–XVI centuries),' *Second International meeting of Anthracology, Paris, France* September 13–16 (2000), pp. 1–10 [online] http://www.academ.edu/5346246/Durand_A._2002_Elements _for_a_cultural_history_of_wood_in_Southern_France_Xth-XVIth_centuries_Thiebault _S._Pernaut_J.-M._Charcoal_Analysis._Methodological_Approaches_Palaeoecological

_Results_and_Wood_Uses_Second_Intern.l_Meeting_of_Anthracology_Paris_13–16 _September_2000_BAR_1063_261–266, accessed November 3, 2013.

Duviols, Pierre, 'Un inédito de Cristobal de Albornoz: La instrucción para descubrir todas las guacas del Pirú y sus camayos y haziendas,' *Journal de la Société des Américanistes* 56 (1967), pp. 7–39.

Dvornik, Francis, *The Slavs in European history and civilization* (Rutgers, 1962).

Dyer, Christopher, 'How urban was medieval England?' *History Today* 47 (1997), pp. 37–43.

Dyson, Stephen L., and Robert J. Rowland Jr., *Archaeology and history in Sardinia, from the Stone Age to the Middle Ages* (Philadelphia, 2007).

Eakin, Marshall C., *British enterprise in Brazil: The St. John d'el Rey Mining Company and the Morro Velho Gold Mine, 1830–1960* (Durham, 1989).

Ebers, John, *The new and complete dictionary of the German and English languages*, vol. 2 (Leipzig, 1798).

Echevarría Arsuaga, Ana, 'Esclavos musulmanes en los Hospitales de cautivos de la Orden Militar de Santiago (siglos XII y XIII),' *Al-Qanṭara* 28 (2007), pp. 465–488.

Echevarría Arsuaga, Ana, 'Explotación y mano de obra en las minas y salinas de al-Andalus,' *Espacio, Tiempo y Forma* 23 (2010), pp. 55–74.

Echevarría Arsuaga, Ana, 'La mayoría "mudéjar" en León y Castilla: legislación real y distribución de la población (siglos XI–XIII),' *En la España medieval* 29 (2006), pp. 7–30.

Edkins, Joseph, *Banking and prices in China* (Shanghai, 1905).

Edmondson, Jonathan C., 'Mining in the later Roman Empire and beyond: continuity or disruption?' *Journal of Roman Studies* 79 (1989), pp. 84–102.

Edwards, Richards, and Keith Atkinson, *Ore deposit geology and its influence on mineral exploration* (New York, 1986).

Ehrenberg, Richard, *Capital and finance in the age of the Renaissance, a study of the Fugger and their connections* (New York, 1923).

Ehrenkreuz, Andrew S., 'Extracts from the technical manual of the Ayyūbid mint in Cairo,' *Bulletin of the School of Oriental and African Studies* 15 (1959), pp. 432–447.

Einaudi, Luigi, *La rendita mineraria: origini e basi della rendita mineraria* (Torino, 1900).

Elbl, Martin M., 'From Venice to the Tuat: trans-Saharan copper trade and Francesco di Marco Datini of Prato,' in *Money, markets, and trade in late medieval Europe*, vol. 1, ed. Lawrin Armstrong et al., pp. 411–459 (Leiden, 2007).

Elliot, John, 'Teaching history in the twenty-first century,' presentation delivered at University of Oxford, January 29, 2013 [online] https://www.youtube.com/watch?v=s52uQqS fAB4, accessed February 12, 2015.

Elsie, Robert, *Early Albania: A reader of historical texts, 11th–17th centuries* (Wiesbaden, Hesse, 2003).

Elvin, Mark, *The retreat of the elephants: An environmental history of China* (New Haven, 2008).

Elwes, Henry J., and Augustine Henry, *The trees of Great Britain and Ireland*, vol. 6 (Cambridge, England, 2014).

Engel, Pál, *The realm of St. Stephen: A history of medieval Hungary, 895–1526* (London, 2001).

Engels, Frederick, *The condition of the working class in England in 1844*, trans. F. Kelley Wischnewetzky (London, 1892).

Engels, Frederick, 'Wanderings in Lombardy' (1841) [online] https://www.marxists.org/ar chive/marx/works/1841/12/lombardy.htm, accessed February 13, 2015.

English, Edward D., *Encyclopedia of the Medieval World*, vol. 1 (New York, 2005).

Enhag, Per, *Encyclopedia of the elements* (Sweden, 2005).

Epalza, Míkel de, 'Estructuras de acogida de los moriscos emigrantes de España en el Mágreb (siglos XIII al XVIII),' *Alternativas, Cuadernos de Trabajo Social* 4 (1996), pp. 35–58.

Ergene, Boğaç A., *Local court, provincial society, and justice in the Ottoman Empire: Legal practice and dispute resolution in Çankiri and Kastamonu (1652–1744)* (Leiden, 2003).

Esposito, Roberto, *Origine e destino della comunità* (Torino, 2012).

Estow, Clara, 'The economic development of the Order of Calatrava, 1158–1366,' *Speculum* 57 (1982), pp. 267–291.

Evans, Arthur J., 'Antiquarian researches in Illyricum, Parts I–II,' *Archaeologia, miscellaneous tracts relating to antiquity* 48 (1883), pp. 3–105.

Evans, Arthur J., 'Antiquarian researches in Illyricum, Parts III–IV,' *Archaeologia, miscellaneous tracts relating to antiquity* 49 (1885), pp. 1–167.

Evans, Chris, and Göran Rydén, *Baltic iron in the Atlantic world in the eighteenth century* (Leiden, 2007).

Evans, E. Estyn, 'Transhumance in Europe,' *Geography* 25 (1940), pp. 172–180.

Evergates, Theodore, ed., *Feudal society in medieval France: Documents from the County of Champagne* (Philadelphia, 1993).

Eyuboglu, Yener, et al., 'The Eastern Black Sea-type volcanogenic massive sulfide deposits: geochemistry, zircon U-Pb geochronology and an overview of the geodynamics of ore genesis,' *Ore Geology Reviews* 59 (2014), pp. 29–54.

Fagan, Brian M., *The Little Ice Age: How climate made history, 1300–1850* (New York, 2000).

Fagnan, Edmond, *Extraits inédits relatifs au Maghreb (géographie et histoire)* (Alger, 1924).

Faroqhi, Suraiya, *Approaching Ottoman history: An introduction to the sources* (Cambridge, England, 1999).

Faroqui Suraiya, *Artisans of empire: Crafts and craftspeople under the Ottomans* (Palgrave, 2009).

Faroqhi, Suraiya, et al., *An economic and social history of the Ottoman Empire* (Cambridge, England, 1994).

Ferluga, Jadran, *Byzantium in the Balkans: Studies on the Byzantine administration and the Southern Slavs from the VIIth to the XIIIth centuries* (Amsterdam, 1976).

Fernández Villegas, Oswaldo, 'La huaca Narihuala: un documento para la etnohistoria de la costa norte de Perú (1000–1200 D.C.),' *Bulletin Institute Frances Études Andines* 19 (1990), pp. 103–127.

Ferrante, Carla, and Antonello Mattone, 'Le comunità rurali nella Sardegna medievale (secoli XI-XV),' *Diritto @ Storia* 3 (2004) [online] http://dirittoestoria.it/3/Lavori-in-Corso /Contributi/Contributi-web/Ferrante-Mattone-Comunita-rurali.htm#_ftnref158, accessed May 1, 2015.

Ferreira Vieira, Alexandra M., 'Christian religious landscapes and earlier archeological evidence in the Trás-os-Montes and Alto Douro Region (Portugal),' *Journal of Iberian Archeology* 12 (2009), pp. 41–54.

Fine, John V. A., *The late medieval Balkans: A critical survey from the late twelfth century to the Ottoman conquest* (Michigan, 1994).

Fivaller De Velaz, José M., *Memoria del olivo y su cultivo, elaboración del aceite, medios que deben emplearse, para que los aceites de España rivalicen con los de Italia* (Palma, 1864).

Fleure, Herbert J., 'Regions in human geography-with special reference to Europe,' *The Geographical Teacher* 9 (1917), pp. 31–45.

Flitch, John E. C., *Mediterranean moods: Footnotes of travel in the islands of Mallorca, Menorca, Ibiza, and Sardinia* (London, 1911).

Fluck, Pierre, and Ancel Bruno, 'Le paysage minier des sites métalliques des Vosges et de la Forêt-Noire,' *Annales de Bretagne et des pays de l'Ouest* 96 (1989), pp. 183–201.

Flynn, Dennis O., 'Born with a "silver spoon": The origin of world trade in 1571,' *Journal of World History* 6 (1995), pp. 201–221.

Flynn, Dennis O., 'China and the Spanish Empire,' *Revista Económica* 14 (1996), pp. 309–338.

Flynn, Dennis O., and Arturo Giráldez, 'Cycles of silver: Global economic unity through the mid-eighteenth century,' *Journal of World History* 13 (2002), pp. 391–427.

Flynn, Dennis O., and Arturo Giráldez, eds., *Metals and monies in an emerging global economy* (London, 1997).

Földváry, Géza Z., *Geology of the Carpathian region* (New Jersey, 1988).

Fonseca, Luís Adão D., and Maria H. Ribeiro da Cunha, *De Vasco a Cabral: Oriente e Ocidente nas navegações oceânicas* (Lisboa, 2001).

Forbes, Robert J., *Metallurgy in Antiquity: A notebook for archeologists and technologists* (Leiden, 1950).

Forbes, Robert J., *Studies in ancient technology*, vol. 7, Ancient Geology: Ancient Mining and Quarrying: Ancient Mining Techniques (Leiden, 1963).

Forci, Antonio, 'Feudi e fuedatari in Trexenta (Sardegna meridionali) agli esordi della dominazione catalano-aragonese (1324–1326),' *Rivista dell'Istituto di Storia dell'Europa Mediterranea* 4 (2010), pp. 151–211.

Forêt, Philippe, *Mapping Chengde: the Qing landscape enterprise* (Honolulu, 2000).

Forslund, William, *Visbys roller i ett växande handelsnätverk: Hur handel koncentrerar sig beroende på teknologiska och institutionella faktorer*, Uppsala University, Department of Economic History (Uppsala, 2011) [online] http://www.diva-portal.org/smash/record.jsf ?pid=diva2:437868, accessed January 22, 2014.

Francovich, Riccardo, and Luisa Dallai, 'Colline Metallifere (Toscane, Italie): recherche et mise en valeur du paysage d'un district minier,' *Archeo Sciences, Revue d'archéométrie* 34 (2010), pp. 277–287.

Francovich, Riccardo, and Roberto Farinelli, 'Potere e attività minerarie nella Toscana altomedievale,' in *La storia dell'altomedioevo italiano (VI–X secolo) alla luce dell'archeologia, Atti del Convegno Internazionale, Siena 1992*, cur. Riccardo Francovich, and Ghislaine Noyé, pp. 1–29 (Florence, 1994).

Frapporti, Giuseppe, *Della storia e della condizione del Trentino* (Trento, 1840).

Freedman, Paul H., *Images of the medieval peasant* (Stanford, California, 1999).

Freeman, Edward A., *The historical geography of Europe*, vol. 1 (London, 1882).

Freshfield, Douglas W., 'The Great Passes of the Western and Central Alps,' *The Geographical Journal* 49 (1917), pp. 2–22.

Freund, Ernst, *The legal nature of corporations* (Chicago, 1897).

Friday, Karl, ed., *Japan emerging: Premodern to 1850* (New York, 2012).

Friedman, Jonathan, and Christopher K. Chase-Dunn, *Hegemonic decline: Past and present* (Boulder, Colorado, 2005).

Frulio, Gabriela, 'Catalan methods for construction in Sardinia,' in *Proceedings of the first International Congress on Construction History*, vol. 2, comp. Santiago Huerta Fernández, pp. 935–941 (Madrid, 2003).

Fuhrmann, Horst, '*Quis Teutonicos constituit iudices nationum?* The trouble with Henry,' *Speculum* 69 (1994), pp. 344–358.

Fumagalli, Vito, *Landscapes of fear: Perceptions of nature and the city in the Middle Ages* (Cambridge, England, 1994).

Fumagalli, Vito, *Uomini e paesaggi medievali* (Bologna, 1989).

Furtado, Celso M., *Development and underdevelopment*, trans. R. W. de Aguiar and E. C. Drysdale (Berkeley, 1964).

Furtado, Celso M., *The economic growth of Brazil*, trans. R. W. de Aguiar and E. C. Drysdale (Berkeley, 1963).

Furtado, Celso M., et al., *A grande esperança em Celso Furtado: ensaios em homenagem aos seus 80 anos* (São Paulo, 2001).

Gabrielli, Francesco, 'Greeks and Arabs in the Central Mediterranean Area,' *Dumbarton Oaks Papers* 18 (1964), pp. 57–65.

Gale, Noël H., and Zofia A. Stos-Gale, 'Ancient Egyptian silver,' *Journal of Egyptian Archaeology* 67 (1981), pp. 103–115.

Gallin, Lenore J., and Robert H. Tykot, 'Metallurgy at Nuraghe Santa Barbara (Bauladu), Sardinia,' *Journal of field archeology* 20 (1993), pp. 335–345.

Gamberini, Andrea, 'La territorialità nel Basso Medioevo: un problema chiuso? Osservazioni a margine della vicenda di Reggio,' *Reti Medievali* 5 (2004) [online] http://www.storia.unifi.it/_RM/rivista/atti/poteri/Gamberini.htm, accessed March 4, 2015.

Gamble, Barry, *Cornish mines: St Just to Redruth* (Cornwall, England, 2011).

García Fernández, Ernesto, 'Viñedo y vino en Álava durante la Edad Media,' in *Mundos medievales: espacios, sociedades y poder*, vol. 2, ed. Beatriz Arízaga Bolumburu et al., pp. 1351–1364 (Santander, 2012).

García Guerra, Elena M., 'Itinerarios mundiales de una moneda supranacional: el 'real de a ocho' o peso durante la Edad Moderna,' *Studia historica* 28 (2006), pp. 241–257.

García Linera, Álvaro, *La potencia plebeya: acción colectiva e identidades indígenas, obreras y populares en Bolivia* (La Paz, 2008).

García Moreno, Luis A., 'Teudemiro de Orihuela y la invasión islámica,' in *Mundos medievales: espacios, sociedades y poder*, vol. 2, ed. Beatriz Arízaga Bolumburu et al., pp. 529–544 (Santander, 2012).

García Pulido, Luis J., 'La red de acequias de Granada, sus pagos agrícolas de origen andalusí,' *Entre Ríos, Revista de Arte y Letras* 15–16 (2011), pp. 151–157.

Garçon, Marion, et al., 'Silver and lead in high-altitude lake sediments: Proxies for climate changes and human activities,' *Applied Geochemistry* 27 (2012), pp. 760–773.

Gardner, John S., *Ironwork: From the earliest times to the end of the medieval period* (London, 1907).

Garegnani, Pierangelo, 'Value and distribution in the classical economists and Marx,' *Oxford Economic Papers* 36 (1984), pp. 91–325.

Garlandini, Alberto, et al., *Il patrimonio storico industriale della Lombardia: censimento regionale* (Brescia, 1991).

Gato Castaño, Purificación, 'La Academia de Metalurgia de Potosí, Obra del Ilustrado Jorge Escobedo, 1775–1785,' in *Minería y metalurgia intercambio tecnológico y cultural entre América y Europa durante el período colonial*, ed. Manuel Castillo Martos, pp. 175–204 (Sevilla, 1993).

Gaud, Henri, and Jean-François Leroux-Dhuys, *Les abbayes Cisterciennes en France et en Europe* (Paris, 1998).

Genovesi, Stefano, 'Lo spostamento di popolazione e persone nelle regioni minerarie delle province occidentali in età imperiale,' in *L'Africa romana*, vol. 2, ed. Aomar Akerraz et al., pp. 755–771 (Roma, 2006).

Geray, Uçkun, and Sezgin Özden, 'Silvopastoralism in Turkey's mountainous Mediterranean region,' *Mountains research and development* 23 (2003), pp. 128–131.

Gerber, Haim, 'The Muslim law of partnerships in Ottoman court records,' *Studia Islamica* 53 (1981), pp. 109–119.

Giacomo Ortu, Gian, 'Famiglia e possesso contadino in contest feudale: il caso sardo,' *Studi Storici* 36 (1995), pp. 1075–1098.

Gibb, Hamilton A. R., et al., eds., *The Encyclopedia of Islam*, vols. 1–8 (Leiden, 1960).

Gierke, Otto, *Political theories of the Middle Ages*, trans. Frederic W. Maitland (Cambridge, England, 1900).

Gilberthorpe, Emma, and Elissaios Papyrakis, 'The extractive industries and development: the resource curse at the micro, meso, and macro levels,' *Extractive industries and society* 2 (2015), pp. 381–390.

Gill, Mike C., 'An outline of the chemistry of lead smelting,' in *Boles and Smeltmills, Historical Metallurgical Society, Matlock, Bath* (1992), p. 3.

Gillingham, John B., 'A historian of the twelfth-century Renaissance and the transformation of English society, 1066-ca. 1200,' in *European transformations: The long twelfth century*, ed. Thomas F. X. Noble and John H. van Engen, pp. 45–74 (Notre Dame, Indiana, 2012).

Gimlette, John, 'Morocco: On the high road in the Atlas Mountains,' *Telegraph online edition*, May 8, 2011 [online] http://www.telegraph.co.uk/travel/destinations/africaandindian ocean/morocco/8498050/Morocco-on-the-high-road-in-the-Atlas-Mountains.html, accessed March 6, 2014.

Giovanelli, Benedetto, *Intorno all'antica zecca Trentina e a due monumenti Reti: lettere tre* (Trento, 1812).

Giráldez, Arturo, *The age of trade: The Manila galleons and the dawn of the global economy* (Maryland, 2015).

Giunta, Francesco, and Alberto Boscolo, 'Geronimo Zurita ed i problemi mediterranei della Corona d'Aragona,' in *VII Congreso de Historia de la Corona de Aragón*, vol. 1, comp. Congrès d'Historia, pp. 187–228 (Barcelona, 1962).

Gjeçov, Shtjefën, *The Code of Lekë Dukagjini*, trans. L. Fox (New York, 1989).

Glahn, Richard V., *The country of streams and grottoes: Expansion, settlement, and the civilizing of the Sichuan frontier in Song times* (Cambridge, Massachusetts, 1987).

Glahn, Richard V., *Fountain of fortune: Money and monetary policy in China, 1000–1700* (Berkeley, 1996).

Glanvil, Joseph, 'On the Mendip lead mines,' *Philosophical Transactions* 28 (1667), p. 525.

Glick, Thomas F., 'Levels and levelers: Surveying irrigation canals in medieval Valencia,' *Technology and Culture* 9 (1968), pp. 165–180.

Goguet, Antoine-Yves, *The origins of laws, arts, and sciences, and their progress among the most ancient nations*, 3 vols. (Edinburgh, 1775).

Gökçe, Ahmet, and Gülcan Bozkaya, 'Lead and sulfur isotope evidence for the origin of the Inler Yaylası lead-zinc deposits,' *Journal of Asian Earth Sciences* 26 (2006), pp. 91–97.

Goldsmith, Oliver, *A history of the earth and animated nature*, vol. 1 (London, 1847).

Gómez Zúñiga, Pastor R., 'Minas de plata y conflictos de poder: el origen de la Alcaldía Mayor de Minas de Honduras (1569–1582),' *Asociación para el fomento de los estudios históricos en Centroamérica, Boletín* 15 (n.d.) [online] http://www.afehc-historia-cen troamericana.org/index.php?action=fi_aff&id=356, accessed February 8, 2013.

González Arévalo, Raúl, 'Cautiverio y esclavitud en el Reino de Granada (siglos XIII–XVI),' *Vínculos de Historia* 3 (2014), pp. 232–257.

Górecki, Piotr, *Parishes, tithes, and society in earlier medieval Poland, ca. 1100–1250* (Philadelphia, 1993).

Gould, Sabine B., *The deserts of southern France*, vol. 2 (London, 1894).

Gozalbes Busto, Guillermo, and Enrique Gozalbes Cravioto, 'Al-Magrib al-Aqsà en los primeros geógrafos árabes orientales,' *Miscelánea de estudios árabes y hebraicos, sección árabe-Islam* 47 (1998), pp. 167–185.

Grañeda Miñón, Paula, 'Los lingotes andalusíes de plata de Hornachuelos (Córdoba),' *Qurtuba: estudios andalusíes* 3 (1998), pp. 65–80.

Grant, Richard, 'Walking with Berber nomads,' *Telegraph Travel* February 9, 2013 [online] http://www.telegraph.co.uk/travel/destinations/africaandindianocean/morocco/9847593 /Morocco-walking-with-Berber-nomads.html, accessed March 6, 2013.

Graulau, Jeannette, 'Finance, industry, and globalization in the early modern period: The example of the metallic business of the House of the Fugger,' *Rivista di Politici Internazionali* 75 (2008), pp. 554–598.

Graulau, Jeannette, 'Ownership of mines and taxation in Castilian laws, from the Middle Ages to the early modern period,' *Continuity and Change* 26 (2011), pp. 13–44.

Green, Joel B., ed., *Dictionary of Jesus and the Gospels* (Illinois, 1992).

Green, Judith, 'King Henry I and Northern England,' *Transactions of the Royal Historical Society* 17 (2007), pp. 35–55.

Greenaway, Frank, 'Thirty centuries of assaying,' *Bulletin of the British Society for the History of Science* 2 (1961), p. 103.

Grierson, Philip, *Monnaies du moyen âge, L'univers des monnaies* (Freiburg, 1976).

Grierson, Philip, and Lucia Travaini, *Medieval European coinage*, vol. 14, *Italy (III) (South Italy, Sicily, Sardinia)* (Cambridge, England, 1999).

Grigelis, Algimantas, 'The first large geological map of Central and Eastern Europe (1815),' *Geologija* 50 (2008), pp. 125–134.

Grigelis, Algimantas, et al., 'Stanisław Staszic: An early surveyor of the geology of Central and Eastern Europe,' *Annals of Science* 68 (2011), pp. 199–228.

Grzés, Marek, and Jan Szupryczyński, 'Large floods in the lower Vistula River,' *GeoJournal* 38 (1996), pp. 235–240.

Guidoboni, Emmanuela, 'Human factors, extreme events, and floods in the Lower Po Plain (Northern Italy) in the 16th century,' *Environment and History* 4 (1998), pp. 279–308.

Guilbert, John M., and Charles Frederick Park, *The geology of ore deposits* (New York, 1986).

Gunder Frank, André, 'Immanuel and me with-out hyphen,' *Journal of World-Systems Research* 6 (2000), pp. 216–231.

Gunder Frank, André, *ReOrient: Global economy in the Asian age* (Berkeley, 1998).

Gunder Frank, André, *World accumulation, 1492–1789* (New York, 1978).

Gunder Frank, André, and Barry K. Gills, *The world system: Five hundred years or five thousand?* (New York, 1993).

Habashi, Fathi, 'The beginnings of mining and metallurgical education in Japan,' *De re metallica* 17 (2011), pp. 85–92.

Hahn, Otto H., 'Ore reduction in the Harz, II,' *Engineering and Mining Journal* 91 (1911), pp. 1163–1166.

Halbout, Patrick, et al., 'Corpus des objets domestiques et des armes en fer de Normandie. Du ler au XVe siècle,' *Cahier des Annales de Normandie* 20 (1986), pp. 1–255.

Hall, Augustin F. C., 'Early West African metallurgies: New data and old orthodoxy,' *Journal of World Prehistory* 22 (2009), pp. 415–438.

Hall, John W., 'Feudalism in Japan: A reassessment,' *Comparative Studies in Society and History* 5 (1962), pp. 15–51.

Hall, Thomas C. F., *Lead ores* (London, 1921).

Hallaq, Wael B., *Authority, continuity, and change in Islamic Law* (Cambridge, England, 2001).

Halleck, Henry W., trans., *A collection of mining laws of Spain and Mexico* (San Francisco, 1859).

Halsall, Paul, 'Medieval source book: Agreement on the exploitation of a silver mine, 1180,' *Internet Medieval Sourcebook, Fordham University* (New York, 1998) [online] http://www.fordham.edu/Halsall/source/1180slvrmine.asp, accessed January 12, 2013.

Hamilton, Eric. J., *American treasure and the price revolution in Spain, 1501–1650* (Cambridge, Massachusetts, 1934).

Hammer, Carl I., *A large-scale slave society of the early Middle Ages: Slaves and their families in early medieval Bavaria* (London, 2017).

Hamouda, O. F., and B. B. Price, 'The justice of the just price,' *European Journal of the History of Economic Thought* 4 (1997), pp. 191–261.

Hannaway, Owen, 'Georgius Agricola as humanist,' *Journal of the History of Ideas* 53 (1992), pp. 553–560.

Hansen, Peter H., 'Albert Smith, the Alpine Club, and the invention of mountaineering in mid-Victorian Britain,' *Journal of British Studies* 34 (1995), pp. 300–324.

Har-El, Shai, *Struggle for domination in the Middle East, the Ottoman-Mamluk War, 1485–1491* (Leiden, 1995).

Harding, Anthony, *Salt in prehistoric Europe* (Leiden, 2013).

Harreld, Donald J., *High Germans in the Low Countries* (Leiden, 2004).

Harrell, James A., and V. Max Bronx, 'The oldest surviving topographical map from ancient Egypt (Turin Papyri 1879, 1899, and 1969),' *Journal of the American Research Center in Egypt* 29 (1992), pp. 81–105.

Harris, Marvin, 'The economy has no surplus,' *American Anthropologist* 61 (1959), pp. 185–199.

Hartwell, Robert, 'A cycle of economic change in Imperial China: Coal and iron in Northeast China, 750–1350,' *Journal of the Economic and Social History of the Orient* 10 (1967), pp. 102–159.

Harvey, Charles, and Jon Press, 'Issues in the history of mining and metallurgy,' *Business History* 32 (1990), pp. 1–14.

Häseler, Ernest, *Das bergwerk in Rammeslberg bei Goslar* (Harzburg, 1981).

Hawqal, Ibn, *Bibliotheca Geographorum Artabicorum. Kitāb al-masālik wa'l-mamālik*, vol. 2, ed. M. J. de Goeje (Leiden, 1873).

Hay, John D., *Morocco and the Moors: Western Barbary* (London, 1861).

Heck, Gene W., 'Gold mining in Arabia and the rise of the Islamic State,' *Journal of the Economic and Social History of the Orient* 42 (1999), pp. 364–395.

Heer, Friedrich, *The Holy Roman Empire*, trans. J. Sondheimer (New York, 1968).

Herbert, Eugenia W., *Red gold of Africa: Copper in precolonial history and culture* (Winsconsin, 2003).

Herlihy, David, 'Church property on the European continent, 701–1200,' *Speculum* 36 (1961), pp. 81–105.

Herlihy, David, 'The history of the rural seigneury in Italy, 751–1200,' *Agricultural History* 33 (1959), pp. 58–71.

Herlihy, David, *Medieval and Renaissance Pistoia: The social history of an Italian town, 1200–1430* (New Haven, 1967).

Hernández Esteve, Esteban, ed., *Moneda y monedas en la Europa medieval, siglos XII–XV* (Pamplona, 2000).

Hess, Andrew C., *The forgotten frontier: A history of the sixteenth century Ibero-African frontier* (Chicago, 2010).

Hilferding, Rudolf, *Finance capital, a study of the latest phase of capitalist development*, trans. T. Bottomore (London, 1981).

Hill, Donald R., trans., *Kitāb al-Ḥiyal: The book of knowledge of ingenious mechanical devices* (Dordrecht, 1974).

Hilton, Rodney H., *English and French towns in feudal society, a comparative study* (Cambridge, England, 1995).

Hinojosa, José, 'Sal, fiscalidad y cultura material en el reino de Valencia a fines de la Edad Media,' in *Mundos medievales: espacios, sociedades y poder,* vol. 2, ed. Beatriz Arízaga Bolomburu, et al., pp. 1467–1478 (Santander, 2012).

Hiroyuki, Yanagihashi, ed., *The concept of territory in Islamic law and thought* (Oxford, 2000).

Hirt, Alfred M., *Imperial mines and quarries in the Roman world, organizational aspects 27 B.C.–A.D. 235* (Oxford, 2010).

Hirth, Friedrich, and William Rockhill, trans., *Chau Ju-kua: His Work on the Chinese and Arab trade in the XII and XIII centuries (Chu-fan-chï)* (St. Petersburg, 1911).

Hochstadt, Steve, 'Migration in preindustrial Germany,' *Central European History* 16 (1983), pp. 195–224.

Hodgson, Marshall G. S., *The venture of Islam*, 3 vols. (Chicago, 1974).

Hoffman, J. Wesley, 'The commerce of the German Alpine passes during the early Middle Ages,' *Journal of Political Economy* 31 (1923), pp. 826–839.

Hoffman, J. Wesley, 'The Fondaco dei Tedeschi: the medium of Venetian-German trade,' *Journal of Political Economy* 40 (1932), pp. 244–252.

Hoffman, Richard C., *An environmental history of medieval Europe* (Cambridge, England, 2014).

Holtfrerich, Carl-Ludwig, *Frankfurt as a financial centre, from medieval trade fair to European banking centre* (Munich, 1999).

Holzer, Herwig F., and Eugen F. Stumpfl, 'Mineral deposits of the Eastern Alps,' *Abhl. Geol. Bundesanstalt* 34 (1980), pp. 171–196.

Hoover, Herbert C., *Principles of mining: Valuation, organization, and administration* (New York, 1909).

Hoover, Herbert C., and Lou H. Hoover, trans., *Georgius Agricola De Re Metallica* (New York, 1950).

Hoppenbrouwers, Peter, and Jan L. Zanden, eds., *Peasants into Farmers?* (Belgium, 2001).

Horák, Jan, and Michal Hejcman, '800 years of mining and smelting in Kutná Hora region (the Czech Republic): Spatial and multivariate meta-analysis of contamination studies,' *Journal of Soils Sediments* 16 (2016), pp. 1584–1598.

Horton, Mark, 'Artisans, communities, and commodities: Medieval exchanges between Northwestern India and East Africa,' *Ars Orientalis* 34 (2004), pp. 62–80.

Huang, Ray, *Taxation and governmental finance in sixteenth-century Ming China* (London, 1974).

Hübner, Rudolf, et al., *A history of Germanic private law* (Boston, 1918).

Humbert, André, 'De l'utilité pour la géographie de l'observation et de la photographie aériennes obliques,' *Mélanges de la Casa de Velázquez* 15 (1979), pp. 485–488.

Humbert, André, '*Suelo y vuelo* au XVIIIe s., les surfaces fictives d'arbres dans le *Catastro de La Ensenada*,' *Mélanges de la Casa de Velázquez* 14 (1978), pp. 511–518.

Humboldt, Alexander v., *Political essay on the Kingdom of New Spain*, vol. 3, trans. John Black (London, 1814).

Hunn, Geoffrey C., *First globalization: The Eurasian exchange* (Maryland, 2003).

Hunt, Christopher J., *The lead miners of the North Pennines in the eighteenth and nineteenth centuries* (Manchester, 1970).

Hunt, Edwin S., and James M. Murray, *A history of business in medieval Europe, 1200–1550* (Cambridge, England, 1999).

Huson, Hugh D., *The rise of the Demidov family and the Russian iron industry in the eighteenth century* (Newtonville, Massachusetts, 1986).

Illés, Iván, *Visions and strategies in the Carpathian Area (VASICA)* (Budapest, 2008).

Imai, Hideki, *Geological studies of the mineral deposits in Japan and East Asia* (Tokyo, 1978).

Imber, Colin, *The Ottoman Empire, 1300–1650: The structure of power* (New York, 2009).

İnalcik, Halil, *An economic and social history of the Ottoman Empire*, vol. 1, *1300–1600* (Cambridge, England, 1994).

İnalcik, Halil, 'Ottoman methods of conquest,' *Studia Islamica* 2 (1954), pp. 103–129.

İnalcik, Halil, and Donald Quataert, eds., *An economic and social history of the Ottoman empire, 1300–1914*, vol. 1 (Cambridge, England, 1994).

Isidore, of Seville Saint, *Isidore of Seville's Etymologies: A complete English translation*, trans. P. Throop (Charlotte, Virginia, 2005).

Issawi, Charles, 'Europe, the Middle East, and the shift in power: Reflections on a theme by Marshall Hodgson,' *Comparative Studies in Society and History* 22 (1980), pp. 487–504.

Jackson, Lowis, *Modern metrology* (London, 1882).

Jackson, Patrick N. W., ed., *Four centuries of geological travel: the search for knowledge on foot, bicycle, sledge, and camel* (London, 2007).

Jackson, Peter, 'Marco Polo and his "Travels,"' *Bulletin of the School of Oriental and African Studies* 61 (1998), pp. 82–101.

James, Edward, *Europe's barbarians*, A.D. *200–600* (Harlow, England, 2009).

Jánošíková, Petra, 'Mining business pursuant to "Ius Regale Montanorum" in the 14th century,' *Journal of European History of Law* 2 (2011), pp. 165–168.

Japan Weekly Mail, 'Trade of Nagasaki for 1903,' *The Japan Weekly Mail*, November 19, 1904, pp. 568–569.

Jayasuriya, Shisan S., *The Portuguese in the East: A cultural history of a maritime trading empire* (New York, 2008).

Jelavich, Charles, and Barbara Jelavich, *The Balkans in transition: essays in the development of Balkan life since the eighteenth century* (Berkeley, 1963).

Jepson, Tim, *National Geographic traveler: Italy* (Washington, D.C., 2010).

Jervis, William P., 'Mineral resources of Tuscany,' *Journal of the Society of Arts*, August (1860), pp. 689–697.

Jiménez Alcázar, Juan Francisco, 'Tierra, propiedad y paisaje agrario en la frontera de Granada: el núcleo medieval de Coy (Lorca, Murcia),' *Anales de la Universidad de Alicante: Historia Medieval* 10 (1996), pp. 169–195.

Jiménez De La Espada, Marcos, and José U. Martínez Carreras, eds., *Relaciones geográficas de Indias*, 4 vols. (Madrid, 1965).

Jiménez Mata, María C., *La Granada islámica: contribución a su estudio geográfico-político -administrativo a través de la toponimia* (Granada, 1990).

Jiménez Puertas, Miguel, and Luis Martínez Vázquez, 'La organización social de un espacio andalusí: reflexiones en torno a la vega de Granada,' in *Mundos medievales, espacios sociale sy poder, homenaje al profesor José Ángel García de Cortázar y Ruiz de Aguirre*, ed. Beatriz Arízaga Bolumburu et al., pp. 159–172 (Cantabria, 2012).

Jireček, Hermenegild, *Codex juris Bohemici*, T. Primus (Prague, 1867).

Jixing, Pan, 'The spread of Georgius Agricola's De re metallica in Late Ming China,' *T'oung Pao*' 77 (1991), pp. 108–118

Johnson, Douglas W., 'The conquest of Rumania,' *Geographical Review* 3 (1917), pp. 438–456.

Johnson, Edgar A. J., 'Just price in an unjust world,' *International Journal of Ethics* 48 (1937/1938), pp. 165–181.

Johnson, Michael R. W., and Simon L. Harley, *Orogenesis: The making of mountains* (Cambridge, England, 2012).

Jones, Michael, ed., *The new Cambridge medieval history*, vol. 6 (Cambridge, England, 2000).

Jones, Peter M., *Politics in the rural society: The southern Massif Central, c.1750–1880* (Cambridge, England, 1985).

Juleff, Gillian, 'Technology and evolution: A root and branch view of Asian iron from first millennium B.C. Sri Lanka to Japanese steel,' *World archaeology* 41 (2009), pp. 557–577.

Jurković, Ivan, 'Bakovići: The biggest gold deposit of Bosnia and Herzegovina,' *Rudarsko-geološko-naftni zbornik* 7 (1995), pp. 1–15.

Jurković, Ivan, 'Barite, hematite, and cinnabar ore deposits in the Dusin area, mid-Bosnian schist mountains,' *Rudarsko-geološko-naftni zbornik* 8 (1996), pp. 51–65.

Kaláb, Zdenkě, et al., 'Mine water movement in shallow medieval Mine Jeroným (Czech Republic),' in *Mine Water and the Environment, 10th International Mine Water Association Congress*, ed. International Mine Water Association, pp. 16–26 (Nova Scotia, Canada, 2008).

Káldy-Nagy, Gyula, 'The first centuries of the Ottoman military organization,' *Acta Orientalia Academiae Scientiarum Hungaricae* 31 (1977), pp. 147–183.

Kalus, Peter, *Die Fugger in der Slowakei* (Augsburg, 1999).

Kamen, Henry, *Empire: How Spain became a world power, 1492–1763* (New York, 2003).

Kamen, Henry, *The Spanish Inquisition, a historical revision* (New Haven, 2014).

Karpat, Kemal H., *Social change and politics in Turkey: A historical-structural analysis* (Leiden, 1973).

Kaser, Karl, *The Balkans and the Near East* (Berlin, 2011).

Katić, Tatjana, 'The *Sancak* of Prizren in the 15th and 16th century,' *OTAM* 33 (2013), pp. 113–138.

Kautsky, Karl, *The economic doctrines of Karl Marx*, trans. Henry J. Stenning (London, 1925).

Kawahata, Hodaka, et al., 'Climate change and its influence on human society in western Japan during the Holocene,' *Quaternary International* 440 (2017), pp. 102–117.

Keall, Edward J., 'The dynamics of Zabid and its hinterland: The survey of a town on the Tihamah Plain of North Yemen,' *World Archeology* 14 (1983), pp. 378–392.

Keiji, Nagahara, and Kozo Yamamura, 'Shaping the process of unification: Technological progress in sixteenth and seventeenth century Japan,' *Journal of Japanese Studies* 14 (1988), pp. 77–109.

Kellenbenz, Hermann, 'The gold mining activities of the Fuggers and the cementation privilege of Kremnitz,' in *Industry and finance in early modern history: Papers presented to George Hammersley to the occasion of his 74th birthday*, ed. I. Blanchard, pp. 186–204 (Stuttgart, 1992).

Kellenbenz, Hermann, *Los Fugger en España y Portugal hasta 1560*, trans. M. Prieto Vilas (Valladolid, 2000).

Kellenbenz, Hermann, ed., *Precious metals in the age of expansion: Papers of the XIV International Congress on Historical Sciences* (Stuttgart, 1981).

Kellenbenz, Hermann, *The rise of the European economy: an economic history of continental Europe from the fifteenth to the eighteenth century* (New York, 1976).

Kern, Anton, et al., *Kingdom of salt: 7,000 years of Hallstat* (Vienna, 2009).

Kerner v. Marilaun, Anton, *The natural history of plants*, vol. 2 (New York, 1895).

Kernot, Charles, *Valuing mining companies: A guide to the assessment and evaluation of assets, performance and prospects* (New York, 2000).

Khaldûn, Ibn, *The Muqaddimah, an introduction to history*, trans. Franz Rosenthal (Princeton, 2005).

Kharajian, Hagop A., *Regional geology and mining of Armenia* (New York, 1915).

Khûri Hitti, Philip, et al., eds., *The origins of the Islamic State, being a translation from the Arabic accompanied with annotations, geographic and historic notes of the Kitâb futûh al-buldân of al-Imâm abu-l ʿAbbâs Aḥmad ibn-Jâbir al-Balâdhuri* (Beirut, 1968–1969).

Kibler, William W., and Grover A. Zinn, *Medieval France: An encyclopedia* (London, 2006).

King, Andy, and Michael Penman, eds., *England and Scotland in the fourteenth century* (Suffolk, England, 2007).

King, Geoffrey R.D., 'Notes on some mosques in Eastern and Western Saudi Arabia,' *Bulletin of the School of Oriental and African Studies* 43 (1980), pp. 251–276.

King, Peter, *The finances of the Cistercian Order in the fourteenth century* (Kalamazoo, Michigan, 1985).

King, Robert J., 'Minerals explained 3: Galena,' *Geology Today* 1 (1985), pp. 188–190.

Kink, Rudolf, *Fontes Rerum Austriacarum: Oesterreichische Geschichts-Quellen, Diplomataria et Acta, V Band, Codex Wangianus* (Wien, 1852).

Kirnbauer, Franz, 'Die Bergordnung von Trient aus dem Jahre 1208 und ihre Beziehung zur Bergbautechnik,' *Blätter für Technikgeschichte* 20 (1958), pp. 1–24.

Klápště, Jan, *The Czech lands in medieval transformation* (Netherlands, 2012).

Klarwill, Victor v., *The Fugger news-letters, second series, being a further selection from the Fugger papers specially referring to Queen Elizabeth and matters relating to England* (London, 1926).

Kluge, Friedrich, *An etymological dictionary of the German language*, trans. John F. Davis (London, 1891).

Knapp, Bernard A., et al., eds., *Social approaches to an industrial past: The archaeology and anthropology of mining* (New York, 1998).

Knorn, Henricus H., et al., *Dissertatio historica de metallifodinarum Hartzicarum: prima origine et progressu et quomodo ad Sereniss* (Helmstadt, 1680).

Kobata, Atsushi, 'The production and uses of gold and silver in sixteenth- and seventeenth-century Japan,' *Economic History Review* 18 (1965), pp. 245–266.

Koeppen, Adolph L., *The world in the Middle Ages: An historical geography*, vol. 1 (New York, 1854).

Kohad, V. P., 'Monitoring environmental impact of ore beneficiation processing at Zawar mines,' in *Proceedings of the international conference on environmental management in metallurgical industries 2000*, ed. Radha C. Gupta, pp. 133–139 (Varanasi, 2000).

Korey, Michael, *The geometry of power, mathematical instruments, and Princely mechanical devices from around 1600* (Munich, 2007).

Kovačević-Kojić, Desanka, 'Les metaux precieux de Serbie et le marche Europeen (XIVᵉ–XVᵉ siècles),' *Recueil des travaux de l'Institut d'études byzantines* XLI (2004), pp. 191–203.

Kovačević-Kojić, Desanka, 'Les mines d'or et d'argent en Serbie et Bosnie,' *Annales: Économies, Sociétés, Civilisations* 15 (1960), pp. 248–258.

Kovacs, Marinel, and Alexandrina Fülöp, 'Baia Mare geological and mining park: A potential new geopark in the northwestern part of Romania,' *Studia Universitatis Babeş-Bloyai* 54 (2009), pp. 27–32.

Koytcheva, Elena, '*Civitates et Castra* on Via Militaris and Via Egnatia: Early Crusaders' view,' *Revue des Études Sud-est Européennes* 44 (2006), pp. 139–145.

Krekić, Bariša, 'Dubrovnik and Spain: Commercial and human contacts, fourteenth–sixteenth centuries,' in *Iberia and the Mediterranean World of the Middle Ages*, vol. 2, ed. Paul E. Chevedden et al., pp. 395–406 (Leiden, 1996).

Kriedte, Peter, *Feudalismo tardío y capital mercantil*, trans. J. L. Vermal (Barcelona, 1994).

Krüger, Joachim, 'Copper mining and metallurgy in prehistoric and the more recent past,' *Sustainable Metals Management* 19 (2006), pp. 417–448.

Kumar Biswas, Arun, 'Minerals and metals in medieval India,' in *History of Indian science, technology, and culture, AD 1000–1800*, vol. 3, ed. Abdur Rahman, pp. 275–313 (Oxford, 1998).

Kumar Biswas, Arun, 'Non-gem minerals in pre-modern India,' *Indian Journal of History of Science* 29 (1994), pp. 421–463.

Kuran, Timur, 'The absence of corporation in Islamic law: Origins and persistence,' *American Journal of Comparative Law* 53 (2005), pp. 785–834.

Kurter, Ajun, 'Glaciers of Turkey.' US Geological Survey Professional Paper 1386-G-1 (1988), pp. 1–29.

Kutzsche, K., 'Silver-smelting in the ore mountains (Erzgebirge),' *Neue Hütte* 36 (1991), pp. 315–316.

Kuwasaburo, Takatsu, et al., *History of the empire of Japan*, trans. F. Brinkley (Tokyo, 1893).

Kysel, Vladimír, 'Representative list of the intangible cultural heritage of Slovakia,' *Slovakia Ethnology* 5 (2013), pp. 561–565.

La Salvia, Vasco, *Iron making during the migration period: The case of the Lombards* (Oxford, 2007).

Lamborn, Robert, *The metallurgy of silver and lead a description of the ores, their assay and treatment, and various constituents* (London, 1878).

Lambton, Ann Katherine S., 'The qānāts of Yazd,' *Journal of the Royal Asiatic Society* 2 (1992), pp. 21–35.

Lampertico, Fedele, *Sulla legislazione mineraria: studi* (Venezia, 1869).

Landes, David S., *The wealth and poverty of nations* (New York, 1998).

Langholm, Odd, 'The German tradition in late medieval value theory,' *European Journal History of Economic Thought* 15 (2008), pp. 555–570.

Large, Duncan, and Wayne E. Walcher, 'The Rammelsberg massive sulphide Cu-Zn-Pb-Ba-deposit, Germany: An example of sediment-hosted, massive sulphide mineralization,' *Mineralium Deposita* 34 (1999), pp. 522–538.

Larner, John, *Marco Polo and the discovery of the world* (New Haven, 1999).

Lawn, James G., *Mine accounts and mining book-keeping* (London, 1904).

Lazzari, Tiziana, 'Comunità rurali nell'alto medioevo: pratiche di descrizione e spie lessicali nella documentazione scritta,' in *Paesaggi, comunità, villaggi medievali: atti del Convegno internazionale di studio*, cur. Paola Galetti, pp. 405–422 (Bologna, 2010).

Le Goff, Jacques, *Intellectuals in the Middle Ages*, trans. T. L. Fagan (Oxford, 1993).

Le Goff, Jacques, *La Baja Edad Media*, trans. L. Ortíz (Madrid, 1971).

Le Roy Ladurie, Emmanuel, *The peasants of Languedoc* (Illinois, 1976).

Le Strange, Guy, *The geographical part of the Nuzhat-al-quluб composed by Hamd-Allāh Mustawfī of Qazwīn in 740 (1340)* (Leiden, 1911).

Le Strange, Guy, *The lands of the eastern Caliphate: Mesopotamia, Persia, and Central Asia from the Moslem conquest to the time of Timur* (New York, 1873).

Lee, Kwang Y., 'Some rare-element mineral deposits in mainland China,' *Geological Survey Bulletin* 1312-N (1970), pp. 1–31.

Lee, Richard E., ed., *The longue durée and world-systems analysis* (New York, 2012).

Lee, Samuel, trans., *The travels of Ibn Batūta* (London, 1829).

Lekai, Louis J., 'Medieval Cistercians and their social environment, the case of Hungary,' *Analecta Cisterciensia* 32 (1976), pp. 251–280.

Leroux-Dhuys, Jean F., and Henry Gaud, *Les abbayes Cisterciennes en France et en Europe* (Paris, 1998).

Leroy, Marc, et al., 'La sidérurgie dans l'est de la Gaule, l'organisation spatial de la production de l'Âge du fer au haut Moyen Age,' *Gallia* 57 (2000), pp. 11–21.

Letts, Malcolm, 'Marco Polo: Discussion,' *The Geographical Journal* 120 (1954), pp. 312–313.

Levi, Doro, 'Sardinia: Isle of antithesis,' *Geographical Review* 33 (1943), pp. 630–654.

Lewis, Archibald R., 'The closing of the medieval frontier, 1250–1350,' *Speculum* 33 (1958), pp. 475–483.

Lewis, Bernard, *Race and slavery in the Middle East: An historical enquiry* (Oxford, 1990).

Lewis, Ewart, *Medieval political ideas*, 2 vols. (New York, 1974).

Lewis, George R., *The stannaries: A study of the English tin miner* (New York, 1907).

Leyser, Karl, 'Ottonian government,' *English Historical Review* 96 (1981), pp. 721–753.

Lieber, Alfred E., 'Eastern business practices and medieval European commerce,' *The Economic History Review* 21 (1968), pp. 230–243.

Liebman, Seymour B., *Réquiem por los olivdados: los judíos españoles en América, 1493–1825* (Madrid, 1984).

Lightfoot, Dale R., and James A. Miller, 'Sijilmasa: The rise and fall of a walled oasis in medieval Morocco,' *Annals of the Association of American Geographers* 86 (1986), pp. 78–101.

Lindner, Rudi P., *Explorations in Ottoman prehistory* (Ann Arbor, 2007).

Lindren, Waldemar, *Mineral deposits* (London, 1919).

Lokkegaard, Frede, 'Islamic taxation in the classical period,' *Studies in Islamic history* 10 (1977), pp. 1–294.

Lombard, Maurice, *The golden age of Islam*, trans. J. Hathaway (Princeton, 2004).

Lombard, Maurice, 'Les bases monétaires d'une suprématie économique, l'or Musulmandu VIIᵉ au XIᵉ siècle,' *Annales Histoire Sciences Sociales* 2 (1947), pp. 143–160.

Long, Pamela O., 'The openness of knowledge: An ideal and its context in 16th-century writings on mining and metallurgy,' *Technology and Culture* 32 (1991), pp. 318–355.

López Dueso, Manuel, 'La Edad Media,' in *Comarca de Sobrarbe*, coord. Severino Pallaruelo Campo, pp. 95–114 (Aragon, 1991).

Lopez, Robert S., *The commercial revolution of the Middle Ages, 950–1350* (Cambridge, England, 2005).

Lopez, Robert S., 'Majorcans and Genoese on the North Sea route in the thirteenth century,' *Revue belge de Philologie et d'Historie* 29 (1951), pp. 1163–1179.

Lopez, Robert S., and Irving W. Raymond, trans., *Medieval trade in the Mediterranean world, illustrative documents* (New York, 2001).

Loudon, John C., *An encyclopedia of agriculture* (London, 1835).

Lucas, Adam, *Ecclesiastical lordship, seigneurial power, and the commercialization of milling in medieval England* (London, 2014).

Lučić, Ivo, 'Shafts of life and shafts of death in Dinaric karst, Popovo polje case (Bosnia & Herzegovina),' *Acta Carsologica* 36 (2007), pp. 321–330.

Ludwin, Ruth S., and Gregory J. Smits, 'Folklore and earthquakes: Native American oral traditions from Cascadia compared with written traditions from Japan,' in *Myth and Geology*, ed. L. Piccardi and W. B. Masse, pp. 67–94 (London, 2007).

Lupi, Mario, *Giuseppe Ronchetti Memorie istoriche della città e chiesa di Bergamo*, vol. 1 (Bergamo, 1805).

Lydon, Ghislaine, 'Goulimine (also Goulimime),' in *Encyclopedia of Jews in the Islamic World* (Leiden, 2013) [online] http://referenceworks.brillonline.com/entries/encyclopedia-of-jews-in-the-islamic-world/goulimine-also-goulimime-SIM_0008600, accessed March 7, 2013.

Lynch, John, *The Hispanic world in crisis and change 1598–1700* (Oxford, 1992).

MacDonald, Colin, 'The ancient mine-workings of Laureion,' *Greece and Rome* 8 (1961), pp. 19–21.

Machiavelli, Niccolò, *The Florentine histories*, vol. 1, trans. Charles E. Lester (New York, 1845).

Macini, Paolo, and Enzo Mesini, 'The evolution of pumping systems through the early Renaissance,' in *Henry P. G. Darcy and other pioneers in hydraulics*, ed. Glenn O. Brown et al., pp. 233–251 (Virginia, 2003).

Mackenzie, Eneas, and Marvin Ross, *An historical, topographical, and descriptive view of the County Palatine of Durham*, vol. 2 (Newcastle, 1834).

Mackenzie, Georgina M., and Adeline P. Irby, *Across the Carpathians* (London, 1862).

MacLeod, Christine, *Inventing the Industrial Revolution, the English patent system, 1660–1800* (Cambridge, England, 1988).

Madgearu, Alexandru, 'Salt trade and warfare in medieval Transylvania,' *Ephemeris Napocensis* 11 (2001), pp. 271–283.

Magdalino, Paul, *The empire of Manuel I Komenos, 1143–1180* (Cambridge, England, 2002).

Magnusson, Roberta, and Paolo Squatriti, 'The technologies of water in medieval Italy,' in *Working with water in medieval Europe*, ed. Paolo Squatriti, pp. 217–266 (Leiden, 2000).

Majer, Jirf, 'Changes in silver mining of the Bohemian lands in the 16th century and their economic consequences,' in *Miniere e Metallurgia, deciottesima settimana di Studio del Instituto Internazionale do Storia Economica 'Francesco Datini,'* cur. Simonetta Cavaciocchi, CD format (Prato, 1986).

Majer, Jirf, 'Ore mining and the town of St. Joachimsthal/Jáchymov at the time of Georgius Agricola,' *GeoJournal* 32 (1994), pp. 91–99.

Malfatti, Bartolomeo, *Degli idiomi parlati anticamente nel Trentino e dei dialetti odierni, note storiche* (Vigo, 1878).

Malfatti, Bartolomeo, 'I confini dei Principato de Trento,' in *Archivio Storico per Trieste, L'Istria e il Trentino* Vol. Sec., ed. S. Morpurgo and A. Zenatti, pp. 1–32 (Roma, 1883).

Malte-Brun, Conrad, *A system of universal geography*, vol. 2 (Boston, 1834).

Malthus, Thomas R., *Definitions of political economy* (London, 1827).

Manca, Ciro, 'Colonie iberiche in Italia nei secoli XIV e XV,' *Anuario de Estudios Medievales* 10 (1980), pp. 505–538.

Mandel, Ernest, *An introduction to Marxist economic theory* (New York, 1973).

Mander, James, *The Derbyshire miners' glossary, or an explanation of the technical terms of the miners* (Bakewell, 1824).

Mango, Marlia M., 'Tracking Byzantine silver and copper metalware, 4th–12th centuries,' in *Byzantine trade: 4th–12th centuries, the archeology of local, regional, and international exchange*, ed. Marlia Mundell Mango, pp. 221–238 (England, 2009).

Maravall, José Antonio, *Estado moderno y mentalidad social (siglos XV–XVII)*, 2 vols. (Madrid, 1972).

Marchese, Eugenio, 'Sopra alcuni vocaboli contenuti nel Breve di Villa di Chiesa di Sigerro,' *Rivista economica della Sardegna*, December 15, 1876, pp. 41–47.

Marcoux, Eric, et al., 'Lead isotope signatures of epithermal and porphyry-type ore deposits from the Romanian Carpathian Mountains,' *Mineralium Deposita* 37 (2002), pp. 173–184.

Marichal, Carlos, *El camino hacia el Euro: el real, el escudo y la peseta* (Madrid, 2001).

Marinelli, Olinto, 'The regions of mixed populations in northern Italy,' *The Geographical Review* 7 (1919), pp. 129–148.

Markham, Clements R. trans., *Narrative of the embassy of Ruy González de Clavijo to the court of Timour at Samarcand, A.D. 1403–6* (London, 1859).

Markham, Clements R., trans., *The travels of Pedro de Cieza de León, A.D. 1532–50, contained in the first part of his Chronicle of Peru* (London, 1864).

Marmelzat, William, 'Lost and found: Agricola's original description of occupational dermatitis (1558),' *Archives of dermatology* 86 (1962), pp. 234–235.

Marques, José, 'A origem do concelho de Ribeira de Pena (1331),' *Revista de Guimarães* 103 (1993), pp. 327–341.

Marshall, Alfred, *Principles of economics*, vol. 1 (London, 1895).

Martín Civantos, José M., 'Alquife, un castillo con vocación minera en el Zenete (Granada),' *Arqueología y territorio medieval* 8 (2001), pp. 325–345.

Martín Civantos, José M., 'El Cerro del Toro y la minería de la Kura de Ilbira (Granada-Almería),' in *Minería y metalurgia histórica en el sudoeste europeo*, ed. Octavio Puche Riart and Mariano Ayarzagüena Sanz, pp. 333–343 (Madrid, 2005).

Martín Gutiérrez, Emilio, 'En los bosques andaluces, los carboneros a finales de la Edad Media,' in *Mundos medievales: espacios, sociedades y poder,* vol. 1, ed. Beatriz Arízaga Bolumburu et al., pp. 1561–1572 (Santander, 2012).

Martínez Frías, Jesús, 'Sulphide and sulphosalt mineralogy and paragenesis from the Sierra Almagrera,' *Estudios Geológicos* 47 (1991), pp. 271–279.

Martínez Girón, Ramón, 'La montaña de Tudmir: introducción etnográfica,' *Gazeta de antropología* 6 (1988), pp. 1–10.

Martiñón-Torres, Marcos, et al., 'Some problems and potentials of the study of cupellation remains: The case of post-medieval Montbéliard, France,' *ArcheoSciences* 32 (2008), pp. 59–70.

Martinón-Torres, Marcos, and Thilo Rehren, 'Ceramics in fire assay practices: A case study of 16th-century laboratory equipment,' in *Understanding people through their pottery*, ed. María I. Prudencio et al., pp. 139–148 (Lisbon, 2005).

Martins, Ana L., 'Breve histórica dos garimpos de ouro do Brasil,' in *Em Busca do Ouro Garimpos e Garimpeiros no Brasil*, ed. Bernardino R. Figuereido et al., pp. 177–215 (São Paulo, 1984).

Martonne, Emmanuel, 'The Carpathians: Physiographic features controlling human geography,' *Geographical Review* 3 (1917), pp. 417–437.

Marx, Karl, *Capital, a critique of political economy*, vol. 1, ed. Frederick Engels (Chicago, 1906–1909).

Massala, Gianandrea, *Sonetti storici sulla Sardegna* (Cagliari, 1808).

Matías Rodríguez, Roberto, 'Ingeniería minera romana,' in *Elementos de ingeniería romana,*

Congreso europeo, Las obras públicas romanas, dir. Raúl Alba, et al., pp. 157–190 (Tarragona, 2004).

Matilla Tascón, Antonio, *Historia de las minas de Almadén, desde la época romana hasta el año 1645* (Madrid, 1958).

Matley, Ian M., 'Transhumance in Bosnia and Herzegovina,' *Geographical Review* 58 (1968), pp. 231–261.

Matte, Phillipe, 'Two geotraverses across the Ibero-Armorican Variscan of Western Europe,' in *Profiles of orogenic belts*, ed. Nicholas Rast and Frances M. Delany, pp. 53–82 (Washington, D.C., 1983).

Matthew, Donald, *Atlas of medieval Europe* (New York, 1983).

Matthews, George T., *News and rumor in Renaissance Europe: The Fugger newsletters* (New York, 1970).

Mayhew, Nicholas J., and Peter J. Spufford, *Later medieval mints: Organization, administration, and techniques* (Oxford, 1988).

Mayor, Adrienne, *The poison king: The life and legend of Mithradates, Rome's deadliest enemy* (Princeton, 2009).

McKinsty, Hugh E., *Mining geology* (New York, 1948).

McNeill, John R., *The mountains of the Mediterranean world, an environmental history* (Cambridge, England, 1992).

McNeill, William, *The rise of the West: A history of the human community* (Chicago, 1991).

Mederer, Johannes, et al., 'Base and precious metal mineralization in Middle Jurassic rocks of the Lesser Caucasus: A review of geology and metallogeny and new data from the Kapan, Alaverdi and Mehmana districts,' *Ore Geology Reviews* 58 (2014), pp. 185–207.

Melechen, Nina, 'Loans and Jewish-Christian relations in the Archdiocese of Toledo,' in *Iberian and the Mediterranean World of the Middle Ages*, vol. 1, ed. Larry J. Simon, pp. 185–215 (Leiden, 1995).

Melis, Federigo, et al., *Industria e commercio nella Toscana medievale* (Florence, 1989).

Melve, Leidulf, "The revolt of the medievalists': directions in recent research on the twelfth-century renaissance,' *Journal of Medieval History* 32 (2006), pp. 231–252.

Menant, François, *Lombardia feudale: studi sull'aristocrazia padana nei secoli X–XIII* (Milano, 1992).

Menant, François, 'Pour une historie médiévale de l'enterprise minière en Lombardie,' *Annales: Économies, Sociétés, Civilisations* 42 (1987), pp. 779–796.

Mensing, Scott, et al., 'Human and climatically induced environmental change in the Mediterranean during the Medieval Climate Anomaly and Little Ice Age: A case from central Italy,' *Anthropocene* 15 (2016), pp. 49–59.

Mentz, Brígida v., coord., *Sultepece en el siglo XIX* (México, D.F., 1989).

Merz, John Theodore, *A history of European thought in the nineteenth century*, vol. 1 (Edinburgh, 1907).

Michaud-Quantin, Pierre, *Universitas Expressions du mouvement communitaire dans le moyen-âge latin* (1970).

Michelet, Jules, *The history of France*, vol. 1 (London, 1844–1846).

Mies, Maria, *Patriarchy and accumulation on a world scale: Women in the international division of labor* (London, 1986).

Mihevc, Andrej, et al., eds., *Introduction to the Dinaric karst* (Ljubljana, 2010).

Miljković, Ema, 'The timar system in the Serbian lands: With a special survey on the timar system in the Sanjak of Smederevo,' *Journal of Ottoman Legacy Studies* 1 (2014), pp. 36–47.

Miller, Edward, and John Hatcher, *Medieval England: Towns, commerce, and crafts, 1086–1348* (New York, 1995).

Miller, John A., *The practical handbook for the working miner and prospector and the mining investor* (London, 1897).

Miller, William, 'Bosnia before the Turkish occupation,' *The English Historical Review* 13 (1898), pp. 643–666.

Milnehome, David, 'Inaugural address, session 1881–1882,' *Transactions of the Edinburgh Geological Society* 4 (1882), pp. 119–133.

Milsom, Stroud F., *The legal framework of English feudalism* (Cambridge, England, 1976).

Minorsky, Vladimir, 'A Persian geographer of A.D. 982 on the orography of Central Asia,' *The Geographical Journal* 90 (1937), pp. 259–264.

Miskimin, Harry A., 'Two reforms of Charlemagne? Weights and measures in the Middle Ages,' *Economic History Review*, New Series 20 (1967), pp. 35–52.

Mispoulet, Jean-Baptiste, *Le régime des mines à l'époque romaine et au Moyen Âge d'après les Tables d'Aljutrel* (Paris, 1908).

Mitchell, Sydney K., *Taxation in medieval England* (New Haven, 1951).

Mokyr, Joel, *The lever of riches: Technological creativity and economic progress* (New York, 1990).

Molenda, Danuta, 'Mining towns in central-eastern Europe in feudal times,' *Acta Poloniae Historica* 34 (1976), pp. 165–188.

Molina López, Emilio, and María C. Jiménez Mata, 'La propiedad de la tierra en la Vega de Granada a finales del siglo XV: el caso del Alitaje,' *Anaquel de Estudios Árabes* 12 (2001), pp. 442–479.

Monge, Carlos, 'High altitude disease,' *Archives Internal Medicine* 59 (1937), pp. 32–40.

Moník, Martin, and Pavel Šlézar, 'An analysis of metalworking by-products from the medieval town of Uničov,' *Interdisciplinaria Archaeologica* 3 (2012), pp. 229–235.

Monroe, Arthur Eli, *Early economic thought: Selections from economic literature prior to Adam Smith* (Cambridge, Massachusetts, 1924).

Moore, Frederick, 'The races of the Balkan peninsula,' *The National Geographic Magazine* 23 (1918), pp. 473–489.

Mor, Carlo G., and Heinrich Schmidinger, *I poteri temporali dei vescovi in Italia e in Germania nel Medioevo* (Bologna, 1979).

Morărescu, Gabriela, 'Geological research in Inner Carpathian Romania up to the 19th century,' *Philobiblon* 14 (2009), pp. 229–249.

Moreno Nieto, D. José, *Discursos leídos ante la Real Academia de la Historia* (Madrid, 1864).

Morini, Domenico, and Piero Bruni, *The Regione Toscana project of geological mapping: Case histories and data acquisition* (Florence, 2004).

Moscheles, Julie, 'Natural regions of Czechoslovakia,' *Geographical Review* 14 (1924), pp. 561–575.

Motzki, Harald, et al., *Analysing Muslim traditions: Studies in legal, exegetical, and Maghazi hadith* (Leiden, 2010).

Mueller, Andreas G., 'The Rammelsberg shale-hosted Cu-Zn-Pb sulfide and barite deposit, Germany: linking SEDEX and Kuroko-type massive sulfides.' Slide presentation and explanatory notes, March 21, 2008 [online] http://www.geoberg.de/wp-content/uploads/2010/06/080322_04.pdf, accessed June 11, 2012.

Mundell, Robert, 'Comment on academic exclusion: The case of Alexander Del Mar,' *European Journal of Political Economy* 20 (2004), pp. 61–68.

Mugueta, Íñigo, 'Explotación minera en el Reino de Navarra: la mina de plata de Urrobi (s. XIV),' *Congrès International RESOPYR* (2005), pp. 3–28.

Müller, Diamillo, *Biografie autografe ed inedite di illustri italiani di questo secolo* (Torino, 1853).

Munro, John H., *Bullion flows and monetary policies in England and the Low Countries, 1350–1500* (Hampshire, Great Britain, 1992).

Munro, John H., 'Industrial energy from water mills in the European economy, 5th to 18th centuries: The limitations of power,' *Economia ed energia, seccoli XIII–XVIII, Atti delle 'Settimane di Studi' e altrie convegni, Istituto Internazionale di storia economica, F. Datini* 34 (2003), pp. 223–269.

Munro, John H., 'The medieval origins of the financial revolution,' *International History Review* 25 (2003), pp. 505–562.

Muratori, Ludovico A., *Annali d'Italia dal principio dell'era volgare sino all'anno 1750,* vol. 6 (Lucca, 1763).

Murray, John, *Handbook for Switzerland and the adjacent regions* (London, 1905).

Mushet, David, *Papers on iron and steel* (London, 1840).

Mutton, Alice F. A., 'The Black Forest: Its human geography,' *Economic geography* 14 (1938), pp. 131–153.

Nagel, Anne-Hilde, 'Norwegian mining in the early modern period,' *GeoJournal* 32 (1994), pp. 137–149.

Nagel, Rob, and Diane Sawinski, *UXL Encyclopedia of landforms and other geologic features,* vol. 1 (Farmington Hills, Michigan, 2004).

Naravane, M. S., *The Rajputs of Rajputana (a glimpse of medieval Rajasthan)* (New Delhi, 1999).

Nardi, Arnoldo, ed., *Condizioni economiche dell'industria mineralogica in Toscana durante il medio evo* (Livorno, 1847).

Narita, Eikichi, 'Geology and ore deposits of the Onikobe-Hosokura district, northeastern Honshu, Japan,' *Journal of the Faculty of Science Hokkaido University* 11 (1963), pp. 651–681.

Nash, George H., *Life of Herbert Hoover, the engineer, 1874–1914* (New York, 1996).

Nash, June, *We eat the mines and the mines eat us: Dependency and exploitation in Bolivian tin mines* (New York, 1979).

Nastich, Vladimir, 'Almaty-town and mint dating back to the 13th century,' *Information Bulletin of the International Association for the Study of the Cultures of Central Asia* 22 (2000), pp. 120–132.

Naumann, Edmund, 'The physical geography of Japan, with remarks on the people,' *Proceedings of the Royal Geographical Society and Monthly Record of Geography* 9 (1887), pp. 86–102.

Nederman, Cary J., 'Sovereignty, war, and the corporation: Hegel on the medieval foundations of the modern state,' *Journal of Politics* 1987 (49), pp. 500–520.

Needham, Joseph, ed., *Science and civilization in China*, vol. 5 (Cambridge, England, 1985).

Needham, Joseph, et al., *Chinese science: Explorations of an ancient tradition* (Cambridge, Massachusetts, 1973).

Nef, John U., 'Industrial Europe at the time of the Reformation,' *Journal of Political Economy* 49 (1941), pp. 1–40.

Nef, John U., 'Silver production in Central Europe, 1450–1618,' *Journal of Political Economy* 49 (1941), pp. 575–591.

Neiva, Ana M. R., et al., 'Antimony quartz and antimony-gold quartz veins from northern Portugal,' *Ore Geology Reviews* 34 (2008), pp. 533–546.

Nerantzis, N., 'Pillars of power: Silver and steel in the Ottoman Empire,' *Mediterranean Archeology and Archaeometry* 9 (2009), pp. 71–85.

Neubauer, Franz, et al., 'Late Cretaceous and Tertiary geodynamics and ore deposit evolution of the Alpine-Balkan-Carpathian-Dinaride orogen,' in *Mineral exploration and sustainable development*, ed. Demetrios Eliopoulos et al., pp. 1133–1136 (Rotterdam, 2003).

New York Times, 'Frommer's Thuringia Forest,' *The New York Times* undated [online] http://travel.nytimes.com/ref/travel/frm_weimar_0130026990.html, accessed March 10, 2013.

Newbigin, Marion I., *Geographical aspects of the Balkans in their relation to the Great European War* (New York, 1915).

Newsweek, 'The miners stand fast,' May 17 (1982), p. 64.

Nicolescu, Stefan, 'Glossary of geological localities in the former Austro-Hungarian Empire, now in Romania,' *Canadian Mineralogist* 36 (1998), pp. 1373–1381.

Niox, Gustave, *Les pays balkaniques* (Paris, 1915).

Nisser, Marie, 'Industrial archaeology in the Nordic countries, viewed from Sweden,' *World Archaeology* 15 (1983), pp. 137–147.

Noble, Thomas F. X., and John V. Engen, eds., *European transformations: The long twelfth century* (Notre Dame, Indiana, 2012).

Nriagu, Jerome O., 'Cupellation: The oldest quantitative chemical process,' *Journal of Chemical Education* 62 (1985), pp. 668–674.

Nriagu, Jerome O., 'Tales told in lead,' *Science* 281 (1998), p. 1622.

Nweeya, Samuel K., *Persia: The land of the Magi* (Philadelphia, 1910).

Nyazee, Imran A. K., *The Book of Revenue Kitāb al-Amwāl* (Reading, UK, 2005).

Oberländer-Târnoveanu, Ernest, 'The coinage of the Genoese settlements of the Western Black Sea shore and on the Danube,' *Peuce Serie Nouă* 2 (2004), pp. 285–296.

O'Dell, Ilse, 'Jost Amman and the *Album Amicorum* drawings after prints in autograph albums,' *Print Quarterly* 9 (1992), pp. 31–36.

Ogden, Jack, 'Metals,' in *Ancient Egyptian materials and technology*, ed. Paul T. Nicholson and Ian Shaw, pp. 148–176 (Cambridge, England, 2006).

Oliveira Marques, António H. R., *Ensáios de história medieval portuguesa* (Lisbon, 1980).

Oliveira Marques, António H. R., *Hansa e Portugal na Idade Média* (Lisbon, 1959).

Oliver, Roland, and Anthony Atmore, *Medieval Africa, 1250–1800* (Cambridge, England, 2001).

Olla Repetto, Gabriella, *Studi sulle istituzioni amministrative e giudiziarie della Sardegna nei secoli 14. e 15* (Cagliari, 2005).

Ollé, Manuel, *La empresa de China: de la armada invencible al galeón de Manila* (Barcelona, 2002).

Ollier, Cliff, and Colin F. Pain, *The origin of mountains* (London, 2000).

Oma, Mary V., 'Silver refinement and debasement, a historical survey,' *Journal of Chemical Education* 65 (1988), p. 153.

Oman, Giovanni, 'Al-Idrīsī,' *Encyclopaedia of Islam,* 2nd ed. (Leiden, 2013) [online] http://referenceworks.brillonline.com/entries/encyclopaedia-of-islam-2/al-idrisi-SIM_3494, accessed March 15, 2013.

Orsi Lázaro, Mario, 'Estrategia, operaciones y logística en un conflicto mediterráneo. La revuelta del Juez de Arborea y la "armada e viatge" de Pedro el Ceremonioso a Cerdeña (1353–1354),' *Anuario de Estudios Medievales* 38 (2008), pp. 921–968.

Ortalli, Gherardo, 'Il mercante e lo stato: structure della Venezia altomedievale,' in *Mercati e mercanti dell'Alto Medioevo: l'area euroasiaica e l'area mediterranea,* ed. Centro Italiano Di studi Sull'Alto medioevo, pp. 85–135 (Spoletto, Itália, 1993).

Osheim, Duane J., 'Countrymen and the law in late-medieval Tuscany,' *Speculum* 64 (1989), pp. 317–337.

Ouseley, William, *The Oriental geography of Ebn Haukal, an Arabian traveller of the tenth century* (London, 1800).

Overbeek, Henk, 'Cycles of hegemony and leadership in the core of the world system,' Working Paper no. 31, Amsterdam International Studies, Department of International Relations and Public International Law, University of Amsterdam (Maarssen, The Netherlands, 1993).

Pack, Spencer J., *Aristotle, Adam Smith, and Karl Marx: On some fundamental issues in 21st century political economy* (Cheltenham, UK, 2010).

Palacios García, Antonio, et al., eds., *VII Congreso internacional sobre patrimonio geológico y minero* (Puertollano, España, 2008).

Palinkaš, Ladislav A., et al., 'Metallogeny of the northwestern and central Dinarides and southern Tisia,' *Ore Geology Reviews* 34 (2008), pp. 501–520.

Palladius, Archimandrite, 'Elucidations of Marco Polo's travels in North-China, drawn from Chinese sources,' *Journal of the North-China Branch of the Royal Asiatic Society* X (1876), pp. 1–54.

Pallares, María C., and Ermelindo Portela, 'El complejo minero-metalúrgico de la granja cisterciense de Constantín. Bases para el desarrollo de una investigación en arqueología medieval,' *Arqueología y territorio medieval* 7 (2014), pp. 81–91.

Palumbo-Liu, David, et al., eds., *Immanuel Wallerstein and the problem of the world: System, scale, culture* (North Carolina, 2011).

Pamuk, Şevket, *A monetary history of the Ottoman empire* (Cambridge, England, 2000).

Park, R. Graham, *Foundations of structural geology* (Oxford, 1997).

Parker Mason, Walter A., 'The beginnings of the Cistercian Order,' *Transactions of the Royal Historical Society* 19 (1905), pp. 169–207.

Pastoreau, Michael, *Una historia simbólica de la Edad Media occidental,* trans. J. Bucci (Buenos Aires, 2006).

Patetta, Francesco, 'La "Lex Frisionum," studi sulla origine e sulla critica del testo,' *Memoria Acc. Torino* 43 (1893), pp. 1–66, 91–98.

Patterson, Clair C., 'Native copper, silver, and gold accessible to early metallurgists,' *American Antiquity* 36 (1971), pp. 286–321.

Paul, Wolfgang, *Mining lore: An illustrated composition and documentary compilation with emphasis on the spirit and history of mining* (Portland, Oregon, 1970).

Paulinyi, O., 'Die anfänglichen Formen des Unternehmens im Edelerzbergbau zur Zeit des Feudalismus, II Teil,' *Acta historica Academiae Scientiarum Hungaricae* 12 (1966), pp. 261–318.

Peattie, Roderick, *Mountain geography: A critique and field study* (Cambridge, Massachusetts, 1936).

Peković, Željko, and Nikolina Topić, 'A late-medieval and post-medieval foundry in the historic-centre of Dubrovnik,' *Post-medieval Archeology* 45 (2011), pp. 266–290.

Pennington, Kenneth, and Melodie H. Eichbauer, eds., *Law as profession and practice in medieval Europe, essays in honor of James A. Brundage* (London, 2011).

Pérez Macías, Juan A., 'Cerro Salomón y la minería hispano-musulmana en Garb Al-Andalus,' *Arqueología Medieval* 6 (1999), pp. 19–43.

Perini, Agostino, *Dizionario geografico, statistico del Trentino* (Trento, 1856).

Perini, Carlo, and Carlo Lurati, *Illustrazione del Tirolo italiano e della Svizzera italiana* (Milano, 1859).

Perry, Consul-General, 'Report by Mr. Consul-General Perry on the trade and commerce of Venice for the year 1867,' in *Commercial reports received at the Foreign Office from Her Majesty's Consuls during the year 1868, August to December*, Foreign Office, pp. 459–465 (London, 1869).

Petersen, Georg G., *Mining and metallurgy in ancient Perú*, trans. William E. Brooks (Boulder, Colorado, 2010).

Petkov, Kiril, *The voices of medieval Bulgaria, seventh–fifteenth century, the records of a bygone culture* (Leiden, 2008).

Petrocchi, Luigi, *Massa Marittima, arte e storia* (Florence, 1900).

Pignotti, Lorenzo, *The history of Tuscany, from the earliest era*, vol. 4, trans. John Browning (London, 1836).

Pinson, Mark, ed., *The Muslims of Bosnia-Herzegovina, their historic development from the Middle Ages to the dissolution of Yugoslavia* (Cambridge, Massachusetts, 1996).

Pipino, Giuseppe, *Oro, miniere, storia. Miscellanea di giacimentologia e storia mineraria italiana* (Ovada, Itália, 2003).

Piqueras Haba, Juan, 'Cartografía islámica, Sharq Al-Andalus, siglos X–XII, Al-Idrisi y los precursores,' *Cuadernos de geografía* 86 (2009), pp. 137–163.

Pirenne, Henri, *Economic and social history of medieval Europe*, trans. I. E. Clegg (New York, 1937).

Pires, Tomé, *Suma Oriental, an account of the East, from the Red Sea to China, written in Malacca and India, 1512–1515*, 2 vols., ed. Armando Cortesão (New Delhi, 2005).

Piskorski, Jan M., 'Medieval colonization in East Central Europe,' in *The Germans and the East*, ed. Charles W. Ingrao and Franz A. J. Szabo, pp. 27–36 (Indiana, 2008).

Pitarakis, Brigitte, 'Mines Anatoliennes exploitées par les Byzantins: recherché récentes,' *Revue numismatique* 153 (1998), pp. 141–185.

Pitcher, Donald E., *An historical geography of the Ottoman Empire: From earliest times to the end of the sixteenth century* (Boston, 1973).

Piterberg, Gabriel, 'The formation of an Ottoman Egyptian elite in the 18th century,' *International Journal of Middle East Studies* 22 (1990), pp. 275–289.

Plesník, Pavol, 'Man's influence on the timberline in the West Carpathian Mountains, Czechoslovakia,' *Arctic and Alpine Research* 10 (1978), pp. 491–504.

Poggi, Enrico, *Discorsi economici, storici e giuridici* (Florence, 1861).

Polanyi, Karl, *Trade and market in the early empires: Economies in history and theory* (Glencoe, Illinois, 1957).

Polwhele, Richard, *A history of Cornwall in seven volumes*, vol. 4 (London, 1816).

Pomeranz, Kenneth, 'Political economy and ecology on the eve of industrialization: Europe, China, and the global conjuncture,' *American Historical Review* 107 (2002), pp. 425–446.

Porée, Charles, Études historiques sur le Gévaudan (Paris, 1919).

Porteous, James M., *God's treasure-house in Scotland: A history of times, mines, and lands in the southern highlands* (London, 1876).

Porteous, John, *Coins in history* (New York, 1969).

Porter, Arthur K., *The construction of Lombard and Gothic vaults* (New Haven, 1911).

Porter, David D., 'Letter of Lieutenant Porter, United States Navy, to Secretary of War, May 28, 1856,' in *Reports upon the purchase, importation, and use of camels and dromedaries to be employed for military purposes*, David D. Porter, pp. 103–133 (Washington, D.C., 1857).

Porter, Vera R., and Dora B. Weiner, 'Historical perspective on cadmium-induced nephro-toxicity,' in *Nephrotoxicity in vitro to in vivo animals to man*, ed. Peter H. Bach, pp. 51–57 (The Netherlands, 1989).

Post, Gaines, 'Parisian Masters as a corporation, 1200–1246,' *Speculum* 1934 (9), pp. 421–445.

Postan, Michael M., *Essays on medieval agriculture and general problems of medieval economy* (Cambridge, England, 1973).

Postan, Michael M., *The medieval economy and society: An economic history of Britain, 1100–1500* (Berkeley, 1973).

Postan, Michael M., and H. John Habakkuk, eds., *The Cambridge economic history of Europe*, vol. 6, *The industrial revolutions* (Cambridge, England, 1989).

Postan, Michael M., and John Hatcher, 'Agrarian class structure and economic development in pre-industrial Europe: Population and class relations in feudal society,' *Past and Present*, 78 (1978), pp. 24–37.

Pounds, Norman J. G., *An historical geography of Europe: 450 B.C.–A.D. 1330* (Cambridge, England, 1973).

Pouqueville, François C., *Travels in the Morea, Albania, and other parts of the Ottoman Empire* [. . .] *and a historical and geographic description of the ancient Epirus*, trans. Anne Plumptre (London, 1813).

Pouwels, Randall L., *The African and Middle Eastern world, 600–1500* (Oxford, 2005).

Powers, David, et al., eds., *Islamic legal thought: A compendium of Muslim jurists* (Leiden, 2013).

Prebisch, Raúl L., *The economic development of Latin America and its principal problems* (New York, 1950).

Preller, Charles S. R., *Italian mountain geology*, parts 1–2 (London, 1924).

Prescher, Hans, 'Dr. Georgius Agricola, 1494–1555,' *GeoJournal* 32 (1994), pp. 85–89.

Price, Derek J., 'Medieval land surveying and topographical maps,' *The Geographical Journal* 121 (1955), pp. 1–7.

Price, Larry W., *Mountains and man: A study of process and environment* (Berkeley, California, 1981).

Prioreschi, Plinio, *Medieval medicine* (Omaha, 2003).

Provero, Luigi, 'Le comunità rurali nel medioevo: qualche prospettiva,' in *Lo spazio politico locale in età medievale, moderna e contemporanea, Atti del convegno internazionale di studi*, cur. R. Bordone et al., pp. 335–340 (Alexandria, 2007).

Pryce, William, *Mineralogia cornubiensis: A treatise on minerals, mines, and mining, containing the theory and natural history of strata, fissures, and lodes* (London, 1778).

Puche Riart, Octavio, 'La minería visigótica y musulmana en la Península Ibérica,' in *Bocamina, Patrimonio minero de la región de Murcia*, ed. Octavio Puche Riart, pp. 87–92 (Murcia, 2005).

Puddu, Giuseppe, et al., 'Spatial-explicit assessment of current and future conservation options for the endangered Corsican Red Deer (*Cervus elaphus corsicanus*) in Sardinia,' *Biodiversity Conservation* 18 (2009), pp. 2001–2016.

Pulszky, Ágost, *The theory of law and civil society* (London, 1888).

Pungetti, Gloria, 'Anthropological approach to agricultural landscape history in Sardinia,' *Landscape and Urban Planning* 31 (1995), pp. 47–56.

Py, Vanessa, and Bruno Ancel, 'Exploitation de smines métalliques de la vallée Freissinières (Hautes-Alpes, France): contribution à l'étude de l'économie sud-alpine aux IXe–XIIIe siècles,' *Preistoria Alpina* 42 (2007), pp. 83–98.

Pyhrr, Stuart W., et al., *Heroic armor of the Italian Renaissance: Filippo Negroli and his contemporaries* (New York, 1999).

Quintana Frías, Ignacio, 'Minería y territorio durante el Califato de Córdoba,' *Boletín Geológico y Minero* 117 (2006), pp. 567–569.

Rachewiltz, Igor, *The secret history of the Mongols*, vol. 3 (Leiden, 2013).

Radosavljević, Slodoban, et al., 'Mineralogy and genetic features of the Cu-As-Ni-Sb-Pb mineralization from the Mlakva polymetallic deposit (Serbia)-new occurrence of (Ni-Sb)-bearing Cu-arsenides,' *Ore Geology Reviews* 80 (2017), pp. 1245–1258.

Radosavljević, Slodoban, et al., '(Pb-S)-bearing sphalerite from the Čumavići polymetallic ore deposit, Podrinje Metallogenic District, East Bosnia and Herzegovina,' *Ore Geology Reviews* 72 (2016), pp. 253–283.

Radosavljević, Slodoban A., et al., 'Polymetallic mineralization of the Boranja orefield, Podrinje metallogenic district, Serbia: Zonality, mineral associations and genetic features,' *Periodico di Mineralogia* 82 (2013), pp. 61–87.

Rădvan, Laurentiu, *At Europe's borders: Medieval towns in the Romanian principalities* (Leiden, 2010).

Raju, Alison, *Via Francigena, pilgrim trail Canterbury to Rome* Part I, *Canterbury to the Great St. Bernard Pass* (Singapore, 2011).

Ramsay, William M., 'Cilicia, Tarsus, and the Great Taurus Pass,' *The Geographical Journal* 22 (1903), pp. 357–410.

Randall-MacIver, David, *Medieval Rhodesia* (New York, 1971).

Read, Thomas T., 'Mineral production and resources of China, II,' *Mining and Scientific Press*, November 11 (1911), pp. 616–619.

Reich, Desiderio, 'Toponomastica storica di Mezocorona,' *Archivio Trentino* 10 (1891), pp. 67–149.

Repetti, Emanuele, *Dizionario geografico, fisico, storico della Toscana*, vols. 1–5 (Florence, 1841).

Reuvid, Jonathan, ed., *Doing business with Slovakia* (London, 2005).

Reynolds, Susan, *Fiefs and vassals: The medieval evidence reinterpreted* (Oxford, 2001).

Reynolds, Terry S., *Stronger than a hundred men: A history of the vertical water wheel* (Baltimore, 1983).

Rhind, William, *A history of the vegetable kingdom* (London, 1874).

Ricardo, David, *Letters of David Ricardo to Thomas Robert Malthus, 1810–1823* (Oxford, 1887).

Richards, J. F., 'Mughal State: Finance and the premodern world economy,' *Comparative Studies in Society and History* 23 (1981), pp. 285–308.

Richardson, Ralph, 'Old Edinburgh geologists,' *Transactions of the Edinburgh Geological Society*, November (1894–1895), pp. 82–99.

Riera Melís, Antonio, 'Monedas y mercados en la Edad Media: el Mediterráneo Noroccidental (c. 1190–1350),' in *Moneda y monedas en la Europa medieval (siglos XII–XV), XXVI Semana de Estudios Medievales*, ed. Antonio Riera Melis et al., pp. 193–256 (Estella, Navarra, 1999).

Riley, Thomas H., *Dictionary of Latin quotations, proverbs, maxims, and mottos, classical and medieval* (London, 1866).

Rippon, Stephen, et al., *Mining in a medieval landscape, the royal silver mines of the Tamar Valley* (Exeter, 2009).

Robb, Laurence J., *Introduction to ore-forming processes* (Oxford, 2004).

Robert, George, *An etymological and explanatory dictionary of the terms and language of geology, designed for the early student, and those who have not made progress in the science* (London, 1839).

Robinson, Chase F., *Empire and elites after the Muslim conquest: The transformation of northern Mesopotamia* (New York, 2000).

Rocke, Alan J., 'Agricola, Paracelsus, and Chymia,' *Ambix* 32 (1985), pp. 38–45.

Rodgers, John, 'Differences between mountain ranges,' in *The anatomy of mountain ranges*, ed. Jean-Paul Schaer and John Rodgers, pp. 11–18 (Princeton, 1987).

Rodolico, Niccolò, cur., *Ordinamenta super arte fossarum rameriae et argenteriae civitatis Massae* (Florence, 1938).

Rogers, J. Michael, 'To and fro: Aspects of Mediterranean trade and consumption in the 15th and 16th centuries,' *Revue du monde musulman et de la Méditerranée* 55–56 (1990), pp. 57–74.

Romero Tallafigo, Manuel, 'Ordenanzas para la explotación de la plata en el Condado de Prades y Baronía de Entenza (años 1343–1352),' *Historia. Instituciones. Documentos* 6 (1979), pp. 325–340.

Rosa, Gabriele, *Delle leggi di Bergamo nel medio evo* (Bergamo, 1856).

Rosen, William, *The Third Horseman: Climate change and the Great Famine of the 14th century* (New York, 2014).

Rosenberg, Gary D., ed., *The revolution in geology: From the Renaissance to the Enlightenment* (Boulder, Colorado, 2009).

Rosenberger, Bernard, 'Autour d'une grande mine d'argent du Moyen Age marocain: le Jebel Aouam,' *Hespéris Tamuda* 5 (1964), pp. 15–78.

Rosenberger, Bernard, 'Tāmdult: citè minière et caravanière pré-saharienne (IXᵉ–XIVᵉ s.),' *Hespéris Tamuda* 11 (1970), pp. 103–141.

Rossi-Doria, Manlio, 'The land tenure system and class in southern Italy,' *American Historical Review* 64 (1958), pp. 46–53.

Rostow, Walter W., *The stages of economic growth: A non-communist manifesto* (Cambridge, England, 1991).

Rowland, Robert, *The periphery in the center: Sardinia in ancient and medieval worlds* (Oxford, 2001).

Royal Geographical Society, *A dictionary of geographical knowledge*, vol. 5 (London, 1856–1859).

Royal Society of London, 'Of a peculiar lead ore of Germany and the use of it,' *Philosophical Transactions,* vol. 1 (1809).

Rubino, Gregorio E., 'Metallurgia e comunitá agro-operaie del Mezzogiorno d'Italia nell'etá della manifatture,' in *Miniere e Metallurgia, deciottesima settimana di Studio del Instituto Internazionale do Storia Economica 'Francesco Datini,'* cur. Simonetta Cavaciocchi, CD format (Prato, Itália, 1986).

Ruíz, Rafael A., 'Panorama de la arqueología medieval de los valles alto y medio del Vinalopó (Alicante),' *Lvcentvm* 2 (1983), pp. 349–383.

Rusu, Andrei A., 'On a possible abbatial crosier from Bizere Monastery (Frumuşeni, Arad county),' *European Journal of Science and Technology* 9 (2013), pp. 211–219.

Ruvinskis, Miriam, *Persecución judía en México* (México, 1977).

Sáez, Reinaldo, et al., 'Geological constraints of massive sulphide genesis in the Iberian Pyrite Belt,' *Ore Geology Reviews* 11 (1996), pp. 429–451.

Saffra, Piero, ed., with Maurice H. Dobb, *The works and correspondence of David Ricardo*, vol. 10 (Cambridge, England, 1973).

Saggioro, Fabio, 'Insediamenti, proprietà ed economie nei territory di pianura tra Adda e Adige (VII–IX secolo),' in *Dopo la fine delle ville: evoluzione nelle Campagne dal VI al IX secolo,* cur. Gian P. Brogiolo et al., pp. 81–104 (Gavi, Itália, 2005).

Saito, Osamu, 'Land, labour, and market forces in Tokugawa Japan,' *Continuity and change* 24 (2009), pp. 169–196.

Salvatori, Antonio, et al., 'The marbles used in the decoration of Hadrian's Villa at Tivoli,' in *Classical marble: Geochemistry, technology, trade,* part 4, ed. Norman Herz and Marc Waelkens, pp. 177–185 (The Netherlands, 1988).

Salvioli, Giuseppe, *Manuale di storia del diritto italiano: dalle invasione germaniche ai nostri giorni* (Torino, 1899).

Sandars, Thomas C., trans., *Institutes of Justinian,* 14th ed. (London, 1917).

Sarris, Peter, *The origins of the manorial economy: New insights from late antiquity* (Oxford, 2004).

Sarti, Giovanni, et al., 'The growth and decline of Pisa (Tuscany, Italy) up to the Middle Ages: Correlations with landscape and geology,' *Il Quaternario* 23 (2010), pp. 311–322.

Sapori, Armando, *The Italian merchant in the Middle Ages* (New York, 1970).

Sapori, Armando, *La Compagnia dei Frescobaldi in Inghilterra* (Florence, 1947).

Savery, Thomas, *The Miner's Friend, or an engine to raise water by fire* (London, 1702).

Say, Jean Baptiste, *Catechism of political economy; or, familiar conversations on the man-*

ner in which wealth is produced, distributed, and consumed in society, trans. John Richter (London, 1816).

Say, Jean Baptiste, *A treatise on political economy, or the production, distribution and consumption of wealth*, ed. Clement C. Biddle, trans. Charles R. Prinsep (Philadelphia, 1848).

Schaer, Jean-Paul, 'Evolution and structure of the High Atlas of Morocco,' in *The anatomy of mountain ranges*, ed. Jean-Paul Schaer and John Rodgers, pp. 107–128 (Princeton, 1987).

Schaer, Jean-Paul, 'Introduction: Comparative anatomy in geology,' in *The anatomy of mountain ranges*, ed. Jean-Paul Schaer and John Rodgers, pp. 3–10 (Princeton, 1987).

Scheinert, Madlen, et al., 'Geochemical investigations of slags from the historical smelting in Freiberg, Erzgebirge (Germany),' *Chemie der Erde* 69 (2009), pp. 81–90.

Scheuermann, Ludwig, *Die Fugger als montanindustrielle in Tirol und Kärnten* (Munich, 1929).

Schevill, Ferdinand, *The history of the Balkan peninsula, from the earliest times to the present day* (New York, 1922).

Schevill, Ferdinand, *The Medici* (New York, 1949).

Schildhauer, Johannes, *The Hansa: History and culture* (London, 1988).

Schmidt, Peter R., and David H. Avery, 'More evidence for an advanced prehistoric iron technology in Africa,' *Journal of Field Archaeology* 10 (1983), pp. 421–434.

Schnell, Scott, *The rousing drum: Ritual practice in a Japanese community* (Honolulu, 1999).

Schneller, Christian, *Quellen und forschungen zur geschichte, litteratur und sprache Osterreichs und seiner Kronländer*, IV, *Tridentinische Urbare aus dem dreizehnten Jahrhundert mit einer urkunde aus judicarien von 1244–1247* (Innsbruck, 1898).

Schorsch, Jonathan, *Swimming the Christian Atlantic: Judeoconversos, Afroiberians, and Amerindians in the seventeenth century* (Leiden, 2009).

Schröcke, Helmut, 'Mining and German settlement in Slovakia, an historical summary,' *GeoJournal* 32 (1994), pp. 127–135.

Schultze, Carol A., et al., 'Direct evidence of 1,900 years of indigenous silver production in the Lake Titicaca Basin of Southern Peru,' *Proceedings of the National Academy of Sciences* 106 (2009), pp. 17280–17283.

Schumacher, Friedrich, 'The ore deposits of Jugoslavia and the development of its mining industry,' *Economic Geology* 49 (1954), pp. 451–492.

Schumpeter, Joseph A., and Elisabeth B. Schumpeter, *History of economic analysis* (London, 1954).

Schurz, William L., *The Manila galleon* (New York, 1959).

Scott, Thom, 'South-west German serfdom reconsidered,' in *Forms of servitude in northern and central Europe: Decline, resistance, and expansion*, ed. Paul H. Freedman and Monique Bourin, pp. 115–128 (Belgium, 2005).

Scoville, Warren C., *The persecution of Huguenots and French economic development, 1680–1720* (Cambridge, England, 1960).

Scrittori di Detta Enciclopedia, *Dizionario generale di scienze, lettere, arti, storia, geografia* [. . .] *Supplimento perenne alla nuova enciclopedia* (Torino, 1869).

Sedlar, Jean W., *East Central Europe in the Middle Ages, 1000–1500* (Seattle, 1994).

Segers-Glocke, Christiane, et al., *Aspects of mining and smelting in the Upper Harz Mountains (up to the 13th/14th century) in the early times of a developing European economy* (St. Katharinen, Germany, 2000).

Séguin, Lisbeth G., *The Black Forest: Its peoples and legends* (London, 1879).

Sella, Quintino, 'Condizione minerarie dell'isola di Sardegna,' *Discorsi Parlamentari di Quintino Sella* 2 (1888), pp. 521–774.

Sella, Quintino, *Relazione del Deputato Sella alla commissione d'inchiesta* [. . .] *condizioni dell'industria mineraria nell'isola di Sardegna* (Florence, 1871).

Sempat Assadourian, Carlos, 'La bomba de fuego de Newcomen y otros artificios de de-sagüe: un intento de transferencia de tecnología inglesa a la minería novohispana, 1726–1731,' *Historia Mexicana* 50 (2001), pp. 385–457.

Serrano Larráyoz, Fernando, '*Item perrexil, mostarda, lechugas et raunos*, notas sobre la alimentación de mineros alemanes en Pamplona a finales del siglo XIV (1392),' *Anuario de Estudios Medievales* 38 (2008), pp. 236–269.

Serrano-Piedecasas Fernández, Luis M., 'El primer siglo de la Meseta bajo el dominio is-lámico, la restructuración del poder,' in *Mundos medievales: espacios, sociedades y poder*, vol. 1, ed. Beatriz Arízaga Bolumburu et al., pp. 901–913 (Santander, 2012).

Serrano Ruano, Delfina, 'Minas en colecciones de feutas y casos jurídicos del occidente Islámico (ss. XII–XIV d.C.), el problema de la propiedad de los yacimientos mineros,' *Espacio, tiempo y forma* 23 (2010), pp. 185–203.

Serrão, Joel, dir., *Dicionário de História de Portugal*. 4 vols. (Porto, 1979).

Settia, Aldo A., 'Assetto del popolamento rurale e coppie toponimiche nell'Italia Padana (secoli IX–XIV),' *Studi Storici* 36 (1995), pp. 243–266.

Sforza, I. Cesarini, 'Italiani non Trentini nel Trentino,' *Archivio Trentino* 22 (1907), pp. 66–76.

Shaer, Jean-Paul, 'Introduction: Comparative anatomy in geology,' in *The anatomy of moun-tain ranges*, ed. Jean Paul Schaer and John Rodgers, pp. 3–10 (Princeton, 1987).

Shaham, Ron, ed., *Law, custom, and statute in the Muslim world: Studies in honor of Aharon Layish* (Leiden, 2006).

Shākir, Aḥmad ibn Mūsá, and Ḥasan ibn Mūsá Ibn Shākir, *The book of ingenious devices (Kitāb al-ḥiyal)*, trans. Donald Routledge Hill (Dordrecht, 1979).

Shealy, Howard, '*Novi cives*: The Frescobaldi and the Florentine republic,' *Proceedings and papers of the Georgia Association of Historians* (1988), pp. 108–118.

Shipton, K. M. W., 'The prices of the Athenian silver mines,' *Zeischrift für Papyrologie und Epigraphik* 120 (1998), pp. 57–63.

Sidiqqi, Iqtidar Husain, *Indo-Persian historiography up to the thirteenth century* (Delhi, 2010).

Sigler, Laurence E., trans., *Fibonacci's Liber abaci* (New York, 2002).

Sijpesteijn, Petra M., et al., *From al-Andalus to Khurasan: Documents from the medieval Muslim world* (Leiden, 2007).

Simmons, Ian G., *The Moors of England and Wales: An environmental history 8000 BC to 2000 AD* (Edinburgh, 2003).

Simonin, Louis, *Underground life; or mines and miners*, ed. H. W. Bristow (New York, 1869).

Simonin, M. Louis, 'De l'ancienne loi des mines de la République Italienne de Massa-Marittima (Toscane),' *Annales des Mines* 8 (1859), pp. 1–15.

Simonin, M. Louis, 'La Maremma Toscana souvenirs de voyage, II,' *Revue des Deux Mondes* 32 (1862), pp. 893–929.

Skilton, Julius A., *Mining districts of Pachuca, Real del Monte, El Chico and Santa Rosa* (Boston, 1882).

Smirke, Edward, 'Original documents: Indenture under which the silver mines of Byrland, Devon, were worked, temp. Edward I,' *Archaeological Journal* 27 (1870), pp. 129–133.

Smith, Adam, *The wealth of nations: An inquiry into the nature and causes of the wealth of nations,* ed. Edwin Cannan and Max Lerner (New York, 1937).

Smith, Cyril S., and Martha T. Gnudi, eds., *The Pirotechnia of Vannoccio Biringuccio, the classic sixteenth century treatise on metals and metallurgy* (Ontario, 1990).

Smith, Elizabeth B., and Michael Wolfe, *Technology and resource use in medieval Europe: Cathedrals, mills, and mines* (Aldershot, 1997).

Smith, John, *A system of modern geography*, 2 vols. (London, 1811).

Smith, Richard L., *Premodern trade in world history* (New York, 2009).

Smith, William, ed., *A dictionary of Greek and Roman geography*, vol. 1 (London, 1872).

Smyth, Warington W., 'Geological features of the country round the mines of the Taurus in the Pashalic described from observations made in the year 1843,' *Proceedings of the Geological Society of London* 4 (1846), pp. 512–522.

Sociedad Anónima Hullera Vasco-Leonesa et al., eds., *Jornadas sobre minería y tecnología en la Edad Media peninsular* (León, España, 1995).

Society for the Diffusion of Useful Knowledge, *A description and history of vegetable substances used in the arts and in domestic economy: Timber trees, fruits* (London, 1830–1833).

Soetbeer, Adolf, *Litteraturnachweis über Geld-und Münzwesen, insbesondere über den Währungsstreit, 1871–1891, mit geschichtlichen und statistischen Erläuterungen* (Berlin, 1892).

Solecki, Ralph S., 'Cave art in Kürtün Ini, a Taurus Mountain site in Turkey,' *Man* 64 (1964), pp. 87–88.

Solórzano y Pereira, Juan De, *Política Indiana*, ed. Francisco R. De Valenzuela (Madrid, 1930).

Soto Company, Ricard, '¿Una oferta sin demanda? La esclavitud rural en Mallorca antes de la peste negra (ss. XIII–XIV),' *Historia agraria* 21 (2000), pp. 11–32.

Soukhanov, Anne H., *Microsoft Encarta college dictionary* (New York, 2001).

Speakman, Fleur, and Colin Speakman, *Walking in the Harz Mountains* (Cumbria, 1994).

Spelman, Edward, et al., trans., *The whole works of Xenophon*, vol. 1 (Philadelphia, 1845).

Sperges, Joseph v., *Tyrolische bergwerksgeschichte* (Vienna, 1765).

Spremić, Momčila, 'I tributi veneziani nel Levante nel XV secolo,' *Studi veneziani* 13 (1971), pp. 221–252.

Spufford, Peter, 'The mint buildings of medieval Europe,' in *Actas del XIII Congreso Internacional de Numismática*, vol. 2, coord. Carmen Alfaro Asins et al., pp. 1059–1065 (Madrid, 2003).

Spufford, Peter, *Money and its use in medieval Europe* (Cambridge, England, 1988).

Spufford, Peter, *Power and profit: The merchant in medieval Europe* (London, 2002).

Squatriti, Paolo, *Water and society in early medieval Italy, A.D. 400–1000* (Cambridge, England, 1998).

Stadel, Christoph, 'The Brenner Freeway (Austria-Italy): Mountain highway and controversy,' *Mountain Research and Development* 13 (1993), pp. 1–17.

Stahl, Alan M., *Zecca, the mint of Venice in the Middle Ages* (Baltimore, 2000).

Stanoyevich, Milivoy S., *Early Jugoslav literature (1000–1800)* (New York, 1922).

Stark, Werner, 'The contained economy: An interpretation of medieval economic thought,' in *The evolution of capitalism*, ed. Leonard Silk and Mark Silk, pp. 18–193 (New York, 1972).

Steane, John, *The archeology of medieval England and Wales* (New York, 1985).

Štefánik, Martin, 'Italian involvement in metal mining in the Central Slovakian region, from the thirteenth century to the reign of King Sigismund of Hungary,' *I Tatti Studies in the Italian Renaissance* 14/15 (2011–2012), pp. 11–46.

Stein, Aurel Sir, *Serindia, detailed report of explorations in Central Asia and westernmost China carried out and described under the orders of H. M. Indian government*, 3 vols. (Oxford, 1921).

Stenton, Frank M., *The first century of English feudalism* (Oxford, 1968).

Stern, Laura I., 'Crime and punishment,' in *Medieval Italy, an encyclopedia*, vol. 1, ed. Christopher Kleinhenz, pp. 557–562 (New York, 2004).

Sternberg, G. Kaspar, *Umrisse der Geschichte des Bergbaues und der Berggesetzgebung des Königreichs Böhmen* (Prague, 1838).

Steuer, Heiko, 'Settlements in the southern Black Forest: Castels and mining (dominance through commerce),' *Hierarchies in rural settlements* 9 (2011), p. 123.

Stojković, Milan D., 'Saxon miners in Serbian medieval laws and written texts,' *Mining History* 17 (2010), pp. 49–54.

Stojsavljević, Rastislav, et al., 'Serbian medieval towns and their tourist potentials,' *Geographica timisiensis* 19 (2010), pp. 189–196.

Stone, David, *Decision-making in medieval agriculture* (Oxford, 2010).

Strieder, Jacob, *Jacob Fugger, the Rich*, trans. M. L. Hartsough (Hamden, Connecticut, 1966).

Stretch, Richard H., *Prospecting, locating, and valuing mines* (New York, 1903).

Stuard, Susan M., 'Dowry increase and increment in wealth in medieval Ragusa (Dubrovnik),' *Journal of Economic History* 41 (1981), pp. 795–811.

Suárez, Thomas, *Early mapping of Southeast Asia, the epic story of seafarers, adventurers, and cartographers who first mapped the regions between China and India* (Singapore, 1999).

Suárez Fernández, Luis, et al., *Historia general de España* (Madrid, 1989).

Subías Pérez, Ignacio, et al., 'Explotaciones mineras del entorno del Hospital de Benasque: geología y encuadre histórico,' *Revista de la Sociedad Española de Minerología* 9 (2008), pp. 239–240.

Sucurro, Maria C., 'Building an identity: King Desiderius, the Abby of Leno (Brescia) and the relics of St. Benedictine (8th. C.),' paper delivered at International Medieval Meeting, University of Lleida, July 1, 2011.

Suess, Eduard, *The face of the earth*, vol. 1, trans. H. B. C. Sollas (Oxford, 1904).

Swetz, Frank J., *Capitalism and arithmetic: The new math of the 15th century* (La Salle, Illinois, 1987).

Taitz, Emily, *The Jews of medieval France, the community of Champagne* (Province, 1994).

Talbert, Richard J. A., *Rome's world: The Peutinger map reconsidered* (Cambridge, England, 2010).

Tanaka, Minoru, and Masatoshi M. Yoshino, 'Re-examination of the climatic change in central Japan based on freezing dates of Lake Suwa,' *Royal Metereological Society* 37 (1982), pp. 252–259.

Tangheroni, Marco, *Commercio, finanza, funzione pubblica: stranieri in Sicilia e Sardegna nei secoli XIII–XV* (Pisa, 1989).

Tangheroni, Marco, *Pisa e il Mediterraneo: uomini, merci, idee dagli Etruschi ai Medici* (Milano, 2003).

Tangheroni, Marco, and C. Giorgioni Mercuriali, *La cittá dell'argento: Iglesias dalle origini alla fine del Medioevo* (Napoli, 1985).

Targioni Tozetti, Giovanni, *Relazioni d'alcuni viaggi fatti in diverse parti della Toscana, per osservare le produzioni naturali, e gli antichi monumenti di essa*, vol. 3 (Florence, 1751).

Taylor, W. Cooke, *The natural history of society in the barbarous and civilized state, an essay towards discovering the origin of human improvement*, vol. 1 (London, 1840).

Tchikhatchev, Petr A., *Asie Mineure: description physique de cette contree* (Paris, 1856).

Tenfelde, Klaus, 'Mining festivals in the nineteenth century,' *Journal of Contemporary History* 13 (1978), pp. 377–412.

Tengberg, Margareta, 'Beginnings and early history of date palm garden cultivation in the Middle East,' *Journal of Arid Environments* 86 (2012), pp. 139–147.

Tennant, Robert, *Sardinia and its resources* (Rome, 1885).

Terreni, Antonio, et al., *Viaggio pittorico della Toscana dell'Abate Francesco Fontani*, vol. 3 (Florence, 1827).

Thibodeau, Alyson M., 'The strange case of the earliest silver extraction by European colonists in the New World,' *Proceedings of the National Academy of Sciences* 104 (2007), pp. 3663–3666.

Thomasius, Harald, 'The influence of mining on woods and forestry in the Saxon Erzgebirge up to the beginning of the 19th century,' *GeoJournal* 32 (1994), pp. 101–102.

Thompson, James W., 'The Cistercian Order and colonization of mediaeval Germany,' *The American Journal of Theology* 24 (1920), pp. 67–93.

Thompson, James W., 'Dutch and Flemish colonization of mediaeval Germany,' *The American Journal of Sociology* 24 (1918), pp. 159–186.

Thompson, James W., 'Early trade relations between the Germans and the Slavs,' *Journal of Political Economy* 30 (1922), pp. 543–558.

Thompson, James W., 'Medieval German expansion in Bohemia,' *The Slavonic Review* 4 (1926), pp. 605–628.

Thomson, Thomas, *Outlines of mineralogy, geology, and mineral analysis*, vol. 2 (London, 1836).

Tierney, Brian, *Foundations of the Conciliar theory, the contribution of the medieval canonists from Gratian to the Great Schism* (Leiden, 1998).

Timberlake, Simon, 'Early leats and hushing remains: Suggestions and disputes of Roman mining and prospection for lead,' *Mining History* 15 (2004), pp. 64–76.

Tizzoni, Marco, et al., eds., *Alle origini della siderurgia lecchese: ricerche archaeometallurgiche ai Piani d'Erna* (Lecco, 2006).

Tizzoni, Marco, and Costanza Cucini, *Il comprensorio minerario e metallurgico delle valli Brembana, Torta ed Averara dal XV al XVII secolo* (Bergamo, 1997).

Tobaruela, Montserrat M., 'Una aproximación a la minería y la metalurgia andalusí en la depresión de Vera (Almería),' *Arqueología y territorio medieval* 7 (2000), pp. 59–79.

Toch, Michael, 'Lords and peasants: A reappraisal of medieval economic relations,' in *The expansion of Latin Europe, 1000–1500*, vol. 2, ed. Felipe Fernández-Armesto and James Muldoon, pp. 281–300 (Farnham, England, 2008).

Tod, James, *Annals and antiquities of Rajast'han*, vol. 1 (London, 1914).

Todd, Malcolm, *The early Germans* (Oxford, 2004).

Toll, Christopher, 'Al-Hamdānī as a scholar,' *Arabica* 31 (1984), pp. 306–317.

Topolski, Jerzy, *The manorial economy in early-modern east-central Europe: Origins, development, and consequences* (Hampshire, Great Britain, 1994).

Torres, Diego, *Relación del origen y suceso de los Xarifes y del estado de los reinos de Marruecos, Fez, y Tarudante, y de los más que tienen usurpados* (Madrid, 1586).

Torres Fuentes, Juan, 'El reino musulmán de Murcia en el siglo XIII,' *Anales de la Universidad de Murcia* 10 (1951–1952), pp. 259–274.

Torres Lázaro, Julio, 'Obreros, monederos y casas de moneda, Reino de Castilla, siglos XIII–XV,' *Anuario de Estudios Medievales* 41 (2011), pp. 673–698.

Totman, Conrad D., *Pre-industrial Korea and Japan in environmental perspective* (Leiden, 2004).

Toul Jurievich, Josephus, *Institutiones juris metallici hungarici*, vol. 2 (Zagreb, 1822).

Tourasse, Patrick, and Charles Obled, 'Dynamique des épisodes pluvieux intenses sur le Sud-Est du Massif Central, aspects météorologiques et applications hydrologiques,' *La Houille Blanche* 7/8 (1981), pp. 559–568.

Toussaint Reinaud, Joseph, *Muslim colonies in France, northern Italy, and Switzerland: Being the English translation of Reinaud's Invasions des Sarrazins en France, et de France en Savoie, en Piémnot et en Suisse* (Lahore, 1964).

Townson, Robert, *Philosophy of mineralogy* (London, 1798).

Townson, Robert, *Travels in Hungary* (London, 1797).

Toynbee, Arnold, *The treatment of Armenians in the Ottoman Empire* (New York, 1916).

Travaini, Lucia, 'Mint organisation in Italy between the twelfth and fourteenth centuries: A survey,' in *Late medieval mints: Organisation, administration, and techniques*, ed. Nicholas J. Mayhew and Peter Spufford, pp. 39–60 (Oxford, 1988).

Trichur, Ganesh K., ed., *The rise of Asia and the transformation of the world-system* (Boulder, Colorado, 2009).

Tringham, Ruth, 'Southeastern Europe in the transition to agriculture in Europe: Bridge, buffer, or mosaic,' in *Europe's first farmers*, ed. T. Douglas Price, pp. 19–56 (Cambridge, England, 2000).

Troisi, Antonio, et al., 'Restauro delle mure antiche tratto CD-DE (III Stralcio), progetto esecutivo architettonico,' Regione Toscana, Commune di Massa Marittima, Provincia di Grosseto (Milano, 2014), pp. 1–20.

Tsang Woo, Yang, 'Silver-mining and smelting in Mongolia,' *Transactions of the American Institute of Mining Engineers* 33 (1902), pp. 755–760.

Tsuna, Masuda, *Kodō Zuroku, illustrated book on the smelting of copper* (Connecticut, 1983).

Tuan, Yi-Fu, *A historical geography of China* (Chicago, 2008).

Turner, William, *A new herball Parts II, III*, ed. George L. Chapman et al. (Cambridge, England, 1995).

Tylecote, Ronald F., 'Roman lead working in Britain,' *British Journal for the History of Science* 2 (1964), pp. 25–43.

Udovitch, Abraham L., *Partnership and profit in medieval Islam* (New Jersey, 1970).

Ullmann, Walter, 'The development of the medieval idea of sovereignty,' *English Historical Review* 64 (1949), pp. 1–33.

Umlauft, Friedrich, *The Alps* (London, 1889).

United States Hydrographic Office, *Mediterranean pilot: The coast of France and Italy from Cape Cabère to Cape Spartivento, together with the Tuscan archipelago* [. . .], vol. 2 (Washington, D.C., 1917).

Upham, Edward, *History of the Ottoman Empire, from its establishment, till the year 1828*, vol. 1 (Edinburgh, 1829).

Ure, Andrew, *A dictionary of arts, manufactures, and mines*, vol. 1 (New York, 1868).

Vargas-Bedemar, Eduard R., *Sulle miniere della Sardegna* (Roma, 1806).

Vasiliev, Alexander A., 'Imperial porphyry sarcophagi in Constantinople,' *Dumbarton Oaks Papers* 4 (1948), pp. 3–26.

Vauchez, André, et al., eds., *Encyclopedia of the Middle Ages* (Chicago, 2000).

Vázquez De Prada, Valentín, 'La coyuntura de la minería y de la metalurgia europeas (siglos XIII–XVIII),' *Revista de Historia Económica* 6 (1988), pp. 257–273.

Vega Martín, Miguel, and Salvador Peña Martín, 'Alternancias epigráficas en las monedas almorávides,' *Al-Andalus Magreb: Estudios Árabes e Islámicos* 10 (2002–2003), pp. 293–316.

Velho, Álvaro, et al., *A journal of the first voyage of Vasco Da Gama, 1497–1499* (Farnham, England, 2010).

Vent, Glenn, and Ronald A. Milne, 'The standardization of mine accounting,' *Accounting Historians Journal* 16 (1989), pp. 57–74.

Verna, Catherine, 'Innovations et métallurgies en Méditerranée Occidentale (XIIIe–XVe siècles),' *Anuario de Estudios Medievales* 41 (2011), pp. 623–644.

Vilar, Pierre, *A history of gold and money, 1450–1920*, trans. J. White (London, 1976).

Villani, Giovanni, et al., *Croniche di Giovanni, Matteo e Filippo Villani: secondo le migliori stampe e corredate di note filologiche e storiche: testo di lingua* (Trieste, 1857–1858).

Vinelli, Marcelo, 'Water conservation in Sardinia,' *Geographical Review* 16 (1926), pp. 395–402.

Virnich, Winand, *De juris regalis metallorum origine ac progressu* (Tubingen, 1871).

Völlnagel, Jörg, *Splendor Solis oder Sonnenglanz* (Munich, 2004).

Volpe, Gioacchino, 'Montieri: Costituzione politica, struttura sociale e attività economica d'una terra mineraria toscana nel XIII secolo,' *Vierteljahrschrift für Social und Wirtschaftsgeschichte* 3/4 (1908), pp. 315–423.

Voltelini, Hans, *Giurisdizione signorile su terre e persone nel trentino medievale*, trans. Vigilio Mattevi (Trento, 1981).

Von Stromer, Wolfgang, 'Nuremberg in the international economics of the Middle Ages,' *Business History Review* 44 (1970), pp. 210–225.

Vryonis, Speros, 'The question of Byzantine mines,' *Speculum* 37 (1962), pp. 1–17.

Vucinich, Wayne S., 'The nature of Balkan society under Ottoman rule,' *Slavic Review* 21 (1962), pp. 597–616.

Wade, John, *British history, chronologically arranged, comprehending a classified analysis of events and occurrences in Church and State* (London, 1839).

Waele, Jo, and Paolo Forti, 'Mineralogy of mine caves in Sardinia,' *Hellenic Speleological Society* 21–28 August 2005, pp. 1–6.

Wagner, Donald B., 'The administration of the iron industry in eleventh-century China,' *Journal of the Economic and Social History of the Orient* 44 (2011), pp. 175–197.

Wallerstein, Immanuel, *The modern world-system*, vol. 1, *Capitalist agriculture and the origins of the European world-economy in the sixteenth century* (New York, 1974).

Wallerstein, Immanuel, *The modern world-system*, vol. 2, *Mercantilism and the consolidation of the European world-economy, 1600–1750* (New York, 1980).

Wallerstein, Immanuel, *The modern world-system*, vol. 3, *The second great expansion of the capitalist world-economy, 1730–1840* (California, 1989).

Walsh, Robert, *Narrative of a journey from Constantinople to England* (London, 1828).

Walters, Steve G., 'Clear the way or Black Hillock Mine, Tideslow Moor,' *Bulletin of the Peak District Mines Historical Society* 7 (1980), pp. 327–332.

Ward, Gerald W. R., *The Grove encyclopedia of materials and techniques in art* (Oxford, 2008).

Waring, L. F., 'Kosovo,' *The Slavonic Review* 2 (1923), pp. 56–70.

Weatherford, Jack, *Genghis Khan and the making of the modern world* (New York, 2004).

Weber, Eugen, 'Introduction to the study of Saxon settlement in Transylvania during the Middle Ages,' *Medieval Studies* 18 (1956), pp. 50–60.

Weber, Max, *General economic history*, trans. F. H. Knight (New York, 2003).

Wedepohl, Karl H., and Albrecht Baumann, 'Isotope composition of medieval lead glasses reflecting early silver production in Central Europe,' *Mineralium Deposita* 32 (1997), pp. 292–295.

West, Charles, *Reframing the feudal revolution: Political and social transformation between Marne and Moselle, c.800–c.1100* (Cambridge, England, 2013).

Westermann, Ekkehard, ed., *Bergbaureviere als Verbrauchszentren im von industriellen Europa* (Stuttgart, 1997).

White, James D., 'Jehol, mostly a wilderness, is land of paupers, bandits,' *The Milwaukee Journal*, January 4, 1946, p. 5.

White, Joseph M., *A new collection of laws, charters and local ordinances of the governments of Great Britain, France, and Spain relating to the concessions of land in their respective colonies*, vol. 1 (Philadelphia, 1839).

White, Sam, *The climate of rebellion in the early Ottoman Empire* (New York, 2011).

White, Sam, 'Little Ice Age crisis of the Ottoman Empire: A conjuncture in Middle East environmental history,' in *Water on sand: Environmental histories of the Middle East and North Africa*, ed. Alan Mikhail, pp. 71–90 (Oxford, 2013).

Whiter, Walter, *Etymologicon universale, or universal etymological dictionary*, vol. 1 (Cambridge, England, 1811).

Wickham, Chris, *The mountains and the city: The Tuscan Apennines in the early Middle Ages* (Oxford, 1988).

Wickham, Chris, 'Paludi e miniere nella Maremma toscana, XI–XIII secoli,' *Castrum* 7 (2001), pp. 451–466.

Wicks, Robert S., 'Monetary developments in Java between the ninth and sixteenth centuries: A numismatic perspective,' *Indonesia* 42 (1986), pp. 42–77.

Wiener, Leo, *Commentary to the Germanic Laws and medieval documents* (Cambridge, Massachusetts, 1915).

Wigen, Kären, 'Discovering the Japanese Alps: Meiji mountaineering and the quest for geographical enlightenment,' *Journal of Japanese Studies* 31 (2005), pp. 1–26.

Williams, A. R., 'The gilding of armour: Medieval and Renaissance techniques,' *Gold Bulletin* 10 (1977), pp. 115–117.

Williams, Alan, 'A note on liquid iron in medieval Europe,' *Ambix* 56 (2009), pp. 68–75.

Willies, Lynn, 'Ancient and post-medieval mining sites in the Khetri Copper Belt and Kolar Gold Field, India,' *Bulletin of the Peak District Mines Historical Society* 11 (1992), pp. 285–295.

Willies, Lynn, 'The mines at Campiglia Marittima, Livorno, Italy,' *Bulletin of the Peak District Mines Historical Society* 11 (1990), pp. 1–4.

Wilson, C. S. Charles W., 'Notes on the physical and historical geography of Asia Minor, made during the journeys in 1879–82,' *Proceedings of the Royal Geographical Society* 6 (1884), pp. 310–325.

Wilson, Eric M., *The savage republic: De Indis of Hugo Grotius, republicanism, and Dutch hegemony within the early modern world-system (c.1600–1619)* (Leiden, 2008).

Wilson, Joseph, *A history of mountains: Geographical and mineralogical*, vol. 3 (London, 1906).

Wilson, Joseph S., 'Production of gold and silver,' *The Bankers Magazine* 23 (1868), pp. 246–292.

Wingate, A. W. S., 'Nine years' survey and exploration in northern and central China,' *The Geographical Journal* 29 (1907), pp. 174–200.

Wischnitzer, Mark, 'Origins of the Jewish artisan class in Bohemia and Moravia, 1500–1648,' *Jewish Social Studies*, October 1954, pp. 335–350.

Wittfogel, Karl A., *History of Chinese society: Liao, 907–1125* (New York, 1949).

Wohlgemuth, Lennart, ed., *The Nordic countries and Africa: Old and new relations* (Uppsala, 2002).

Wolloch, Nathaniel, 'Facts or conjectures: Antoine-Yves Goguet's historiography,' *Journal of the history of ideas* 68 (2007), pp. 429–449.

Woodward, Horace B., *The history of the Geological Society of London* (London, 1908).

Worth, Richard N., *Historical notes concerning the progress of mining skill in Devon and Cornwall* (Cornwall, 1872).

Wright, George N., *A new and comprehensive gazetteer*, vol. 4 (London, 1837).

Wright, J. B., et al., *Geology and mineral resources of West Africa* (London, 1985).

Wulff, Hans E., 'The qanats of Iran,' *Scientific American* 218 (1968), pp. 94–105.

Wyckoff, Dorothy, 'Albertus Magnus on ore deposits,' *Isis* 49 (1958), pp. 109–122.

Yamamura, Kozo, 'The development of *Za* in medieval Japan,' *Business History Review*, 47 (1973), pp. 438–465.

Yamey, Basil S., 'Fifteenth and sixteenth century manuscripts on the art of bookkeeping,' *Journal of Accounting Research* 5 (1967), pp. 51–76.

Yang, Bin, 'Horses, silver, and cowries: Yunnan in global perspective,' *Journal of World History* 15 (2004), pp. 281–322.

Yate, Asadullah, *Al-Ahkam as-Sultaniyyah, the laws of Islamic governance, 'Alī ibn Muhammad Māwardi* (London, 1996).

Yener, K. Aslihan, 'The archaeometry of silver in Anatolia: The Bolkardağ Mining District,' *American Journal of Archaeology* 90 (1986), pp. 469–472.

Yule, Henry, trans., *The book of Ser Marco Polo the Venetian, concerning the kingdoms of the East*, vol. 1 (London, 1874).

Yule, Henry, et al., *Cathay and the way thither: Being a collection of medieval notices of China*, 2 vols. (London, 1866).

Yule, Henry, and Arthur Coke Burnell, *A glossary of colloquial Anglo-Indian words and phrases and kindred terms* (London, 1903).

Yuste López, Carmen, *Emporios transpacíficos: comerciantes mexicanos en Manila* (México, D.F., 2007).

Zaitsev, Evgeny A., 'The meaning of early medieval geometry: From Euclid and surveyors' manuals to Christian philosophy,' *Isis* 90 (1999), pp. 522–553.

Zammatteo, Paolo, 'A Luserna e Faedo sulle tracce di una storia mineraria millenaria. Una pagina affascinante del nostro passato,' *Il Trentino* 40 (2004), pp. 67–70.

Zavoianu, Ion, 'Romania's water resources and their uses,' *GeoJournal* 29 (1993), pp. 19–30.

Zhiqin, Xu, et al., eds., *Orogenic Belts: Geological mapping* (Utrecht, The Netherlands, 1997).

Zulawski, Ann, 'Wages, ore sharing, and peasant agriculture: Labour in silver mines, 1607–1720,' in *Mines of silver and sold in the Americas (An expanding world: The European impact on world history, 1450–1800, Vol. 19)*, ed. Peter Bakewell, pp. 199–224 (London, 1997).

Zycha, Adolf, *Das Böhmische Bergrecht des Mittelalters auf Grundlage des Bergrechts von Iglau* (Berlin, 1900).

INDEX

Page numbers in *italic* type indicate illustrations or charts. Page numbers followed by *n* indicate notes. Page numbers followed by *t* indicate tables.